THE CORE REPERTORY
OF
EARLY AMERICAN
PSALMODY

D1609466

RECENT RESEARCHES IN AMERICAN MUSIC

H. Wiley Hitchcock, general editor

A-R Editions, Inc., publishes six quarterly series—

Recent Researches in the Music of the Middle Ages and Early Renaissance
Margaret Bent, general editor

Recent Researches in the Music of the Renaissance
James Haar, general editor

Recent Researches in the Music of the Baroque Era
Robert L. Marshall, general editor

Recent Researches in the Music of the Classical Era
Eugene K. Wolf, general editor

Recent Researches in the Music of the Nineteenth and Early Twentieth Centuries
Rufus Hallmark, general editor

Recent Researches in American Music
H. Wiley Hitchcock, general editor—

which make public music that is being brought to light
in the course of current musicological research.

Each volume in the *Recent Researches* is devoted
to works by a single composer or to a single genre of composition,
chosen because of its potential interest to scholars and performers,
and prepared for publication according to the standards that govern
the making of all reliable historical editions.

Subscribers to this series, as well as patrons of subscribing institutions,
are invited to apply for information about the "Copyright-Sharing Policy"
of A-R Editions, Inc., under which the contents of this volume
may be reproduced free of charge for study or performance.

Correspondence should be addressed:

A-R EDITIONS, INC.
315 West Gorham Street
Madison, Wisconsin 53703

RECENT RESEARCHES IN AMERICAN MUSIC • VOLUMES XI and XII

THE CORE REPERTORY
OF
EARLY AMERICAN
PSALMODY

Edited by Richard Crawford

A-R EDITIONS, INC. • MADISON

Library of Congress Cataloging in Publication Data

The Core repertory of early American psalmody.

    (Recent researches in American music, 0147–0078 ;
v. 11–12)
    Bibliography : p.
    1. Hymns, English—18th century. I. Crawford, Richard,
1935— . II. Series.
M2.3.U6R4   vol. 11–12   [M2116]   84-757677
ISBN 0–89579–198–6

Contents

Preface

Introduction

The repertory of sacred music published in early America is marked by growth and change. From the thirteen tunes in the ninth (1698) edition of "The Bay Psalm Book," the first music printed in the English-speaking American colonies, the number of sacred pieces in print grew to nearly 7,500 by the beginning of 1811.[1] From a selection of pieces out of British tune-books, a true Anglo-American repertory developed, with some two-thirds of its pieces composed by musicians living and working in this country. From an assortment of textless psalm tunes, moving in block chords, the repertory came to encompass more elaborate pieces, many written as expressive settings of particular texts.[2] From a strictly congregational repertory, it gradually came to admit pieces that would challenge the skill of experienced choir singers. Thus, during the eighteenth and early nineteenth centuries, American psalmody evolved into a vigorous musical enterprise as new compositions, new tunebooks, new compilers, and new composers appeared in a widening, increasingly competitive market.

Beneath this ever-changing surface, however, ran a strong current of continuity. In sacred music the impulse to change was balanced and sometimes outweighed by the will to resist change. Like people in many other places, early American Protestants favored familiar music for singing in public worship. Most congregations sang without accompaniment. Few church members owned tunebooks or could have read the music in them if they had, and, therefore, a small stock of tunes was preferred. Even singing-schools, choirs, and musical societies, whose members sang from books and professed some measure of musical literacy, consistently mixed old favorites with the new pieces they explored. "Good musick never wearies the correct and cultivated taste," wrote one connoisseur of sacred music. "Like old wine," he continued, "it gathers goodness by age, and the more it is tried, the more it is approved."[3]

The metaphor that likens a piece of sacred music to "old wine" is surely more suggestive than precise. Perhaps changes in a fine bottle of wine do improve its quality with age. A piece of music, however, accumulates impact over time not because it changes itself, but because it stores more and deeper cultural meanings for those who sing and hear it.

Protestant sacred music of early America is admirably designed to carry such meanings. Usually cast in rhymed meter, the stylized form of a psalm- or hymn-tune's text makes it easy to remember and also separates it from other kinds of verbal communication. Set to a tune and sung, the text draws added impact from the music, which both governs the tempo and helps to establish and intensify a mood. Sung by a group, the music creates a strong, if temporary, community of shared purpose; as words flow in measured pace from many lips, they release meanings for all to feel and to ponder. When introduced as part of a religious ritual, a sacred piece appears in a context of high significance to the participants. Finally, when repeated again and again—and it should be remembered that Americans in 1800 and after were raising their children to sing and hear sung many of the same sacred pieces that they themselves had learned in their youth—a sacred piece can store and focus the singers' and listeners' emotional experience, which then stands ready to be tapped and, perhaps, also changed and enriched by the next repetition. Because so much of the power of sacred music is tied to familiarity and memory, it is no wonder that sacred music tends to be conservative— that people, Christians included, have seldom welcomed the replacement of well-known sacred styles and pieces with new ones.

The following work, containing representative versions of the 101 sacred pieces most often printed in America between 1698 and 1810, documents persistence and continuity in a context of change. Chosen not for attractiveness to modern ears, nor for representation of style trends in early American music, nor for theological range or denominational emphasis, but simply for the statistical frequency with which its compositions appeared in print, the group of pieces included in this Core Repertory registers at least one measure of the musical preferences of an earlier age.

As well as containing the music of the Core Repertory, the present edition offers detailed information on each of its compositions. Appendix I is devoted to tune biographies, in which the authorship, sources, publication statistics, pattern of American circulation, and musical form and style of each Core Repertory piece are discussed. Appendix II lists (with sigla) American sacred collections from the period 1698–1810 in which Core Repertory compositions appear. And the tables in Appendix III measure other aspects of the frequency of Core Repertory printings.

Three Stages of American Tunebook Publishing: 1698–1810

The publication history of early American Protestant sacred music seems to divide into three stages, each dominated by a different emphasis.

I. (1698–1760)—During this period the printed repertory grew slowly. Most musical publications were tune supplements: anthologies of textless tunes designed to be bound in at the backs of metrical psalters. Many supplements came out in edition after edition with little or no change in content (e.g., Bay 1698ff, Tufts 1723ff).[4] Almost all of the compositions in such publications were British psalm- and hymn-tunes for congregations to sing in public worship. By 1760, only about eighty-five sacred compositions had appeared in print in the English-speaking colonies; of that number, twenty-three tunes, or twenty-seven percent, are included here as Core Repertory pieces.[5]

II. (1761–1790)—Several important changes took place during the next period. First, the larger oblong tunebook with didactic introduction, rare before this time (though see, e.g., Walter 1721ff), came more and more to replace the smaller, more limited, tune supplement, signalling a shift in emphasis from the congregation to the singing-school as a market for tunebooks. Second, as musical learning spread and musical literacy increased, more choirs were formed, and tunebooks began to include more and more elaborate music—especially fuging-tunes and anthems for choirs to sing—as well as congregational favorites.[6] Third, many of the singing-school and choir pieces published in these tunebooks were pieces whose tunes usually circulated with the same texts, in contrast to the congregational tunes, few of which were linked with any single text.[7] Fourth, the period also witnessed the advent of American-born composers, whose pieces were published in ever-growing numbers in the tunebooks. An important result of these changes was that a typical tunebook was now "eclectic" in the musical forms and styles that it contained. Newer pieces in fresh styles—the English parish style of William Knapp or William Tans'ur, for example, or the Methodist style of Martin Madan, or the Yankee style of Daniel Read or Timothy Swan—took their places next to older British plain tunes. As the size and variety of the available repertory grew, the act of compiling, of choosing which pieces to print and deciding which texts to set to which tunes, grew more complicated. Compiling became something of an art in itself. Compilers of tunebooks weighed and balanced artistic, religious, educational, and economic factors, consulting both personal and community tastes in selecting their music. Their selections produced the beginnings of a new canon. By 1790, the sacred repertory in print in America included at least 1,469 compositions; 73 of the 1,222 pieces known to have been introduced between 1761 and 1790 are in the present Core Repertory.

III. (1791–1810)—Sacred music publication in America reached a grander scale in the next two decades, when approximately five times as many new sacred pieces were printed as had appeared in the previous 90 years. To the list of factors that had affected circulation earlier, three new ones were added. The first was legal: the earliest Federal Copyright Law was passed in 1790, which no doubt slowed the unrestricted flow of pieces from tunebook to tunebook without composers' knowledge or consent.[8] The second was musical and ideological: the rise of a reform movement aimed at discrediting the supposedly faulty training and technique of American-born psalmodists, and favoring music by European composers, or at least music in a more "chaste," less lively, more Europeanized idiom. The third was technological and ultimately economic. While most earlier tunebooks had been printed from engraved plates by small entrepreneurs, letterpress printers working with movable type now took over the sacred music industry, and professional publishers, discovering that profits were there to be made, entered the field.[9] Each of these three factors helped to keep newer compositions out of the Core Repertory. Copyright restrained their circulation, encouraging compilers to stick with familiar pieces in the public domain. Reform ideology encouraged the publication of "reform" collections (e.g., Salem 1805f, Deerfield 1808) to rival the "eclectic" tunebooks; the former often specialized in the "ancient," European-style pieces that had flourished during the early part of the century. Finally, tunebooks published by book-trade professionals and printers tended to stress salable, hence already familiar, music, thereby ratifying the notion of a Core Repertory while helping to shape it. A startling statistic supports this point: of nearly 6,000 new compositions published during this period, only five are in the present Core Repertory.

Choosing the Core Repertory

The present list was compiled by counting tune printings, with a printing defined as the appearance of a composition in one edition or state of one tunebook. That definition is not as simple as it may seem, for it is not always obvious what constitutes a separate edition or state of a book. On the one hand, for example, Andrew Law's *Select Harmony* was printed more than fifteen different times from essentially the same copper plates, but without any separate edition numbers. Among all these printings, only three significant changes of musical content are found: Law published part of *Select Harmony* late in 1778, issued the complete book a few months later, in early 1779, and published an edition early in 1782 with small but noteworthy musical changes. He continued to print the last version into the 1790s, issuing it at least twelve times with no significant musical alterations. For the purpose of this study, only the two printings for tunes appearing in the 1779 and 1782 issues were counted. Since the 1778 publication was so obviously makeshift, it was not counted separately. And since only close bibliographical scrutiny can detect variations among the dozen issues of the 1782 version—Law gave no separate designation to any of them—they are treated in the Core Repertory count as a single edition. On the other hand, although Andrew Adgate's *Philadelphia Harmony* was published eight times with *Rudiments of Music* (second through ninth editions) between 1789 and 1807 with the same music on the first fifty-six pages in all editions, for reasons explained below, each tune's printing has been counted.

Law and Adgate represent extreme cases, but the tune count in both reflects a basic rule of thumb that is followed here: if there is evidence that a compiler has rethought the identity of a collection, either by bringing out an identified new edition, or by bringing out an altered issue that amounts to a new edition (even if it is not called one), the tunes in that issue are counted as new printings. Therefore, appearances of a tune in separately designated editions of a single tunebook are counted as printings. Likewise, appearances of a tune in a substantially altered issue not designated as a separate edition are also counted as printings.

The size of the Core Repertory, 101 compositions, has turned out to be workable and convenient. It is large enough to provide a characteristic sample (nearly 1.5 percent of the entire repertory) and small enough to be encompassed in a single, hefty tunebook. Admittedly, a claim that the list also represents *the* 101 "most popular" sacred pieces of the period could be disputed, because a cumulative total reached by cataloguing music published during the course of more than a century will not necessarily reflect what music was popular at any given moment within that time-span. There is also a practical objection to equating "most frequently printed" with "most popular." If one puts his trust entirely in numbers, he may well find himself making a distinction as decisive as that between the quick and the dead—between, for example, tunes printed forty-four times and tunes printed forty-three times, the former being canonized in the Core Repertory, the latter consigned to loser's oblivion.

The present Core Repertory may later be subject to slight changes. Collections and issues now undiscovered seem certain to turn up in the future, and when they do, they may bring about the replacement of a tune or two on the list. Such difficulties and possible unfairness are part of any attempt to choose a sample. However, the advantages of identifying a central, representative core of tunes for observation, analysis, and interpretation should outweigh reservations about the way they have been chosen. In fact, the method of

choice used here may enjoy a certain advantage over one accounting for more variables. Its very simplicity may help to remind the user of the list's limitations, while a more sophisticated, more complicated method might beguile him into thinking he is working with a repertory of tunes scientifically proven "most popular."

The Music of the Core Repertory

The music of the Core Repertory was composed over a period of nearly two-and-a-half centuries: from the 1550s to the 1790s. During that time great changes took place in the music of Western Europe and England. During that time, too, British Protestant sacred music gained a foothold in the New World. In view of these events and others, the stylistic diversity that exists among Core Repertory compositions is to be expected.

That diversity has been documented and analytically described by John Worst.[10] Identifying four composer groups, Worst makes it possible to sort out the 101 pieces of the Core Repertory into the following style categories:[11]

STYLE CATEGORY	TUNES CONTRIBUTED
1. Tunes by English and French composers of the sixteenth and early seventeenth centuries	10
2. Tunes by English and German composers of the seventeenth and early eighteenth centuries	12
3. Tunes by English composers of the mid-to-late eighteenth century	42
4. Tunes by American composers of the late eighteenth to early nineteenth centuries	37

Nicholas Temperley's recent work on English psalmody clarifies matters further, so that one is tempted to adjust Worst's style categories a bit:[12] (1) English and French "common tunes" of the sixteenth and seventeenth centuries.[13] (2) English parish tunes of the eighteenth century, both homophonic and fuging.[14] (3) English Methodist-inspired pieces of the mid-eighteenth century and later.[15] (4) American compositions by New Englanders working from 1770 on.

Even after the adjustments, Worst's analytical and stylistic framework still holds for the music of the Core Repertory, and there seems no need to rehash his work here.

There is, however, a perspective on the Core Repertory that approaches the music on a more basic level than the style categories suggested above, and this concerns the level of rhythmic motion. Important for any kind of music, motion is fundamental in the field of hymnody, because it is precisely the function of a hymn tune to shape the delivery of a sacred text by guiding it through time. If one approaches the compositions of the Core Repertory as agents of motion and thinks of the music of Anglo-American Protestantism as representing a gradual process of discovering new and different ways in which sacred texts can move through time, then a somewhat altered view of the history of the music suggests itself. As a collection of some of the most successful compositions of Anglo-American Protestantism, drawn from several centuries' time, the Core Repertory seems to provide an ideal basis from which the outline of that history might be sketched.

The Common-Tune Style

The oldest style of song in the American Core Repertory is that of the "common tune," introduced into English Protestant congregations during the sixteenth century as a tune to which a variety of texts could be sung, as distinguished from a "proper tune," which was linked with just one set of words. The common tunes that found their way into American tunebooks are distinguished by duple meter, by through-composed melodic structure (ABCD) wherein each phrase receives a different melody (almost always carried in the tenor), by delivery of the text in notes of equal value, and by a lack of written embellishment.[16] To reform-minded psalmodists after 1800, tunes like Psalm 100 [Old], Windsor, Canterbury, Psalm 148, and Southwell represented "the old slow church music,"[17] and a sober gravity of motion was singled out as their chief trait. Moving in measured gait, the common tunes assign equal stress to each text syllable.[18] The result is a piece that in performance can resemble the clanging of a great church bell, with each note and syllable sounding in a separate attack, and the slower the tempo, the more disconnected the syllables. It is no wonder that both in England and America the "old way of singing"—in which congregational singers freely decorated the notes of the original psalm tunes, slowing the tempo even further—grew up in the seventeenth and eighteenth centuries within the framework of the duple common tunes.[19]

The simple impressiveness of the common tunes and the absence of rhythmic difficulties that might trouble the singers, make their stately, foursquare movement the heart of Anglo-American congregational performance—the touchstone from which other kinds of motion proceeded. The seventeenth and early eighteenth centuries saw more common tunes composed: St. David's, London New, York, Coleshill, St. James, Standish, and St. Anne. Isle of Wight, Walsall, and Bangor, composed in the British Isles in the 1720s and 1730s, all maintain the old measured duple tread; but all show their more modern provenance through the addition, here and there, of passing tones that fill melodic gaps and soften the angular melodic contour often found in such tunes. The appearance in 1770 of two more pieces (one by an American and the other by an Englishman) in the common-tune mold—William Billings's Lebanon and Aaron Williams's St. Thomas—proves that the old

convention could still reward the composer who had a feel for it.

In 1700 an Anglo-American psalm tune, almost by definition, proceeded in slow duple meter; but by 1800, Anglo-American sacred pieces moved in widely varied ways. No innovation was more striking or more basic to the repertory's transformation than the process of increasing rhythmic animation that touched psalmody during the course of the eighteenth century. The tunes of the Core Repertory illustrate something of that process and even suggest the order in which changes took place.

Dactylic Tunes

Early in the eighteenth century a new, more incisive way of declaiming text appeared in duple-time tunes. In contrast to the common-tune style, in which all syllables receive equal value, phrases began to be organized into patterns of long and short notes, especially dactyls (♩♪♪).[20] Aylesbury, Rochester, and Wells—tunes in Short Meter (6.6.8.6),[21] Common Meter (8.6.8.6), and Long Meter (8.8.8.8), respectively, all of which were first published between the years of 1718 and 1724— derive a sharp rhythmic thrust from the dactyl, which suggests that this pattern was a device newly rediscovered at about that time. Aylesbury manages five, Rochester six, and Wells eight dactyls in four phrases. The dactyl introduces an element of rhythmic propulsion into duple meter that must have encouraged singers to take a faster tempo. However, in New England the performance of sacred music was an issue so tradition-bound that worshippers were known to leave the meeting-house in protest if singing departed in any way from custom. Perhaps it was an unwontedly brisk tempo that explains an incident during public worship at Canton, Massachusetts, on 11 February 1770: "Some tunes were not relished. On the striking up of Ailesbury . . . old William Wheeler got up and went out of meeting."[22]

Dactylic patterns persisted into the second half of the century. Funeral Thought (1763) employs the pattern with special effectiveness by lengthening the long notes and speeding up the short ones, turning the exaggerated verbal accent into the dominating force in the tune. Here is a clearcut case of a tune's being composed with specific words in mind. The title suggests as much; the circulation of tune and text as a pair strengthens the suggestion further; and the musical phrase of the beginning confirms it: "Hark!" is set to a long E, high in the tenor range; "tombs" is stressed by the next long note; and "sound" resonates on a sustained E-major dominant triad. The dactylic pattern made strong impact on American composers of the 1770s and 1780s. Both Chester and Windham, the best-known tunes of Billings and Daniel Read, themselves the best-known Yankee composers of their time, rely on the dactylic pattern. Billings's AMHERST, Alexander Gillet's PSALM 25, and Amos Bull's PSALM 46 also draw their rhythmic organization from this pattern. Even Billings's LEBANON, the only American Core Repertory tune in the common-tune mold, begins with a half-note and two quarters before proceeding in half-notes; its beginning is thus made more decisive by the dactyl's shaping power. In all, fully a tenth of the tunes in the Core Repertory are dominated by dactyls, showing that dactylic rhythm, with its driving declamatory force, helped to preserve duple time as a framework for the composition of psalm- and hymn-tunes through most of the century.

Triple-Time Tunes

A second discovery made by eighteenth-century psalmodists was that sacred texts could be sung in iambs (♩ ♩), the pattern that most easily fits the accents of English words, and hence "overwhelmingly the commonest type [of motion] in all English verse."[23] Texts began to be scanned as alternations of strong and weak syllables, tunes were composed in which the former consistently received two beats to the latter's one, and triple time was introduced into parish church music. Judging from the dates of triple-time Core Repertory tunes, iambic declamation and triple time made their first decisive impact in the decade of the 1710s.[24] The iambic, triple-time approach to motion persisted through much of the rest of the century and is evident in nearly a quarter of the tunes of the Core Repertory.

If the triple-time tunes in the Core Repertory are examined in chronological order, one can observe how psalmodists gradually transformed a rather rigid formula into a means of achieving flexibility and grace. PORTSMOUTH (1711) and BATH (1713), the two earliest triple-time tunes, stick almost entirely to one note per syllable, alternating whole-notes and halves in $\frac{3}{2}$ time.[25] BURFORD, composed later in the decade, loosens the formula a bit, as a few of the whole-notes on downbeats are subdivided into halves. BROMSGROVE, from the late 1720s, turns that tendency into something like another formula, as it subdivides the whole-note downbeat of almost every other measure into half-notes, which fill in gaps in the tenor melodic line, making intervals within phrases almost entirely stepwise. In this tune and in Tans'ur's COLCHESTER (1735), also in Common Meter (8.6.8.6), whole-notes on the fourth syllable of the poetic line subdivide the first and third phrases into halves, and a sense of movement is established that seems almost facile when compared with the more old-fashioned motion of Tans'ur's PLYMOUTH (also introduced in 1735).

William Knapp developed the possibilities of triple-time motion even further in two tunes introduced in 1738. ALL SAINTS is a study of stepwise tenor melodic motion, with most of its strong beats subdivided into half-notes and a few weak beats in the second half of the piece further divided into quarters. In WESTON FAVEL the composer seems to have spared no effort to produce the liveliest triple-time piece possible. Instead of the usual $\frac{3}{2}$, the time signature is $\frac{3}{4}$, quickening the tempo. The notes on the strong downbeats are dissolved in that they are reduced not simply from half-notes to quarters, but even further, to a sharply etched rhythmic motive—a dotted-eighth-and-sixteenth-note figure (♪. ♪) that becomes something of a mannerism. (Of the first thirteen measures in the tenor, ten begin with that figure.) The tune's range, an eleventh, is unusually wide, and the tenor melody is full of skips. Rhythmic subdivision in WESTON FAVEL is not, as in earlier tunes, primarily a way of smoothing out the melody line. It is, instead, a means of enlivening the motion. The rhythmic motive, in fact, often decorates one pitch, rather than moving the line either upward or downward. Taken together, the dotted rhythms and the melodic skips give the tune an energy unusual in congregational sacred music of the time. Its acceptance in England doubtless owed much to the novelty of its motion.[26] WESTON FAVEL was apparently conceived with the text (by Isaac Watts) in mind. The concluding text repetitions are written into the tune, and the pervasive cheerfulness of the text is well supported by the tune's bumptious gait.

By the 1740s psalmodists had found several different ways to treat triple time, and their successors took over most of them. Tunes like IRISH (1749) and KINGSBRIDGE (ca. 1760) are written in $\frac{3}{4}$ and dissolve many of their strong-beat half-notes—there is even some use of the dotted-eighth-and-sixteenth motive, though in more restrained fashion than in WESTON FAVEL. However, although LITTLE MARLBOROUGH (1763) and ST. HELEN'S (ca. 1763) are also in $\frac{3}{4}$, they avoid any ornamental tendency, and stick to movement in half-notes and quarters. ST. MARTIN'S (1735), MORNING HYMN (ca. 1760), and PUTNEY (1763), all in $\frac{3}{2}$, show considerable flexibility in their melodic decoration, breaking up many strong beats with the dotted-rhythm motive (♩. ♪ ♩). The first SUTTON of the Core Repertory (ca. 1760) and WANTAGE (1763) move almost entirely in whole-notes and halves in $\frac{3}{2}$, recalling the sobriety of the earlier PORTSMOUTH and BATH. And in BUCKINGHAM (ca. 1763) and, especially, BROOKFIELD (1770), the intermixing of whole-notes, half-notes, and the dotted rhythmic motive on downbeats, coupled with an expansive melodic sweep in the third phrase, combine to produce an especially supple, imaginative use of triple time.

By the mid-eighteenth century, then, Anglo-American psalmodists had mastered half-note patterns and dactylic patterns of motion in duple time, as well as iambic motion in triple time. It remained for musicians of the century's second half to explore duple time further. This they did, chiefly by discovering new modes of quarter-note motion.

Decorated Duple Tunes

The first discovery in duple-time quarter-note motion seems to have been spearheaded by the Methodists, a reformist sect that grew up within the Anglican Church under the leadership of John Wesley. Believing that singing "should be a heartfelt and spontaneous act of worship by the people,"[27] Wesley and the Methodists brought a new kind of music into use among their followers, a music that borrowed some of its more immediately appealing features from popular secular music. The Core Repertory tune AMSTERDAM (1742), published in the first Methodist tunebook, illustrates many traits of the type. Its time signature, $\frac{2}{4}$, calls for a fast tempo. It moves in quarter-notes with occasional melodic embellishments in eighths and sixteenths. Its text is trochaic rather than iambic, with the strong syllables appearing on down-beats.[28] Its melody is organized according to the kinds of repetition often found in instrumental dance music. The first phrase is stated, then repeated almost exactly, and after a digression it returns, creating a melodic form of AABA. An observer writing early in the nineteenth century about sacred music noted that some of the lighter-weight pieces of the previous age had tunes inspired by the march: that AMSTERDAM was one such piece named by this observer provides evidence that its motion made it seem lighter than most others, at least within its field of sacred music.[29]

AMSTERDAM is the earliest of a group of fourteen Core Repertory pieces that are here called "decorated duple tunes." Within that group certain qualities characterize both music and text. Earlier psalm- and hymntunes had been written according to metrical rather than expressive dictates, and few were linked with any single text, except for tunes in unusual meters to which few texts would fit. From mid-century on, however, more and more tunes were composed with specific words in mind—composed not simply to match a text's metrical accents, but also to underline and intensify its meaning and, hence, its expressive power. Most of the decorated duple tunes in the Core Repertory are linked with specific texts; and most speak messages of joy and good cheer, replete with references to the skies and to heaven. AMSTERDAM, BETHESDA, PORTSMOUTH (also called TRUMPET), ST. GEORGE'S, CHRISTMAS, and MIDDLETOWN are sung to texts with martial elements—either military commands or images of the splendors of heaven. The texts of ADESTE FIDELES, ENFIELD, JORDAN, and PORTUGAL all recount heavenly splendors more fully. The optimistic messages of the texts to PSALM 33 and DUNSTAN confirm the general character, leaving only HOTHAM and WINTER, both sung to texts of a somewhat different, though certainly not contradictory tone.

The music of the decorated duple tunes shows a corresponding family resemblance. Every one of the fourteen is in major mode. All but two (PSALM 33 and WINTER) display melodic repetition in the tenor; several repeat the first phrase (e.g., AMSTERDAM), several the last phrase (e.g., CHRISTMAS), and others repeat according to some other scheme (e.g., ST. GEORGE'S, ABACD and PORTUGAL, ABCA). Together with their repetitions of melodic phrases, most of these tunes show some other formal trait that separates them from earlier tunes: AMSTERDAM, BETHESDA, PORTSMOUTH, CHRISTMAS, HOTHAM, and MIDDLETOWN have texts in Particular Meters that exceed the conventional four-line stanza; PSALM 33, ENFIELD, and JORDAN each set two stanzas (rather than the normal one) of Common Meter; ST. GEORGE'S, DUNSTAN, and ADESTE FIDELES all repeat the last part of the text, thus drawing out the length of the piece and giving special weight to the concluding words; and only PORTUGAL and WINTER are set to four-line stanzas without repetition. Some of the decorated duple tunes are written in $\frac{2}{4}$, and some are in $\frac{4}{4}$ time.[30] JORDAN is written in $\frac{2}{2}$; yet its other earmarks relate it so strongly to the decorated duple type that the observer feels justified in saying it should have been, or at least might well have been, notated in $\frac{2}{4}$.[31]

Of the four through-composed pieces in the Core Repertory, three—DENMARK, DYING CHRISTIAN, and HABAKKUK—set metrical text in decorated duple style. The first two introduce contrasting sections in triple time: this may have been done in DENMARK (mm. 21–41) to bring some variety to a non-dramatic, four-stanza text; it seems to have been done in DYING CHRISTIAN because the narrative text invites a contemplative contrast (mm. 68–79) before the triumphant close. Both tunes also pursue rhetorical emphasis through repetition of sections, of whole phrases, and of parts of phrases. In contrast to these two pieces, HABAKKUK maintains its original pattern of movement throughout, and is, in fact, unified by a four-note rhythmic figure (♪ | ♩ ♩ ♩.) that appears in almost every phrase in the piece.

Declamatory Duple Tunes

The second kind of duple-time movement that arrived with the second half of the century encompasses more Core Repertory pieces than any other type. Like the kind of movement brought in by the Methodists, this one also relies heavily upon the quarter-note. However, unlike the decorated duple tunes, in this group the half-note is the basic unit of motion, and quarter-note bursts appear as disruptions that are like a shifting of gears. The Methodist-inspired decorated duple tunes have about them an air of novelty and fashion: their character marks them as interlopers from outside the tradition. The second kind of tune, however, here called "declamatory duple," shows all the earmarks of an inside job. Written in the $\frac{2}{2}$ of the old common tunes, the declamatory duple style does not propose the faster beat that $\frac{2}{4}$ would imply; rather, the stolid tread of traditional duple time is enlivened with explosions of quarter-notes.

Joseph Stephenson's PSALM 34 (1760), one of the earliest examples of the declamatory duple type in the Core Repertory, displays the characteristic features well. Immediately after a whole-note beginning that allows them to gather themselves and tune their voices, the singers launch out in quarter-note motion to the first cadence. After a brief second phrase, mostly in half-notes, quarter-note motion begins again, this time through fuging, with the voices entering successively. The fuging lasts some six measures, with each quarter-note beat articulated by at least one of the voices singing one syllable per note. The forward march of the fuging section is further intensified by its melody, which consists almost entirely of repeated notes. Much has been made of the fuging-tune as the musical form that brought counterpoint to English parish psalmody and thereafter to American music. However true that may be, the fundamental fact remains that in fuging sections the voices often declaim quarter-notes syllabically and frequently sing a subject that involves repeated notes as well. The result was a newly aggressive kind of rhythmic movement. (The idea that fuging involves a kind of motion as well as a kind of texture may be implicit in the Latin word *fugere*—to fly—from which *fugue* is derived.)

Some thirty pieces in the Core Repertory are declamatory duple tunes. Most of these reach their declamatory climax in a "fuge." But several, in fact, are not fuging-tunes at all—if a fuging-tune is defined as a piece containing one or more sections in which voices enter successively, producing text overlap. Even more basic to the declamatory duple type than fuging is sectional structure, with at least one section dominated by declamatory quarter-note motion. In fact, almost all of the declamatory duple Core Repertory pieces are cast in two sections, with the second marked off by repeat signs.[32]

In some declamatory duple tunes, the second section contrasts sharply with the first. One obvious element of contrast is the texture change built into the fuging-tune, where four voices give way suddenly to one. Another area of contrast is in the rhythm of the text delivery. In MAJESTY, NORWICH, and BRISTOL, for example, the text in the first part of the piece is set flexibly before the incisive quarter-note beat of the second section's beginning abruptly introduces a new, more regular motion. MILFORD and CALVARY begin with fuges in dactylic rhythm; but the second section of each swings into a fuge in quarter-notes that brings a sense of acceleration. WORCESTER achieves a similar effect through a second section that fuges in quarter-notes and eighth-notes. MONTGOMERY introduces two fuges in its second section, the first in the characteristic repeated quarters and the second in quarters and eighths. In each of these pieces, and in others as well, the second section brings a more vigorous motion.[33]

In other tunes the contrast between sections is not very great at all. The fuging sections of BRIDGEWATER

and of NEWBURY, for example, move in dactyls, just as do the beginnings of both. In RAINBOW the fuge, with its brief melismas and downward melodic gesture, seems more a continuation than a digression. And two elements make the fuge of the second section of MARYLAND less aggressive than most: the voices enter with half-notes rather than quarters, and the subject of the fuge avoids repeated notes almost entirely. Thus, some psalmodists reduced the sectional contrast of declamatory duple tunes by composing second sections that avoid the sharply marked rhythm of quarter-note declamation.

A more common way to reduce sectional contrast, however, was to introduce declamatory quarter-note motion into both sections, anticipating the second's aggressive thrust in the first.[34] Of the thirty declamatory duple tunes in the Core Repertory, no fewer than seventeen begin with a melody in which either a half-note or a whole-note is followed by syllabic quarter-notes. PSALM 34 and DALSTON, in the 1760s, and MARYLAND, HARTFORD, and SUFFIELD, in the 1770s, are early examples of a technique that blossomed in the 1780s with such tunes as GREENFIELD, LENOX, VIRGINIA, MONTAGUE, LISBON, SHERBURNE, GREENWICH, and RUSSIA, and in the 1790s with MONTGOMERY, CORONATION, the 1793 SUTTON, and NEW JERUSALEM. Even where quarter-note declamation pervades both sections of a piece, however, the design of the sectional form emphasizes the second part. Not only is the second section repeated in full; it is also longer than the first section. Moreover, the beginning of the second section often brings both a texture change and a rhythmic acceleration, and it is thus the piece's most striking event. In fact, it is typical of the declamatory duple tunes of the Core Repertory that, by one means or another, the second section generates more energy than the first, building into each stanza a kind of dramatic plan in which motion plays a decisive role.

Since the decorated duple style described above is linked with the Methodists and shows a strong preference for texts of a certain kind, one may wonder whether an examination of the texts of the declamatory duple tunes in the Core Repertory might shed any light on the origin of that style. Is there anything distinctive about the texts of these declamatory duple pieces that might have encouraged the composers to work out a new way of treating them? For example, are the stanzas written to stress opposites, so that they invite sharp sectional contrasts? Do the texts of these pieces contain more than their share of images that seem to require vigorous declamatory motion? Do they favor a particular mood?

The answer to all of these questions is no. The texts of the declamatory duple pieces in the Core Repertory form a representative cross-section of the text-types of the Core Repertory as a whole.[35] Most are psalm paraphrases, chiefly by Watts, with some hymns mixed in; the emotional range goes all the way from the mournful Psalm 69 ("Save me, O God, the swelling flood," the 1793 SUTTON) to the ebullient Psalm 148 ("Ye tribes of Adam join," LENOX). Major and minor modes are quite equally divided, and although the most somber texts are sung in minor (e.g., "Teach me the measure of my days," SUFFIELD), so are some of the joyful (e.g., "This spacious earth is all the Lord's," HARTFORD, and "Ye sons of men with joy record," MONTAGUE). Most declamatory duple pieces are linked and circulated with specific texts, and as a group they show many examples of expressive text setting. Yet the fondness for sectional contrasts, quarter-note declamation, and repeated notes—all distinctive traits of the declamatory duple style—could seemingly be applied just as well to any other group of texts.

Though first introduced by English psalmodists, the declamatory duple model was cultivated with special skill by New Englanders. Its rise coincided with the advent of pieces by American composers in American-published tunebooks. The innate vigor of the declamatory duple style recommended it to singing-school scholars and choir singers, by whom it was joyfully embraced. Nevertheless, when a movement to reform American sacred music began in the 1790s, sparked by the clergy and certain musicians, the declamatory duple tunes were among the first to be purged. The reasons given are well known: the harmonic smoothness of European practice was missing from these tunes; and the text overlap of fuging-tunes produced verbal confusion. But the overriding complaint of reformers, governed by notions of religious and musical propriety, was that declamatory tunes encouraged spirited, even rambunctious, performances. Singers sailed into quarter-note declamation with a gusto that caused one psalmodist to caution: "Singing and vociferation are not the same thing."[36] Thus, the new style of movement that declamatory duple tunes had brought to psalmody proved the cause of their undoing: to the reformers who sought to control and remake American taste in sacred music, these tunes had too much spirit to be spiritual.

A Note on Performance

To sing the pieces in the Core Repertory, modern performers may need guidance on three issues.

The first is tempo. During the period in which the Core Repertory compositions were in circulation, each time signature stood for its own "mood of time" and hence implied a particular tempo. Some compilers gave precise instructions on the subject of tempo, although it is hard to know how closely their directions were followed. Time signatures in the present edition, which have been converted to modern equivalents, should nevertheless be taken as tempo suggestions. Metronomic translations of the basic beat have been worked out as follows:[37]

TIME SIGNATURE IN THIS EDITION	MM EQUIVALENT
4/4	♩ = 60
2/2	♩ = 60
2/4	♩ = 120
3/2	♩ = 60
3/4	♩ = 80

The second performance issue concerns the disposition of voices. In most of the settings printed here, the melody appears in the tenor voice. Although evidence is scanty, there is reason to think that eighteenth-century Americans who sang these settings doubled the tenor melody an octave higher, in the treble (soprano) part.[38] Certainly that was done in congregational singing, as it is today; moreover, Billings 1794 recommended as much,[39] and the southern shape-note singers, who have preserved some of this music in living tradition, commonly double both treble and tenor parts at the octave, producing a six-voice texture. Modern singers are therefore encouraged to explore doublings; singing the pieces as written can also be recommended.

The third issue is accompaniment. The music of the Core Repertory was all published in its own time, as it is here, to be sung unaccompanied. That does not mean, however, that instruments never played along with psalm-singing. Nor does it mean that modern performances must be given without instruments. Present-day singers interested in trying to recapture the sound and spirit of earlier performances might want to double the voice parts with instruments, because after theological disapproval of instruments began to erode in the 1780s and 1790s, flutes, clarinets, violins, cellos, and organs were used in churches, singing-schools, and musical societies to accompany singing. If an organ is used, however, the organist ought not to be encouraged to reharmonize pieces.[40]

Editorial Policy

The Core Repertory of Early American Psalmody has been edited according to the following principles and practices.

1. Since each piece was printed at least forty-four times, and many received more than 100 printings,[41] and since, therefore, "popularity" is the chief criterion for inclusion, the goal here has been to find a representative form of each piece—one that circulated widely. Some pieces change very little from printing to printing, but others change a good deal. No attempt is made here to catalogue variants or to produce composite versions; rather, many printings of each piece have been examined, a representative version from the period has been chosen, and that version is included in the present edition. (Repeats are added to a few pieces on the authority of printings other than the

one selected; these are noted in the Critical Commentary.)

2. Composer attributions from original sources are made on the music pages for all pieces whose composers are definitely known. For pieces whose composers have not been identified, the country or place of origin is cited on the music page. Dates on the music pages are those of the composition's first printing.

3. The text chosen here is the one most closely linked with the tune during the period. In Anglo-American sacred music of the seventeenth and eighteenth centuries, tunes and texts often carried on separate lives. While some of the pieces printed here virtually always appeared with the same texts, other tunes carried many different texts. A survey of the sources revealed a favorite text for each tune in all but a small number of cases; even where no clearcut consensus text could be identified, a text was chosen that is printed with the tune at least twice during the period.

4. Multiple stanzas of text are provided for all except the through-composed pieces. Although most musical sources carry only one stanza of text, most of the texts come from well-known hymnbooks of which many eighteenth-century Americans had copies, and there is reason to believe that several stanzas of text were often sung. Rather than suggesting that every stanza of every piece ought to be sung, the goal here has been to make available to the twentieth-century performer and scholar the full text that was easily accessible to his or her eighteenth-century predecessor. Performers can then choose stanzas as they please.

5. The tunes are chosen from a variety of sources. The collections from which tunes are transcribed for the edition show a wide chronological range (printed between 1761 and 1810) and a wide geographical spread (compiled or printed as far north as Exeter, New Hampshire; as far west and south as Harrisburg, Pennsylvania), and many are works that went through several editions (e.g., Adgate's *Philadelphia Harmony, The Worcester Collection,* and *The Village Harmony*). The general intent was: (1) to take the tune after it had passed from the composer's control and through the hands and compilations of several editors; and (2) to demonstrate that the repertory flourished for a rather long time over a rather wide territory. The few pieces taken here from their first printings or from works compiled by their composers all appeared in that form in many other printings as well.

6. Underlaid texts may be divided into three classes:

Class I: texts appearing in the same form in which they are printed in the musical sources.

Class II: texts which in the musical sources contain inconsistencies of capitalization, punctuation, or spelling that might confuse the modern reader and performer; these are edited here for clarity.

Class III: texts incomplete or absent from the musical sources; these are supplied here from text sources

and follow the capitalization, punctuation, and spelling found there.

If no mention of changes in the underlaid text is made in the Critical Commentary, the text has been taken *verbatim* from the musical source (Class I) or the text source (Class III). Changes in Class II texts are noted in the Critical Commentary. The following editorial changes have been made tacitly in all three classes of text.

    a. First words in poetic lines are capitalized.
    b. Proper nouns are capitalized.
    c. Ampersands (&) are changed to "and"; the article "ye" is modernized to "the."
    d. The verb "shew" is modernized to "show."
    e. Italics indicating quotations are replaced by quotation marks; italicized proper names are left in roman type.

7. Additional stanzas are taken from text sources cited in Appendix I, also with original capitalization, punctuation, and spelling unless otherwise noted in the Critical Commentary or covered by the list of changes noted in no. 6 above.

8. Time signatures are from the sources except where noted in the Critical Commentary. In pieces where the musical accents conflict strongly with the barring in the source, alternative barrings are suggested above the staff (see Plate I and no. [99] WINTER).

9. In the original printings, groups of two or more notes sung to the same syllable are connected by slurs. In the present edition, text underlay, the beaming of eighth- and/or sixteenth-notes together, and the use of extender lines after final syllables substitute for the source slurs. (Cf. Plate I and no. [64], PSALM 25.)

10. Accidentals in parentheses are cautionaries and have been added by the editor. Everything else on the music pages that is surrounded by square brackets is also of editorial origin.

11. Clefs for the treble (soprano) and bass parts are from the sources. The tenor, originally written in standard G clef, is here written in octavating G clef, showing that it is to be read an octave lower than it is notated. Unless otherwise noted in the Critical Commentary, the counter (alto) was originally written in C clef. Dynamic markings written in the original sources as "soft," "piano," "loud," or "forte" are here modernized to "*p*," and "*f*" without comment; the dynamic indication "increase" is similarly modernized to "cresc." here.

12. The melody is usually sung by the tenor. Wherever another voice carries the tune, that voice is identified in the score as "[melody]."

Acknowledgments

No edition of the Core Repertory of early American psalmody would ever have appeared had not someone first suggested that one be attempted. That suggestion came in the summer of 1972 from H. Wiley Hitchcock, whose support and encouragement have been indispensable to the project during its long gestation period.

The first serious work on the edition was done in 1974 during my term as Senior Research Fellow at the Institute for Studies in American Music at Brooklyn College, City University of New York. Editorial principles were sketched out and versions of most of the pieces tentatively chosen by members of my seminar, including Mason Martens, Laurie Spiegel, Robin Warren, Angelo Corbo, Stuart Chasnoff, and Rita Mead, all of whose contributions I gratefully acknowledge.

The music was put into final form at the University of Michigan in 1977–78 with the careful and dependable help of Thomas L. Riis, and with financial support from the John Simon Guggenheim Foundation. Several graduate students in the musicology program at Michigan have also contributed suggestions and information to the project, most notably Nym Cooke, David Warren Steel, and Paul Osterhout. The staff of the William L. Clements Library has consistently been helpful during the years I have worked there on this project.

My indebtedness to the published work of Nicholas Temperley is manifest in the following pages, but his generous willingness to share unpublished data and to offer advice and moral support through the course of this project should also be acknowledged. With the support of the University of Michigan's Rackham School of Graduate Studies, Gail Dapogny and Eleanor Benjamin assisted me with indexing the repertory. Other colleagues who have helped at one stage or another are Karl Kroeger, David A. Sutherland, Bruce Gustafson, Walter L. Powell, Allen P. Britton, and the late Irving Lowens. As my collaborators on a forthcoming bibliography of American sacred music imprints, made between 1698 and 1810, the latter two men began the bibliographical study out of which first came the notion of a Core Repertory.

Finally, thanks are due to the staff of A-R Editions, Inc., whose passion for clarity and consistency has left me much in their debt.

Richard Crawford

Notes

1. Composer-compiler Stephen Jenks wrote in 1804 of the "great torrent of music which is continually pouring upon the public from almost every quarter" (Jenks 1804). The count and much of the information presented below are taken from the present editor's unpublished index of American tunebooks. The index was completed in the course of work on an as yet untitled bibliography of American sacred music imprints, from between 1698 and 1810, written in collaboration with Allen P. Britton and Irving Lowens, forthcoming from the American Antiquarian Society, Worcester, Massachusetts.

2. Anglo-American sacred music encompasses both strophic and through-composed pieces. Among strophic compositions, which set one or more stanzas of verse and provide music to which additional stanzas can be sung, the simplest is the plain tune, which sets its text without repetition of words or sections. The tune-with-extension repeats words or sections within the course of setting its text. The fuging-tune includes at least one section where contrapuntal voice entries produce text overlap. Through-composed forms are represented by anthems and set-pieces. The anthem sets a prose text and the set-piece a verse text.

3. *The Monthly Anthology and Boston Review*, I (December, 1804); quoted in Richard Crawford, *Andrew Law, American Psalmodist* (Evanston: Northwestern University Press, 1968), p. 179.

4. The sigla used here to refer to publications of sacred music are identified in Appendix II, below.

5. If the German-language repertory, which at this period showed very little overlap with the English, is added to the group of 85, 247 different sacred pieces were in print in the American colonies by 1760, dropping the proportion of Core Repertory pieces to 9 percent. See Appendix III, Table 1, for a list of Core Repertory pieces in order of their first American printings.

6. The Core Repertory contains such congregational favorites as PSALM 100 [OLD], WINDSOR, and MEAR; such fuging-tunes as PSALM 34, SHERBURNE, and LENOX; and such through-composed anthems and set-pieces as the ANTHEM FOR EASTER and DENMARK. There is no evidence that early American congregations sang anything but the congregational music.

7. See Richard Crawford, liner notes for *Make a Joyful Noise: Mainstreams and Backwaters of American Psalmody (1770–1840)*, (New World Recording, NW 255).

8. David P. McKay and Richard Crawford, *William Billings of Boston: Eighteenth-Century Composer* (Princeton: Princeton University Press, 1975), pp. 221–30, traces Billings's own efforts to obtain copyrights and recommends that historians of American music study the subject further.

9. Richard Crawford and D. W. Krummel, "Early American Music Printing and Publishing," *Printing and Society in Early America*, ed. William L. Joyce et al. (Worcester: American Antiquarian Society, 1983), pp. 195–99, 215–22.

10. John Worst, "New England Psalmody 1760–1810: Analysis of an American Idiom" (Ph.D. diss., University of Michigan, 1974).

11. Ibid., p. 300.

12. Nicholas Temperley, *The Music of the English Parish Church*, 2 vols. (Cambridge: Cambridge University Press, 1979).

13. Ibid., 1: 65–71.

14. Ibid., 1: 190–96. This category encompasses the dactylic

and triple-time tunes described below, as well as the declamatory duple pieces by English composers.

15. Ibid., 1: 207–14.

16. Ibid., 1: 76. Noting the changes that took place in the common tunes over time, Temperley describes them as being "ironed and flattened by hard use."

17. Bartholomew Brown and others, *Columbian and European Harmony* (Boston: Isaiah Thomas and Ebenezer T. Andrews, 1802), p. [4].

18. The last syllable in each phrase, however, may receive slightly more stress by being held longer.

19. See Temperley, *The Music*, 1: 91–98; see also Idem, "The Old Way of Singing: Its Origins and Development," *Journal of the American Musicological Society* 34 (Fall 1981): 511–44.

20. Patterned rhythm in psalm-singing was not an eighteenth-century invention. In fact, the oldest English psalm tunes—the proper tunes of the Anglo-Genevan psalter, Sternhold and Hopkins's "Old Version," and the later "Ainsworth Psalter," many of which are eight-line structures—had been organized according to rhythmic patterns. But, as Temperley has shown (*The Music*, 1: 63ff), during the later sixteenth century most of these tunes gave way to the four-line common tunes, which lost rhythmic snap under congregational use. Perhaps the inability of congregations to sing with rhythmic precision had as much to do with the eight-line tunes falling from favor as did their length. LANDAFF, the only sixteenth-century proper tune in the Core Repertory, rigidly applies dactylic rhythm to the beginnings of each of its six lines (four of ten syllables, two of eleven). Perhaps its rhythm explains why LANDAFF did not appear in American tunebooks until the second half of the eighteenth century, when it began to circulate with shorter dactylic tunes that came into favor at the same time.

21. The numerals refer to the number of syllables per line in each of these familiar four-line stanza structures.

22. Daniel T. V. Huntoon, *History of the Town of Canton* (Cambridge: John and Son, 1893), p. 312.

23. Alex Preminger, ed., *Princeton Encyclopedia of Poetry and Poetics*, enl. ed. (Princeton: Princeton University Press, 1974), p. 300.

24. The classic triple-time tune PSALM 149 had appeared in print in 1708. However, it gives its text, in Particular Meter (i.e., a pattern other than the usual Common, Short, or Long meters), a spondaic setting, assigning a syllable to each half-note in $\frac{3}{2}$ time. Another triple-time tune, ANGELS HYMN, dates back all the way to 1623. However, in this original (1623) version, printed as No. 336 in *Historical Companion to Hymns Ancient & Modern*, ed. Maurice Frost (London: William Clowes & Sons, 1962), the iambic movement that eighteenth-century compilers gave it had not yet appeared. (See also ANGELS HYMN in Appendix I.)

25. They share this property with MEAR, BEDFORD, and PSALM 100 [NEW].

26. See Erik Routley, *The Music of Christian Hymnody* (London: Independent Press, 1957), pp. 89ff.

27. Temperley, *The Music*, I: 209.

28. Temperley, *The Music*, I: 212, calls "the new trochaic metres . . . the Wesleys' chief contribution to English sacred prosody."

29. See Appendix I, s.v. AMSTERDAM.

30. See A Note on Performance, p. xvi, about the relationship between time signatures and tempos. CHRISTMAS and DUNSTAN were both notated with a quarter-note beat in England and in some American publications too.

31. Billings 1786, the collection in which JORDAN was introduced, contains many pieces similar in style to JORDAN that are notated in $\frac{2}{4}$ (e.g., HARTFORD, PHILANTHROPY, PETERSBURGH, MORIAH, and others), suggesting that Billings had himself become acquainted with Methodist hymnody and was exploring its possibilities.

32. The declamatory duple tunes that lack repeated second sections are NEWBURY, DALSTON, and JUDGMENT.

33. Perhaps no examples of duple declamatory motion are more striking than a pair found in the Core Repertory's lone through-composed setting of prose: Billings's ANTHEM FOR EASTER. The first example occurs well into the piece (mm. 46–51), after much antiphonal singing and movement in fits and starts. "Did he rise?" comes the question, to which the answer resounds: "Hear, o ye nations, Hear it, o ye dead!" with all four voices joining under a *forte* marking, and with a rhythmic snap sure to rouse the somnolent. The second noteworthy passage consists of the stream of consecutive repeated eighth-notes on which the chorus announces with Monteverdian *parlando*: "Then first humanity triumphant passed the crystal ports of light, and seized eternal youth" (mm. 77–85).

34. A different way of doing the same thing is demonstrated in PSALM 136. Because its first section concludes with a fuge based on repeated quarter-notes, the beginning of the second in similar fashion brings no strong sense of contrast.

35. Of the one hundred verse texts in the Core Repertory, sixty are psalm paraphrases and forty are hymns. Isaac Watts contributed fifty of the sixty psalm paraphrases, and the rest come from Brady and Tate's *New Version* (eight), Sternhold and Hopkins's "Old Version" (one), and the "Bay Psalm Book" (one). Watts also wrote twenty-two of the hymns; Charles Wesley contributed four, Philip Doddridge two, and Joseph Addison, Thomas Flatman, Edward Perronet, Alexander Pope, Elizabeth Rowe, Robert Seagrave, Anne Steel, and Nahum Tate one apiece. Watts's texts dominate the Core Repertory as a whole, since there are seventy-two in all.

36. This admonition, noted down from an American tunebook published between 1785 and 1810, seems too apt to discard even though I must admit to having lost track of where I found it.

37. See also McKay and Crawford, *William Billings*, pp. 241–46.

38. Only William Billings, *The Continental Harmony* (Boston: Isaiah Thomas and Ebenezer T. Andrews, 1794), p. xv, and Isaac Lane, *An Anthem: Suitable to Be Performed at an Ordination* (Northampton: Daniel Wright and Company, 1797), p. [2], describe the practice of doubling in print before 1810.

39. See McKay and Crawford, *William Billings*, pp. 232–33.

40. For more on instruments and their role in psalmody, see Ibid., pp. 348–55.

41. For a list of Core Repertory pieces according to the number of printings they received, see Appendix III, Table 2.

Appendix I:
Core Repertory Compositions:
Historical Commentary

Entry Format

Information about each Core Repertory composition is given in a section of textual-historical commentary. These sections are arranged in alphabetical order by tune title. Commentary on each tune includes the following information in the following order.

Title

Tunes are listed alphabetically by title. The title used is normally the one under which the tune was first published in America. A few pieces, however, came to be closely identified with titles different from those of their first American printings. In such cases, the later, more prevalent title is used here. Additional titles given to the piece in American printings are listed in parentheses below the main title. Composer attribution appears immediately after the title.

Paragraph 1: Sources

1. Source, authorship, and meter (designated C.M. = Common Meter; S.M. = Short Meter; L.M. = Long Meter; or P.M. = Particular Meter) of the text underlaid with the tune in this edition.[1]

2. Source(s) of first publication—If the composition is not American, both the source in which it was first published and source of its first American publication are given.

3. Source from which the version of the tune in this edition is taken and the title under which it appeared, if that differs from the present title—The sigla used in this section are the same as those found elsewhere in the edition (see Appendix II).

Paragraph 2: Form and Publication Statistics

1. Category of musical form (i.e., anthem, set-piece, fuging-tune, tune-with-extension, plain tune) and textual meter (designated C.M., S.M., L.M., or P.M.).

2. Number of printings in America between 1698 and 1810.[2]

3. Comment about text-tune relationship—Some pieces were closely linked with certain texts, while others appeared with many different texts.

Paragraph 3: Circulation

1. Proportion of printings in New England, where most sacred music of the eighteenth and early nineteenth centuries was published.[3]

2. Pattern of circulation—A report is made of the tunebooks (cited according to the sigla listed in Appendix II) in which the piece appeared, in the hope of revealing any geographic or stylistic pattern that might be evident. Places listed are the places where compilers lived and worked at the time their books appeared. (Thus, in Appendix II, Pilsbury 1799, for example, is assigned to its compiler's home base of Charleston, South Carolina, even though it was printed in Boston, where letterpress printing technology for music was available.) For most pieces, all of the collections in which they appeared are listed; for some with many printings, however, findings are summarized.[4] (See, e.g., DENMARK, ST. MARTIN'S, and WELLS; though, for the sake of including a complete census of the most widely printed piece of all, the entry on PSALM 100 [OLD] names every collection.) Collections with only one edition are given with an author's name or a designating title and date (e.g., Billings 1786, Sacred 1806). If a piece appeared in a subsequent edition of a collection, an "f" is added to the siglum (e.g., Law 1779f). If a collection was published in more than one subsequent edition and the piece appeared in all, "ff" is added to the siglum (e.g., Worcester 1786ff). If, on the other hand, a collection enjoyed more than one subsequent edition and the piece appeared in some but not all of them, the latest printing is also indicated in the siglum (e.g., Village 1795–1803). References are sometimes made to "eclectic" and "reform" tunebooks, especially from the years 1800 to 1810. The former means books containing a mixture of American and European compositions, the latter, books devoted mostly or entirely to European pieces harmonized according to "correct" principles derived from European practice.[5]

3. Circulation in the period between 1811 and 1820—Some seventy American tunebooks published in the decade after 1810 have been canvassed to see how the Core Repertory tunes fared in print during that decade; the number of printings found in them is reported.

4. Appearance in retrospective collections—Between 1829 and 1879, a number of "historical" tunebooks were printed in New England: these are publications consciously harking back to earlier tastes and advertising themselves as specializing in favorite sacred pieces of times past. A sample of eight such books (listed below in chronological order) has been canvassed to see which Core Repertory pieces survived in them.

Stoughton Collection of Church Music. Boston: Marsh & Capen, 1829.

The Billings and Holden Collection of Ancient Psalmody. Boston: Marsh, Capen & Lyon, 1836.

Symphonia Grandaeva Rediviva. Ancient Harmony Revived. Hallowell, Maine: Masters, Smith & Co., 1847.

Mansfield, Rev. D. H. *The American Vocalist.* Boston: W. J. Reynolds, 1849.

Marshall, Leonard. *The Antiquarian.* Boston: C. H. Keith, 1849.

Continental Harmony. Boston: Oliver Ditson, 1857.

[Kemp, Robert H.] *Father Kemp's Old Folks Concert Music.* Boston: Oliver Ditson, 1874.

Cheney, Simeon Pease. *The American Singing Book.* Boston: White, Smith & Co., 1879.

5. Appearance in southern tunebooks—While most of the music of the Core Repertory fell out of fashion in the north, where it flourished in the eighteenth and early nineteenth centuries, some of these pieces were kept in living tradition in the south, chiefly in shape-note tunebooks. Five southern tunebooks were canvassed to see which Core Repertory pieces appealed to later southern compilers and singers.

Carden, Allen D. *The Missouri Harmony.* Revised and improved. Cincinnati: Morgan and Sanxay, 1832.

Walker, William. *The Southern Harmony.* Philadelphia: T. Cowperthwait, 1847. (Compiled in Spartanburg, South Carolina.)

McCurry, John G. *The Social Harp.* Philadelphia: T. K. Collins for the proprietor, John G. McCurry, 1855. (Compiled in Hart County, Georgia.)

White, B. F., and E. J. King. *The Sacred Harp.* New and much improved and enlarged edition. Philadelphia: S. C. Collins for the proprietors, White, Massengale & Co., Hamilton, Ga., 1860.

Swan, M. L. *The New Harp of Columbia.* Nashville: W. T. Berry, 1867.

Paragraph 4: Musical Style, Performances, Reputation

1. Some comment about the composition as a piece of music.

2. Evidence of eighteenth- and early nineteenth-century performances, if any is available. (Sources documenting evidence in this section are listed below under References for Appendix I. When towns are named without citation, the source of information will be found under the name of the town in the References list.)

3. Statements about the piece, if available, dealing with its composition, history, character, or reputation.

Additional References

1. EARLY NINETEENTH-CENTURY MANUSCRIPTS

Alderdice — Alderdice, Catherine. Manuscript of sacred music, written out near Emmitsburg, Maryland, 1800–29. William Clements Library, University of Michigan, Ann Arbor.

Eckhard — *Jacob Eckhard's Choirmaster's Book of 1809.* Copied in Charleston, South Carolina. A facsimile with introduction and notes by George W. Williams. Columbia: University of South Carolina Press, 1971.

Read — Read, Daniel. "Musica Ecclesia." Manuscript tunebook prepared in New Haven, Connecticut, ca. 1829–32. New Haven Colony Historical Society, New Haven.

2. TWENTIETH-CENTURY REFERENCE WORKS

AH — Christ-Janer, Albert, Charles W. Hughes, and Carleton Sprague Smith. *American Hymns Old and New.* New York: Columbia University Press, 1980.

AMR — Frost, Maurice, ed. *Historical Companion to Hymns Ancient & Modern.* London: William Clowes & Sons, for the Proprietors, 1962.

A&M — *Hymns Ancient and Modern.* Historical edi-

tion. London: William Clowes and Sons, for the Proprietors, 1909.

Fisher — Fisher, William Arms. *Ye Olde New-England Psalm-Tunes 1620–1820.* Boston: Oliver Ditson, 1930.

Frost — Frost, Maurice. *English & Scottish Psalm & Hymn Tunes c. 1543–1677.* London: Oxford University Press, 1953.

Hall — Hall, James William, Jr. "The Tune-Book in American Culture: 1800–1820." Ph.D. diss., University of Pennsylvania, 1967. (Pp. 133–36 present a "List of Most Popular Tunes"—191 titles chosen from a sampling of 50 tunebooks, 1880–20.)

Hitchcock — *American Music Before 1865 in Print and on Records: a Biblio-Discography.* Preface by H. Wiley Hitchcock. Brooklyn: Institute for Studies in American Music, 1976. (Numbers in parentheses refer to recordings.)

MinA — Marrocco, W. Thomas, and Harold Gleason. *Music in America: An Anthology from the Landing of the Pilgrims to the Close of the Civil War, 1620–1865.* New York: Norton, 1964.

Temperley — Temperley, Nicholas. *The Music of the English Parish Church.* 2 vols. Cambridge: Cambridge University Press, 1979. (Vol. 2 is "an anthology of English church music and its sources.")

3. CURRENT REPRESENTATIVE PROTESTANT HYMNALS

Baptist — Sims, Walter Hines, ed. *Baptist Hymnal.* Nashville: Convention Press, 1956.

Congregational — *Pilgrim Hymnal.* [Congregational Church]. Boston: Pilgrim Press, 1958.

Episcopal — *The Hymnal of the Protestant Episcopal Church in the United States of America, 1940.* New York: The Church Pension Fund, 1940.

Lutheran — *The Lutheran Book of Worship.* Minneapolis: Augsburg Publishing House, 1978.

Methodist — *The Methodist Hymnal.* Nashville: The Methodist Publishing House, 1966.

Presbyterian — *The Hymnbook.* Richmond, Philadelphia, New York: John Ribble, for The Presbyterian Church in the United States, The United Presbyterian Church in the U.S.A., and The Reformed Church in America, 1955.

Cross-References

If one Core Repertory tune is cited in an entry on another tune, the reader is directed to the additional citation by a cross-reference.

Notes to Entry Format

1. The sigla used to cite text sources are expanded either in the section References for Appendix I—Sources for Underlaid Texts or in Appendix II. The E-numbers following some of these expansions refer to Charles Evans's *American Bibliography* (see introduction to Appendix II).

The most prevalent textual meters in Anglo-American sacred music are four-line stanzas with the following arrangement of syllables:

Common Meter (C.M.)	8. 6. 8. 6.
Long Meter (L.M.)	8. 8. 8. 8.
Short Meter (S.M.)	6. 6. 8. 6.

Other patterns may be referred to as Particular Meters (P.M.), meaning patterns other than the commonplace four-line stanzas. One that carries its own label is:

Hallelujah Meter (H.M.)   6. 6. 6. 6. 4. 4. 4. 4.

Because the three set-pieces (DENMARK, DYING CHRISTIAN, and HABBAKUK) are settings of specific texts, meters are not indicated for these in the commentary.

2. Appendix III, Table 2, lists Core Repertory tunes by the number of times they were printed. The totals given here supersede those in Crawford MM (see References for Appendix I).

3. For a list of Core Repertory pieces according to their proportion of New England printings, see Appendix III, Table 3.

4. The summarizing involves two groups of works: tunebooks compiled or published by Daniel Bayley of Newburyport, Massachusetts, who between 1764 and 1788 was responsible for many collections (see Appendix II under the names of Bayley, Stickney, Tans'ur, and Williams), and tunebooks published in Massachusetts between 1800 and 1810. Tunebooks issued outside Massachusetts are listed in full in almost every case.

5. For a list of the tunebooks that carried the most Core Repertory pieces, see Appendix III, Table 4.

Tune Biographies

[1.] ADESTE FIDELES, by J. F. Wade
(LISBON, OPORTO, PORTUGAL NEW, PORTUGUESE HYMN)

Text from Watts, Psalm 92, L.M., 2d part. First published in [Samuel Webbe], *An Essay or Instruction for Learning the Church Plain Chant* (London, 1782). First published in America in Nehemiah Shumway, *The American Harmony*, 2d ed. (Philadelphia, 1801). Mann 1807, p. 31, as PORTUGUESE HYMN.

ADESTE FIDELES, a L.M. tune-with-extension in major mode, was printed 48 times. It was published with at least a dozen different texts, but more frequently with the present one than with any other.

Introduced in Philadelphia (Shumway 1801), ADESTE FIDELES received slightly less than half of its printings in New England. Its first printing is later than that of any other Core Repertory piece to appear in an American publication, and it enjoyed instant vogue, appearing in thirty-nine different tunebooks in just a decade's time. ADESTE FIDELES was picked up by other collections printed in Philadelphia (Sacred 1803, Carr 1805, Aitken 1806, Sacred 1806, Woodward 1806ff, Law 1807f, Addington 1808); in Baltimore (Cole S 1803, Cole 1804f, Gillet 1809); in Massachusetts (Brown 1802ff, Essex 1802, Worcester 1803, Boston First 1805f, Salem 1805f, Hill 1806, Holyoke 1807, Mann 1807, Suffolk 1807, Deerfield 1808, Boston Hymns 1808, Sanger 1808, Shaw 1808, Huntington 1809); in Connecticut (Griswold 1807); and in New York City (Evans 1808f, Seymour 1809). Perhaps the most dramatic evidence of the near-universal acceptance of this piece, however, is the list of tunebooks—urban and rural, reform and eclectic, from New Hampshire to Maryland—that printed it in 1810: Blake, Boston Brattle, Boston West, Cole, Doll, Jenks, Peck, Sacred, Village, Wyeth. It was also one of a small handful of sacred pieces to be published in sheet-music form: Richard J. Wolfe, *Secular Music in America, 1801–1825* lists several sets of piano variations and embellishments based on the tune (Nos. 2639, 2698, 7481, 9230). Circulation continued briskly in the decade 1811–1820, with appearances in at least twenty-nine tunebooks from those years. ADESTE FIDELES also appeared in four northern retrospective collections and three southern tunebooks.

Temperley documents ADESTE FIDELES's English popularity (Temperley, 1:236), and notes that its alternative titles stem from "its association with the Portuguese Embassy Chapel" in London (1:245). He also describes the "repeating tune" as a tune-type favored by English Methodists of the late eighteenth century: repeating tunes employ textural contrast and text repetition to achieve an unusually strong climax at the end of the piece (Temperley, 1:212; also see Routley 1959, pp. 147–48, for more on the tune's composition). The tune seems to have originated as a setting, dating from ca. 1743, of the Latin Christmas hymn, *Adeste Fideles*. The close identification of the tune with the translation of the text of that hymn, "O come, all ye faithful," dates in America at least as far back as the 1850s, for William Henry Fry's "Santa Claus" Symphony (1853) concludes with quotations of it. As reported in the composer's program of the symphony, after Santa Claus has paid his visit and has flown away, there

is heard in the highest regions of the Violins with fluttering ecstasy of hovering angels, the Christmas Hymn, *Adeste Fideles* . . . The hymn runs then into a swelling note of the whole orchestra, the perfect major chord. . . . This betokens the break of day. We are now introduced to the happy household. Knockings awaken the little sleepers with the cries of "Get up! get up! get up!" imitated on the Horn; and so roused, the children rush with joy and seize their toys, and the orchestra now plays *Little Bo-peep* on toy-trumpets, drums, and so forth. A trait from the Introduction of the Symphony, leads to the *Adeste Fideles (Hither, ye Faithful)* Hymn which, with grand chorus and orchestra, concludes the piece (quoted from Upton, p. 338).

Additional References

1. Alderdice, p. xx; Eckhard, No. 12; Read, No. 380
2. AMR 593; A&M 59; Hall (as PORTUGUESE HYMN)
3. Baptist; Congregational; Episcopal; Lutheran; Methodist; Presbyterian

[2.] ALL SAINTS, by William Knapp
(BOLTON, KNAP'S 100, WAREHAM)

Text from Watts, Psalm 19, L.M. First published in William Knapp, *A Sett of New Psalm Tunes* (London, 1738). First published in America in [*Collection of Psalm Tunes, with an Introduction, "To Learn to Sing"*] (Boston, [1763–67]), or Josiah Flagg, *A Collection of the Best Psalm Tunes* (Boston, 1764), or Thomas Walter, *The Grounds and Rules of Musick*, [8th ed.] (Boston, 1764). Boston 1799, p. 66.

ALL SAINTS, a triple-time L.M. plain tune in major mode, was printed 58 times. Textless until 1786, it appeared with at least a dozen different texts and was linked closely with none, though three collections did set it to the present text.

Introduced in Boston (see above), ALL SAINTS received more than 85 percent of its printings in New England, most of them in Massachusetts. The tune appeared in six of Daniel Bayley's publications before the war (Bayley 1766f, Bayley 1767f, Tans'ur 1767f, Tans'ur 1769ff, Bayley 1770ff, Stickney 1774ff), as well as in Walter 1764a, Gilman 1771, and New England 1771. Jocelin 1782 and Law 1783 introduced ALL SAINTS in Connecticut, Dearborn 1785 introduced it in New Hampshire, while another group of Massachusetts works printed it in the 1780s and 1790s (Bayley 1784, Mass 1784f, New 1784, Worcester 1786, Bayley 1788, Sacred 1788, Federal 1790ff, Boston 1799). Not until Cole 1799 (Baltimore) was the tune printed outside New England, and only a handful of appearances in Pennsylvania (Cumberland 1804, Woodward 1806ff, Law 1807f) and New York City (Evans 1810) followed that up. In the meantime, however, ALL SAINTS held its place in Massachusetts (Holyoke 1803, Law 1803, Salem 1805f, Boston First 1806, Middlesex 1807f, Deerfield 1808, Huntington 1809, Boston Brattle 1810, Brown 1810, Sacred 1810), mostly in reform collections. Circulation continued strong in the decade 1811–1820, with printings in twenty-eight different tunebooks. ALL SAINTS appeared in three later retrospective northern collections, but it was in no southern tunebook.

While the melody of ALL SAINTS is built up from four distinctly different phrases, ABCD, the tune is integrated in another way by a single motive (see mm. 1–2 of the tenor): three descending half-notes, followed by a fourth note, which lies a step away in either direction. That motive, in one form or another, occurs every other measure in phrases 1, 2, and 4; its absence from the third phrase creates a sense of digression. Temperley shows the tune (as WAREHAM) to have been an English favorite (1:236) and describes it as one of a group of "homophonic . . . country psalm tunes . . . with a tendency to elaboration," that "show the country psalmodist's grasp of simple melody" (1:176). In the colonies, ALL SAINTS was chosen by a congregation in Wilbraham, Massachusetts, for singing in public worship (22 October 1770; 1 of 23 tunes).

Additional References

1. Read, No. 169
2. AH, p. 152; AMR 245; A&M 345; Hall (as ALL SAINTS and WAREHAM); Temperley 2:ex. 44
3. Baptist; Congregational; Episcopal; Lutheran; Methodist; Presbyterian

Cross-Reference

See entry on ST. THOMAS.

[3.] AMHERST, by William Billings
Text from New Version, Psalm 148, P.M. First published in William Billings, *The New-England Psalm-Singer* (Boston, [1770]). Worcester 1788, p. 54.

AMHERST, a duple-time P.M. plain tune in major mode, was printed 74 times. It was more often set to the present text than to any of the three others with which it was printed, including the composer's own choice, "To God the mighty Lord," Psalm 136 from New Version.

Introduced in Boston by the composer's own works (Billings 1770, 1778ff, 1779), AMHERST received slightly less than two-thirds of its printings in New England. Picked up in Connecticut by Law 1779 and Jocelin 1782, it passed thereafter into a series of collections from Massachusetts (Mass 1784f, New 1784, Worcester 1786ff, Federal 1788ff, Sacred 1788, and in the 1790s, Mann 1797f and Boston 1799) and Philadelphia (Selection 1788ff, Adgate 1789ff, Shumway 1793f). By 1800 AMHERST had appeared in Virginia (Sandford 1793), New Hampshire (Village 1795ff, Merrill 1799), South Carolina (Pilsbury 1799) and New York State (Huntington 1800); a few years later, Arnold 1803 introduced it in Maryland. After 1800 AMHERST was most often found in eclectic compilations from Massachusetts (Belknap 1802, Cooper 1804, Albee 1805, Boston First 1806, Mann 1807, J. Read 1808, Sanger 1808) and Pennsylvania (Sacred 1806, Woodward 1806ff, Chapin 1808f, Wyeth 1810). It appeared in Law 1801, unaccountably attributed to a "Mr. Coleman" (Crawford, p. 323). Modest circulation continued in the next decade with printings in at least a dozen collections from the years 1811–1820. AMHERST appeared in four retrospective northern collections and in two southern tunebooks.

Though repeated dactyls make it square-cut and perhaps even a bit monotonous, AMHERST was by far the most frequently printed H.M. tune of the period. It rated favorable mention in 1835 from Thomas Hastings, who, describing Billings as owning "some genius, but very little learning," admitted: "his Amherst is on the whole a decent tune" (*Musical Magazine* I; quoted in McKay & Crawford, p. 203).

Additional References

1. Alderdice, p. vv; Read, No. 279
2. AH, p. 234; Hall

[4.] AMSTERDAM
Text from Law 1779; written by Robert Seagrave (see Julian, p. 1036). First published in *The Foundery Collection* (London, 1742). First published in America by Josiah Flagg, *A Collection of Psalm Tunes* (Boston, 1764) or Thomas Walter, *The Grounds and Rules of Musick*, [8th ed.] (Boston, 1764). Law 1779, p. 7.

AMSTERDAM, a P.M. tune-with-extension in duple time and in major mode, was printed 48 times. Closely linked with the present text, AMSTERDAM—the only Core Repertory piece with this meter—also appeared with at least three other texts, though none was in more than one other collection.

Introduced in Boston (by Flagg 1764 or Walter 1764a), AMSTERDAM received some 56 percent of its printings in New England, many of these in the publications of Daniel Bayley in Newburyport, Massachusetts (Tans'ur 1767f, Williams 1769ff, Stickney 1774ff, Bayley 1784, Bayley 1788), and Andrew Law in Cheshire, Connecticut (Law 1779f, Law 1792, Law 1794f). The only Massachusetts tunebook of the 1790s to carry it was Worcester 1791–97, followed by a handful after 1800 (Cooper 1804, Holyoke 1804, Boston Hymns 1808, Brown 1810). Elsewhere, it flourished in Philadelphia (Adgate 1791ff, Shumway 1793f, Poor 1794, Selection 1794f, Aitken 1806, Law 1807f, Woodward 1809, Blake 1810), appearing also in single items to the south in Baltimore (Cole 1799) and Charleston (Pilsbury 1799), and also in New York City (Evans 1808f). Circulation continued in the next decade, with printings in at least twenty-three collections from the years 1811–1820. AMSTERDAM also appeared in four retrospective northern collections and in two southern tunebooks.

AMSTERDAM represents the tendency of Wesleyan Methodism to enlist secular musical techniques in the service of sacred music. The notation itself—quarter-note motion in $\frac{2}{4}$, with eighth-note- and even a few sixteenth-note-decorations—suggests a sprightlier movement than most of the other pieces in the collection (see A Note on Performance, p. xvi of Preface). And the structure of the melody, with its immediate repetition of the first period and the same music's return at the end (AABA), hints strongly at instrumental origin. Writing in the 1820s, Thomas Hastings commented that Americans enjoyed "a general fondness for rhythmical movements," and pointed out that some "light compositions" of church music were in fact "made up of ideas derived more or less remotely from military movements," which is to say from marches. Among the pieces he named, all English in origin, was AMSTERDAM (Hastings, Dissertation, p. 205). Karl Kroeger, noting the tune's resemblance to the Moravian tune SERVICE, suggests that AMSTERDAM was originally Moravian (Kroeger 1973).

Additional References

1. Read, No. 365
2. Hall
3. Baptist; Methodist; Presbyterian

Cross-Reference

See entry on BETHESDA.

[5.] ANGELS HYMN, by Orlando Gibbons
(ANGELS SONG, ANGELS TUNE, OLD ANGELS HYMN)

Text from New Version, Psalm 95. First published in Wither, *Hymns and Songs of the Church* (London, 1623). Gibbons's first phrase differs from the one printed here, which was a product of eighteenth-century tinkering. Temperley, in a personal communication, assigns the change to Michael [and John] Broom[e], *Michael Broom's Collection of Church Musick* (n.p., 1725). First published in America in James Lyon, *Urania* (Philadelphia, 1761). Selection 1788, p. 52.

ANGELS HYMN, a triple-time L.M. plain tune in major mode, was printed 73 times. Appearing frequently without text, and set to at least eleven different texts in all, it was printed with the present one in most of its Philadelphia printings from 1788 on.

Introduced in Philadelphia (Lyon 1761f), ANGELS HYMN received only a third of its printings in New England—less than any other Core Repertory tune save one. The tune appeared before 1800 in no more than three Massachusetts tunebooks (Flagg 1764, Tans'ur 1767f, Tans'ur 1769ff) and four more in Connecticut (Law 1781, Jocelin 1782f, Law 1791f, Read 1794f), receiving most of its circulation in collections from New York City (Psalms 1767, Collection 1774, Amphion 1789) and especially Philadelphia (Tunes 1763f, Tunes 1786, Selection 1788ff, Adgate 1789ff, Shumway 1793f). Moving in the 1790s into New York State (Atwill 1795f) and South Carolina (Pilsbury 1799), ANGELS HYMN reappeared after 1800 in a few reform collections in Massachusetts (Law 1803, Salem 1805f, Middlesex 1807f, Sacred 1810) and Maryland (Cole 1804f, Cole 1808, Gillet 1809, Cole 1810), and also in an assortment of books from Connecticut (Read 1807f), New York (Huntington 1800, Atwill 1804, Erben 1806, Erben 1808, Evans 1808f, Little 1809f, Seymour 1809), and Pennsylvania (Cumberland 1804, Sacred 1806, Woodward 1806ff, Addington 1808, Blake 1810), as well as in the reform-minded Village 1810 from New Hampshire. Circulation continued in the next decade, with printings in more than fifteen tunebooks from the years 1811–1820. ANGELS HYMN appeared in three retrospective northern collections, but none of the southern tunebooks examined included it.

ANGELS HYMN exemplifies one of the many ways in which early English hymn-tune composers could achieve a balanced melodic shape. After each of the first three phrases traces a stepwise ascent—to the fourth degree (m. 3), then the fifth (m. 6), then the sixth (m. 10)—the last completes a melodic arch by beginning high and, again via step, settling on the tonic. A congregation at Harwinton, Connecticut, voted on 4 June 1776 to make ANGELS HYMN one of twenty-two tunes it sang in public worship.

Additional References

1. Eckhard, No. 6; Read, No. 154
2. AMR 336; A&M 6; Frost 364 (cf. 362a–c); Hall (attributed to *Harmonia Sacra*); Hitchcock (489)?
3. Episcopal

[6.] ANTHEM FOR EASTER: THE LORD IS RISEN INDEED, by William Billings
(EASTER ANTHEM)

Text, probably compiled by Billings himself, begins with an exhortation whose first five words are taken from Luke 24:34; mm. 15–30 set I Corinthians 15:20 from the New Testament, minus the first word; the rest is from Young, pp. 56–57. First printed in William Billings, *An Anthem for Easter* ([Boston, 1787]), an eight-page pamphlet that contains three pieces for the Easter season. A version of the anthem "with an addition entirely new inserted in the middle" was advertised for sale by Billings in 1795, in a separate publication that has yet to be located (Independent Chronicle, 26 November 1795, quoted in McKay & Crawford, p. 182). Holden 1793, p. 107; additional section from Village 1800, p. 172.

Billings's ANTHEM FOR EASTER, a through-composed duple-time setting of prose text in major mode, was printed 46 times, making it the most frequently published anthem of the period. All pre-1811 printings are set to the same text, though from the time of Joseph Doll's *Leichter Unterricht in der Vokal Music,* 2d ed. (Harrisburg, 1815), it also appeared in German translation: "Der Herr ist erstanden."

Introduced in Boston (Billings 1787), the ANTHEM FOR EASTER received more than two-thirds of its printings in New England. In Massachusetts it appeared in multi-edition works like Federal 1791ff, Holden 1793f, Worcester 1794ff, and Mann 1797f, and after 1800 in French 1802, Boston First 1806, and Huntington 1807. Picked up in Connecticut (Brownson 1797, Read 1798, Terril 1800, Read 1807f), it appeared further north as well (Village 1796, Maxim 1805f, Robbins 1805). Outside New England it first appeared in Virginia (Sandford 1793) and then New York (Atwill 1795f, Atwill 1804, Erben 1806, Little 1809f, Seymour 1809). Stammers 1803 introduced it in Pennsylvania, followed by Aitken 1806, Chapin 1808f, Blake 1810, and Wyeth 1810. Circulation slowed in the next decade, with fewer than a dozen printings discovered in tunebooks from the years 1811–1820. However, the EASTER ANTHEM appears in all eight northern retrospective collections and in all five of the southern tunebooks canvassed.

Rather than offering a coherent narrative, Billings's ANTHEM FOR EASTER delivers a series of assertions and questions about Jesus's resurrection, each with its own response, and with each section marked off from the next by a measure of silence. Typically, the assertions are announced by one or two voices, while the full chorus delivers the responses. (I. Bass: "The Lord is risen indeed"; Chorus: "Hallelujah." II. Bass: "Now is Christ risen . . . "; Chorus: "Hallelujah!" III. Fuging chorus led by bass: "And did he rise?"; Chorus: "Hear, o ye nations . . . He burst the bars of death and triumphed o'er the grave." IV. Tenor & bass: "Then I rose"; Chorus: "Then first humanity triumphant . . ." V. Counter & bass: "Man all immortal, hail . . ."; Chorus: "Thine all the glory, man's the boundless bliss.") With its many separate sections, its fondness for reduced scoring, and its frequent text repetition, the ANTHEM FOR EASTER emphasizes clarity of structure and audibility of text over sustaining high energy and momentum, though the latter qualities are not entirely missing. (See Preface; note that the one fuging section, mm. 39–45, avoids text overlap, as does the fuging portion of the "additional section"; see no. [6a], mm. 7–15.)

Billings's ANTHEM FOR EASTER was one of the few early American compositions famous enough to inspire a story about its origin. As reported by Alexander Thayer, later Beethoven's biographer:

> The story goes that [Billings] composed his Easter Anthem one Evening after his return from a [singing-school]—lying flat on the hearth, and writing by the light of the coals, raked open for the purpose; however that may be, it is even now, to an ear not over nice, a spirit-stirring composition (Thayer, quoted in McKay & Crawford, p. 150n).

Indications are that Billings reaped little monetary reward for his highly successful anthem, coming to regret that he had not protected it by copyright. In 1797 he noted in a newspaper advertisement that others had published it in their collections, "and I am credibly informed, that their collections did not sell the worse for it." Explaining that he had made an addition to the piece (see no. [6a]), he appealed for patronage in a burst of mixed metaphor:

> As I own the Vineyard, and have done *all* the labor in it myself—I beg the Community to grease the Rollers of the Press, so as to enable me to eat some of the fruit thereof (Independent Chronicle, 3 April 1797; quoted in McKay & Crawford, pp. 183–84).

The appeal was fruitless, however, and in all but a small handful of printings it was the version without the additional section that circulated. William Bentley's diary reports a successful performance at a Thanksgiving service in Salem: "Our Choir did

2. AMR 320; A&M 477; Hall
3. Episcopal

Cross-Reference

See entry on ST. THOMAS.

[11.] BETHESDA

Text from Watts, Psalm 84, P.M. First published in *Harmonia Sacra, or a Choice Collection of Psalm and Hymn Tunes* (London, ca. 1760), or before. First published in America by A. Williams, *The American Harmony, or Universal Psalmodist*, Vol. II of [Daniel Bayley], *The American Harmony*, 5th ed. (Newburyport, 1769). Bayley 1784, p. 79.

BETHESDA, a duple-time H.M. plain tune in major mode, was printed 50 times. Almost never printed textless, BETHESDA appeared with at least six different texts but was linked more frequently with the present one than any other.

Introduced in Massachusetts (Williams 1769ff), BETHESDA received 90 percent of its printings in New England, mostly in Massachusetts tunebooks. The tune appeared in one more of Daniel Bayley's colonial collections (Stickney 1774ff) and two more after the war (Bayley 1784, Bayley 1788), as well as in Mass 1784f and New 1784 in the 1780s. Only two Massachusetts tunebooks of the 1790s carried it (Federal 1790ff, Boston 1799); but after 1800 it appeared in fourteen more, most but not all of them reform-oriented items (Brown 1802ff, Law 1803, Cooper 1804, Holyoke 1804, Salem 1805f, Boston First 1806, Huntington 1807a, Mann 1807, Middlesex 1807f, Suffolk 1807, Deerfield 1808, Boston Brattle 1810, Boston West 1810, Sacred 1810). Poor 1794, printed in Philadelphia, introduced BETHESDA outside New England, but only Cole 1805, Law 1807f, and Erben 1808, each from a different city, picked it up. Bull 1795 and Griswold 1798 in Connecticut and Village 1795–1800, Village 1808f, and Blanchard 1808 in New Hampshire accounted for the rest of its New England appearances. Circulation continued widely in the next decade, as BETHESDA was picked up by some thirty collections published in the years 1811–1820. The tune was included in three retrospective northern collections but no southern tunebooks.

BETHESDA, which moves almost entirely within the range of a fifth, is cast melodically in AA¹B form, if its six phrases are paired and reduced to three—the repetition of the opening phrase suggests the tune's possible secular or instrumental origin, as in AMSTERDAM.

Additional References

1. Read, No. 278
2. Hall (attributed to Green)

[12.] BRIDGEWATER, by Lewis Edson

Text from Watts, Psalm 104, L.M. First published in [Simeon Jocelin], *The Chorister's Companion* (New Haven, 1782). Village 1810, p. 16.

BRIDGEWATER, a L.M. fuging-tune in major mode, was printed 99 times. Published with at least fourteen different texts, it was linked most frequently with the present one, although its independence from any single text is dramatized by its textless printing in the composer's son's collection, Edson 1801.

First published in Connecticut (Jocelin 1782f), BRIDGEWATER, which received only 46 percent of its printings in New England, was the most widely printed sacred piece of the 1780s. It appeared in fifteen different tunebooks in that decade, divided among Massachusetts (Bayley 1784, Bayley 1785, Worcester 1786–91, Bayley 1788, Federal 1788–93, Sacred 1788, Worcester 1794), Connecticut (Brownson 1783ff, Langdon 1786, Law 1786ff, Read 1787ff), New Hampshire (Dearborn 1785), Penn-

sylvania (Selection 1788ff, Adgate 1789ff), and New York (Amphion 1789). In the next decade, circulation widened southward, to include Baltimore (Ely 1792), Alexandria (Sandford 1793), and Charleston (Pilsbury 1799), and northward as well (Village 1795ff), while maintaining a moderate level (French 1793, Shumway 1793f, Read 1794f, Atwill 1795f, Brownson 1797, Mann 1797, Boston 1799) in territory in which it had already appeared. Printings after 1800 were few in New England (Gamut 1807 and Read 1807f in Connecticut; Brown 1804, Bushnell 1807, and Huntington 1807 in Massachusetts; Robbins 1805 in Maine) but many outside (nine collections in Pennsylvania: Little 1801, Cumberland 1804, Sacred 1806, Woodward 1806ff, Rothbaust 1807, Chapin 1808f, Blake 1810, Doll 1810, Wyeth 1810; eight in New York: Huntington 1800, Edson 1801f, Seymour 1803f, Atwill 1804f, Little 1805ff, Erben 1806, Evans 1808f, Seymour 1809; one in Maryland: Arnold 1803), balancing the totals among several states—twelve different collections from Pennsylvania, eleven from Massachusetts, ten from New York, eight from Connecticut—more closely than almost any other Core Repertory tune. Modest circulation continued in the next decade, with printings in more than a dozen collections from the years 1811–1820. BRIDGEWATER later appeared in seven retrospective northern collections and in two later southern tunebooks.

BRIDGEWATER follows the standard fuging-tune form, setting a single four-line stanza with a fuge on the third line. Its rhythm, however, departs from the model: though notated in duple time, it follows a triple pattern rather consistently until m. 14, when, with an outburst of quarter-note declamation, it shifts strikingly into duple time. Writing of Lewis Edson late in the nineteenth century, Cheney reported:

> He composed a number of excellent tunes which remained popular; among them, Bridgewater and Lenox, tunes which will last as long as any of the old American compositions. They have been published in very many of the collections which have flooded the country since his day (Cheney, p. 171).

Additional References

1. Alderdice, p. 122
2. Hall

[13.] BRISTOL, by Timothy Swan

Text by Joseph Addison; appeared in *The Spectator*, 23 August 1712 (see Julian, pp. 17ff); the version here is slightly altered from the original, taken from Boston West, p. 44. First published in Oliver Brownson, *Select Harmony* (n.p., [1785]). Village 1796, p. 178.

BRISTOL, a fuging-tune setting two stanzas of L.M. text in major mode, was printed 79 times. The tune appeared more frequently by far with the present text than with any of the other four with which it was published, though Swan's own *New England Harmony* (1801) assigns it "Rejoice ye shining worlds on high" (Watts, Psalm 24, L.M., stanza 5f).

Introduced in Connecticut (Brownson 1785f), BRISTOL received 59 percent of its printings in New England. The tune immediately caught the fancy of compilers, appearing in ten different collections before the end of the decade: Langdon 1786, Law 1786ff, Read 1787ff, and Jocelin 1788 in Connecticut; Worcester 1786–1800, Bayley 1788a, and Federal 1788ff in Massachusetts; and Selection 1788ff and Adgate 1789ff in Pennsylvania. In later years circulation broadened southward to include Maryland (Ely 1792), South Carolina (Pilsbury 1799), and New Jersey (Smith 1803f), westward to the Hudson Valley (Huntington 1800, Little 1805ff), and northward to New Hampshire (Village 1796ff). In Connecticut only two new tunebooks picked it up in the years 1790–1810: Read 1794ff and Swan 1801. During the same period, its printings in Massachusetts showed a decline (French 1793, Holden 1793ff, Stone 1793, Mann 1797, Boston 1799, before 1800; Collection 1804 and J. Read 1808, after), while the opposite occurred in Pennsylvania (Shumway 1793f, before 1800; Little 1801, Sacred 1806, Chapin 1808f, Blake 1810, Wyeth 1810, after). Circulation fell off in the next decade to fewer than a dozen appearances in collections from the years 1811–1820. Bristol later appeared in four retrospective northern collections, but none of the southern tunebooks carried it.

Bristol stands out among fuging-tunes in the Core Repertory because of its texture changes (mm. 9ff, 13ff, 17ff), its unusually long section of verbal conflict in the fuge, and its expressive text-setting (m. 3 "pillars" extending from high to low; m. 5, "sky" on a high note; mm. 17ff, "th'unweary'd sun" set to a stream of declaimed quarter-notes). On 4 July 1798, Bristol was sung under Daniel Read's direction at an Independence Day celebration in New Haven (Bushnell, p. 190). Many years later it was haughtily dismissed by "A Country Clergyman," writing to the *Boston Musical Gazette*:

> Is it possible that [anyone] . . . can feel any religious impression, or at all be edified, by singing, or hearing sung, such musical fiddlefaddle, as the tunes of . . . Bristol . . . and fifty others of similar ridiculous cast, to be found in more or less singing books of [an earlier] day? (Quoted in Bushnell, pp. 454–55)

Additional References

1. Alderdice, p. 122
2. Hall

[14.] Bromsgrove
(Broomsgrove, Crowle, Crowley)

Text from Watts, Hymns II, no. 61. First published in James Green, *A Book of Psalmody*, 6th ed. (London, ca. 1729). First published in America in Thomas Walter, *The Grounds and Rules of Musick*, [7th ed.] (Boston, 1760). Boston 1799, p. 23.

Bromsgrove, a triple-time C.M. tune in minor mode, was printed 61 times. Appearing with at least seventeen different texts, it was never closely linked with any single one, and more than half of its printings were textless.

Introduced in Boston (Walter 1760f), Bromsgrove received more than three-quarters of its printings in New England, all but two of that number (Gilman 1771 and Wood 1810, both from Exeter, New Hampshire) in Massachusetts. A favorite of Daniel Bayley's (nine of his publications between Bayley 1764ff and Bayley 1788 included it), Bromsgrove was also carried by such New England collections as Johnston 1763, Flagg 1764, New England 1771, Mass 1784f, and New 1784. It appeared in colonial Philadelphia as well (Lyon 1761f, Tunes 1763f). Around the turn of the century its popularity picked up again in Massachusetts (Boston 1799, French 1802, Holyoke 1803, Law 1803, Salem 1805f, Boston First 1806, Middlesex 1807f, Deerfield 1808, Huntington 1809, Boston West 1810, Brown 1810, Wood 1810) and Pennsylvania (Stammers 1803, Cumberland 1804, Woodward 1806ff, Law 1807f), widening southward to include single appearances in Charleston (Pilsbury 1799), Baltimore (Cole 1808), and Norfolk, Virginia (Tomlins 1810). Modest circulation continued in the next decade, with appearances in about a dozen collections from the years 1811–1820. Bromsgrove appeared neither in later retrospective collections in the north, nor in southern tunebooks.

Bromsgrove achieves prevailing stepwise motion within the range of a minor sixth by dissolving into half-notes the expected whole-note in almost every other measure (mm. 1, 3, 5, 8, 10, 12). The tune was chosen on 22 October 1770 by the congregation at Wilbraham, Massachusetts, for singing in public worship (1 of 23 tunes).

Additional References

1. Eckhard, No. 44; Read, No. 103
2. A&M 601; Hall (as Broomsgrove, attributed to Knapp)

[15.] Brookfield, by William Billings

Text from Watts, Hymns I, no. 82. First published in William Billings, *The New-England Psalm-Singer* (Boston, [1770]). Worcester 1786, p. 36.

A triple-time L.M. tune in minor mode, Brookfield, with 88 printings, was Billings's most widely published piece in his own time. Some printings were textless, and in all eight different texts were printed with Brookfield, most often the present one—though Billings himself, in Billings 1778ff, linked it with "Twas on that dark, that doleful night" (Watts, Hymns III, no. 1).

First published in the composer's hometown of Boston (Billings 1770), Brookfield received nearly 60 percent of its printings in New England. The tune caught on quickly, appearing in the next two decades in thirteen new Massachusetts tunebooks alone (New England 1771, Stickney 1774f, Billings 1778ff, Billings 1779, Bayley 1784, Mass 1784f, New 1784, Bayley 1785, Worcester 1786–92, Bayley 1788, Federal 1788ff, Sacred 1788), as well as three in Connecticut (Law 1779, Jocelin 1782f, Law 1786), two in Philadelphia (Selection 1788ff, Adgate 1789ff), and one in New York City (Amphion 1789). The rate of circulation slowed in central New England during the 1790s (Brownson 1797, Griswold 1798, Boston 1799) and also in New York (Atwill 1795f) and Pennsylvania (Shumway 1793f) but broadened northward (Village 1795ff) and to the south as well (Sandford 1793, Pilsbury 1799). After 1800, Brookfield appeared in a number of eclectic New England collections (Holyoke 1803, Cooper 1804, Read 1804f, Boston First 1806, Bushnell 1807, Gamut 1807, Huntington 1807, Suffolk 1807, Sanger 1808) but no reform ones; it also circulated in New York (Huntington 1800, Atwill 1804, Little 1805ff, Erben 1806, Seymour 1809) and Pennsylvania (Sacred 1806, Woodward 1806ff, Blake 1810, Wyeth 1810). Circulation continued strong in the next decade, with some two dozen printings in works published during the years 1811–1820. Brookfield also appeared in five later retrospective northern tunebooks, though none of the southern collections picked it up.

The structure of Brookfield is unusual for a four-line plain tune: its fourth phrase is an almost exact repetition, in all voices, of the second, creating the form ABCB. Writing in the 1830s, the reformer Thomas Hastings had at least faint praise for the tune. Describing Billings as a composer of "some genius, but very little learning," Hastings continued: "his Brookfield has been deservedly popular" (Musical Magazine I; quoted in McKay & Crawford, p. 203). A few years later, a correspondent to the *Boston Musical Gazette* wrote:

> The writer is not among those who would reject every piece of music composed by our American authors of former days. Jordan and Brookfield, by Billings . . . are excellent, and not discreditable to musical genius, and their insertion in the Boston publications is honorable to the compilers (Quoted in Bushnell, p. 457).

Additional References

1. Alderdice, p. 325; Read, No. 209
2. Hall; Hitchcock 175

Cross-References

See entries on Buckingham, Coronation, Kingsbridge, Putney, Windham.

[16.] BUCKINGHAM

Text from Watts, Psalm 4, C.M. Probably first published shortly before its first known appearance in Aaron Williams, *The Universal Psalmodist* (London, 1763). First published in America in William Tans'ur, *The Royal Melody Complete*, vol. I of [Daniel Bayley], *The American Harmony*, 5th ed. (Newburyport, 1769); or A. Williams, *The American Harmony, or Universal Psalmodist*, vol. II of [Daniel Bayley], *The American Harmony*, 5th ed. (Newburyport, 1769). Village 1796, p. 91.

A triple-time C.M. tune in minor mode, BUCKINGHAM was printed 74 times. Of the eight different texts with which BUCK-INGHAM was printed, the one most frequently linked with it, besides the present one, is Psalm 12: in the Old Version, "Help, Lord, for good and godly men," printed in Tans'ur 1769 and elsewhere; or in Watts's version, "Help, Lord, for men of virtue fail," printed in most post-1800 books.

BUCKINGHAM, introduced in Newburyport (Tans'ur 1769 or Williams 1769ff) received more than 90 percent of its printings in New England. In the 1770s and 1780s, it appeared in a sub-stantial number of Massachusetts collections (Bayley 1770ff, New England 1771, Stickney 1774ff, Billings 1779, Bayley 1784, Mass 1784f, New 1784, Worcester 1786f, Bayley 1788, Federal 1788ff, Sacred 1788) and in the only two Connecticut tunebooks to include it (Jocelin 1782f, Brownson 1783ff). Village 1795ff picked it up in northern New England. Atwill 1795f, Pilsbury 1799, and Atwill 1804 introduced it, respectively, to the Hud-son Valley and Charleston, South Carolina, while Massachu-setts printings were restricted to just two new works in the 1790s (Holden 1793ff, Boston 1799). After 1800 BUCKINGHAM re-gained a place in New England, appearing in seventeen collec-tions from Massachusetts, one from New Hampshire and one from Maine, including both eclectic items (Brown 1802ff, Hol-yoke 1803, Cooper 1804, Holyoke 1804, Albee 1805, Robbins 1805, Boston First 1806, Holyoke 1807, Mann 1807, Suffolk 1807, Sanger 1808) and reform tunebooks (Salem 1806, Middle-sex 1807f, Blanchard 1808, Deerfield 1808, Huntington 1809, Boston Brattle 1810, Boston West 1810, Sacred 1810). It was also printed in Baltimore (Gillet 1809) and Harrisburg (Wyeth 1810). Circulation continued in the next decade, with at least two dozen printings accumulated in collections published in the years 1811–1820. BUCKINGHAM also appears in five northern retrospective collections, though not in any of the southern tunebooks.

The triple-time motion and melodic contour of BUCKINGHAM is close enough to that of Billings's BROOKFIELD to have served as the latter's model. Also noteworthy is the differing function of each voice part: the treble shadowing the wide-ranging tenor melody, the bass providing an active and often independent support below, and the counter, restricted to moving within a fifth, playing no melodic role at all.

Additional References

1. Alderdice, p. hh; Read, No. 120
2. Hall (attributed to Williams)

[17.] BURFORD
(BUFORD, HEXHAM, NORWICH, UXBRIDGE)

Text from Hymns, no. 103, p. 294; authorship untraced. First published in John Chetham, *A Book of Psalmody* (London, 1718). First published in America by Thomas Walter, *The Grounds and Rules of Musick*, [6th ed.] (Boston, [1759?]). Suffolk 1807, p. 52.

A triple-time C.M. tune in minor mode, BURFORD was printed 45 times. Most printings before 1800 were textless; thereafter almost every printing was set to a different text, though the present one—one of at least thirteen with which BURFORD appeared—is found in several tunebooks.

Introduced in Boston (Walter 1759ff), BURFORD received more than 80 percent of its printings in New England. Its publi-cation history falls into two phases. The first consists of BUR-FORD's appearances in ten tunebooks and supplements in colo-nial New England (Johnston 1763, Bayley 1764ff, Flagg 1764, Bayley 1767f, Tans'ur 1767f, Tans'ur 1769ff, Bayley 1770f, Gilman 1771, New England 1771). The second began around the turn of the century, when Cole 1799 (Baltimore) introduced it outside New England, followed by Cumberland 1804 and Law 1807f in Pennsylvania, Jackson 1804 and Erben 1808 in New York City, and Cole 1808 and Cole 1810 again in Balti-more. As with the first phase, however, New England print-ings, especially Massachusetts works, dominated the second (Essex 1802, Holyoke 1803, Law 1803, Salem 1805f, Boston First 1806, Middlesex 1807f, Suffolk 1807, Shaw 1808, Boston Brattle 1810), though a pair of New Hampshire reform items (Blan-chard 1808, Village 1810) also carried it. Moderate circulation continued in the next decade with appearances in more than a dozen collections from the years 1811–1820. BURFORD shows up, however, in no more than two retrospective northern col-lections and in none of the later southern tunebooks.

Although lacking outright repetition of whole phrases, BUR-FORD is a tightly integrated little piece: mm. 1–3 and mm. 5–7 are almost identical in all voices, and m. 8–m. 12 harks back to m.1–m. 5. Temperley describes BURFORD as one of a group of "homophonic . . . country psalm tunes . . . with a tendency to elaboration," which "show[s] the country psalmodist's grasp of simple melody" (p. 176).

Additional References

1. Eckhard, No. 85; Read, No. 95
2. A&M 456; Hall (attributed to Purcell)
3. Episcopal

Cross-Reference

See entry on ST. THOMAS.

[18.] CALVARY, by Daniel Read

Text from Watts, Horae, pp. 21f. First published in Daniel Read, *The American Singing Book* (New Haven, 1785). Federal 1788, p. 76.

CALVARY, a C.M. fuging-tune in minor mode, received 46 printings, apparently all with the present text, though the quo-tation below suggests that the tune-text link was not ironclad.

Introduced in Connecticut (Read 1785ff), CALVARY received nearly two-thirds of its printings in New England. Picked up within a few years of its first publication by five other tune-books in Connecticut and Massachusetts (Worcester 1786–97, Law 1787, Bayley 1788, Federal 1788–93, Sacred 1788), and find-ing its way thereafter into Village 1795ff in northern New En-gland, the tune soon lost its hold on its original home turf. French 1793 and Boston 1799 were the only other Massachu-setts tunebooks to print it, it was omitted from Worcester 1786 after 1797, and in Connecticut it appeared later only in Read 1794. Outside New England it received printings in Philadel-phia (Shumway 1793f), New Jersey (New Jersey 1797), South Carolina (Pilsbury 1799), and the Hudson Valley (Little 1805ff). Only in early nineteenth-century Pennsylvania (Little 1801, Sa-cred 1806, Chapin 1808f, Blake 1810, Wyeth 1810) did it hold a firm place in the repertory. Circulation dropped off sharply in the next decade, and only three printings have been discovered in tunebooks from the years 1811–1820. CALVARY appeared in four retrospective northern collections and in one southern tunebook.

With its first and third lines of text given over to fuging, the first part of CALVARY emphasizes verbal conflict (especially mm. 2–5 and 8–11), which makes the clearing of the texture and the drawn-out word repetitions of the second part a most striking effect (mm. 13ff). An early nineteenth-century reference, almost surely written as a satire by a correspondent calling himself "Ichabod Beetlehead," praised CALVARY. "What a sort of dying melancholy possesses me," he wrote, "when Cavalry [*sic*] has been performed to the words of Watts' Funeral Thought! My flesh has been all over goose pimples" (Columbian Centinel; quoted in McKay & Crawford, p. 199).

Additional References

1. Alderdice, p. 190
2. Hitchcock (447)

[19.] CANTERBURY
(CANTABURY, LOW DUTCH)

Text from Watts, Hymns II, no. 3. First published in John Cosyn, *Musike of Six and Five Partes* (London, 1585). First published in America in *The Psalms Hymns, and Spiritual Songs*, 9th ed. (Boston, 1698). Mass 1784, p. 81, as CANTABURY.

A C.M. duple-time common tune in major mode, CANTERBURY was printed 90 times. Most often appearing without text, it also was printed with at least eight different ones during the period surveyed, most frequently with the text supplied here.

Introduced in Boston (Bay 1698ff), CANTERBURY received 86 percent of its printings in New England, where it appeared in more than thirty Massachusetts collections and in only three others from elsewhere in New England (Gilman 1771, Jenks 1804f, and Village 1810). A fixture in the publications of colonial Massachusetts (Brady 1713f, Walter 1721ff, Tufts 1723ff, Turner 1752, Johnston 1755f, Bayley 1764ff, Flagg 1764, Williams 1769ff, Bayley 1770f, New England 1771, Stickney 1774f), CANTERBURY appeared in colonial Philadelphia as well (Dawson 1754, Lyon 1761f, Hopkinson 1763). While later Philadelphia printings were limited to only two new works (Tunes 1786, Adgate 1791ff), the parade of Massachusetts collections continued briskly in the 1780s (Bayley 1784, Mass 1784f, New 1784, Bayley 1788, Sacred 1788), slacked off in the 1790s (Boston 1799), then resumed after 1800, especially but not exclusively in reform tunebooks (Essex 1802, Holyoke 1803, Brown 1804f, Boston First 1805f, Salem 1805f, Holyoke 1807, Middlesex 1807f, Suffolk 1807, Deerfield 1808, Huntington 1809, Boston Brattle 1810, Boston West 1810, Sacred 1810). Cole 1810, published in Baltimore, was the lone printing outside New England in the years 1800–1810. Circulation continued in the next decade, with some two dozen appearances in collections from the years 1811–1820. CANTERBURY was picked up by two retrospective northern collections, but none of the southern tunebooks has it.

CANTERBURY, whose melody encompasses no more than a perfect fourth, has the narrowest range of any Core Repertory tune. Moreover, its cadence on the subdominant (first phrase) makes it one of only two major-mode plain tunes in the Core Repertory to end a phrase on any chord except tonic and dominant (see ST. ANNE). Temperley notes that Playford's CANTERBURY (Frost 19a, 19b) is a later, somewhat altered version of Ravenscroft's LOW DUTCH (Frost 19; Temperley, 1:72), though both versions are included in the present count of printings. Samuel Sewall of Boston reported in his diary of having heard Thomas Walter, nephew of Cotton Mather and later a tunebook compiler himself, "set Low Dutch very well" at a gathering attended by Massachusetts Governor Dudley (Sewall Diary, 24 October 1718, p. 906). As an early congregational favorite, CANTERBURY was sung in the embellishmental "old way" before the singing-school reform of the 1720s. According to Thomas Symmes, that mode of performance demanded "supernumerary Notes & Turnings of the voice," and he went on to say:

An Ingenious Gentleman, who has prick'd [i.e., notated] Canterbury, as some . . . Sing it, finds (as I remember) no less than 150 Notes, in that Tune . . . whereas [when sung as it is usually notated], there are but 30 (Symmes, pp. 44–45; quoted in McKay & Crawford, p. 14).

Several congregations adopted CANTERBURY as one of the tunes sung in public worship: in Massachusetts, Weston (1724; 1 of 14), Needham (7 January 1729; 1 of 8), and Wilbraham (22 October 1770; 1 of 23). In a controversy about musical suitability in Westborough, Massachusetts, at mid-century, a foe of triple-time psalm tunes ignored the minister's instruction to sing MEAR, substituting CANTERBURY instead (Parkman Diary, 29 April 1750, p. 215).

Additional References

1. Eckhard, No. 38; Read, No. 43
2. AH, p. 225; Fisher, pp. 3, 5; Frost 19b; Hitchcock 115, 119, 122, 148, 157, 175, 194; MinA, p. 34; Temperley, 2:ex. 15b

Cross-Reference

See entry on PSALM 100 [OLD].

[20.] CHESTER, by William Billings

Text by Doddridge (Julian, pp. 305f.), taken here from Hymns, no. CII, p. 293, stanzas 2–6. First published in William Billings, *The New-England Psalm-Singer* (Boston, [1770]). Worcester 1788, p. 25.

CHESTER, a duple-time L.M. plain tune in major mode, and probably the most famous early American musical composition today, was printed 56 times. Published first with Billings's own "Let tyrants shake their iron rod," and sometimes printed without text as well, CHESTER from 1786 on was most frequently linked with the present text—one of three with which it appeared.

First published in Boston (Billings 1770), CHESTER received 88 percent of its printings in New England—a higher proportion than any other American-composed Core Repertory piece. In the 1770s and 1780s CHESTER was taken into a dozen tunebooks in Massachusetts and Connecticut (Stickney 1774f, Billings 1778ff, Billings 1779, Law 1779, Jocelin 1782, Brownson 1783ff, Bayley 1784, New 1784, Law 1786, Worcester 1786ff, Federal 1788ff, Sacred 1788), though in the next two decades its appearances there fell off to just half-a-dozen in the composer's home state of Massachusetts: Holden 1793ff, Mann 1797, Boston 1799, Holden 1800, Cooper 1804, Holyoke 1804. In the meantime, Village 1795ff had introduced it in the north, followed later by Maxim 1805 and Robbins 1805. CHESTER was introduced outside New England by Ely 1792 in Baltimore, receiving printings thereafter in the Hudson Valley (Atwill 1795f, Atwill 1804), South Carolina (Pilsbury 1799), Delaware (Fobes 1809) and Pennsylvania (Wyeth 1810). Circulation fell off sharply in the next decade, when CHESTER appeared in fewer than half-a-dozen collections from the years 1811–1820. It appeared, however, in seven northern retrospective collections, though in only one southern tunebook.

Even though its four phrases are distinct from each other (ABCD), CHESTER is unified in a most ingenious way. The dactylic beginnings, rhythmic continuation, and four-measure length of all four phrases make each seem like a fresh start on the same melodic subject. The harmonic plan—with phrases cadencing on V, V, I, I, in that order—suggests, however, not four fresh beginnings but two eight-measure segments, one an antecedent and the other a consequent. At the same time, the first and third phrases of the melody, with their upward movement, seem like a pair, as do the second and fourth, with their complementary downward movement. So mm. 1–4 and

9–12 belong together melodically, just as do mm. 5–8 and 13–16, except that in mm. 13–14 the ascending motive heard earlier in the tenor melody in mm. 1–2 and 9–10 is found in the treble voice. CHESTER thus displays a clever balance of rhythm, harmony, and gesture, drawing its variety and coherence from the way its very simple elements diverge and interlock. Set originally to a defiantly patriotic text, CHESTER is remembered as an emblem of Americans' resistance of British domination before and during the War of Independence. The political weight of CHESTER had already begun to be tapped in other ways before the end of the eighteenth century, when a group of "Republicans" in Canton, Massachusetts, sought to break up a Federalist Independence Day rally by marching around the meeting site singing CHESTER (McKay & Crawford, p. 70n). The Reverend William Bentley, describing an Independence Day meeting at Marblehead, Massachusetts in 1801, noted that CHESTER was sung "in Billings's own verses," and that "this was as appropriate as the Marseilles Hymn or the French ca ira" (Bentley Diary, 5 July 1801, vol. II:378). Its appearance as the "Death Beat" in James Hulbert's *The Complete Fifer's Museum* (Northampton, 1807) dramatizes its unique role as a hymn tune whose associations made it suitable for double duty as a piece of functional patriotic music. Its current status as a recognizable piece of early Americana owes much to its fiery original text and to its appearance in William Schuman's *New England Tryptich* (1956), composed for orchestra and arranged for band the next year. Familiar to both choral directors and bandmasters, CHESTER today is more likely to be heard at a choral concert or a football halftime show than to be sung in public worship.

Additional References

1. Alderdice, p. kk
2. AH, p. 143; Fisher, p. 7; Hall; Hitchcock 56, 59, 62, 63, 64, 116, 119, 120, 121, 122, 151, 157, 175, 184, (34); MinA, p. 112

[21.] CHRISTMAS, by Martin Madan
(BRISTOL)

Text from Law CH; authorship unknown. First published in [Martin Madan], *A Collection of Psalm and Hymn Tunes . . . To Be Had at the Lock Hospital* (London, [1769]). First published in America in Andrew Law, *A Collection of Hymn Tunes* (Cheshire, Connecticut, [1783]). Law 1794, p. 46, as BRISTOL.

CHRISTMAS, a P.M. major-mode duple-time tune-with-extension of the kind favored by eighteenth-century English Methodists, was printed 52 times. The tune was sung to at least nine different texts, almost all of them relating to the birth of Jesus, with the present one being the most frequently found.

Introduced in Connecticut (Law C 1783), CHRISTMAS received almost two-thirds of its printings in New England. Its second appearance (Sandford 1793) was removed by hundreds of miles and a decade's time from its first, and before 1800 only three more tunebooks had picked it up: Law 1794ff and Federal 1794 in Boston, and Pilsbury 1799 in Charleston, South Carolina. After the turn of the century it was a different story, as more than thirty new collections printed CHRISTMAS. Village 1800ff in the north, Read 1807f and Peck 1808 in Connecticut, and a host of Massachusetts items (including both eclectic works like Brown 1802ff, Mann 1807, Suffolk 1807, and J. Read 1808; and reform works like Salem 1805f, Middlesex 1807f, Shaw 1808, and Madan 1809, among others) kept it before the New England public. South of there, circulation broadened to Maryland (Cole 1804, Gillet 1809, Cole 1810), New York City (Erben 1806, Erben 1808, Evans 1808f, Seymour 1809), Philadelphia (Woodward 1806ff, Law 1807f, Addington 1808, Peck 1810), and Delaware (Fobes 1809). Moderate circulation contin-

ued in the next decade with a dozen or more printings in collections published in the years 1811–1820. CHRISTMAS was included in two northern retrospective collections but in none of the southern tunebooks.

Madan's original was set for three voice parts with the melody in the treble. Law's setting, in an arrangement considered progressive for its time, keeps the melody on top, adding a fourth voice—a kind of second treble—below the melody. (Some other compilers shifted the melody to the tenor, e.g., Village 1800, whose attribution reads: "Altered from Madan.") The appoggiaturas in the melody are typical of the "Methodist" style, as are the repetitions—of text to new music (mm. 5–10), and of both text and music (mm. 15–20), especially the latter, with its climax in volume.

Additional Reference

1. Read, No. 32

[22.] COLCHESTER, by William Tans'ur
(COLCHESTER NEW)

Text from New Version, Psalm 122. First published in William Tans'ur, *A Compleat Melody*, 2d ed. (London, 1735). First published in America in Thomas Walter, *The Grounds and Rules of Musick*, [7th ed.] (Boston, 1760). Worcester 1788, p. 17.

A triple-time C.M. tune in major mode, COLCHESTER was printed 96 times. Before the late 1780s it customarily appeared without text; thereafter it was set to at least nine different texts, most frequently the present one and "My never-ceasing songs shall show" (Watts, Psalm 89).

Introduced in Boston (Walter 1760f), COLCHESTER received some 93 percent of its printings in New England, most of them in Massachusetts. The tune was established there by its appearances in nine of Daniel Bayley's publications (from Bayley 1764ff to Bayley 1788) and a series of Boston collections (Johnston 1763, Flagg 1764, New England 1771, Billings 1779, Mass 1784f, New 1784, Federal 1788ff, Sacred 1788), as well as Worcester 1786–1800 from central Massachusetts, Gilman 1771 and Dearborn 1785 from New Hampshire, and a smaller group of Connecticut tunebooks (Law 1779, Law 1781, Jocelin 1782f, Read 1787ff). Village 1795–1803 introduced COLCHESTER in the north, while Atwill 1795f introduced it outside New England, followed after the turn of the century by Atwill 1804 in Albany, and three Pennsylvania works (Stammers 1803, Law 1807f, Wyeth 1810). In the meantime, moderate circulation continued in central New England, both in Connecticut (Law 1791f, Read 1794ff) and Massachusetts (Holden 1793f, Mann 1797, Boston 1799), picking up dramatically after 1800, as COLCHESTER appeared in eighteen new Massachusetts tunebooks, both eclectic (Brown 1802ff, Cooper 1804, Albee 1805, Boston First 1806, Mann 1807, J. Read 1808) and reform (Essex 1802, Salem 1805f, Middlesex 1807f, Boston West 1810, and others). It was also printed in Village 1810. Circulation was vigorous in the next decade, as COLCHESTER appeared in more than thirty collections from the years 1811–1820. It was also picked up by five northern retrospective collections, but no southern tunebooks printed it.

COLCHESTER is made from the simplest materials, emphasizing the major scale, from which the first three phrases are built almost entirely, and the tonic triad, which is sounded for some 60 percent of the tune's duration. When he was preparing the second edition of *The Columbian Harmonist* in 1804, Daniel Read wrote his brother: "I have no objection to have you substitute a good long meter tune in the place of . . . Colchester" (quoted in Bushnell, p. 283), but when the work appeared in print, Tans'ur's tune remained part of it.

Additional References

1. Alderdice, p. c; Read, No. 38
2. Hall (attributed to Williams)

Cross-Reference

See entry on PSALM 100 [OLD].

[23.] COLESHILL
(DUBLIN)

Text from Watts, Psalm 144, C.M., 2d Part. First published in [William Barton], *The Book of Psalms in Metre* (London, 1644). First published in America in William Dawson, *The Youths Entertaining Amusement* (Philadelphia, 1754). Lyon 1761, p. 11.

A C.M. common tune in minor mode, COLESHILL was printed 45 times. Sometimes published textless, it appeared with five different texts, all doleful in mood, but most frequently with the present one. (Cumberland 1804 sets it to William Billings's "Death with his warrant in his hand," sung in the composer's own publications to his Core Repertory tune LEBANON.)

Introduced in Philadelphia (Dawson 1754), COLESHILL received only about one-fourth of its printings in New England—the lowest proportion by far of any Core Repertory piece. COLESHILL appeared in twenty different tunebooks, fifteen of them published in Pennsylvania at rather widely spaced intervals of time. Picked up by three Philadelphia collections of the 1760s (Lyon 1761f, Hopkinson 1763, Tunes 1763f), the tune did not appear there again for more than two decades (Tunes 1786, Selection 1788ff, Adgate 1789ff); after another break, this time of some fifteen years, it found its way into a succession of later Pennsylvania items (Cumberland 1804, Woodward 1806ff, Law 1807f, Rothbaust 1807, Sanno 1807, Chapin 1808f, Blake 1810, Wyeth 1810), both urban and rural, including two in the German language. In Maryland, Arnold 1803 and Gillet 1809 printed COLESHILL. Its only appearances in New England came in tunebooks by Connecticut compilers known to have taught singing-schools in Pennsylvania: Law 1783, Benham 1790ff, and Law 1793ff. Modest circulation continued in the next decade, with appearances in roughly a dozen collections published in the years 1811–1820. None of the northern retrospective collections carry COLESHILL, but it appeared in three southern tunebooks, and Jackson includes it on his list of eighty "most popular" southern folk hymns (Jackson, p. 135).

COLESHILL is closely related to WINDSOR, also in the Core Repertory. Noting Erik Routley's discovery of the relationship, Temperley shows that "more than half the notes are identical" in the tunes of COLESHILL and WINDSOR (2:ex. 15a), proposing that COLESHILL began its existence as an "improvised descant" to WINDSOR (Temperley, 1:74, 96). In the Hutchinson Partbook (1763; probably copied in Pennsylvania), the following text was provided for a two-voice setting of COLESHILL (here entitled DUBLIN):

> Brave George the third then is our King
> Which sits on Brittain's Throne
> God Prosper him long for to Reign
> His lawfull heirs Each One[.]

Additional References

1. Alderdice, p. 131; Eckhard, No. 39; Read, No. 96
2. Frost 392a; Temperley 2:ex. 15a, 18

Cross References

See entries on LEBANON and WINDSOR.

[24.] CORONATION, by Oliver Holden
Text from Smith; written by Edward Perronet (see Julian, p. 41). First published in Oliver Holden, *The Union Harmony*, vol. I (Boston, 1793). Worcester 1800, p. 25.

A duple-time C.M. tune-with-extension in major mode, CORONATION was printed 47 times. Originating as a setting of the present text, it was consistently linked with it, appearing with no other text during the period covered here.

Introduced in Massachusetts (Holden 1793ff), CORONATION received more than 80 percent of its printings in New England. In the decade after its first publication, it appeared only in Massachusetts (Mann 1797f, Worcester 1797ff, Boston 1799, Holden 1800, Belknap 1802, Brown 1802f, French 1802), but from 1803 on, its circulation broadened dramatically. It was picked up by several tunebooks in Connecticut (Jenks 1803, Jenks 1804f, Read 1804ff, Griswold 1807, Jenks 1810) and New York (Seymour 1803f, Atwill 1804f, Little 1809f, Seymour 1809). It also appeared in northern New England (Village 1803ff, Child 1804, Maxim 1805f, Robbins 1805) and later, to the south, in Delaware (Fobes 1809) and Pennsylvania (Wyeth 1810) without losing its place in Massachusetts, where eclectic tunebooks continued to print it (Holyoke 1804, Boston First 1806, Bushnell 1807, Huntington 1807, Suffolk 1807, J. Read 1808). Modest circulation continued in the next decade, with appearances in ten collections published in the years 1811–1820. CORONATION was included in seven northern retrospective collections, and three southern tunebooks printed it as well.

Beginning in quarter-note motion, CORONATION climaxes on the half-note delivery, marked *"forte,"* of the last line of each stanza ("And crown him Lord of all"), which is also the source of the title. Balancing contrast (the abrupt changes of texture and volume after the double-bar) with repetition (the second-half repeat; the recurrent last-line refrain), Holden composed a tune whose endurance has surpassed that of any other eighteenth-century American sacred piece. A writer in the 1830s singled out CORONATION, together with Billings's JORDAN and BROOKFIELD and Read's WINDHAM, as "excellent" (Boston Musical Gazette; quoted in Bushnell, p. 457). Cheney later praised it prophetically as a tune that "will live for many generations yet to sing and admire" (Cheney, p. 178). Jones's *Handbook* (1886) gave CORONATION its own entry as "one of the most popular church tunes ever composed" (p. 43), predicting also that it would "perpetuate [Holden's] name to the end of time" (p. 76). Charles Ives made a fugue subject from the melody of the third line ("Bring forth the royal diadem") for the original first movement of String Quartet No. 1 (1896), which he later transferred to his Symphony No. 4, as the third movement. As noted in AH, CORONATION "has enjoyed general and uninterrupted popularity to the present day" (p. 419), and it is found in many current Protestant hymnals with its original text, though in musical arrangements somewhat altered from Holden's original. CORONATION was collected ca. 1980 from oral tradition singing of Primitive Baptists in the Blue Ridge region of Virginia and North Carolina (Sutton, p. 15).

Additional References

1. Alderdice, p. n
2. AH, p. 419; Hall; Hitchcock 119, 150, 166, 175, 177, (318); MinA, p. 143
3. Baptist; Congregational; Episcopal; Lutheran; Methodist; Presbyterian

[25.] DALSTON
(PSALM 122)

Text from Watts, Psalm 122, P.M. First published in Aaron Williams, *The Universal Psalmodist* (London, 1763). First published in America in Josiah Flagg, *A Collection of the Best Psalm Tunes* (Boston, 1764). Sacred 1788, p. 51.

DALSTON, a duple-time P.M. tune in major mode, was printed 71 times. Although textless in its first printing and occasionally thereafter, DALSTON was linked with the present text in Tans'ur 1767 and in most later appearances, though some use the variant "How does my heart rejoice" from Belknap's *Sacred Poetry* (Boston, 1795).

First published in Boston (Flagg 1764), DALSTON received 80 percent of its printings in New England, most of those in Massachusetts (31 of 41 tunebooks). The tune appeared in seven of Daniel Bayley's publications (from Bayley 1766f to Bayley 1788) and also in several supplements (Gilman 1771, New England 1771, Law 1781, New 1784) as well as in other New England tunebooks of the 1780s (Jocelin 1782, Mass 1784f, Worcester 1786, Sacred 1788), before being picked up in Philadelphia (Adgate 1789ff, Selection 1790ff, Poor 1794). Printings in Virginia (Sandford 1793) and, much later, Maryland (Gillet 1809) round out the brief roster of appearances outside New England. In the meantime, eighteen Massachusetts collections of the period 1790–1810—from eclectic works like Federal 1790ff, Holden 1793f, Mann 1797, Boston 1799, Boston First 1806, Huntington 1807a, and Mann 1807, to reform items like Salem 1805f, Deerfield 1808, and Sacred 1810, among others—carried it, as did Village 1795–96, Blanchard 1808, and Village 1810 in New Hampshire. Wide circulation continued in the next decade, with printings in at least thirty-four collections from the years 1811–1820. DALSTON appeared in seven retrospective northern collections and one southern tunebook.

Narrow in range—after its first note the melody covers just a minor sixth—and rhythmically obsessive, with all six phrases following almost exactly the same pattern, DALSTON owes its popularity to its metrical structure: it is the only Core Repertory tune in the meter 6.6.8.6.6.8. It may have been the tune referred to when, in Westfield, Massachusetts, on 27 May 1772, the choir sang "Dalton" after a singing lecture. On 4 June 1776, DALSTON was adopted at Harwinton, Connecticut, for singing in public worship (1 of 22 tunes). William Bentley's diary contains a parody of the text of DALSTON, which he explains as follows:

> At Beverley the Deacon was solicitous with a certain Clergyman to read a certain Psalm. How pleased & blest was I. The Psalm being found, & read, the following parody was written on the Deacon's motion.
>
> How pleased & blest was I,
> To make the people cry,
> This mighty deed their favor gains.
> May God grant me power
> To lengthen prayer an hour,
> And have a parish for my pains.

This has often been a subordinate wish (Bentley Diary, 27 March 1790, vol. II:156).

Additional References

1. Read, No. 308
2. Hall (attributed to Williams)

[26.] DENMARK, by Martin Madan
(ANTHEM, BEFORE JEHOVAH'S, HYMN)

Text is John Wesley's paraphrase of Watts's Psalm 100, L.M., 2d Part (see Julian, p. 1059). First published in [Martin Madan], *A Collection of Psalm and Hymn Tunes . . . To Be Had at the Lock Hospital* (London, [1769]). First published in America in Andrew Law, *Select Harmony* ([Cheshire, Connecticut, 1781–82]). Holden II 1793, p. 77.

DENMARK, a major-mode set-piece, was printed 93 times—far more than any other through-composed sacred piece of its time. Composed to the present text, it appeared with no other.

Introduced in Connecticut (Law 1782), DENMARK received some 61 percent of its printings in New England. It was picked up before 1790 in Massachusetts (Mass 1784f, Worcester 1786 III), New York City (Amphion 1789), and Philadelphia (Adgate 1789ff). Then, during the century's last decade, printings appeared in seven states: Massachusetts (Federal 1790ff, Worcester 1791ff, Holden II 1793, Mann 1797f), Connecticut (Law M 1793ff, Bull 1795, Read 1795), Pennsylvania (Shumway 1793f), Virginia (Sandford 1793), New York (Atwill 1795f), New Hampshire (Village 1796ff, Merrill 1799), and South Carolina (Pilsbury 1799). In the years 1800–1810, DENMARK appeared in thirty-eight different new collections, a total matched or exceeded by only a half-dozen other Core Repertory pieces. Broadening into northern New England (Hill 1801, Maxim 1805, Robbins 1805), its circulation extended southward into Maryland (Cole 1803, Cole 1804) and Virgina (Tomlins 1810) and as far west as Harrisburg (Wyeth 1810). Urban music publishers included it in their tunebooks (Graupner 1806 in Boston, Sacred 1803 and Carr 1805 in Philadelphia, New York 1803 and Erben 1806 in New York), and sheet music editions appeared in Philadelphia and New York as well (Wolfe 5498-5500A). At the same time, books intended for small town and rural populations also carried it: Griswold 1807 and Read 1807f in Connecticut; Huntington 1800 and Little 1809f in the Hudson Valley. It appeared in reform collections as well (Olmsted 1805, Salem 1805f, Addington 1808, Shaw 1808, Boston West 1810). Wide circulation continued in the next decade, with appearances in at least twenty-eight collections from the years 1811–1820. DENMARK was published in six northern retrospective tunebooks, and one southern tunebook carried it.

Temperley notes that DENMARK was a favorite in England as well as America, citing it as evidence that "Methodist and Evangelical psalmody" was a "popular source for country church music" (Temperley, 1:240). Indeed, DENMARK bears all the earmarks of the English "Methodist" style, including a three-voice texture with the melody on top; a florid, highly ornamented melodic line supported with orthodox European-style harmonies; and, toward the end, frequent repetition of text phrases in hopes of generating a climactic effect (see Temperley, 1:210–13). William Bentley's diary records performances of DENMARK over three decades' time: in Salem on 22 March 1787 "at fast," and on 15 December 1796 for "the Thanksgiving Day of our Commonwealth"; at a Masonic meeting in Worcester on 24 June 1798; and at "annual fast" services in Salem on 5 April 1810 and 3 April 1817 (Bentley Diary, vol. III: 508; vol. IV:445). Hastings, Dissertation comments that "though made up of common-place ideas," DENMARK is "chaste" and "unaffected" in style, and that it sets the text so that "the poet's ideas are enforced, his accents and his diction are properly preserved; and from these causes, more than from any other, we apprehend, the musick has so long continued to please us" (pp. 209–10). Among the many printings of DENMARK, some variations are to be found. Perhaps the two most notable are a simplification and revision in Bull 1795, where it is set for four voices rather than three ("the alterations . . . are made with a view of adapting [the piece] to the use of New-england Choirs; and not from a supposition that [it was] faulty as printed in other books," Bull 1795, p. 7), and Elias Mann's supplementary middle section, apparently first published in AMM 1800, and dismissed by Andrew Law as a "miserable ragged patch which is stuck into Denmark" (Law Essays, p. 14). See Wienandt & Young, pp. 220–23, which reproduces Mann's "addition," and also facsimiles of DENMARK as printed in Little and Smith's *The Easy Instructor* (claimed as a 1798 edition, but actually is some unidentified issue from after 1810) and Lowell Mason's *Carmina Sacra* (1842).

Additional References

1. Eckhard, No. 30
2. Fisher, p. 44; Hall

Cross-References

See entries on ENFIELD, HABAKKUK, JORDAN, PSALM 100 [OLD], PSALM 149.

[27.] DUNSTAN, by Martin Madan

Text from Watts, Psalm 72, L.M. First published in [Martin Madan], *A Collection of Psalm and Hymn Tunes . . . To Be Had at the Lock Hospital* (London, [1769]). First published in America in Andrew Law, *A Collection of Hymn Tunes* (Cheshire, Connecticut, [1783]). Law 1794, p. 19.

DUNSTAN, a L.M. tune-with-extension in major mode, was printed 54 times. Closely linked with no single text, it appeared with at least eleven different ones, though most frequently with the present choice.

Introduced in Connecticut (Law C 1783), DUNSTAN received 83 percent of its printings in New England, most of them in Massachusetts. Its second printing (Federal 1790ff) followed its first by seven years, but thereafter their frequency increased in New England (French 1793, Law 1794f, Worcester 1794ff, Village 1795ff, Mann 1797f, Boston 1799), and before the decade was over DUNSTAN had also appeared in South Carolina (Pilsbury 1799). After the turn of the century, printings in Maryland (Cole 1804) and Pennsylvania (Aitken 1806, Woodward 1806ff, Law 1807f, Blake 1810) made DUNSTAN available outside New England, while seventeen Massachusetts tunebooks—including a few eclectic works (Brown 1802ff, Belknap 1806f, Mann 1807, Suffolk 1807) but more reform items (Law 1803, Salem 1805f, Deerfield 1808, Shaw 1808, Boston West 1810, and others)—accounted for the rest of its appearances. Circulation continued in the next decade, with printings in at least eighteen collections in the years 1811–1820. Only one northern retrospective collection picked up DUNSTAN, however, and no southern tunebooks included it.

Sometimes appearing in three and sometimes in four voices in its various sources—Law seems to have been the first to add a fourth voice to Madan's original—DUNSTAN reflects its English Methodist origin in its orthodox harmony and its florid treatment and forceful repetition of the text's last line.

Additional References

1. Read, No. 177
2. Hall

[28.] THE DYING CHRISTIAN, by Edward Harwood
(NEW YORK, VITAL SPARK)

Text by Alexander Pope, who wrote it in 1712 under inspiration from two classical sources—the Roman Emperor Hadrian's supposed deathbed utterance, and a fragment of a lyric ode by the Greek poetess Sappho—and who concluded his poem with words from St. Paul (I Corinthians 15:55; see Julian, p. 1226). First published in Edward Harwood, *A Set of Hymns and Psalm Tunes* (London, ca. 1770). First published in America in Andrew Law, *The Rudiments of Music*, 2d ed. ([Cheshire, Connecticut, 1786]). Village 1800, p. 24, as NEW-YORK.

THE DYING CHRISTIAN, a set-piece in major mode, was printed 46 times, always with the present text.

Introduced in Connecticut (Law 1786ff), THE DYING CHRISTIAN received two-thirds of its printings in New England. An added complication of its printing history is that it circulated in two different versions. The more prevalent—the one included in the present edition—was an arrangement by Andrew Law that stays in major mode throughout. The other, closer to Har-

wood's original, begins in minor mode, shifting to major at the words "Hark! They whisper." Law's version, usually entitled NEW YORK (but given its more distinctive title in this edition), appeared in many of his own works, including Law M 1794 and Law 1800 in Cheshire, Law 1804 in Boston, and Law 1807f in Philadelphia. It was also printed several times in Massachusetts tunebooks (Holden 1793, Worcester 1794ff, Mann 1797), though it owes most of its circulation to Village 1795ff in New Hampshire. Atwill 1795f introduced it in the Hudson River Valley, Atwill 1804 also printed it, and Hill 1801 carried it to Vermont. As for the second setting, usually published as THE DYING CHRISTIAN, it seems to have been introduced to the U.S. in Massachusetts (Federal 1794, Gram 1795, Holden 1796f, Worcester 1797ff), maintaining a place there after the turn of the century (Cooper 1804, Boston First 1806, Graupner 1806, Shaw 1808) but also appearing in several other large cities: Charleston (Pilsbury 1799), Philadelphia (Aitken 1806, Woodward 1806ff, Blake 1810), New York City (Seymour 1809), and Baltimore (Cole 1810). A sheet-music edition appeared in New York in 1806 (Wolfe 3450). Brisk circulation continued in the next decade, with more than twenty appearances in collections published in the years 1811–1820. THE DYING CHRISTIAN also appeared in five retrospective northern collections and one southern tunebook.

THE DYING CHRISTIAN dramatizes a believer's thoughts as his earthly body dies and he is reborn in heaven. Musical contrasts support the miracle: stately, half-note motion as death approaches (more lugubrious in Harwood's original, where mm. 1–25 are in minor mode); an abrupt stir of bustling excitement as angel voices beckon (mm. 26–67); an arching, swelling gesture in triple time as the thread of life is broken (mm. 68–79); and a long, fast, repetitive paen of celebration of the Christian's new state of being. Temperley reports the popularity of Harwood's setting in England, noting as well that Pope's text enjoyed at least fifteen different through-composed settings in Britain and America (Temperley, 1:213–14). In 1801, Andrew Law, answering a critic who had complained in print about his arrangement of Harwood's piece, had some valuable things to say about that arrangement. Although he was silent about his changing of the mode, melody, and harmony of the first section, he did report that he had renamed the piece ("it was never called New-York till I gave it that name"), and he recommended that if people objected to his adding a fourth voice, a tenor, to the piece, they could simply leave it out—which is what the version published in the present edition does.

> If the Tenor I have added is found to have injured the piece, is it not very easy to drop it, and sing the tune in three parts, according to its original design? (Philadelphia Repository, 20 September 1801; quoted in Crawford, pp. 151–54)

Thomas Hastings made the following comments on the piece in 1822:

> The musick of the "Dying Christian" consists wholly of the most common-place ideas, and this, perhaps, as it leaves the attention at leisure to dwell on the sentiments of the poet, is the most fortunate circumstance in the composer's style of designing. The movement is adapted to the purposes of narration; and the poet, in language that could scarcely be heightened by any species of imaginative painting, is not prevented by musical *impertinences,* from bringing before us the scene he attempts to describe. An effect that was never contemplated by the composer, can sometimes be advantageously superinduced by the skilful executant; hence in the present instance, when the scene, which the poet alludes to, is presented to our imaginations, a particular method of uttering some of the lines, produces the true effect of the imita-

tive, on those who admire the piece. No degree of sentimental illusion, however, can fully redeem the impropriety that occurs at the words, "Hark! they whisper," &c. We are so repeatedly told to *hark,* and so often reminded to *whisper,* as to become impatient to know the sequel; and before what the "angels say" is actually communicated to us, our emotions so far subside as to deprive the substance of their message of its proper influence. From some fortunate circumstances in designing, the piece has been found to produce a good effect on the generality of listeners, though as a musical composition it falls in other respects below mediocrity (Hastings, Dissertation, pp. 210–11; see also Carr).

Additional References

1. Eckhard, No. i
2. Hall (as NEW YORK; no attribution); Temperley, 2:ex. 47

[29.] ENFIELD, by Solomon Chandler

Text from Rowe, p. 44; written by Elizabeth Rowe. First published in Oliver Brownson, *Select Harmony* (n.p. [Connecticut, 1785]). Law 1791, p. 19.

ENFIELD, a setting of two stanzas of C.M. text in major mode, was printed 57 times. Its identification with the present text was very close; in only two tunebooks does it appear with different texts.

Introduced in Connecticut (Brownson 1785f), ENFIELD received nearly 80 percent of its printings in New England. Picked up almost immediately in its home state (Law 1787ff), ENFIELD won a solid place in the repertory through appearances in New England collections of the 1790s: French 1793, Holden 1793ff, Law 1794f, Mann 1797f, Worcester 1797ff, Village 1798ff, Boston 1799, Merrill 1799. Pilsbury 1799 introduced it outside New England, where it appeared most often in collections from New York (Huntington 1800, Little 1805ff, Atwill 1806, Seymour 1809, Evans 1810). Two other collections in Pennsylvania (Little 1801, Wyeth 1810) also carried it. Except for Law 1803 and Salem 1806, the post-1800 New England collections in which ENFIELD appeared form a roster of the region's more eclectic offerings: Holden 1800, Brown 1802ff, Holyoke 1803, Albee 1805, Maxim 1805f, Robbins 1805, Boston First 1806, Holyoke 1807, Mann 1807, Read 1807f, Suffolk 1807, J. Read 1808, Sanger 1808. Circulation was maintained in the next decade with appearances in at least fifteen collections from the years 1811–1820. ENFIELD was included in four northern retrospective collections and in two later southern tunebooks.

ENFIELD's melodic structure is unusual among American-composed tunes of its time. Its repetition of the first phrase at the start of the second and, less directly, the fourth (AA¹BA²) and the ornamentation and secondary-dominant cadence in the third phrase suggest that it was inspired either by an instrumental melody or by Madan's Methodist style (see, e.g., DENMARK). A memoir by composer Timothy Swan's daughter explains the tune's title and supplies all that is now known about its composer and origin:

Father was well acquainted with Chandler who made several tunes tho' he was no singer. He has the credit of making Enfield. . . . He lived in Enfield[,] Tailor by trade. By some it is said that two others assisted Chandler in making the tune of Enfield. Tis a sweetly soft air (Swan, p. [2]).

Additional References

1. Alderdice, p. 302; Read, No. 91
2. Hall

Cross-Reference

See entry on JORDAN.

[30.] FUNERAL THOUGHT
(FUNERAL HYMN, RADNOR, WALDEN)

Text from Watts, Hymns II, no. 63. First published in Aaron Williams, *The Universal Psalmodist* (London, 1763). First published in America in [Daniel Bayley], *A New and Compleat Introduction to the Grounds and Rules of Musick* (Newburyport, 1764) or Josiah Flagg, *A Collection of the Best Psalm Tunes* (Boston, 1764). Williams 1769, p. 80, as A FUNERAL THOUGHT.

FUNERAL THOUGHT, a C.M. minor-mode plain tune notated in duple time, was printed 95 times. Several were textless, but from the beginning of its circulation in America its identification with Watts's text, which the text source labels "A funeral thought," was firm.

First printed in Massachusetts (see above), FUNERAL THOUGHT received more than three-quarters of its printings in New England. Massachusetts printings before 1790 include Walter 1764a, six of Daniel Bayley's publications, and New England 1771, Mass 1784f, New 1784, Worcester 1786–88, Federal 1788–93, and Sacred 1788. Appearances in New Hampshire and Connecticut (Gilman 1771, Law 1781, Jocelin 1783f), added to Selection 1788ff and Adgate 1789ff, which introduced FUNERAL THOUGHT outside New England, bring the number of pre-1790 collections in which it appeared to twenty, a figure matched or topped by only nine other Core Repertory tunes. Circulation over the next two decades broadened to include Maryland (Ely 1792, Cole 1804f, Cole 1808), Charleston (Pilsbury 1799), and New York City (Erben 1806, Erben 1808), as well as maintaining a scattering of printings in Pennsylvania (Poor 1794, Wyeth 1810), New Hampshire (Village 1795ff, Merrill 1799, Blanchard 1808), and Connecticut (Jenks 1806, Read 1810). But the lion's share of appearances in the last two decades came in Massachusetts, where Worcester 1800f and seventeen new collections, some eclectic and some reform, carried it: Gram 1795, Boston 1799, Holden 1800, Holden 1801, Brown 1802ff, Holyoke 1803, Cooper 1804, Holyoke 1804, Albee 1805, Boston First 1806, Holyoke 1807, Mann 1807, Middlesex 1807f, Suffolk 1807, Deerfield 1808, Sanger 1808, Sacred 1810. Circulation continued in the next decade, with at least two dozen appearances in collections from the years 1811–1820. FUNERAL THOUGHT appeared in five northern retrospective collections and in two later southern tunebooks.

The rhythmic notation of FUNERAL THOUGHT suggests that the tune was traditionally performed in a slow, flexible triple-time, alternating long-held syllables with quickly declaimed ones (see Preface, p. xii, above). FUNERAL THOUGHT appeared most often in four-voice settings but occasionally in three voices. Evidence for its performance is abundant. When, in the summer of 1782, the wife of New Haven minister Jonathan Edwards drowned, "Watts's Funeral Thought ('Hark from the tombs . . .')" was sung at her funeral (Connecticut Journal; quoted in Bushnell, pp. 63–64). The diary of the Reverend Ezra Stiles of New Haven mentions five funerals between 1778 and 1788 at which FUNERAL THOUGHT was sung, including that of the Reverend Chauncey Whittlesey, which began with its presentation "by the singers of the three Galleries" (Stiles Diary, 26 July 1787; the others occurred on 28 January 1778, 27 November 1780, 25 June 1782, and 19 June 1788; see Stiles Diary, vol. II: 245, 483; vol. III:28, 272, 319). William Bentley's diary records two more singings at funerals in Salem in 1798 (Bentley Diary, 20 March, 8 April; vol. II:262, 264). During the Revolution, instrumental performances were given. At a military funeral in 1775, the fifes played "the tune called the Funeral Thoughts. At the end of each line in the tune the Drums beat one Stroke" (Diary of Benjamin Boardman; quoted in Camus, p. 116). Giles Gibbs's manuscript fife book (Ellington, Connecticut, 1777) contains the tune with the direction: "to be played at the burial"

(Gibbs, p. 26). Mark Twain's *Huckleberry Finn*, Chapter 26, suggests that by the middle of the nineteenth century, the first phrase of Watts's text was circulating on its own. Huck, floating down the Mississippi, has joined up with a pair of swindlers who are conniving to cheat the three Wilks sisters out of their inheritance. Joanna ("Hare-lip"), the youngest of the sisters, seems suspicious of the travelers' claim to be from England, and she questions Huck closely. But her oldest sister, Mary Jane, chides her for being rude to Huck, a guest. Then the second sister, Susan, "*she* waltzed in," Huck recalls, "and if you'll believe me she did give Hare-lip hark from the tomb!" Shortly after the Civil War, however, a Chicago music periodical edited by Henry Clay Work predicted that the new generation of singing-school scholars would no longer be satisfied with tunes like FUNERAL THOUGHT.

> "Hark from the tombs a doleful sound" will hardly be the style of music that will find favor in [modern] singing schools, and the old style of books will hardly be adapted to the rhythm of the popular pulse. . . . The music in demand will be mostly secular, largely patriotic, and all must be fresh, elastic, and full of nerve (Song Messenger, p. 56).

Nevertheless, in 1941 Vance Randolph collected FUNERAL THOUGHT in oral tradition in the Ozarks:

> sung by Mrs. May Kennedy McCord, Springfield, Missouri. . . . The beginning of an old hymn which she heard in a church in Stone County, Mo., in the 90s. Mrs. McCord says that facetious young folk sometimes sang the word *doleful* as if it were *dodel-fiddle*, which was regarded as very daring and a great joke (Randolph, No. 638).

Additional References

1. Alderdice, p. 88; Read, No. 110
2. Hall (attributed to Williams)

Cross-References

See entries on CALVARY, PSALM 100 [OLD].

[31.] GREENFIELD, by Lewis Edson
    Text from New Version, Psalm 46. First published in [Simeon Jocelin], *The Chorister's Companion* (New Haven, 1782). Little 1801, p. 33.
    GREENFIELD, a duple-time P.M. piece in minor mode, was—together with Edson's LENOX—the most frequently published American fuging-tune, with 103 printings. The present text was by far the most preferred, though the tune was printed with three others, and the composer's own son brought it out with no text at all (Edson 1801).
    First published in Connecticut (Jocelin 1782f), GREENFIELD received 57 percent of its printings in New England. It appeared in thirteen different tunebooks in the 1780s, a total matched or topped by only a half-dozen other pieces. Those appearances were divided among Massachusetts (Bayley 1785a, Worcester 1786–97, Bayley 1788, Federal 1788ff, Sacred 1788), Connecticut (Brownson 1783ff, Langdon 1786, Law 1786ff, Read 1787ff), New York City (Amphion 1789), and Philadelphia (Selection 1788ff, Adgate 1789ff). Widening circulation from the 1790s on introduced GREENFIELD to Maryland (Ely 1792), Virginia (Sandford 1793), New York's Hudson Valley (Atwill 1795f, Huntington 1800, Atwill 1804, Little 1805ff), northern New England (Village 1795ff, Hill 1801, West 1802f, Robbins 1805, Maxim 1808), New Jersey (New Jersey 1797), South Carolina (Pilsbury 1799), and New York City (Edson 1801f, Seymour 1803f, Seymour 1809). In the meantime, printings continued through the decade in Massachusetts (French 1793, Holden 1793f, Mann 1797f, Boston 1799), Connecticut (Read 1794ff),

and Philadelphia (Shumway 1793f). After 1800, city printings in the latter areas were restricted to Philadelphia (Little 1801, Sacred 1806, Woodward 1806ff, Chapin 1808f, Blake 1810), while books intended for smaller communities in western Pennsylvania (Cumberland 1804, Wyeth 1810) and Massachusetts (Albee 1805, Belknap 1806f, Huntington 1807, J. Read 1808, Sanger 1808) accounted for a slightly larger number. Circulation in the next decade dropped to fewer than a dozen appearances in collections from the years 1811–1820. GREENFIELD was included in four northern retrospective collections and in two southern tunebooks.
    With its alternation between a minor dominant (mm. 2, 3, 5, 14, 17) and a major dominant (mm. 9, 19), its open perfect consonances (mm. 1, 12, 13, 15, 20), and its dissonant clashes (mm. 3, 4, 8, 11, 15), GREENFIELD exemplifies the harmonic style developed by rural Yankee psalmodists. And its stretches of quarter-note declamation exemplify the possibilities for robust, accented singing that the fuging-tune opened up.

Additional References

1. Alderdice, p. 50
2. Hall; Hitchcock 156, 162, (122)

Cross-References

See entries on LENOX, PSALM 46.

[32.] GREENWICH, by Daniel Read
    Text from Watts, Psalm 73, L.M. First published in [Amos Doolittle & Daniel Read], *The American Musical Magazine* (New Haven, 1786–87). Read 1797, p. 50.
    GREENWICH, a minor-mode L.M. fuging-tune in duple time, setting two stanzas of text, was printed 82 times, making it, together with STAFFORD, Read's most widely published piece in his own time. It was closely linked with the present text, appearing with only one other, and that in just one collection. (Vinson Bushnell has suggested that Read chose this text as a condemnation of other compilers for their unauthorized borrowings or pirating of his tunebooks [Bushnell, pp. 95–97].)
    Introduced in Connecticut (Doolittle 1786), GREENWICH received 55 percent of its printings in New England. The tune won immediate acceptance, appearing in at least seven different tunebooks within five years of its first printing: in Connecticut (Law 1786, Read 1787ff), Massachusetts (Bayley 1788a, Worcester 1788ff, Federal 1790ff), and Pennsylvania (Adgate 1789ff, Selection 1789). In the next decade, GREENWICH solidified its place in the central New England repertory (French 1793, Holden 1793ff, Read 1794ff, Griswold 1796f, Mann 1797f, Boston 1799), moving northward (Village 1795ff), west to the Hudson Valley (Atwill 1795f), and south of New England to Virginia (Sandford 1793), New Jersey (New Jersey 1797), South Carolina (Pilsbury 1799), and Philadelphia (Shumway 1793f). After 1800, printings in new Massachusetts tunebooks were few (Holden 1800, Huntington 1807, J. Read 1808), but GREENWICH flourished on the periphery: in the north (Hill 1801, Robbins 1805, Maxim 1808), the Hudson Valley (Huntington 1800, Atwill 1804, Little 1805ff), New Jersey (Smith 1803f), and Harrisburg (Wyeth 1810), as well as in New York City (Seymour 1803f, Seymour 1809) and Philadelphia (Little 1801, Sacred 1806, Blake 1810). Circulation was modest in the next decade, with appearances in ten new collections from the years 1811–1820. GREENWICH was included in six northern retrospective collections and in two southern tunebooks.
    GREENWICH sets two stanzas of text, with lines 1-3 of the second stanza fuged in an unusually long section of verbal conflict (nine measures). Perhaps because both the texture and the textual mood change with the second stanza—the first verse re-

gretting envy of the wicked, the second seeming to gloat over their fall—southern shape-note singers take the first section slowly, then shift into a faster tempo at the fuge. Note, e.g., the performance of GREENWICH by the Alabama Sacred Harp Convention on the recording "White Spirituals from *The Sacred Harp*" (New World 205). Read published a "corrected" version of GREENWICH in *The New Haven Collection* (New Haven, 1818).

Additional References

1. Alderdice, p. 108
2. Fisher, p. 26; Hall; Hitchcock 122

Cross-Reference

See entry on STAFFORD.

[33.] HABAKKUK
(BOWDEN, LEOMINSTER)

Text by Charles Wesley (see Julian, p. 104). First published in *Harmonia Sacra, or a Choice Collection of Psalm and Hymn Tunes* (London, ca. 1760), or before. First published in America in Andrew Law, *A Collection of Hymn Tunes* (Cheshire, Connecticut, [1783]) or John Stickney, *The Gentleman and Lady's Musical Companion* (Newburyport, [1783]). Worcester 1800, p. 142.

HABAKKUK, a duple-time set-piece in major mode, was printed 55 times, always with the present text.

Introduced either in Connecticut or Massachusetts (see above), HABAKKUK received nearly three-quarters of its printings in New England. In the years before 1800, it appeared in several eclectic New England works (Bayley 1784, Jocelin 1788, Worcester 1788–1800, Federal 1790–93, Village 1796ff), as well as in others with more specialized content (Holden II 1793, Bull 1795, Law 1796ff, Benjamin 1799). A similar pattern persisted in the next decade, as both eclectic items (AMM 1800, Holden 1800, Brown 1802f, Jenks 1803, Cooper 1804, Albee 1805, Boston First 1806) and reform works (Essex 1802, Salem 1805f, Blanchard 1808) carried it. Shumway 1793f, printed in Philadelphia, introduced HABAKKUK outside New England, and it subsequently appeared in the Hudson River Valley (Atwill 1795f, Atwill 1804, Little 1805ff), Philadelphia (Sacred 1803, Law 1807f), and Norfolk, Virginia (Tomlins 1810). Circulation continued on a small scale in the next decade, with printings in at least eleven collections from the years 1811–1820. HABAKKUK appeared in three northern retrospective collections but in no southern tunebooks.

HABAKKUK shares with DENMARK some traits of Methodist hymnody, though its melody appears in the middle voice rather than on top, and it avoids text repetition. In its extremely wide range (the tune occupies a thirteenth), its sometimes angular skips (mm. 11, 13–14), its ornamentation, and its form (first phrase repeated, mm. 5–8; internal repetitions in both brief sequences, cf. mm. 16–17 and mm. 18–19, and larger chunks, cf. mm. 9–12 and mm. 20–24) suggest that it originated as an instrumental piece. That suggestion is strengthened by the bass line, devoted in some places to pedal-points (mm. 16–21) and elsewhere to standard cadential figures (mm. 28ff). HABAKKUK was sometimes published in four-voice arrangements, including a simplified one by Amos Bull, about which the arranger wrote:

The alterations in Denmark and Habakkuk, and some other tunes, are made with a view of adapting them to the use of the Newengland Choirs; and not from a supposition that they were faulty as printed in other Books (Bull 1795, p. 7).

Additional Reference

2. Hall (attributed to Madan)

[34.] HARTFORD, by Elihu Carpenter

Text from Watts, Psalm 24, L.M. First published in Andrew Law, *Select Harmony* ([Cheshire, Connecticut], 1779). Law 1779, p. 58.

A duple-time setting of two stanzas of L.M. text, HARTFORD was printed 46 times. It is consistently linked with the present text, though it did appear with at least two others.

Introduced in Connecticut (Law 1779f), HARTFORD received only half of its printings in New England. The tune's period of peak circulation occurred in the decade after its debut in print, when it appeared in Massachusetts (Bayley 1784, Mass 1784f, Worcester 1786f, Bayley 1788, Federal 1788–93, Sacred 1788), Connecticut (Law 1786ff, Read 1787ff), and Pennsylvania (Selection 1788ff, Adgate 1789ff). Thereafter, New England circulation declined sharply (Holden 1793, Collection 1804 in Massachusetts; Read 1794, Gamut 1807 in Connecticut; West 1802 in Vermont), but HARTFORD did appear in a succession of later Philadelphia tunebooks (Shumway 1793f, Sacred 1806, Chapin 1808f, Blake 1810), and also in Charleston (Pilsbury 1799) and New York City (Seymour 1803f). Circulation stopped almost completely in the next decade, as HARTFORD appeared in fewer than five collections from the years 1811–1820. It is not found in any northern retrospective collections but did appear in one southern tunebook.

Without introducing fuging or text overlap, HARTFORD employs the steady quarter-note declamation characteristic of the fuging-tune. Grouping the notes mostly in repeated pairs, the tune generates strong rhythmic momentum, especially in the second half, where twenty-five consecutive beats go by before a cadential break. HARTFORD, which lacks accidentals, exemplifies American modal harmony, being in Aeolian mode on D.

Additional Reference

1. Alderdice, p. 288

[35.] HOTHAM
(HYMN)

Text by Charles Wesley (see Julian, p. 590, who writes: "During the past hundred years few hymns have been so extensively used. . . . It is given in the hymn-books of all English-speaking countries, and has been translated into many languages"), quoted here from Law Collection, p. 10. First published in [Martin Madan], *A Collection of Psalm and Hymn Tunes . . . To Be Had at the Lock Hospital* (London, [1769]). First published in America in Andrew Law, *A Collection of Hymn Tunes* (Cheshire, Connecticut, [1783]). Brownson 1797, p. 11.

HOTHAM, a duple-time P.M. hymn tune in major mode, was printed 59 times, consistently with the present text.

HOTHAM received roughly 60 percent of its printings in New England. Introduced in Connecticut (Law C 1783), it was not reprinted for eight years, until Worcester 1791–97 and Adgate 1791ff introduced it in Boston and Philadelphia, respectively. During the 1790s the tune received fairly wide distribution, both in New England (Holden II 1793, Federal 1794, Law 1794, Brownson 1797, Village 1798ff, Benjamin 1799, Boston 1799) and southward in Virginia (Sandford 1793) and Baltimore (Cole 1799). A favorite of post-1800 reformers in New England and elsewhere (Law 1805, Salem 1805f, Law 1807f, Blanchard 1808, Boston Brattle 1810, Boston West 1810, Brown 1810, Sacred 1810), HOTHAM also appeared in works compiled by urban members of the secular music trade: Graupner 1806 in Boston; Erben 1806 in New York City; Sacred 1803 and a sheet-music edition by Raynor Taylor (Wolfe 9259) in Philadelphia. Specialized European-based tunebooks (Addington 1808, Madan 1809) also carried it. But so did more eclectic items: Holden 1800, Cooper 1804, Huntington 1807a, and Mann 1807 in Massachusetts; Jenks 1810 in Connecticut; Evans 1808f in New York City; and Aitken 1806, Woodward 1806ff, Chapin 1808f, and Blake 1810 in Philadelphia. Circulation in the next decade was widespread, as Hotham appeared in at least forty collections from the years 1811–1820. It was picked up by six northern retrospective collections, but no southern tunebooks included it.

Temperley notes the popularity of Hotham in England in the years 1790 to 1860 (Temperley, 1:236). He also describes the tune as an exemplar of the "Methodist" style, quoting an English author's complaint in 1819 about that style's "theatrical embellishments" and "galant cadence, long since obsolete in the theater but still common in psalm tunes." In its three-fold presentation of the beginning of the last line of text, Hotham seeks to achieve a climactic effect, noted by Temperley as typical of Methodist "repeating tunes" (1:212).

Additional References

1. Read, No. 319
2. Hall (attributed to Madan); Temperley, 2:ex. 45

Cross-Reference

See entry on Jordan.

[36.] Irish
(Dublin, St. Patrick's)

Text from Watts, Hymns II, no. 72. First published in *A Collection of Hymns and Sacred Poems* (Dublin, 1749). First published in America in Josiah Flagg, *A Collection of the Best Psalm Tunes* (Boston, 1764). Mann 1797, p. 27.

Irish, a triple-time C.M. tune in major mode, was printed 82 times. Worcester 1788 was the first to give it its present text, one of at least sixteen with which it was published.

Introduced in Massachusetts (Flagg 1764), Irish received nearly two-thirds of its printings in New England. The tune was rather slow to catch on, appearing during the colonial period only in a pair of Massachusetts works besides Flagg (Bayley 1770ff, New England 1771) and during the 1780s in just a handful of others (Law 1781, Mass 1784f, New 1784, Sacred 1788, Worcester 1788–97). Circulation continued at a similar pace in New England during the 1790s (Law 1791f, Federal 1790–93, Village 1795ff, Mann 1797, Boston 1799), widening to include Virginia (Sandford 1793), the Hudson River Valley (Atwill 1795f, Huntington 1800, Atwill 1804, Little 1805ff), Baltimore (Cole 1799, Cole 1808, Cole 1810), and Charleston (Pilsbury 1799). After 1800 Irish, with appearances in thirty-three new collections, came to be one of the dozen most widely printed Core Repertory pieces. A new favorite in Pennsylvania (Shumway 1801, Stammers 1803, Cumberland 1804, Sacred 1806, Woodward 1806ff, Law 1807f, Addington 1808, Blake 1810, Wyeth 1810), it also appeared in New York City (Erben 1806, Erben 1808, Evans 1808f). Its place in the New England repertory remained secure, both among more eclectic tunebooks (Brown 1802ff, Holyoke 1804, Albee 1805, Robbins 1805, Boston First 1806, Griswold 1807, Mann 1807, Sanger 1808) and reform collections (Essex 1802, Law 1803, Salem 1805f, Middlesex 1807f, Blanchard 1808, Deerfield 1808, Boston West 1810, Sacred 1810). Circulation continued strong in the next decade, with appearances in at least twenty-five collections from the years 1811–1820. Irish appeared in five northern retrospective collections but in none of the southern tunebooks canvassed.

Temperley shows Irish to have been an English favorite (Temperley, 1:236). The tune exemplifies the musical idiom of one branch of mid-century British psalmody. Its lightly decorated, triple-time melody is supported by an often stepwise bass line, producing stepwise root movement from time to time

(e.g., mm. 9–10, 12–13), and chords sometimes lack the expected third (mm. 2, 11, and 14).

Additional References

1. Alderdice, p. m; Eckhard, No. 61; Read, No. 35
2. AMR 263; A&M 404; Hall (attributed to Williams)
3. Episcopal; Methodist; Presbyterian

Cross-Reference

See entry on Psalm 100 [Old].

[37.] Isle of Wight
(Isle White, Sharon)

Text from Watts, Hymns II, no. 63. First published in *A Sett of Tunes in 3 Parts* ([London, ca. 1720]). First published in America in John Tufts, *An Introduction to the Singing of Psalm-Tunes*, 5th ed. (Boston, 1726). Shumway 1793, p. 23.

Isle of Wight, a duple-time C.M. tune in minor mode, was printed 62 times. Usually textless before the late 1780s, it appeared with ten different texts in all; the present text is one of two with which it was published more than once.

Introduced in Boston (Tufts 1726ff), Isle of Wight received 58 percent of its printings in New England. Published in a succession of supplements and tunebooks from colonial and wartime New England (Bay 1737f, Turner 1752, Johnston 1755f, Flagg 1764, Bayley 1767f, Bayley 1770ff, Gilman 1771, New England 1771, Billings 1779), Isle of Wight also appeared in colonial Philadelphia (Dawson 1754, Lyon 1761f, Tunes 1763f). Circulation continued steadily in both places during the century's last two decades: in Massachusetts and Connecticut (Mass 1784f, New 1784, Law 1786ff, Jocelin 1788, Sacred 1788, Law 1794f, Boston 1799), New York City (Amphion 1789), and in Philadelphia (Selection 1788ff, Adgate 1789ff, Shumway 1793f). It broadened after 1800 to include New York State (Huntington 1800, Erben 1806), maintaining a modest place as well in Massachusetts and Pennsylvania (Law 1803, Cooper 1804, Cumberland 1804, Sacred 1806, Middlesex 1807f, Blake 1810). Circulation was moderate in the next decade, with appearances in more than a dozen collections from the years 1811–1820. Isle of Wight appeared in one northern retrospective collection and no southern tunebooks.

The present setting, published in the 1790s, provides open sonorities for the first and last notes of every phrase but one (m. 14), simplifying tuning for the singers; but harmonic progressions are still treacherous in the first phrase, and unwonted dissonances creep in (mm. 4, 7, 13). It seems possible that the E-flats in the key signature might have been ignored by the singers, raising the sixth scale degree and throwing the mode into Dorian, a practice followed by some shape-note singers today. Colonial American singers most likely had some difficulty with the tune, for it was nicknamed "Isle of Shoals . . . in Derision," according to the Reverend Thomas Symmes, minister in Bradford, Massachusetts (Symmes, p. 37). Nevertheless, the congregation at Weston, Massachusetts, chose it in 1738 to sing in public worship (1 of 15 tunes).

Additional References

1. Read, No. 116
2. Hall (attributed to Tans'ur)

[38.] Jordan, by William Billings
Text from Watts, Hymns II, no. 66. First printed in William Billings, *The Suffolk Harmony* (Boston, 1786). Little 1801, p. 45.

Jordan, a duple-time setting of two stanzas of C.M. text, was printed 71 times. The present text, whose reference to the River Jordan obviously inspired the tune's title, is found in all except a very few collections; four other texts also appeared with the tune.

First published in Boston (Billings 1786), JORDAN received some 63 percent of its printings in New England. Picked up by a pair of Massachusetts-based tunebooks soon after its introduction (Federal 1788, Worcester 1788ff), JORDAN nevertheless circulated more widely outside New England during the 1790s than inside, appearing in Maryland (Ely 1792), Virginia (Sandford 1793), New York State (Atwill 1795f, N. Billings 1795), New Jersey (New Jersey 1797), and South Carolina (Pilsbury 1799), as well as in Massachusetts (Holden 1793ff, Mann 1797f, Boston 1799) and New Hampshire (Village 1795ff, Merrill 1799). After 1800, several more collections from northern New England printed JORDAN (Hill 1801, Maxim 1805f, Robbins 1805). Read 1807f supplied the tune's lone Connecticut appearance, while in Massachusetts it was picked up by quite a number of eclectic tunebooks (Holden 1800, Brown 1802f, Holyoke 1803, Cooper 1804, PSA 1804, Belknap 1806f, Boston First 1806, Holyoke 1807, Mann 1807, Suffolk 1807), one hard-core reform work (Boston West 1810), and a compilation by a Boston sheet-music publisher (Graupner 1806). Outside New England JORDAN was a favorite in New York City (Edson 1801f, Erben 1808, Seymour 1809, Evans 1810), appearing also in the Hudson Valley (Atwill 1804f, Little 1805ff), Baltimore (Cole 1804, Cole 1808), and in a trio of Pennsylvania tunebooks (Little 1801, Chapin 1808f, Wyeth 1810). Steady circulation continued in the next decade, with appearances in at least seventeen collections from the years 1811–1820. JORDAN was included in six northern retrospective collections and one southern tunebook.

The melodic structure of the tune is unusual among American sacred pieces of its time. Its second phrase begins by repeating the start of the first, creating an antecedent-consequent parallel; and, after a digressive third phrase, the fourth begins with a brief suggestion of the first. The resulting form (AA¹BA²; cf. ENFIELD) suggests that JORDAN was inspired either by an instrumental melody or by the so-called "Methodist" style (see DENMARK, HOTHAM). Long after most New England favorites had fallen from fashion, JORDAN continued to appear in respectable company. Writing in the mid-1830s, the reformer Thomas Hastings clearly felt some conflict about the tune:

> Jordan, if indeed the melody was ever invented by [Billings], had claims somewhat beyond mediocrity. It has lately found its way into one of the leading publications of Boston, an honor, however, of which it is not worthy (Musical Magazine, I; quoted in McKay & Crawford, p. 202).

A slightly later account, more willing to grant JORDAN its due, called it and some other early New England compositions "excellent, and not discreditable to musical genius," and praised its appearance in recent Boston publications as "honorable to the compilers" (Boston Musical Gazette; quoted in Bushnell, p. 457). As late as 1879, Cheney could name JORDAN as one of Billings's tunes that "continue popular" (Cheney, p. 169). In Melville's *Moby Dick* (Chapter 22), when the *Pequod* sets sail from Nantucket on an icy Christmas evening, Captain Bildad, the pious Quaker who owns part of the ship, pilots her out of the harbor. The narrator describes the scene as follows:

> As the old Craft deep dived into the green seas, and sent the shivering frost all over her, and the winds howled, and the cordage rang, [Bildad's] steady notes were heard,
>
> > "Sweet fields beyond the swelling flood,
> > Stand dressed in living green.
> > So to the Jews old Canaan stood,
> > While Jordan rolled between."
>
> Never did those sweet words sound more sweetly to me than then.

The "sweet words" Bildad sang were those of the second half of William Billings's JORDAN.

Additional References

1. Alderdice, p. 323
2. AH, p. 211; Hall

Cross-Reference

See entry on CORONATION.

[39.] JUDGMENT, by Daniel Read

Text from Watts, Psalm 50, P.M., 1st Part. First published in Daniel Read, *The American Singing Book* (New Haven, 1785). Worcester 1788, p. 41.

JUDGMENT, which was printed 48 times, is one of only two Core Repertory pieces in the ten-syllable lines of Psalm 50 (six 10s; the structure of LANDAFF, the other—four 10s, two 11s—differs slightly, representing the "old" rather than the "new" 50th meter; see Lyon 1761, pp. 56–59, where the two meters are so identified). The present text appears with most printings, though Smith 1803, Huntington 1807, and Little 1809 assign texts in the "old" meter of Watts's Psalm 50, Part II. (Unaccountably, Bayley 1788 gives it a C.M. text. One regrets missing a chance to hear singers trying to make that incongruous match fit.)

Introduced in Connecticut (Read 1785ff), JUDGMENT received 83 percent of its printings in New England. Picked up by four Massachusetts items of the 1780s (Bayley 1788a, Federal 1788, Worcester 1788, Worcester 1797ff), JUDGMENT during the next two decades was reprinted in more than a dozen eclectic tunebooks in Massachusetts (Holden 1793ff, Mann 1797f, Boston 1799, Holden 1800, Brown 1802f, Boston First 1806, Huntington 1807, Mann 1807, J. Read 1808), Connecticut (Read 1804ff), and northern New England (Village 1796–1800, Merrill 1799, Robbins 1805, and Village 1807ff). Elsewhere, JUDGMENT circulated in the Hudson Valley (Atwill 1795f, Huntington 1800, Atwill 1804, Little 1809f), and southward to South Carolina (Pilsbury 1799), New Jersey (Smith 1803f), and Delaware (Fobes 1809), and westward to Harrisburg (Wyeth 1810). The printing history of JUDGMENT is closely related to that of LANDAFF. Federal 1790ff replaced JUDGMENT with LANDAFF; conversely, Worcester 1786 printed LANDAFF, but Worcester 1788 and 1797ff substituted JUDGMENT. Village 1796ff printed only JUDGMENT, adding LANDAFF from the 1807 edition on. Only five collections (Bayley 1788, Pilsbury 1799, Brown 1802ff, Mann 1807, and Village 1807ff) contain both pieces. Circulation in the next decade was slow, with perhaps as few as a half-dozen appearances in collections from the years 1811–1820. JUDGMENT appeared in three retrospective northern collections but in none of the southern tunebooks.

Read's JUDGMENT is notable for the flexibility of its text declamation. Setting six ten-syllable lines, it varies the rhythm of all, except that line 5 repeats the rhythm of line 3. (Cf. LANDAFF for a different approach to declamation.) One noteworthy appearance of JUDGMENT in the decade 1811–1820 came in *The New Haven Collection* (New Haven, [*recte*] 1818), where it was headed "corrected by the author."

Additional References

1. Alderdice, p. aa; Read, No. 310
2. Hall

Cross-Reference

See entry on LANDAFF.

[40.] KINGSBRIDGE

Text from Watts, Psalm 24 and Psalm 107. First published in

Harmonia Sacra, or a Choice Collection of Psalm and Hymn Tunes (London, ca. 1760), or before. First published in America in Josiah Flagg, *A Collection of the Best Psalm Tunes* (Boston, 1764). Federal 1790, p. 23.

KINGSBRIDGE, a triple-time L.M. tune in minor mode, was printed 51 times. The present text, one of twelve with which it appeared, was linked with it in many tunebooks before 1800, though not in later ones.

Introduced in Boston (Flagg 1764), KINGSBRIDGE received some three-quarters of its printings in New England. The tune's circulation before 1790 depended on a succession of Massachusetts tunebooks (Bayley 1768, Williams 1769ff, Stickney 1774ff, Mass 1784f, Bayley 1784, Bayley 1785, Bayley 1788, Worcester 1786–94, Federal 1788–93, Sacred 1788) and three in Connecticut (Law 1779, Jocelin 1782, Law 1783f). The only books to pick it up in the 1790s were compiled elsewhere: in Maryland (Ely 1792), New Hampshire (Village 1795–1803), and South Carolina (Pilsbury 1799). After the turn of the century, KINGSBRIDGE reappeared in a handful of New England works (Holyoke 1803, Robbins 1805, Boston First 1806, Mann 1807, Blanchard 1808), making its way as well into Philadelphia (Shumway 1801, Sacred 1806, Woodward 1806ff, Law 1807f, Blake 1810) and New York City (Erben 1806, Erben 1808). Steady circulation continued in the next decade with at least fourteen appearances in collections from the years 1811–1820. KINGSBRIDGE appeared neither in any northern retrospective collections nor in southern tunebooks.

The structure of KINGSBRIDGE is unusual for a four-line plain tune: its fourth phrase is an exact repetition, in all voices, of its second, creating the form ABCB (cf. Billings's BROOKFIELD for a similar form with a less literal repeat). In a letter from Charleston, South Carolina, Andrew Law reported attending a worship service in which, when the organ would not work, "we collected four or five and sung Norwich and Kingsbridge. Mr. Nott says a number of people have told him since that they wish the Organ might never go again" (Andrew Law to William Law, 11 January 1787; quoted in Crawford, p. 55).

Additional Reference

1. Read, No. 217

[41.] LANDAFF
(FRANCE, KINGSTON, OLD 50, PSALM 50)

Text from Watts, Psalm 50, 2d Part. First published in *Psalmes of David in English Metre,* 2d ed. ([Geneva], 1558). First published in America in *Neu-vermehrt-und vollständiges Gesang-Buch* (Germantown, Pennsylvania, 1753), printed for the Reformed Church in the U.S. Lyon 1761, p. 84, as "The Old 50th Psalm Tune."

LANDAFF, in minor mode, duple time, and one of two Core Repertory tunes with ten-syllable lines, was printed 84 times (See JUDGMENT, above, for a note distinguishing its "new" 50th meter from LANDAFF's "old" one—the latter concluding with a pair of eleven-syllable lines). Most early printings are textless, but from Mass 1784 on, the present text is usual, though LANDAFF was printed with at least four others.

Introduced in Pennsylvania (Neu 1753ff), LANDAFF received 62 percent of its printings in New England. After being first published in America in a German language hymnbook, LANDAFF also appeared in such later Pennsylvania imprints as the Reformed Church's Neue 1797ff and two Mennonite works (Mennonite 1803, Mennonite 1804f). English-language tunebooks from colonial Philadelphia also carried it (Dawson 1754, Lyon 1761f, Tunes 1763f), but it appeared in none printed there after Selection 1788ff and Adgate 1789ff. Except for Ely 1792

(Baltimore), New Jersey 1797, and Pilsbury 1799 (compiled in Charleston, South Carolina), the rest of LANDAFF's printing history took place in New England. There, after being introduced in Boston (Flagg 1764), the tune passed into Daniel Bayley's publications (Bayley 1767f, Tans'ur 1767f, Tans'ur 1769ff, Bayley 1770ff, Stickney 1774, Bayley 1788) as well as into New England 1771 and works of several Connecticut compilers (Law 1779, Law 1781, Jocelin 1782f, Brownson 1783f, Law 1791f). LANDAFF also appeared in Massachusetts in Mass 1784f, Worcester 1786, Sacred 1788, and Federal 1790ff. After the turn of the century, LANDAFF appeared in a roster of Massachusetts collections, including a few eclectic items (Brown 1802ff, Cooper 1804, Holyoke 1804, Albee 1805, Hill 1806, Holyoke 1807, Mann 1807) and several reform works (Essex 1802, Blanchard 1807, Middlesex 1807f, Deerfield 1808, Huntington 1809). Village 1807ff also picked it up. It enjoyed a brisk circulation in the next decade, with appearances in at least twenty-five collections in the years 1811–1820. LANDAFF was published in two later northern retrospective collections but appeared in none of the southern tunebooks examined.

LANDAFF achieves its strong sense of coherence more by its application of the same rhythm to each of its six lines (with a small adjustment on the last two to accommodate the extra syllable) than by its repetition of one internal melodic phrase (ABCCDE). References report the singing of "the old·50th" in Canton, Massachusetts, "the first time" on 19 March 1766 (p. 307), and by a choir in Westfield, Massachusetts, after a singing lecture in 1772. The congregation at Harwinton, Connecticut, chose it for singing in public worship (4 June 1776; 1 of 22 tunes).

Additional References

1. Alderdice, p. 100; Read, No. 316
2. A&M 334; Frost 69; Hall

Cross-Reference

See entry on JUDGMENT.

[42.] LEBANON, by William Billings

Text from Watts, Psalm 144, C.M., 2d Part. First printed in William Billings, *The New-England Psalm-Singer* (Boston, [1770]). Village 1796, p. 63.

LEBANON, a duple-time C.M. tune in minor mode, was printed 48 times. It is linked more frequently with the present text than with any of the other six with which it appeared. (Next in frequency is Billings's own "Death with his warrant in his hand.")

Introduced in Boston (Billings 1770), LEBANON received more than two-thirds of its printings in New England. In the two decades that followed its first publication, it appeared only in Massachusetts (Billings 1778ff, Billings 1779, Worcester 1786ff, Federal 1788, Sacred 1788). During the 1790s the Philadelphia tunebook Selection 1790ff introduced it outside New England, followed there by Shumway 1793f. Village 1795ff picked it up in northern New England, while in Massachusetts Mann 1797 and Boston 1799 provided the tune's only new appearances. After 1800, circulation broadened to the west and south to include the Hudson Valley (Little 1805ff), Baltimore (Cole 1805), Delaware (Fobes 1809), and Harrisburg (Wyeth 1810), as well as one more Philadelphia appearance (Little 1801), while half-a-dozen eclectic items kept LEBANON before the singing public in central New England: Holden 1800, Holden 1801, Cooper 1804, Holyoke 1804, Griswold 1807, and Janes 1807. Circulation fell off in the next decade, with appearances in perhaps as few as seven collections from the years 1811–1820. However, LEBANON appeared in six retrospective northern collections, although none of the southern tunebooks carried it.

In LEBANON, Billings composed his most frequently published reincarnation of the traditional English minor-mode common tune. Except for its dactylic opening and decorated final cadence, LEBANON stands as a latter-day successor to the likes of COLESHILL, STANDISH, and WINDSOR, all of which, perhaps not accidentally, share its key of A minor.

Additional References

1. Alderdice, p. 304; Read, No. 124
2. Hall; Hitchcock 194

Cross-Reference

See entry on COLESHILL.

[43.] LENOX, by Lewis Edson

Text from Watts, Psalm 148, P.M. First published in [Simeon Jocelin], *The Chorister's Companion* (New Haven, 1782). Jocelin 1782, p. 59.

LENOX, which shares with GREENFIELD the honor of being the most frequently published American fuging-tune, was printed 105 times. The tune is in major mode. Of the seven texts with which LENOX appeared, the present one was the clearcut favorite. Watts's Psalm 84, P.M. ("Lord of the worlds above"), also appeared in many collections; and in Edson's son's lone tunebook (Edson 1801f) LENOX was textless.

Introduced in Connecticut (Jocelin 1782f), LENOX received about half its printings in New England. Its circulation was especially vigorous during the 1780s and 1790s, when it appeared in twenty-three different tunebooks, a total matched or topped by only eight other Core Repertory pieces. In those years LENOX established itself firmly in New England with appearances in Connecticut (Law 1783ff, Langdon 1786, Read 1787ff, Read 1794ff), Massachusetts (Bayley 1785a, Worcester 1786ff, Bayley 1788, Sacred 1788, Federal 1790ff, French 1793, Holden 1793ff, Mann 1797, Boston 1799), and New Hampshire (Village 1795ff), while Amphion 1789 printed it in New York City and a Philadelphia tunebook (Selection 1788ff) introduced it there, followed by Adgate 1789ff, Shumway 1793f, and Poor 1794. At the same time, the circulation of LENOX broadened to Maryland (Ely 1792), Virginia (Sandford 1793), the Hudson Valley (Atwill 1795f), New Jersey (New Jersey 1797), and South Carolina (Pilsbury 1799). After 1800, new printings were concentrated in New York (in Hudson Valley collections like Huntington 1800, Atwill 1804f, Little 1805ff, and New York City collections like Edson 1801f, Seymour 1803f, Erben 1806, Evans 1808f, Seymour 1809) and Pennsylvania (including both English language items—Little 1801, Cumberland 1804, Sacred 1806, Woodward 1806ff, Blake 1810, Wyeth 1810—and German ones—Rothbaust 1807, Doll 1810). In addition, LENOX appeared in a small group of eclectic tunebooks from Massachusetts (Holden 1800, Cooper 1804, Holyoke 1804, Boston First 1806, Huntington 1807, J. Read 1808) and the north (Maxim 1805f, Robbins 1805). Circulation was modest in the next decade, with only about a dozen appearances in works from the years 1811–1820. LENOX was included in seven northern retrospective collections, and four of the sampling of southern collections carried it.

LENOX sets one stanza of H.M. The fuge, which continues for twenty-six beats the quarter-note motion broken up earlier in the piece into five-beat spurts, occupies lines 5–7 of the text. The tune's first four phrases provide a fine illustration of how some Yankee composers handled harmony. Each phrase begins and ends with a consonance; but within each phrase, a harmonic collision or unexpected chord occurs: an F/F-sharp clash, generated contrapuntally (m. 2); a submediant chord where the bass movement leads one to expect a tonic (m. 4, beat

3); a second-inversion dominant and submediant, both in the same measure (m. 7, beats 2 and 4); and a free-floating 7th (m. 9, beat 2, counter). Nevertheless, the natural vitality of LENOX served to invite reformers to "improve" rather than discard it (see Cooper 1804, Erben 1806). An 1809 manuscript version of the Charleston organist Jacob Eckhard reduced LENOX to two voices and omitted the fuge. Thomas Hastings's *Church Melodies* (New York, 1858) prints a reharmonization in which the fuge remains intact (see Stevenson, p. 67). Cheney named LENOX among Edson's "excellent tunes which remained popular" in 1879 (Cheney, p. 171).

Additional References

1. Alderdice, p. 56; Eckhard, No. 79
2. AH, p. 218; Hall; Hitchcock 119, 174, 175, 194; MinA, p. 124
3. Baptist; Methodist

Cross-References

See entries on BRIDGEWATER, GREENFIELD, PORTSMOUTH.

[44.] LISBON, by Daniel Read

Text from Watts, Hymns II, no. 14. First published in Daniel Read, *The American Singing Book* (New Haven, 1785). Read 1797, p. 66.

LISBON, a S.M. fuging-tune in major mode, was printed 65 times. It appeared with at least five different texts, but from its first printing to 1810 it was by far most often linked with the present one.

Introduced in Connecticut (Read 1785ff), LISBON received nearly two-thirds of its printings in New England. After being reprinted only in Law 1787 during the 1780s, the tune caught on in the next decade. Ely 1792 (Baltimore) introduced it outside New England, followed by New Jersey 1797. In New England, LISBON was picked up by several collections in Massachusetts (French 1793, Holden 1793ff, Worcester 1794ff, Mann 1797f, Boston 1799) and was reprinted as well in Connecticut (Read 1794ff) and New Hampshire (Village 1795ff). After 1800 circulation broadened to include New York City (Edson 1801f, Seymour 1803f, Atwill 1806, Evans 1808f, Seymour 1809), the Hudson Valley (Little 1805ff), Philadelphia (Little 1801, Stammers 1803, Chapin 1808f, Blake 1810) and rural Pennsylvania (Rothbaust 1807, Wyeth 1810), and Delaware (Fobes 1809). At the same time, LISBON stayed in print in areas where it had enjoyed its earlier popularity: northern New England (Maxim 1805f, Robbins 1805); central New England (Holden 1800, Jenks 1804ff, Graupner 1806, Jenks 1806, Bushnell 1807, Huntington 1807, Suffolk 1807, J. Read 1808); New Jersey (Smith 1803f); and Baltimore (Gillet 1809). Circulation in the next decade was modest, with fewer than a dozen printings in collections from the years 1811–1820. LISBON appeared in seven retrospective northern collections and two southern tunebooks.

LISBON is the shortest fuging-tune in the Core Repertory. Its straightforward, diatonic brevity seems better suited to the present text than its declamation, which twice accents the second syllable of "welcome." Later stanzas, however, scan more suitably. Read "corrected" LISBON, together with several of his other tunes, when he had it printed in *The New Haven Collection* (New Haven, 1818); yet the tune in its "original" form stayed in print through much of the nineteenth century. In 1878 George Hood, an early historian of New England psalmody, named it and WINDHAM as the tunes that "have embalmed the memory of the good man [Read] for generations to come" (Cheney, p. 173). Several years later, F. O. Jones named LISBON as one of five pieces by Read that were "in general use at the present day . . . [and] are known to almost every church singer" (Jones, p. 143).

Additional References

1. Alderdice, p. 318; Read, No. 243
2. Hall; Hitchcock 175

Cross-References

See entries on SHERBURNE, WINDHAM.

[45.] LITTLE MARLBOROUGH

Text from Watts, *Hymns II*, no. 14. First published in Aaron Williams, *The Universal Psalmodist* (London, 1763). First printed in America by [Daniel Bayley], *A New and Compleat Introduction to the Grounds and Rules of Musick* (Newbury, 1764). Worcester 1797, p. 47.

A triple-time tune in minor mode, LITTLE MARLBOROUGH was printed 135 times—more than any other S.M. tune in the Core Repertory. Often appearing textless, LITTLE MARLBOROUGH was linked with at least twelve different texts; though the present choice was easily the most frequent, Watts's Psalm 90, S.M., "Lord what a feeble piece," was another to which LITTLE MARLBOROUGH was often sung.

Introduced in Boston (Bayley 1764ff), LITTLE MARLBOROUGH received 73 percent of its printings in New England. The tune appeared in six more of Daniel Bayley's publications (from Bayley 1767f to Bayley 1788), as well as in nearly a dozen other New England works (Flagg 1766, Gilman 1771, New England 1771, Law 1779, Law 1781, Jocelin 1782f, Mass 1784f, New 1784, Worcester 1786ff, Federal 1788ff, Sacred 1788) before being introduced in Philadelphia (Selection 1788ff, Adgate 1789ff) and New York (Amphion 1789f). In the 1790s, it continued to appear in Massachusetts (Holden 1793ff, Mann 1797, Boston 1799), Connecticut (Law 1791f, Law 1794f, Bull 1795, Brownson 1797), and Philadelphia (Poor 1794) as well, but its circulation broadened to northern New England (Village 1795ff) and southward to Virginia (Sandford 1793), the Hudson Valley (Atwill 1795f), and South Carolina (Pilsbury 1799). After the turn of the century, printings outside New England were restricted to New York and Pennsylvania (Huntington 1800, Atwill 1804, Little 1805ff, Erben 1806, Woodward 1806ff, Law 1807f, Erben 1808, Wyeth 1810). In central New England it positively flourished. Half-a-dozen Connecticut works carried it (Read 1804ff, Olmsted 1805, Jenks 1806, Gamut 1807, Griswold 1807, Jenks 1810) and so did twenty-two Massachusetts tunebooks, including works of every stripe, from eclectic (French 1802, Holyoke 1804, PSA 1804, Boston First 1806, Janes 1807, Sanger 1808) to reform (Law 1803, Salem 1805f, Deerfield 1808, Sacred 1810, and many others). Blanchard 1808, a reform collection from New Hampshire, also printed LITTLE MARLBOROUGH. Circulation continued briskly in the next decade, with appearances in more than forty collections from the decade 1811–1820. LITTLE MARLBOROUGH appeared in four retrospective northern collections, and one of the southern tunebooks also carried it.

The tune of LITTLE MARLBOROUGH concludes with a reference to the first phrase, producing a melody structured ABCA[1]. Each of the tune's four voice-parts has its own separate function, seeming to suggest that the parts were composed successively rather than simultaneously. The tenor presents a tune whose arch-like phrases fill an octave; the treble shadows the tune, either at the tenth or the sixth; the bass moves consistently by skip to provide harmonic support, usually as the root of a triad; the counter, restricted to the range of a minor third, fills in harmony. Congregations at Wilbraham, Massachusetts (22 October 1770; 1 of 23 tunes), and Harwinton, Connecticut (4 June 1776; 1 of 22), chose it for congregational singing. After a reform in Atkinson, New Hampshire, around 1800, LITTLE MARLBOROUGH was one of the tunes brought in as a new favorite (Memoirs, p. 84).

Additional References

1. Alderdice, p. 318; Read, No. 267
2. Hall (attributed to Williams)

Cross-References

See entries on AYLESBURY, PSALM 100 [OLD].

[46.] LONDON NEW
(LONDON)

Text from Watts, Psalm 145, C.M., 3d Part. First published in *The Psalmes of David in Prose and Meeter* (Edinburgh, 1635). First published in America in Thomas Walter, *The Grounds and Rules of Musick* (Boston, 1721). Lyon 1761, p. 17.

A C.M. common tune in major mode, LONDON NEW was printed 52 times, usually without text. Never linked closely with any single text, it appeared with at least six different ones in the years 1804–1810, twice with the present one.

Introduced in Boston (Walter 1721ff), LONDON NEW received three-quarters of its printings in New England. The tune regularly appeared there in the tune supplements and tunebooks of the colonial era (Tufts 1723ff, Bay 1737f, Turner 1752, Johnston 1755f, Bayley 1764ff, Bayley 1767f, Bayley 1770ff, Gilman 1771, New England 1771) and also in Philadelphia (Dawson 1754, Lyon 1761f, Hopkinson 1763). In the two decades following the war, circulation dropped sharply, with appearances only in Law 1783 (Connecticut) and Adgate 1791ff (Philadelphia). After 1800 LONDON NEW made something of a comeback, being picked up by several reform tunebooks in Massachusetts (Salem 1805f, Middlesex 1807f, Deerfield 1808, Boston Brattle 1810, Brown 1810), and appearing also in Jackson 1804 (New York City) and Cumberland 1804 (Shippensburg, Pennsylvania). Modest circulation continued in the next decade, with appearances in at least a dozen collections from the years 1811–1820. LONDON NEW also appeared in two retrospective northern collections and in one southern tunebook.

In a repertory with so many smoothly etched melodic lines, LONDON NEW stands out for its disjunct profile—especially in the tune-carrying tenor, where skips outnumber steps by almost two-to-one, and in the bass, which covers a twelfth. Temperley notes the tune's wide circulation in England (Temperley, 1:125, 236). The Reverend Thomas Symmes, writing in a Regular Singing tract published in Boston in 1723, notes that LONDON NEW "was Sung at the Publick Election, incomparably well, and to good acceptance above a year ago" (Symmes, p. 25). In the Hutchinson Partbook (1763; probably copied in Pennsylvania), the following text was provided for a two-voice setting of LONDON NEW (here entitled NEWTON):

> The kisses of his lips most Sweet
> Let him to me Impart
> For why thy Love more charming is
> Then wine unto my Heart[.]

Additional References

1. Eckhard, No. 31; Read, No. 2
2. A&M 490; Frost 222; Temperley, 2:ex. 52, 82
3. Episcopal

[47.] MAJESTY, by William Billings

Text from Psalm 18, Common Prayer; written by Thomas Sternhold (see Julian, p. 863), and published in the Old Version, Psalm 18, stanzas 9–16. First published in William Billings, *The Singing Master's Assistant* (Boston, 1778). Village 1800, p. 34.

A duple-time, major mode setting of two stanzas of C.M. text, MAJESTY was printed 75 times. A few tunebooks published

MAJESTY with Watts's Psalm 147, but the present text appears with almost all others.

Introduced in Boston (Billings 1778ff), MAJESTY received 56 percent of its printings in New England. It was not published again in Massachusetts until the 1790s (Holden 1793ff, Mann 1797f, Boston 1799), by which time the Connecticut tunebooks Langdon 1786 and Read 1787ff had picked it up, as had Selection 1788ff and Adgate 1789ff in Philadelphia. In the same decade circulation widened southward to Virginia (Sandford 1793) and South Carolina (Pilsbury 1799), westward to the Hudson Valley (Atwill 1795f), and northward as well (Village 1795ff, Merrill 1799), while appearances in Shumway 1793f and Read 1794ff maintained its availability in Philadelphia and Connecticut, respectively. After the turn of the century, MAJESTY was reestablished as a New England favorite, with printings in the north (Hill 1801, Robbins 1805), and especially in eclectic or American-oriented Massachusetts collections: Belknap 1800; Holden 1800; Worcester 1800f; Belknap 1802; Belknap 1806; Boston First 1806; Huntington 1807; Mann 1807; J. Read 1808; Sanger 1808. Outside New England, MAJESTY received several more printings in the Hudson Valley (Huntington 1800, Atwill 1804f, Little 1809f) and Philadelphia (Sacred 1806, Blake 1810) and also appeared in New York City (Seymour 1809), New Jersey (Smith 1803f), and western Pennsylvania (Rothbaust 1807, Wyeth 1810). MAJESTY continued to circulate in the next decade, with more than a dozen printings in collections from the years 1811–1820. It appeared in seven northern retrospective collections and in two of the southern tunebooks as well.

The music of MAJESTY is closely coordinated with the text, with obvious word-painting in the melody on "descended" (mm. 2–3), "above" (m. 4), and "high" (m. 7), and rapid quarter-note declamation on the last two lines of the text, which describe "flying." Although the quotation below seems to claim it as a fuging-tune, MAJESTY achieves the contrasts that give it much of its energy without fuging—that is, without the text overlap that a true fuge creates. Harriet Beecher Stowe, born in Litchfield, Connecticut, in 1811, recalled in the story "Poganuc People" the singing in the meetinghouse when she was a girl:

There was a grand, wild freedom, an energy of motion in the old "fuging tunes" of that day, that well expressed the heart of the people courageous in combat & unshaken in endurance. . . . Whatever the trained musician might say of such a tune as old Majesty, no person of imagination or sensibility could hear it well rendered by a large choir without deep emotion. And when back and forth from every side of the church came the different parts shouting—

On cherubim and seraphim
Full royally He rode,
And on the wings of mighty winds
Came flying all abroad,

there went a stir and thrill through many a stern and hard nature, until the tempest cleared off in the words—

He sat serene upon the floods
Their fury to restrain,
And He as Sovereign Lord and King
For evermore shall reign.

(Quoted in Chase, p. 142)

Later in the century, MAJESTY was singled out by Cheney as one of Billings's tunes that "continue popular" (Cheney, p. 169) and by F. O. Jones as still "being frequently sung at the present day" (Jones, p. 14).

Additional References

1. Alderdice, p. 210
2. AH, p. 24; Fisher, p. 11; Hall; Hitchcock 59, 122, 175

[48.] MARYLAND, by William Billings

Text from Watts, Hymns II, no. 110. First published in William Billings, *The Singing Master's Assistant* (Boston, 1778). Jocelin 1788, p. 20.

MARYLAND, a S.M. fuging-tune in minor mode, was printed 60 times. Most compilers followed the composer's lead and published MARYLAND with the present text, though it did appear with two others (see, e.g., Read 1787ff for an alternative).

Introduced in Boston (Billings 1778ff), MARYLAND received 57 percent of its printings in New England. In the decade following its first publication the tune circulated briskly in Massachusetts (Billings 1779, Bayley 1785, Worcester 1786–97, Bayley 1788, Sacred 1788) and Connecticut (Jocelin 1783f, Langdon 1786, Read 1787ff), appearing also in Philadelphia (Selection 1788ff, Adgate 1789ff). During the 1790s MARYLAND stayed in print in these places: in Massachusetts (Holden 1793, Federal 1794, Mann 1797f, Boston 1799); in Connecticut (Read 1794); and in Philadelphia (Shumway 1793f). It appeared in a wide scattering of collections elsewhere: in Maryland (Ely 1792); Virginia (Sandford 1793); New Hampshire (Village 1795–1803); and South Carolina (Pilsbury 1799). MARYLAND had begun to fall out of fashion by 1800. In the years 1800–1810 only five new collections carried it (Hill 1801 and Janes 1807 in New England; Little 1801–08, Sacred 1806, and Wyeth 1810 outside New England), and it was dropped from many multi-edition tunebooks: Read after 1794, Worcester after 1797, Village after 1803, Little after 1808. The tune virtually disappeared in the decade 1811–1820, with only two printings found in that period. Only two northern retrospective collections carried it, and none of the southern tunebooks has it.

MARYLAND is a fuging-tune—the only one in the Core Repertory—of the fuging chorus type. The first section sets all of the text and cadences on the tonic (mm. 1–9 of MARYLAND were published as a complete piece in Billings 1779). Then the last two lines of the earlier text receive contrapuntal treatment in an added section. The fuging section in MARYLAND is composed in free counterpoint, being imitative only in that the rhythm of the opening subject is reflected in each entering voice.

Additional Reference

1. Alderdice, p. 176

[49.] MEAR
(NEW MEAR)

Text from Watts, Psalm 96, C.M. First published in *A Sett of Tunes in 3 Parts* ([London, ca. 1720]). Introduced into the American colonies in the tune supplement at the end of *The Psalms, Hymns, and Spiritual Songs of the Old and New Testament*, 24th ed. (Boston, 1737). Adgate 1789, p. 15.

A C.M. triple-time tune in major mode, MEAR was printed 121 times. Before the 1780s it usually appeared without text; from that time on, at least nineteen different texts were sung to MEAR, most frequently the present one.

Introduced in Boston (Bay 1737f), MEAR received 55 percent of its printings in New England. The tune held a spot in most of the tune supplements of colonial and early federal New England (Turner 1752, Johnston 1755f, Bayley 1767f, Bayley 1770ff, Gilman 1771, New England 1771, Law 1781, New 1784) and Philadelphia (Dawson 1754, Hopkinson 1763, Tunes 1763f, Tunes 1786), and some important oblong tunebooks as well (in Connecticut, Jocelin 1782f; in Philadelphia, Lyon 1761f, Selection 1788ff, and Adgate 1789ff; and in New York City, Amphion 1789). MEAR received no new Massachusetts printings between 1785 and 1801; but during the 1790s it was a favorite in Connecticut (Benham 1790ff, Law 1791f, Law 1794f, Read 1794ff, Bull 1795, Griswold 1796f), appearing also in Philadelphia (Shumway 1793f) and the Hudson River Valley (Atwill 1795f), to the north (Village 1798ff), and southward in Virginia (Sandford 1793) and South Carolina (Pilsbury 1799). After the turn of the century MEAR appeared in thirty-eight new tunebooks, a total matched or topped by only six other collections. Printings in thirteen new Massachusetts tunebooks, both eclectic (French 1802, Cooper 1804, Boston First 1806, Huntington 1807, and Suffolk 1807) and reform (among others, Law 1803, Salem 1805f, Deerfield 1808, Boston Brattle 1810), led the way. But elsewhere, circulation was balanced among Connecticut (eight new collections: Terril 1800, Jenks 1801, Jenks 1803, Jenks 1804f, Olmsted 1805, Gamut 1807, Griswold 1807, Jenks 1810), New York State (seven new collections: Huntington 1800, Seymour 1803f, Atwill 1804, Little 1805ff, Erben 1806, Erben 1808, Seymour 1809), and Pennsylvania (nine new collections: Little 1801, Stammers 1803, Cumberland 1804, Sacred 1806, Woodward 1806ff, Law 1807f, Chapin 1808f, Blake 1810, Wyeth 1810), with a few additional appearances: Arnold 1803 in rural Maryland and Robbins 1805 and Blanchard 1808 in northern New England. In the decade 1811–1820 MEAR remained a widely accepted favorite, appearing in nearly fifty works published in that period. All of the retrospective northern collections and southern tunebooks consulted carry MEAR, which also appears in Jackson's list of the "most popular" southern folk hymns (Jackson, pp. 130, 144).

MEAR, a triple-time tune virtually without decoration (the A in the tenor, m. 3, is the lone exception), invites consideration as a chain of slow-moving sonorities rather than an interweaving of melodic voices. Its harmonic climax, cutting across the phrase structure, is reached near the middle, where (mm. 6–8) a circle-of-fifths progression leads resonantly to the first subdominant triad in the piece, supporting the highest note in the tenor. The Reverend Ebenezer Parkman of Westborough, Massachusetts, chose MEAR as one of the first triple-time tunes his congregation sang in public worship (Parkman Diary, 29 April 1750; 30 November 1752). Congregations in several other towns included it in their approved repertory: Weston, Massachusetts (1 of 17 tunes; 1753), Wilbraham, Massachusetts (1 of 23 tunes; 22 October 1770), and Harwinton, Connecticut (1 of 22 tunes; 4 June 1776). When, around the turn into the nineteenth century, musical reform was effected in Atkinson, New Hampshire, MEAR was one of the tunes favored by the reform advocates (Memoirs, p. 84). On 7 July 1804, Daniel Read commented in a letter to his brother: "I have no doubt that some of the old tunes (as Old Hundred, Mear &c) will live when hundreds of modern pieces will be buried in oblivion" (quoted in Bushnell, p. 273). MEAR was collected ca. 1980 from oral tradition singing of Primitive Baptists in the Blue Ridge region of Virginia and North Carolina (Sutton, p. 15).

Additional References

1. Alderdice, p. 89; Eckhard, No. 47; Read, No. 1
2. AH, p. 540; Fisher, p. 4; Hall (attributed to "Unknown"); Hitchcock 174, (384); MinA, p. 41

Cross-References

See entries on CANTERBURY, PSALM 100 [OLD].

[50.] MIDDLETOWN, by Amos Bull

Text from Whitefield, p. 35, written by Charles Wesley (see Julian, p. 478). First published in Andrew Law, *Select Harmony* ([Cheshire, Connecticut], 1779). Law 1791, p. 17.

MIDDLETOWN, a major-mode P.M. tune in duple time, was printed 64 times. It was closely identified with the present text, with which it was paired in virtually all publications.

Introduced in Connecticut (Law 1779f), the home state of its composer, MIDDLETOWN received half of its printings in New England. Picked up in half-a-dozen Massachusetts tunebooks of the 1780s (Bayley 1784, Mass 1784f, Worcester 1786–92, Bayley 1788, Federal 1788–93, Sacred 1788), MIDDLETOWN then dropped temporarily out of the New England repertory; its only later Connecticut printing was in a tunebook of Andrew Law (Law 1791f), the holder of its copyright. MIDDLETOWN appeared in New York City (Amphion 1789), and in Philadelphia in Adgate 1789ff and Selection 1790ff, then in Shumway 1793f and Poor 1794, followed later by Little 1801, Sacred 1806, and Chapin 1808f. It was also picked up in Charleston (Pilsbury 1799) and continued to circulate in New York (Seymour 1803f, Evans 1808f, Seymour 1809). After 1800 MIDDLETOWN made something of a comeback in New England, appearing in several Massachusetts tunebooks (Brown 1802ff, Mann 1802, Cooper 1804, Albee 1805, Boston First 1806, Mann 1807), while being printed to the north in Village 1800ff, westward in the Hudson Valley (Little 1805ff), and to the southwest in Harrisburg (Wyeth 1810). Moderate circulation (11 printings) continued in the decade 1811–1820. MIDDLETOWN appeared in four of the retrospective northern tunebooks examined, and in two of the southern tunebooks as well.

Melodic embellishment and a march-like, declamatory rhythm hint that MIDDLETOWN was inspired by Methodist hymnody, a suggestion strengthened by the repetition of the last two lines and the texture changes brought about by antiphony rather than fuging.

Additional References

1. Alderdice, p. 110
2. Hall

[51.] MILFORD, by Joseph Stephenson

Text from Arnold, p. 395; authorship untraced. First published in Joseph Stephenson, *Church Harmony Sacred to Devotion*, 3d ed. (London 1760). First published in America in Andrew Law, *Select Harmony* ([Cheshire, Connecticut], 1779). Federal 1790, p. 25.

A C.M. major-mode fuging-tune with both the first and third lines of its four-line text presented in imitation, MILFORD was printed 68 times. Although three other texts were sung to MILFORD, the present text was by far the most frequently printed with it.

Introduced to America in Connecticut (Law 1779f) by Andrew Law, who also apparently named it (after his home town of Milford, Connecticut?) and who held its copyright, MILFORD received almost four-fifths of its printings in New England. The tune caught on swiftly in Massachusetts (Bayley 1784, Mass 1784f, Bayley 1785, Worcester 1786ff, Bayley 1788, Federal 1788–93, Sacred 1788) and Connecticut (Law 1786ff, Read 1787ff, Jocelin 1788) and was introduced in New York City by Amphion 1789. It continued in print in both New England states in the next decade (Holden 1793ff, Law 1794f, Read 1794, Boston 1799), while also appearing in six more states: Maryland (Ely 1792), Pennsylvania (Shumway 1793f), Virginia (Sandford 1793), New York (Atwill 1795f), New Hampshire (Village 1795ff), and South Carolina (Pilsbury 1799). After the turn of the century, MILFORD maintained its wide circulation, appearing in central New England (Holden 1800, Holyoke 1803, Collection 1804, Cooper 1804, Griswold 1807, Holyoke 1807), northern New England (Maxim 1805f, Robbins 1805), Philadelphia (Stammers 1803, Sacred 1806, Chapin 1808f, Blake 1810), and scattered points elsewhere (Huntington 1800, Gillet 1809, Wyeth 1810). Very few printings (three) occurred in the decade 1811–1820. However, MILFORD did appear in most (seven) northern retrospective collections and in two of the southern tunebooks as well.

With fuges on three of its four lines including the first, MILFORD showed American composers that contrapuntal writing need not be restricted to the second half of a fuging-tune. Its harmonic vocabulary also shows that some English psalmodists, like their American counterparts, did not shrink from open intervals (in mm. 3, 4, 5, 8, and 11) or unexpected clashes (m. 7, beat 2; m. 16, beat 1). Its brief modulation (mm. 10–11) also shows a harmonic adventurousness matched by few, if any, American composers of the period. According to Thomas Hastings, "Old Milford" and other tunes by "Stevenson," drawn from "some of the most insignificant publications of England," served William Billings as "models" when he set about writing his "fuguing music" in colonial Boston (Musical Magazine I; quoted in McKay & Crawford, p. 203). A similar claim appeared a few years later in the *Boston Musical Gazette* I (1838–39) (quoted in Bushnell, p. 465n).

Additional References

1. Alderdice, p. ff
2. Hitchcock (389)

Cross-Reference

See entry on PSALM 34.

[52.] MONTAGUE, by Timothy Swan

Text from Hymns, no. CII, p. 293; written by Philip Doddridge (see Julian, pp. 305f). First published in John Stickney, *The Gentleman and Lady's Musical Companion* (Newburyport, [1783]). Worcester 1788, p. 49.

MONTAGUE, a minor-mode fuging-tune setting two stanzas of L.M. text, was printed 60 times. Of the four different texts with which the tune was published, the present one was by far the most prevalent, and it is also the one that appeared in Swan 1801, the composer's own tunebook.

Introduced in Massachusetts (Stickney 1783), MONTAGUE received 57 percent of its printings in New England. MONTAGUE was quick to catch on, appearing shortly after its introduction in a flurry of tunebooks in Massachusetts (Bayley 1784, Worcester 1786–97, Federal 1788–93, Sacred 1788), Connecticut (Langdon 1786, Law 1786ff, Read, 1787ff), and Philadelphia (Adgate 1789ff, Selection 1789ff). Amphion 1789 introduced it in New York City. During the 1790s tunebooks in the first three places continued to carry it (Holden 1793f, Mann 1797, Boston 1799; Read 1794; Shumway 1793f), while its circulation widened to Baltimore (Ely 1792), northern New England (Village 1796–1800), and South Carolina (Pilsbury 1799). After 1800 the circulation of MONTAGUE declined somewhat. Most of its new appearances were in collections from the geographical periphery: Hill 1801 and Robbins 1805 from the north; Swan 1801, Bushnell 1807, and J. Read 1808 from central New England; Huntington 1800 and Little 1805ff from the Hudson Valley, as well as the Philadelphia collections, Little 1801 and Sacred 1806. Telling evidence of MONTAGUE's declining popularity is that it was dropped from several multi-edition works in which it had earlier appeared: Federal after 1793, Read after 1794, Holden after 1796, Worcester and Mann after 1797, and Village after 1800. Very few printings (four) are found in the decade 1811–1820. However, MONTAGUE appeared in five retrospective northern collections, though it is in only one southern tunebook.

MONTAGUE makes its impact from the energy required of the singers—the high tessitura and frequent flourishes in the tenor melody are notable—and the complexity of the fuge, which sustains text overlap for nine full measures. Swan's own copy of *New England Harmony*, owned by the American Antiquarian Society, contains, next to MONTAGUE, the following note in the composer's hand: "oldest tune, 1777." An 1842 memoir by his daughter reports: "Montague was one of his first tunes—name given on account of his friend Rufus Carver with whom he visited Montague where Carver's mother lived—It was made in [Northfield] when he was 17 yrs old [i.e., 1774]" (Swan, p. [1]; quoted in Murray, p. 436). Writing in 1879, Cheney described MONTAGUE as Swan's "first tune in four parts," adding that it was "sung everywhere so long so minor fugues were fashionable" (Cheney, p. 173), thus suggesting that the tune by that time had outlived its day.

Additional References

1. Alderdice, p. 96
2. Fisher, p. 37; Hitchcock 122

[53.] MONTGOMERY, by Justin Morgan

Text from Watts, Psalm 63, C.M., 1st Part. First published in Asahel Benham, *Federal Harmony* (New Haven, 1790). Shumway 1793, p. 134.

MONTGOMERY, a major mode fuging-tune setting two stanzas of C.M. text, and including a pair of fugal sections, was printed 55 times. The present text was closely identified with MONTGOMERY, though at least two other texts did appear with it.

Introduced in Connecticut (Benham 1790ff), MONTGOMERY received slightly more than half of its printings in New England. The tune won a remarkable degree of acceptance in the 1790s, when it appeared in fourteen different tunebooks—a total matched or topped by only five other Core Repertory pieces, all introduced in the 1780s or earlier. Printings during the 1790s occurred in seven states: Massachusetts (French 1793, Holden 1793ff, Mann 1797, Boston 1799), Connecticut (Law 1791f, Griswold 1796f), Pennsylvania (Adgate 1791ff, Shumway 1793f, Selection 1794f), New York (N. Billings 1795), New Hampshire (Village 1795–1808), New Jersey (New Jersey 1797), and South Carolina (Pilsbury 1799). Circulation fell off during the next decade. In New England, only the Read brothers (Read 1804ff, J. Read 1808) kept MONTGOMERY before the singing public. Elsewhere, the tune stayed in print in the Hudson Valley (Huntington 1800, Little 1805ff), in Philadelphia (Little 1801, Blake 1810), and in rural Pennsylvania (Rothbaust 1807, Doll 1810, Wyeth 1810). Only about a half-dozen printings appeared in the decade 1811–1820. But MONTGOMERY is included in six retrospective northern tunebooks and in three additional southern collections as well.

MONTGOMERY contains two fuges, the first beginning in the bass and moving upward through the voices to the treble, and the second reversing the procedure. Because quarter-note motion is established at the beginning of both major sections of this piece, the dactylic quarter-and-two-eighths figure in m. 6 and mm. 18ff make an especially striking declamatory effect; but no one who has heard the piece performed by southern singers will forget the expressive impact of the sustained notes sung by the counters in mm. 15–16. MONTGOMERY was well enough known in 1811 to be referred to in a letter published in the Boston *Columbian Centinel*. The correspondent, writing under the pseudonym "Ichabod Beetlehead," praised Yankee psalmody at the expense of the more fashionable European sacred music. In what was perhaps a parody of rustic approval, "Beetlehead" confided: "But oh, when I listen to the exstatic strains in Montgomery, I am carried away with rapture, particularly at the treble *solo* in the words Long for a *cooling*.—Here are discovered the wonderful ingenuity of the author together with his delicate and devotional feelings" (quoted in McKay & Crawford, p. 199). Samuel Goodrich, a native of Ridgefield, Connecticut, recalled in his memoirs (ca. 1840?) that during his boyhood he occasionally overheard a neighbor's daughter attempting a one-woman performance of MONTGOMERY while she spun wool in the attic of her home.

> In her solitary operations aloft I have often heard her send forth, from the attic window, the droning hum of her wheel, with fitful snatches of a hymn, in which the bass began, the tenor followed, then the treble, and, finally, the counter— winding up with irresistable pathos, Molly singing to herself, and all unconscious of eavesdroppers, carried on all the parts thus:—
>
> Bass.   "Long for a cooling—
> Tenor.   "Long for a cooling—
> Treble.   "Long for a cooling—
> Counter.   "Long for a cooling stream at hand, And they must drink or die!" (Quoted from Steel, p. 11)

Writing toward the end of the century, S. P. Cheney said of Justin Morgan: "If we test his music by public opinion, Montgomery is his best tune, and one of the very few tunes of this world's music having the vitality for long life" (Cheney, p. 171).

Additional References

1. Alderdice, p. 106
2. Fisher, p. 23; Hitchcock 96, 119, 122, (404); MinA, p. 151

[54.] MORNING HYMN

Text from Hymns & Songs, p. 183, written by Thomas Flatman and published in his *Poems and Songs* (London, 1674). Probably first published in James Lyon, *Urania* (Philadelphia, 1761). Williams 1771, p. 61, as THE MORNING HYMN.

MORNING HYMN, a triple-time L.M. tune in major mode, was printed 45 times. Some were textless; of the half-dozen different texts that appeared with MORNING HYMN, the present was the most frequently found.

Introduced in Philadelphia (Lyon 1761f), MORNING HYMN received some 53 percent of its printings in New England, all of them in Massachusetts. The dates of its appearances in Pennsylvania (in the 1760s, Lyon and Tunes 1763f; in the 1780s, Tunes 1786, Selection 1788ff, and Adgate 1789ff; and in 1810 Blake and Wyeth 1810) demonstrate its checkered printing history. In Massachusetts, meanwhile, MORNING HYMN appeared in five of Daniel Bayley's publications (Williams 1769ff, Bayley 1770ff, Stickney 1774ff, Bayley 1784, Bayley 1788) as well as in Flagg 1764, New England 1771, Mass 1784f, New 1784, and Sacred 1788. Then, after a break of twenty years, it was picked up by a handful of reform tunebooks: Middlesex 1807f, Deerfield 1808, Huntington 1809, Boston West 1810. The only book outside Pennsylvania and Massachusetts to contain MORNING HYMN is Pilsbury 1799, compiled in Charleston, South Carolina. Moderate circulation continued in the decade 1811–1820, with at least a dozen printings. But MORNING HYMN does not appear in any of the northern retrospective collections, nor is it in any of the southern tunebooks published later in the century.

MORNING HYMN decorates its bold, high-lying melodic line in the manner of ST. MARTIN'S, another triple-time favorite. Its harmonic idiosyncrasies range from unexpected progressions (mm. 1–2, 6–7, 12–13) to salty clashes between parts (m. 3, beat 3; m. 6, beat 3; m. 9, beat 3; m. 11, beat 1), to a missing accidental that would have brought a secondary dominant to its anticipated completion (m. 7). Hints abound that the voice parts were conceived separately rather than simultaneously.

Additional Reference

2. Hall (attributed to Tans'ur)

[55.] NEW JERUSALEM, by Jeremiah Ingalls

Text from Watts, Hymns I, no. 21, stanzas 2–60. First published in *The Village Harmony*, 2d ed. (Exeter, 1796). Worcester 1800, p. 22.

NEW JERUSALEM, a major-mode fuging-tune in duple time with the last two lines fuged, was printed 52 times. All printings were underlaid with text; the present one, closely related to the tune's title, is by far the most frequently printed of the three that appeared with NEW JERUSALEM.

Introduced in New Hampshire (Village 1796ff), NEW JERUSALEM received nearly 70 percent of its printings in New England. Of the thirty-one new tunebooks in which the tune appeared during the years 1800–1810, more than two-thirds were New England compilations. Most were from Massachusetts, including collections aimed at Boston singers—Holden 1800, Holden 1801, Cooper 1804, Graupner 1806—and books intended also for rural or small-town markets—AMM 1800, Worcester 1800f, Belknap 1802, French 1802, Mann 1802, Collection 1804, Bushnell 1807, Huntington 1807, J. Read 1808. Several Connecticut compilations also printed NEW JERUSALEM (Terril 1800, Jenks 1803, Read 1804ff, Jenks 1805); more unusual was its appearance in half-a-dozen collections compiled for singers in Maine, New Hampshire, and the composer's home state of Vermont: Village 1796ff, West 1802f, Child 1804, Ingalls 1805, Maxim 1805f, Robbins 1805. Outside New England, NEW JERUSALEM appeared in New York City (Seymour 1803f, Seymour 1809), Philadelphia (Chapin 1808f), Wilmington, Delaware (Fobes 1809), the Hudson Valley (Atwill 1804f, Little 1805ff), and Pennsylvania (Doll 1810, Wyeth 1810). Approximately half-a-dozen printings are found in tunebooks from the decade 1811–1820. NEW JERUSALEM also appears in six retrospective northern collections and in two of the sample of southern tunebooks.

With a second section three times as long as the first, NEW JERUSALEM's proportions favor fuging over block-chord texture. The fuge climaxes with a subject harmonized neatly with a II-V-I progression (mm. 14–15), even as the subject in the tenor contradicts the words to which it is sung. Ingalls's tune circulated in both three and four parts. Daniel Read was one compiler who expressed indecision about which version to publish. "Should you prefer . . . New Jerusalem with Counters," he asked his brother in a letter of 14 August 1804, "and the consequent alterations as they appear in the H. of H. [French 1802] and the V.H. [Village 1796ff] or as originally published?" (quoted in Bushnell, p. 276). In Atkinson, New Hampshire, according to one account, when musical reform was introduced around 1800 or shortly thereafter, the choir director proposed that the fashionable ST. MARTIN'S be sung; but the choir members voted instead for NEW JERUSALEM (Memoirs, p. 77). Finally, "Ichabod Beetlehead," a pseudonym for a putative lover of Yankee psalmody, praised "the sweet warbling notes of New-Jerusalem" in a letter to a Boston newspaper in 1811. Apparently this outspoken rustic admired the fuging section

> where every part goes on independent of the rest in an animating confusion of delightful sounds, which fashionable fools call gingle, but which I call the very criterion of good psalmody. Here is none of your disgusting *expression,* none of your *crescendo* and *diminuendo,* but all is most elevating and delightful (Columbian Centinel; quoted in McKay & Crawford, p. 199).

Additional References

1. Alderdice, p. 182
2. Hall

[56.] NEWBURY
(PSALM 5)

Text from Watts, Psalm 77, C.M. 2d part. First published in

xlvi

Joseph Watts, *A Choice Collection of Church Music* (n.p., 1749). First published in America in James Lyon, *Urania* (Philadelphia, 1761). Bayley 1788, p. 51.

NEWBURY, a C.M. fuging-tune in minor mode with the last line of its four-line stanza fuged, was printed 53 times. Some are textless, and in all, at least eight different texts appeared with NEWBURY; nevertheless, the present one is the most frequently found, especially in tunebooks printed before 1790.

Introduced in Philadelphia (Lyon 1761f), NEWBURY received nearly 60 percent of its printings in New England. The tune's printing history seems to describe a path leading, in the colonial period, from Philadelphia to Massachusetts (Flagg 1764, Tans'ur 1767f, Williams 1769ff, Stickney 1774f), then to Connecticut (Law 1779, Law 1781, Jocelin 1782f), then, after the war, to Massachusetts again (Mass 1784f, New 1784, Worcester 1786f, Bayley 1788, Sacred 1788), and back to Philadelphia (Selection 1788ff, Adgate 1789ff). In the 1790s circulation widened, and printings were scattered between Connecticut (Law 1791f, Brownson 1797), Philadelphia (Shumway 1793f), and Charleston (Pilsbury 1799). Diffusion continued in the next decade, as NEWBURY appeared in the Hudson Valley (Huntington 1800), northern New England (Holyoke 1803, Village 1803ff, Wood 1810), Baltimore (Cole 1805), Philadelphia (Blake 1810), and even back in Boston (Boston First 1806). NEWBURY fell out of use thereafter. A few (three or four) printings are found in collections from the decade 1811–1820; but the tune appears in none of the retrospective northern tunebooks, nor in nineteenth-century southern collections.

NEWBURY, which fuges the last line of the text, is the only Core Repertory fuging-tune whose subject begins with a melisma of any length. It is also the most dissonant: in m. 10, three consecutive sevenths are sounded between counter and bass, and the treble entrance of the fuge subject (m. 15) clashes with the bass in sevenths and a ninth.

Additional References

1. Read, No. 113
2. Hitchcock 162 (as Ps. 5)

[57.] NEWTON
(FALCON STREET, HYMN, SILVER STREET, SKEENSBOROUGH)

Text from Watts, Psalm 95, S.M. First published in Isaac Smith, *A Collection of Psalm Tunes* (London, [ca. 1780]). First published in America in [Simeon Jocelin], *The Chorister's Companion*, 2d ed. (New Haven, 1788). Jocelin 1788, p. 79.

NEWTON, a duple-time S.M. tune in major mode, was printed 61 times. Set to at least thirteen different texts, NEWTON was most often sung to the present one, though "Come we that love the Lord" (Watts, Hymns II, no. 30) was also a favorite.

Introduced in Connecticut (Jocelin 1788), NEWTON received 61 percent of its printings in New England. It caught on more slowly than some other tunes, appearing before 1800 in only seven more works, scattered among Boston (Federal 1792f, Holden 1793ff, Worcester 1797ff, Boston 1799), Charleston, South Carolina (Pilsbury 1799), and the Hudson Valley (Atwill 1795f, N. Billings 1795). After the turn of the century, however, NEWTON's popularity boomed; the tune appeared in thirty-four new tunebooks, a number topped by only ten other Core Repertory compositions. By 1810, it had won a firm place in the New England repertory, with printings in many Massachusetts works—both eclectic items (Holden 1800, Brown 1802ff, Holyoke 1803, Boston First 1806, Graupner 1806, Holyoke 1807, Mann 1807, Suffolk 1807, Sanger 1808) and reform works (Essex 1802, Salem 1805f, Middlesex 1807f, Huntington 1809, Boston Brattle 1810, Boston West 1810, Sacred 1810)—and pairs in Connecticut (Olmsted 1805, Jenks 1810) and New Hampshire (Vil-

lage 1806ff, Blanchard 1808). Outside New England, widening circulation introduced NEWTON to Philadelphia (Shumway 1801, Sacred 1803, Carr 1805, Aitken 1806, Woodward 1806ff, Addington 1808, Chapin 1808f, Blake 1810), Baltimore (Cole 1804f, Gillet 1809, Cole 1810), and New York City (Erben 1806, Erben 1808, Evans 1808f), while Atwill 1804 kept it in print in the Hudson Valley. Vigorous circulation continued in the decade 1811–1820, with printings in nearly forty tunebooks from those years. Each of the later retrospective northern collections carries NEWTON, which also appears in three of the southern tunebooks.

NEWTON blends up-to-date style traits (e.g., angular, rhetorical melodic phrases set off by rests; orthodox use of the secondary dominant) with more archaic, even sometimes awkward ones (e.g., open sonorities in mm. 1, 4, 9, 14; parallel perfect intervals in mm. 11–12; unexpected root movement in mm. 10–13) to dramatize the gap between the figured-bass progressions of eighteenth-century European harmony and the idiom of unaccompanied Anglo-American choral singing.

Additional References

1. Read, No. 231
2. Hall (as SILVER STREET, attributed to Smith)
3. Episcopal

Cross-Reference

See entry on PSALM 100 [OLD].

[58.] NORWICH, by Hibbard?
(PSALM 24)

Text from Belknap, p. 18[6], 2d group, where it is attributed to Watts. First published in Andrew Law, *Select Harmony* ([Cheshire, Connecticut], 1779). Little 1807, p. 95.

NORWICH, a minor-mode fuging-tune which sets a single S.M. stanza, was printed 85 times. Of the five different texts with which it was printed, the present was the one with which it was most closely identified.

Introduced in Connecticut (Law 1779f), NORWICH received more than 60 percent of its printings in New England. The tune had its heyday in the 1780s, when it appeared in sixteen different collections, a total matched or topped during that decade by only two other Core Repertory pieces. Printed in a high concentration of works compiled both in Connecticut (Jocelin 1782f, Brownson 1783ff, Langdon 1786, Read 1787ff) and Massachusetts (Stickney 1783, Bayley 1784, Mass 1784f, Bayley 1785, Worcester 1786–97, Bayley 1788, Federal 1788–93, Sacred 1788), NORWICH also found its way to New Hampshire (Dearborn 1785), Philadelphia (Selection 1788ff, Adgate 1789ff), and New York City (Amphion 1789). In the 1790s its circulation continued strong in outlying areas (Ely 1792, Sandford 1793, and Pilsbury 1799 to the south; Shumway 1793f in Philadelphia; Village 1795ff and Merrill 1799 in northern New England; Atwill 1795f in the Hudson Valley). But in central New England its only new printings in Connecticut were Law 1791f and Read 1794f, and in Massachusetts, Mann 1797f. After the turn of the century, NORWICH appeared in a scattering of New England tunebooks (Cooper 1804 and Boston First 1806 in Boston; also Holyoke 1804, Jenks 1804f, and Read 1807f), and in another half-dozen outside, including Atwill 1804 and Evans 1810 from New York; Sacred 1806, Blake 1810, and Wyeth 1810 from Pennsylvania, and Little 1801ff, published first in Philadelphia and then in Albany. Approximately a dozen printings can be found in tunebooks from the years 1811–1820. NORWICH appears, however, in only three retrospective northern collections and in none of the sampling of southern tunebooks.

NORWICH, which fuges the third of its four lines, is notable for its cross-relations (mm. 7–8, 14–15), its parallel motion between voice parts (treble and counter, mm. 2, 6, 16–17), and its imaginative use of chords on the seventh scale degree: as a triad in root position (mm. 6, 16), as a major-minor seventh chord (m. 12), and even as a triad in second inversion (m. 7). In a letter from Charleston, South Carolina, Andrew Law reported attending a worship service in which, when the organ would not work, "we collected four or five and sung Norwich and Kingsbridge. Mr. Nott says a number of people have told him since that they wish the Organ might never go again" (Andrew Law to William Law, 11 January 1787; quoted in Crawford, p. 55). NORWICH had been in print without attribution for more than a decade before compilers began to assign it to a composer. Candidates are Brownson (Federal 1790; unlikely, since Brownson 1783ff printed NORWICH with no attribution), King (Ely 1792; unlikely, because Law, the first to print NORWICH, assigned one piece to King and NORWICH to "unknown" in Law 1782), Deaolph (Mann 1797; unlikely for exactly the same reason that the attribution to King is), and Hibbard (Sandford 1793, Atwill 1795f, Atwill 1804, Jenks 1804f, Read 1807), who seems the most likely because there is no evidence to contradict it. Hibbard's identity is not known.

Additional References

1. Alderdice, p. 121
2. Hall (attributed to Brownson)

[59.] Ocean
  Text from Watts, Psalm 107, C.M., 4th Part. First published in Andrew Law, *The Rudiments of Music*, 2d ed. ([Cheshire, Connecticut, 1787–90]). Worcester 1797, p. 69.
  OCEAN, a major-mode fuging-tune setting two stanzas of C.M. text, was printed 76 times. Of the two texts with which the tune appeared ("With songs and honours sounding loud," Watts's Psalm 147, C.M., was the other), the present one is found in more collections.
  Introduced in Connecticut (Law 1787ff, a variant issue of Law 1786, q.v. for later eds.), OCEAN received 55 percent of its printings in New England. Published in the 1780s only in Law 1787, Adgate 1789ff, and Selection 1789ff, OCEAN was the most widely circulated Core Repertory piece of the 1790s, appearing in sixteen different tunebooks from eight states: Massachusetts (Federal 1792ff, Worcester 1792ff, French 1793, Holden 1793ff, Mann 1797, Boston 1799), Connecticut (Brownson 1791, Benham 1792ff, Read 1794ff, Willard 1796), Pennsylvania (Shumway 1793f), Virginia (Sandford 1793), New York (Atwill 1795f), New Hampshire (Village 1795ff), New Jersey (New Jersey 1797), and South Carolina (Pilsbury 1799). After 1800, circulation fell off sharply in New England, where OCEAN was carried only by Hill 1801 and Robbins 1805 in the north and by Belknap 1802 and Huntington 1807 in Massachusetts; OCEAN remained in print, however, in the Hudson Valley (Huntington 1800, Atwill 1804, Little 1805ff), in rural Pennsylvania (Cumberland 1804, Rothbaust 1807, Wyeth 1810), and in Philadelphia (Little 1801, Sacred 1806) and New York City (Seymour 1809). Printings continued to slack off in the decade 1811–1820, with just seven appearances in that period. However, OCEAN was published in seven of eight retrospective northern collections and in all five of the southern tunebooks.
  OCEAN has an unusual fuging section. Because the bass entry is accompanied by the counter, only three voices sing overlapping text (m. 16), and the whipping up of the waves is depicted not by textural complication, but by a treble flourish sung over sustained lower notes. The composer, whoever he may have been, was fond of, or unworried about, open sonorities (mm. 6–7, 14–15), weak-beat dissonances (m. 5, beat 2; m.

7, beat 4; m. 8, beat 4; m. 13, beat 4; m. 14, beat 4), and parallel motion between voices—especially tenor and bass (mm. 4–9, 22–24). OCEAN was apparently a favorite piece in New Haven. It was performed at an Independence Day celebration there (4 July 1798), under Daniel Read's leadership (Bushnell, p. 190), and at a "Republican Festival" on 9 March 1803, it was sung to the text "With songs and honors" (Bushnell, p. 250). More than three decades later, however, "A Country Clergyman," writing to *The Boston Musical Gazette*, ridiculed the notion that such a piece of music could serve a sacred purpose.

> Is it possible that [anyone] . . . can feel any religious impressions, or at all be edified, by singing, or hearing sung, such musical fiddlefaddle, as the tunes of . . . Ocean and fifty others of similar ridiculous cast, to be found in more or less singing books of the day? (Quoted in Bushnell, pp. 454–55)

Shumway 1793 was the first of many collections to attribute OCEAN to Timothy Swan. However, the failure of Swan's own *New England Harmony* (1801) to carry the tune provides reason to doubt that attribution. Read 1794ff assigns OCEAN to "Smith"—perhaps the singing master William H. Smith in New York City with whom Read corresponded between 1794 and 1802. The introduction to Sandford 1793 treats American psalmody in verse, singling out OCEAN as a piece whose composer was unknown to the poet: "The author of *Ocean*, we are sorry to tell, / Is unknown, tho' its beauties are known very well."

Additional References

1. Alderdice, p. 54
2. Hall (attributed to Swan); Hitchcock (499) (attributed to Swan)

[60.] PLYMOUTH, by William Tans'ur
  Text from Watts, Psalm 51, C.M., 2d Part. First published in William Tans'ur, *A Compleat Melody*, 2d ed. (London, 1735). First published in America in [*Collection of Psalm Tunes, with an Introduction "To Learn to Sing,"*] (Boston, [1763–67]), or Josiah Flagg, *A Collection of the Best Psalm Tunes* (Boston, 1764). Federal 1790, p. 70.
  PLYMOUTH, a triple-time C.M. tune in minor mode, was printed 100 times. More than a dozen different texts appeared with PLYMOUTH, but the present was the most frequently paired with it.
  Introduced in Boston (Walter 1764a, as well as Johnston 1763 and Flagg 1764), PLYMOUTH received more than three-fourths of its printings in New England. It was published in tune supplements (Bayley 1767f, Bayley 1770ff, Gilman 1771, New England 1771) and oblong collections (Bayley 1764ff, Flagg 1764, Stickney 1774f) of colonial New England. It achieved special popularity in the 1780s, when it appeared in fourteen different tunebooks, a total matched or topped by only four other Core Repertory pieces. Printings in the 1780s include works from Connecticut (Jocelin 1782f, Brownson 1783ff, Law 1783ff, Langdon 1786, Read 1787ff), Massachusetts (Bayley 1784, Mass 1784f, New 1784, Worcester 1786–92, Bayley 1788, Federal 1788–93, Sacred 1788), New York City (Amphion 1789), and Philadelphia (Adgate 1789ff). Though circulation widened geographically to include Baltimore (Ely 1792), the Hudson Valley (Atwill 1795f), and New Hampshire (Village 1798ff), it slowed in the 1790s (Law 1794f and Read 1794ff in Connecticut; Selection 1790ff in Philadelphia), only to pick up again in the next decade. Between 1800 and 1810, PLYMOUTH appeared in fourteen new Massachusetts tunebooks, both eclectic (French 1802, Holyoke 1803, Holyoke 1804, PSA 1804, Boston First 1806, Huntington 1807, J. Read 1808) and reform (Law 1803, Salem 1805f, Middlesex 1807f, Deerfield 1808, Boston Brattle 1810,

Boston West 1810, Brown 1810), as well as three other New England collections (Gamut 1807, Griswold 1807, Blanchard 1808). Elsewhere, the tune was printed in the Hudson Valley (Huntington 1800, Atwill 1804, Little 1809f), New Jersey (Smith 1803f), New York City (Erben 1808), and Harrisburg (Wyeth 1810). In the decade 1811–1820, PLYMOUTH continued to circulate widely, with more than thirty printings in collections of those years. It appeared in three northern retrospective collections, but it is in none of the southern tunebooks.

PLYMOUTH, a tune in four phrases, hones in gradually on its final dominant-tonic cadence with earlier half-closes on the fifth scale degree: an open fifth (m. 4), a minor triad (m. 7), and a major triad (m. 11). The conflict between lowered and raised leading-tones stays unresolved in a piquant clash in the tune's final phrase (m. 12, beat 3). On 4 June 1776, the congregation at Harwinton, Connecticut, chose PLYMOUTH as one of the twenty-two tunes it would sing in public worship. Some years later, Jonathan Huntington cited it as an example of proper musical solemnity:

> By long experience . . . I find that there is as many different tastes for music, as other things. Some will be pleased with Old Hundred, Bath, Plymouth, Wantage, &c. Others would prefer light and airy tunes (Huntington 1807, p. [ii]).

Additional References

1. Alderdice, p. cc; Read, No. 102
2. Hall

Cross-References

See entries on BATH, WANTAGE, PSALM 100 [OLD].

[61.] PORTSMOUTH
(NAMURE)

Text from Watts, Psalm 84, C.M., stanzas 2–9. First published in S[amuel] S[henton], *The Devout Singer's Guide* (London, 1711). First published in America in John Tufts, *An Introduction to the Singing of Psalm-Tunes*, 5th ed. (Boston, 1726). Village 1798, p. 201, as NAMURE.

PORTSMOUTH, a triple-time C.M. tune in major mode, was printed 53 times. Most were textless. However, of the four different texts with which PORTSMOUTH did appear, the present one was the most common.

Introduced in Boston (Tufts 1726ff), PORTSMOUTH received nearly 90 percent of its printings in New England, most of them in Massachusetts. The tune appeared in a steady succession of supplements and tunebooks in colonial New England (Bay 1737f, Turner 1752, Johnston 1755f, Walter 1759ff, Bayley 1764ff, Flagg 1764, Bayley 1767f, Williams 1769ff, Bayley 1770ff, Gilman 1771, New England 1771, Stickney 1774f) and Philadelphia (Dawson 1754, Lyon 1761f, Hopkinson 1763). But after 1775 the pace slowed considerably. In the next fifteen years only Billings 1779, Jocelin 1782, and New 1784 carried PORTSMOUTH in New England, and only Selection 1788f (Philadelphia) included it outside. Nor did circulation pick up dramatically in the years 1790–1810, when only Federal 1790, Holden 1793f, Boston 1799, and Middlesex 1808 carried the tune in Massachusetts, Village 1798f and Law 1805 in northern New England, and Law 1810 in Philadelphia. Modest circulation continued in the decade 1811–1820 (approximately ten appearances). However, none of the retrospective northern collections nor the southern tunebooks carried PORTSMOUTH.

With its orthodox handling of the secondary dominant (mm. 3–4, 6–7), its use of full triads rather than open intervals after m. 1, and its active, disjunct bass-line, the present setting of PORTSMOUTH shows a smoothness of idiom lacking in many Core Repertory tunes. One unusual feature is a counter part that descends at times below the tenor (mm. 5–7, 12) and has a wider range than the melody.

[62.] PORTSMOUTH
(FALMOUTH, MONMOUTH, MONVERT, PORTSMOUTH NEW, TRUMPET)

Text from New Version, Psalm 148. First published in *Harmonia Sacra, or a Choice Collection of Psalm and Hymn Tunes* (London, ca. 1760), or before. First published in America in [Simeon Jocelin], *The Chorister's Companion*, Part Third (New Haven, [1783]), or Andrew Law, *A Collection of Hymn Tunes* (Cheshire, Connecticut, [1783]). Brown 1802, p. 64.

PORTSMOUTH, a major-mode duple-time tune-with-extension that sets one stanza of H.M. text, was printed 47 times. Of the eleven different texts with which it appeared, the present one had two close rivals for frequency: "Ye tribes of Adam join" (Watts's Psalm 148, P.M., closely identified with Edson's LENOX) and "Blow ye the trumpet, blow" (Charles Wesley; see Julian, p. 151).

Introduced in Connecticut (Jocelin 1783f, Law C 1783), PORTSMOUTH received some 55 percent of its printings in New England. The tune enjoyed no special popularity at first, being picked up in the 1780s only by Selection 1788 (Philadelphia), and in the next decade it appeared in Philadelphia (Adgate 1791ff), in New England (Federal 1794 and Bull 1795), and in South Carolina (Pilsbury 1799). After 1800, however, twenty-eight new collections printed PORTSMOUTH. In Massachusetts, both eclectic (Brown 1802ff, Mann 1802, Holyoke 1803, Holyoke 1804, Albee 1805, Huntington 1807, Janes 1807, Mann 1807, and Sanger 1808) and a few reform collections carried it (Middlesex 1807f, Deerfield 1808, Boston West 1810); in Connecticut it appeared in Jenks 1803, Jenks 1805, and Griswold 1807; and in northern New England, it was picked up by Law 1805 and Village 1810. Elsewhere, circulation widened to Maryland (Arnold 1803, Cole 1804, Cole 1810) and New York City (Evans 1808f), while in Philadelphia it held its already established place, appearing in Law 1807f, Addington 1808, Chapin 1808f, Woodward 1809, and Blake 1810. PORTSMOUTH continued to circulate in the next decade, appearing in more than fifteen collections from the years 1811–1820. It was included in two retrospective northern collections, but none of the southern tunebooks carried it.

PORTSMOUTH, with its alternate title "Trumpet," its opening melodic gesture drawn from the harmonic series used by brass instruments, its snappy, march-like strut enlivened with dotted rhythms, and its melodic returns (mm. 9–25 is an extension of mm. 1–8; mm. 34–39 refer back to the beginning), shows ample evidence of instrumental origins.

Additional References

1. Read, No. 281
2. Fisher, p. 21; Hall (attributed to Handel); Hitchcock 122 (attributed to Law)

[63.] PORTUGAL, by Thomas Thorley

Text from Rippon, no. 343; written by Anne Steel (see Julian, p. 1089). Perhaps first published some time before its first known appearance in Thomas Williams, *Psalmodia Evangelica* (London, 1789). First published in America in Samuel Holyoke, Oliver Holden, and Hans Gram, *The Massachusetts Compiler* (Boston, 1795). Essex 1802, p. 40.

PORTUGAL, which sets one stanza of L.M. text to a duple-time tune in major mode, was printed 54 times. It appeared with at least seventeen different texts, but, with appearances in more than a dozen different collections, the present one was linked with it more closely than any other.

Introduced to America in Boston (Gram 1795), PORTUGAL received 54 percent of its printings in New England, most of them in Massachusetts. Although it was printed only once more before 1800 (Pilsbury 1799), the tune appeared in thirty-nine new tunebooks between 1800 and the end of 1810, a total matched or bettered by only four other Core Repertory pieces. Massachusetts tunebooks dominated PORTUGAL's roster of printings, including many eclectic works (Holden 1800, Worcester 1800f, Holden 1801, Brown 1802ff, Holt 1803, Holyoke 1803, Belknap 1806f, Boston First 1806, Holyoke 1807, Huntington 1807a, Mann 1807, Suffolk 1807) and a smaller number of reform items (Essex 1802, Law 1803, Boston First 1805f, Salem 1805f, Deerfield 1808, Middlesex 1808, Boston West 1810). Other New England printings were limited to one in New Hampshire (Village 1808f) and two in Connecticut (Jenks 1810, Read 1810). Outside New England, PORTUGAL enjoyed its most vigorous circulation in Pennsylvania (Shumway 1801, Woodward 1806ff, Law 1807f, Chapin 1808f, Blake 1810, Peck 1810, Wyeth 1810), New York City (Atwill 1806, Erben 1806, Erben 1808, Evans 1808f, Seymour 1809), and Baltimore (Cole 1804f, Cole 1808, Gillet 1809, Cole 1810), though it was also printed in Delaware (Fobes 1809) and Virginia (Tomlins 1810). One of the most widely accepted tunes of the next decade, PORTUGAL appeared in at least forty different tunebooks in the years 1811–1820. It was also included in four of the retrospective northern collections and in four of the five nineteenth-century southern tunebooks canvassed.

PORTUGAL, the latest English-composed Core Repertory tune, shows its up-to-date character in its three-voice texture, with the treble shadowing the tenor melody, mostly at the sixth, while the bass takes an independent, supporting role (except in mm. 11–12). Also unusual is the tune's melodic structure, the fourth phrase being a note-for-note repetition of the first in all voices, making the structure ABCA.

Additional References

1. Alderdice, p. oo; Eckhard, No. 0.1; Read, No. 172
2. Hall

Cross-Reference

See entry on PSALM 100 [OLD].

[64.] PSALM 25, by Alexander Gillet
(GOSHEN, GLASTONBURY)

Text from Watts, Psalm 25, S.M., 1st Part. First published in Andrew Law, *Select Harmony* ([Cheshire, Connecticut], 1779). Holden 1793, p. 29.

PSALM 25, a S.M. tune-with-extension in minor mode, was printed 46 times. As the title suggests, it was linked with the present text, though it also appeared with two others, neither a version of Psalm 25.

Introduced in Connecticut (Law 1779f), PSALM 25 received 87 percent of its printings in New England, a higher proportion than any other American-composed Core Repertory piece except one. During the 1780s, PSALM 25 appeared in a series of Massachusetts tunebooks (Bayley 1784, Mass 1784f, Bayley 1788, Federal 1788ff, Sacred 1788), followed in the next decade by several more there and in Connecticut (Law 1791f, Holden 1793ff, Law 1794f, Worcester 1794f), while Village 1798ff introduced it to New Hampshire. Atwill 1795f, published near Albany, was the first work to print PSALM 25 outside New England, followed by Pilsbury 1799 (Charleston, South Carolina) and several more printings in the Hudson Valley (Huntington 1800, Atwill 1804, Little 1809f), while a scattering of works in Massachusetts (Brown 1802ff, Holyoke 1804, Boston First 1806, Middlesex 1807f), Connecticut (Gamut 1807), and the north (Robbins 1805) kept it before the New England singing public. It enjoyed modest circulation in the decade 1811–1820, appear-

ing in at least a dozen tunebooks in that period. Only one retrospective northern tunebook carried it, however, and it is in none of the southern collections.

PSALM 25 is anything but mechanical in its text delivery, each phrase receiving its own rhythm, including the repetition of the fourth line. Harmonically, when not sounding open intervals, the piece relies almost entirely on four chords: the tonic and dominant, and the relative major and *its* dominant, with one subdominant chord (and its seventh) appearing in the approach to the last cadence.

Additional Reference

2. Hall

[65.] PSALM 33, by William Tuckey

Text from Watts, Psalm 33, C.M., 1st Part. Apparently first printed in James Lyon, *Urania* (Philadelphia, 1761). Jocelin 1788, p. 30.

PSALM 33, which sets two stanzas of C.M. text in major mode, was printed 45 times. Its first printing was textless, but thereafter it consistently appeared with the present text.

Introduced in Philadelphia (Lyon 1761f), PSALM 33 received 62 percent of its printings in New England, where its first appearance took place in Law 1779f (Connecticut). PSALM 33 owed most of its circulation to tunebooks of the 1780s, when it appeared in eleven new collections—a total surpassed by only seven other Core Repertory pieces. In that decade it was picked up by three Connecticut collections (Jocelin 1782f, Brownson 1783ff, and Langdon 1786), seven in Massachusetts (Bayley 1784, Mass 1784f, Bayley 1785, Worcester 1786–94, Bayley 1788, Federal 1788ff, Sacred 1788) and one more in Philadelphia (Selection 1788ff). After it passed into Adgate 1791ff (Philadelphia), however, it received only three more widely scattered printings: Pilsbury 1799 in Charleston, Brown 1802ff in Boston, and Blake 1810 in Philadelphia. PSALM 33 dropped out of the repertory almost completely thereafter. Only one printing from the next decade (1811–1820) has been discovered, and none of the retrospective northern collections or southern tunebooks carry it.

With its modulation to the submediant (mm. 15–16) and its generally orthodox European harmonic vocabulary—the unorthodox fourth in m. 25 and the dissonant clash in m. 28 may have originated as typographical errors—PSALM 33 shows more musical sophistication than most American-composed Core Repertory pieces. Its texture changes and the repetition of the second half show an awareness of up-to-date Methodist practice, though its composer seems not to have been a Methodist. The attribution to Tuckey, which appeared first in Jocelin 1788, seven years after Tuckey's death, is discussed in Crawford, *Lyon*, p. xx, no. 32.

Additional Reference

1. Alderdice, p. 98

[66.] PSALM 34, by Joseph Stephenson
(CREATION, STEVENSON, THRO'ALL THE CHANGING, WILTSHIRE, WISBEACH)

Text from New Version, Psalm 34. First published in Joseph Stephenson, *Church Harmony Sacred to Devotion*, 3d ed. (London, 1760). First published in America in Josiah Flagg, *Sixteen Anthems* (Boston, [1766]). Shumway 1793, p. 32.

PSALM 34, a C.M. fuging-tune in major mode, was printed 115 times—more than any other Core Repertory fuging-tune. Almost all printings link it with the present text, though isolated publications do print it with four others.

Introduced in Boston (Flagg 1766), PSALM 34 received 63 percent of its printings in New England. Appearances in the colonial and wartime period were limited to two of Daniel Bayley's publications (Williams 1769ff, Stickney 1774ff) and to Law 1779f. But in the 1780s, PSALM 34 appeared in fourteen new collections, a total exceeded by only two other Core Repertory pieces. In Massachusetts it was printed by Bayley 1784, Mass 1784f, New 1784, Bayley 1785, Worcester 1786ff, Bayley 1788, Federal 1788ff, and Sacred 1788; in Connecticut by Jocelin 1782f, Brownson 1783ff, and Read 1787ff; Philadelphia by Selection 1788ff and Adgate 1789ff; and in New York City by Amphion 1789. In the 1790s tunebooks from these areas continued to carry PSALM 34—Holden 1793ff, Mann 1797, and Boston 1799 in Massachusetts; Law 1791f, Read 1794ff, and Benjamin 1799 in Connecticut; Shumway 1793f and Poor 1794 in Philadelphia—while circulation broadened into Maryland (Ely 1792), Virginia (Sandford 1793), New Hampshire (Village 1795ff), New York (Atwill 1795f), and South Carolina (Pilsbury 1799). In the next decade, circulation of PSALM 34 extended northward (Maxim 1805f, Robbins 1805) and also southward into New York City (Erben 1806, Erben 1808, Evans 1808f), rural Maryland (Arnold 1803), and Pennsylvania (Wyeth 1810), while maintaining itself in Massachusetts (Holden 1800, Brown 1802f, Holyoke 1803, Cooper 1804, Holyoke 1804, Albee 1805, Boston First 1806, Sanger 1808), the Hudson Valley (Little 1805ff), Baltimore (Cole 1804f), and Philadelphia (Little 1801, Sacred 1806, Chapin 1808f, Blake 1810). Its circulation declined in the decade 1811–1820, when it appeared in fewer than ten collections in the sample. However, it was published in six of the retrospective northern collections, though none of the later southern items picked it up.

PSALM 34 is the English prototype of the kind of fuging-tune that took hold in New England: a chordal beginning is followed by a fuging section that is later repeated, in which bass, tenor, treble, and counter enter in turn with quarter-note declamation, and where the resulting text overlap clears as the final cadence is approached. While American composers borrowed all of those features, few also followed Stephenson's practice of turning levels other than the tonic into temporary tonics, as he does in mm. 6–7 (supertonic) and mm. 13–14 (dominant). According to Thomas Hastings, PSALM 34, together with MILFORD, served William Billings as compositional "models" when the New Englander began to compose in the 1760s and 1770s (Musical Magazine I; quoted in McKay and Crawford, p. 203). In the words of a slightly later writer, Billings, rather than being a great innovator, "fell in with the general taste and took his cue and style from such tunes . . . and many other similar fuging and lively compositions, then just becoming popular" (Boston Musical Gazette I; quoted in Bushnell, p. 465n). The tune was well enough known by 1784 that the anonymous compiler of The Massachusetts Harmony, issued in that year, complained: " 'Tis very seldom that I hear . . . 34 Psalm . . . sung right," apparently in reference to choristers' failure to sing the F-sharp (counter, m. 13) correctly. A memoir describing sacred music-making in Rockingham County, New Hampshire, early in the nineteenth century, notes that by that time PSALM 34 was one of the favorite tunes of the older generation (Memoirs, p. 113).

Additional References

1. Alderdice, p. 62; Read, No. 30
2. Hall; Hitchcock 174

Cross-Reference

See entry on ST. HELEN'S.

[67.] PSALM 46, by Amos Bull
(PSALM 146)

Text from Watts, Psalm 146, P.M. Apparently first pub-

lished in Daniel Bayley, *Select Harmony* (Newburyport, 1784). Read 1797, p. 63.

PSALM 46, a major-mode setting of one P.M. stanza, was printed 44 times. Of the four texts with which it appeared, the present one, though not PSALM 46 as the title would seem to promise, was by far the commonest.

Introduced in Massachusetts (Bayley 1784), PSALM 46 received 57 percent of its printings in New England. It gained quick circulation, with appearances in Massachusetts (Mass 1784f, Worcester 1786f, Bayley 1788, Federal 1788–92, Sacred 1788), Connecticut (Read 1787ff, Jocelin 1788), and Philadelphia (Adgate 1789ff, Selection 1790ff), all within a half-dozen years of its first known printing. Soon thereafter, it appeared in Baltimore (Ely 1792). But although Law 1791f and Read 1794 kept it before the public in Connecticut, as did Shumway 1793f in Philadelphia, PSALM 46 appeared in no new Massachusetts works of the 1790s; it was discarded from Worcester after 1788, Federal after 1792, Read after 1794, and *The Village Harmony* never printed it at all until the tenth edition (Village 1810). After the turn of the century it enjoyed a mild comeback in eclectic Massachusetts tunebooks (Brown 1802ff, Boston First 1806, Mann 1807, J. Read 1808), appearing also in Pennsylvania (Sacred 1806, Blake 1810, Wyeth 1810) and New York City (Erben 1806, Erben 1808). Modest circulation continued thereafter, with perhaps as many as a dozen printings in tunebooks from the years 1811–1820. However, PSALM 46 appeared in only one retrospective northern collection and one of the southern tunebooks examined.

PSALM 46, whose six eight-syllable lines represent the same meter as the fuging-tune GREENFIELD and the iambic ST. HELEN'S, is cast in a rhythmic straight-jacket: each line is built up of two adjacent dactyls (♩ ♪ ♪ ♩│♩ ♪ ♪ ♩).

Additional References

1. Read, No. 295
2. AH, p. 232; Hall

[68.] PSALM 100 [OLD]
(OLD HUNDRED, OLD SAVOY, PSALM 134)

Text from New Version, Psalm 57, stanzas 5–11. First published in *Pseaumes de David* (Geneva, 1551). First published in America in *The Psalms Hymns, and Spiritual Songs*, 9th ed. (Boston, 1698). Village 1800, p. 33, as OLD HUNDRED.

PSALM 100 [OLD], an L.M. common tune in major mode, was printed 226 times, more by far than any other Core Repertory piece, and in fact nearly 30 percent more than its next closest rival. Many of its printings—in fact, all but one before 1786 and quite a number after—were textless; of the sixteen different texts with which OLD HUNDRED appeared, several are found in ten or more different collections. The present text was chosen because it was widespread and because it appeared in significant multi-edition tunebooks of New England, including Worcester 1786ff, Federal 1788ff, and Village 1795ff.

Introduced in Boston (Bay 1698ff), PSALM 100 [OLD] received 64 percent of its printings in New England. In the years before 1760, the tune appeared in eight collections in Massachusetts (Bay 1698, Brady 1720, Walter 1721ff, Tufts 1723ff, Turner 1752, Johnston 1755f) and Pennsylvania (Neu 1753ff, Dawson 1754), more than other Core Repertory tunes of similar vintage (CANTERBURY, PSALM 148, ST. DAVID'S, SOUTHWELL, WINDSOR, YORK), none of which was printed in Neu 1753ff. In the next three-decade period (1760–1789), the tune's circulation broadened to include New York City (Psalms 1767, Collection 1774, Amphion 1789), New Hampshire (Gilman 1771), and Connecticut (Law 1781, Jocelin 1782f). More importantly, however, it quickened in Massachusetts and Pennsylvania (Bayley 1764ff, Flagg 1764, Bayley 1767f, Tans'ur 1767f, Tans'ur 1769ff, Bayley

1770ff, New England 1771, Stickney 1774f, Billings 1779, Mass 1784f, New 1784, Worcester 1786ff, Bayley 1788, Federal 1788ff, Sacred 1788; and in Lyon 1761f, Hopkinson 1763, Tunes 1763f, Tunes 1786, Selection 1788ff, Adgate 1789ff), for a total of twenty-six new works, a figure matching or outstripping that of the eighteenth-century tunes that had become its chief rivals for popularity in those years (AYLESBURY, BANGOR, COLCHESTER, FUNERAL THOUGHT, LITTLE MARLBOROUGH, PLYMOUTH, PSALM 149, ST. ANNE, ST. MARTIN'S, WELLS). During the last two decades of the period (1790–1810), OLD HUNDRED appeared in no fewer than seventy-seven new collections. Its range had broadened to include Maryland (Ely 1792, Cole 1799, Arnold 1803, Cole 1804f, Cole 1808, Gillet 1809, Cole 1810), Virginia (Sandford 1793), South Carolina (Pilsbury 1799), and New Jersey (Smith 1803f). It also appeared in another trio of New Hampshire imprints (Village 1795ff, Robbins 1805, Blanchard 1808), in many collections from the Hudson Valley (Atwill 1795f, Huntington 1800, Atwill 1804f, Little 1805ff) and New York City (Edson 1801f, Seymour 1803f, Erben 1806, Erben 1808, Evans 1808f, Seymour 1809), and in Connecticut (Benham 1790ff, Law 1791f, Law 1794f, Read 1794ff, Bull 1795, Jenks 1801, Jenks 1803, Jenks 1804f, Olmsted 1805, Jenks 1806, Gamut 1807, Griswold 1807, Jenks 1810). Pennsylvania printings include Philadelphia items (Shumway 1793f, Neue 1797ff, Stammers 1803, Sacred 1806, Woodward 1806ff, Law 1807f, Chapin 1808f, Blake 1810, Peck 1810) and several outstate, including German-language collections (Mennonite 1803, Cumberland 1804, Mennonite 1804f, Rothbaust 1807, Wyeth 1810). In the same period, more than two-dozen new tunebooks compiled or printed in Massachusetts carried OLD HUNDRED, including books of all stylistic persuasions (Holden 1793ff, Mann 1797f, Boston 1799, Holden 1800, Brown 1802ff, French 1802, Essex 1802, Holyoke 1803, Law 1803, Cooper 1804, Holyoke 1804, Albee 1805, Salem 1805f, Boston First 1806, Graupner 1806, Hill 1806, Holyoke 1807, Huntington 1807, Mann 1807, Middlesex 1807f, Suffolk 1807, Deerfield 1808, J. Read 1808, Sanger 1808, Boston Brattle 1810, Boston West 1810, Sacred 1810). During the years 1790–1810, nearly a dozen tunes, including old favorites like AYLESBURY, BANGOR, LITTLE MARLBOROUGH, ST. MARTIN'S, WELLS, and WINDSOR, and some newer favorites, such as DENMARK, IRISH, MEAR, NEWTON, and PORTUGAL, were printed in nearly forty different collections. But none came close to matching the near-universal acceptance that OLD HUNDRED received. Circulation continued unabated in the next decade, with printings in more than fifty collections from the years 1811–1820. All of the later retrospective northern collections and southern tunebooks that have been examined also contain PSALM 100 [OLD]. Jackson lists it as one of the most popular "standard hymns" in southern tunebooks (Jackson, p. 130).

It is tempting to search for musical traits that might help to explain PSALM 100 [OLD]'s extraordinary popularity. Surely its rhythm—a series of slow-moving long notes—opened it up to a wide range of tempos and interpretations. Also noteworthy is the careful balance of its melodic shape. The first three phrases each move by step for five notes, then leap into the sixth note— the first phrase continuing upward in the direction of the leap, the second and third changing directions to fill in the gap. The fourth phrase, however, behaves quite differently: after the tune's largest leap to its highest note, it moves downward by two successive leaps, then upward again by leap; its angularity balances the stepwise beginnings of the three earlier phrases, and its final descent helps to compensate for the upward thrust of the first phrase. As early as 1724, the congregation at Weston, Massachusetts, chose OLD HUNDRED as one of its approved tunes (1 of 14), worshippers in Needham did the same in a vote of 7 January 1729 (1 of 8 tunes), and the congregation at

Wilbraham followed suit on 22 October 1770 (1 of 23 tunes). Choir singers, eager for stiffer musical challenges, were not always enthusiastic about OLD HUNDRED. A newspaper account of an incident that took place in Boston during the 1760s reports that a clergyman had asked members of the choir

> to sing the Old Hundredth Psalm. Was his request granted Think you? By no Means. After looking upon him with a smile of Pity for his want of Taste, they told him that was out of Date but they would give him the new Tune to the same Words, which was much better for that it consisted of four or five Parts, and had many Fuges (*New Hampshire Gazette*, January, 1764; quoted in Bushnell, p. 35).

By the end of the century, however, the tide had turned against fuges and musical complexity. Compilers eulogized the most ancient, simplest psalm tunes as repositories of the highest virtues of sacred music. Bartholomew Brown wrote: "After passing through all the grades of improvement, men will at last come to admire the old slow church Music; and will consider the use of Old Hundred and Windsor, as evidence of a correct taste" (Brown 1802, p. [3]). Daniel Read, himself a composer of nine Core Repertory pieces, most of them quite lively, came in his later years to share Brown's opinion: "I have no doubt that some of the old tunes (as Old Hundred, Mear, &c) will live, when hundreds of modern pieces will be buried in oblivion" (Daniel Read to Joel Read, 1804; quoted in Bushnell, p. 273). Andrew Law, in his later years an arch-reformer whose imagination seems to have been liberated by reform rhetoric, offered the most extreme endorsement of PSALM 100 [OLD]: "I have been informed," he wrote, "that Handel said, he would give all his oratorios, if he might be the author of Old Hundred" (Law, Essays, p. 26; quoted in Crawford, p. 244). Approval of OLD HUNDRED, however, was not restricted to the rhetoric of reformers or the borrowings of compilers eager to turn a profit. As well as at regular worship services, the tune was sung on special occasions: at a New Haven memorial service for Gen. George Washington, for example, on 22 February 1800, to Watts's Psalm 89, "Think, mighty God, on feeble man" (Bushnell, pp. 215–16); or on Independence Day in Salem (see Bentley Diary, 4 July 1804; vol. III:96); or at a farewell ceremony for a group of missionaries bound for duty in the field. As William Bentley wrote: "all four [missionaries] with wives . . . left Newbury Port last week. A prayer on the wharf & two thousand sang Old Hundred as they departed" (Bentley Diary, 29 October 1815; vol. IV:358).

Additional References

1. Alderdice, p. m; Eckhard, No. 9; Read, No. 153
2. AH, p. 52; AMR 166; A&M 316; Frost 114; Hall (as OLD HUNDRED; attributed to Luther); Hitchcock 109, 119, 148, 165, 168, 174, 175, 177, 192, (398); MinA, pp. 27–28, 30, 36; Temperley, 2: ex. 76
3. Baptist; Congregational; Episcopal; Lutheran; Methodist; Presbyterian

Cross-References

See entries on BATH, MEAR, PLYMOUTH, PSALM 149, WANTAGE, WINDSOR.

[69.] PSALM 100 [NEW]
(ANTHEM, ANTHEM TO 100, NEW HUNDRED)

Text from Watts, Psalm 90, L.M., stanzas 5–8. First known publication is John Tufts, *An Introduction to the Art of Singing Psalm-Tunes*, 3d ed. (Boston, 1723). Selection 1788, p. 76.

PSALM 100 [NEW], a triple-time L.M. tune in minor mode, was printed 52 times. It is suggested by Lowens to be the earliest American musical composition to reach print (Lowens, pp. 53–55). Most printings before the late 1780s are textless; of the five texts with which the tune appeared, this one and "Ye nations round the earth, rejoice" (Watts, Psalm 100, L.M.) are found the most frequently.

Introduced in Boston (Tufts 1723ff), PSALM 100 [NEW] received 56 percent of its printings in New England. Its publication history falls into two distinct periods. It was a regular in tune supplements and tunebooks of colonial New England and Philadelphia: Bay 1737f, Walter 1740, Turner 1752, Dawson 1754, Johnston 1755f, Walter 1759ff, Lyon 1761f, Hopkinson 1763, Tunes 1763f, Flagg 1764, Bayley 1767f, Bayley 1771, Gilman 1771, New England 1771. Then, after nearly two decades with no printings at all, it was reintroduced into Philadelphia by Selection 1788ff, passing thereafter into several more Philadelphia items (Adgate 1791ff, Shumway 1793f, Sacred 1806), one from rural Pennsylvania (Cumberland 1804), and three from Connecticut (Read 1794, Bull 1795, Griswold 1798). It reappeared in Massachusetts after the turn of the century (Mann 1802, Law 1803, Mann 1807, Middlesex 1808). Moderate circulation continued in the next decade, with more than a dozen appearances in works from the years 1811–1820. However, no northern retrospective tunebooks carried PSALM 100 [NEW], and it appeared in just one of the southern collections canvassed.

PSALM 100 [NEW], the earliest American-composed tune in the Core Repertory, has a certain awkwardness about it, revealed in the relationship between the counter and tenor voices, where a couple of clashes (mm. 3, 7) and several doublings (mm. 6, 7–9, 10, 13, 14) occur. The tune gained approval in at least one New England community soon after its publication: parishioners in Weston, Massachusetts, voted in 1724 to include it among the fourteen tunes approved for congregational singing. Some half-a-century later, the congregations at Wilbraham, Massachusetts (22 October 1770; 1 of 23 tunes), and Harwinton, Connecticut (4 June 1776; 1 of 22 tunes), did the same. In the 1750s, however, in Westborough, Massachusetts, controversy broke out when the precentor set the tune in a worship service. As reported in the Reverend Ebenezer Parkman's diary: "Mr. David Batherick was so displeas'd that at the Next Singing he rose up and set a Tune that would please himself better" (Parkman Diary, 16 November 1752, p. 263). Other entries in Parkman's diary (29 April 1750, p. 215; 30 November 1752, p. 264; 25 August 1755, p. 293) reveal that Batherick and others objected to psalm tunes in triple-time.

Additional References

1. Read, No. 223
2. AH, p. 123; Hitchcock 115, 119, 162, 174; MinA, p. 50

[70.] PSALM 136, by Deaolph

Text from Watts, Psalm 121, P.M., stanza 4. First published in Andrew Law, *Select Harmony* (Cheshire, Connecticut, 1778). Federal 1790, p. 35.

PSALM 136, a major-mode fuging-tune in H.M., was printed 49 times. It was linked in most tunebooks with the present text, though it did appear with two others.

Introduced in Connecticut (Law 1779f), PSALM 136 received almost two-thirds of its printings in New England. The tune won immediate favor in Massachusetts, appearing in eight new tunebooks there during the 1780s: Stickney 1783, Bayley 1784, Mass 1784f, Bayley 1785, Worcester 1786–91, Bayley 1788, Federal 1788–90, Sacred 1788, Worcester 1794ff; as well as in the New Hampshire-published Dearborn 1785 and Amphion 1789 in New York City. After 1790 the circulation of PSALM 136 in New England was restricted to Village 1795–1808 in the north, Law 1791f and Jenks 1804f in Connecticut, and Holden 1793f

and Cooper 1804 in Massachusetts. Outside New England, however, it achieved wide distribution during the same period, appearing in works published in Maryland (Ely 1792), Pennsylvania (Shumway 1793f, Little 1801, Sacred 1806, Wyeth 1810), New York (Atwill 1795f, Little 1805ff), South Carolina (Pilsbury 1799), and Delaware (Fobes 1809). Circulation dropped off sharply in the next decade, with only two appearances recorded in the years 1811–1820. PSALM 136, however, was printed in three northern retrospective collections, though none of the sampling of southern tunebooks carried it.

PSALM 136, the only Core Repertory fuging-tune in H.M., introduces two fuges: one on the third line of text and the other on the fifth and sixth. Of special note is the counter in the second fuge, especially in m. 19, where it covers a whole octave and, for a moment, becomes the most prominent voice in the texture—an opportunity rare for singers of the counter voice in Anglo-American psalmody.

Additional Reference

1. Alderdice, p. 266

[71.] PSALM 148
(OLD 148)

Text from Bay Psalm Book, Psalm 148. First published in *Psalmes of David in English Metre*, 2d ed. ([Geneva], 1558). First published in America in *The Psalms Hymns, and Spiritual Songs*, 9th ed. (Boston, 1698). Lyon 1761, p. 84, as THE OLD 148TH PSALM TUNE.

PSALM 148, a duple-time H.M. tune in major mode, was printed 51 times. Most were textless; but the present text, applied to it in the tune's earliest American printing, and probably sung to it through much of the colonial period, seems a suitable choice.

Introduced in Boston (Bay 1698ff), PSALM 148 received more than 90 percent of its printings in New England, most of them in Massachusetts publications of the colonial period. It appeared in a succession of Massachusetts tune supplements and tunebooks (Brady 1720, Walter 1721ff, Tufts 1723ff, Turner 1752, Johnston 1755f, Bayley 1764ff, Flagg 1764, Williams 1769ff, New England 1771, Stickney 1774f) and was also picked up by three Philadelphia items (Dawson 1754, Lyon 1761f, Hopkinson 1763) for its only printings outside New England. Ignored by compilers during the next three decades, it reappeared in Salem 1805f, whose reform policy was hospitable to "venerable" European psalm tunes, however far out of fashion they may have fallen. PSALM 148 was published in only about a half-dozen of the collections from the decade 1811–1820, in just one retrospective northern collection, and in none of the southern tunebooks.

PSALM 148 gives the impression of covering an even wider range than a ninth (D-E) by virtue of its frequent leaps, especially at the beginning, and its bold downward gesture at the end (mm. 20–26). Harmonically, it stands out among Core Repertory tunes for its favoring of the subdominant.

Additional References

1. Read, No. 285
2. AH, p. 49; Frost 174; Hitchcock 119, 148, 175, (20); MinA, pp. 31, 38

Cross-Reference

See entry on PSALM 100 [OLD].

[72.] PSALM 149
(AILIFF STREET, ALIFF STREET, HANOVER, ST. MICHAEL'S)

Text from New Version, Psalm 149. First published in Nicholas Brady and Nahum Tate, *A Supplement to the New Version of*

Psalms by Dr. Brady and Mr. Tate, 6th ed. (London, 1708). First published in America in John Tufts, *An Introduction to the Singing of Psalm-Tunes*, 5th ed. (Boston, 1726). Worcester 1788, p. 54, as St. Michael's or Ps. 149.

Psalm 149, a triple-time P.M. tune in major mode, was printed 121 times. Customarily printed without text before the 1780s, it thereafter came to be linked closely with the present one, appearing with only two others, neither in more than a single tunebook.

Introduced in Boston (Tufts 1726ff), Psalm 149 received some three-quarters of its printings in New England, most of them in Massachusetts. The tune appeared in a succession of tune supplements and tunebooks of the colonial period, both in New England (Bay 1737f, Turner 1752, Johnston 1755f, Walter 1760f, Bayley 1764ff, Flagg 1764, Bayley 1767f, Tans'ur 1767f, Tans'ur 1769ff, Williams 1769ff, Bayley 1770ff, Gilman 1771, New England 1771, Stickney 1774) and Philadelphia (Dawson 1754, Lyon 1761f, Hopkinson 1763). In the 1780s it was picked up in Connecticut by Jocelin 1782f and Law 1783ff, appearing also in Massachusetts (Bayley 1784, Worcester 1786ff, Bayley 1788, Federal 1788, Sacred 1788, Federal 1794) and in Philadelphia (Tunes 1786, Adgate 1789ff, Selection 1789ff). In the 1790s, circulation slowed in New England (Law 1794f, Boston 1799) but broadened southward to include Virginia (Sandford 1793), Baltimore (Cole 1799), and Charleston (Pilsbury 1799). After 1800 Psalm 149 was reaffirmed as a favorite by New England eclectic compilers (Jenks 1801, Brown 1802f, Mann 1802, Cooper 1804, Albee 1805, Boston First 1806, Village 1806ff, Mann 1807, Read 1807f) and reformers alike (Essex 1802, Law 1803, Salem 1805f, Middlesex 1807f, Deerfield 1808, Huntington 1809, Boston Brattle 1810, Boston West 1810, Sacred 1810) and also by compilers in New York State (Huntington 1800) and City (Erben 1806, Erben 1808, Evans 1808f), Philadelphia (Woodward 1806ff, Law 1807f, Blake 1810), and Baltimore (Cole 1804, Cole 1808). Psalm 149 maintained much of its popularity in the decade 1811–1820, when it appeared in more than twenty-five collections. However, only two retrospective northern collections carried it, and one southern tunebook.

Psalm 149, the only Core Repertory tune setting this particular combination of ten- and eleven-syllable lines, features a high-lying, widely arching melody, inviting energy and enthusiasm from its singers—especially those singing the tune, and the basses, whose part ranges over an eleventh. Temperley praises the tune, along with others composed apparently by William Croft for the *Supplement* of 1708. "They have a majestic dignity," he writes, "that contrasts with the emotional fervour of Jeremiah Clarke's tunes in the Divine Companion," adding: "for the first time it is possible to speak of individual character in psalm tunes: they begin to be miniature works of art" (Temperley, 1:124). In Massachusetts, on 22 October 1770, the congregation at Wilbraham voted Psalm 149 as 1 of 23 tunes it would sing in public worship. Some years later, in Salem, the Reverend William Bentley noted in his diary that a "new version of CXLIX for St. Michael's was sung before sermon" (Bentley Diary, 13 November 1787, vol I:80). On 3 April 1817, the annual fast day celebration in Salem featured the singing of Psalm 149 as well as Denmark and Old Hundred (Bentley Diary, vol. IV:445).

Additional References

1. Eckhard, No. 81; Read, No. 381
2. AMR 167 (2); A&M 326; Hall (as Hanover); MinA, p. 49
3. Congregational; Episcopal; Lutheran; Methodist; Presbyterian

Cross-References

See entries on Psalm 100 [Old], St. Anne.

[73.] Putney, by Aaron Williams

Text from Watts, Hymns II, no. 146. First published in Aaron Williams, *The Universal Psalmodist* (London, 1763). First published in America in William Tans'ur, *The Royal Melody Complete*, 3d ed. (Boston, 1767). Mass 1784, p. 33.

Putney, a triple-time L.M. tune in minor mode, was printed 69 times. Though textless in many earlier printings, it was closely identified with the present text, one of five with which it appeared.

Introduced in Massachussets (Tans'ur 1767f), Putney received three-quarters of its printings in New England. It soon appeared in other works published or compiled by Daniel Bayley (Williams 1769ff, Bayley 1770ff, Stickney 1774f) and in several tune supplements (Gilman 1771, Billings 1779, Law 1781, New 1784). During the 1780s its Massachusetts printings were in Mass 1784f, Worcester 1786f, Bayley 1788, Federal 1788, and Sacred 1788. Jocelin 1782f also printed it in New Haven, and Adgate 1789ff introduced it to Philadelphia. Law 1791f, Law 1794f, and Bull 1795 kept it alive in Connecticut in the 1790s, as did Boston 1799 in Massachusetts. Pilsbury 1799 accounted for only its second appearance outside New England, followed later by Cole 1805 and Cole 1808 in Baltimore, Woodward 1806f and Law 1807f in Philadelphia, and Wyeth 1810 in Harrisburg. Meanwhile, Village 1803ff and Blanchard 1808 printed it in northern New England, while Massachusetts tunebooks—from the eclectic Brown 1802ff, Boston First 1806, and Mann 1807, to the reform-oriented Law 1803, Salem 1805f, Middlesex 1807f, Deerfield 1808, Huntington 1809, Boston Brattle 1810, Boston West 1810, and Sacred 1810—also carried it. Putney was included in at least twenty-five collections of the period 1811–1820, and in four northern retrospective collections, though it appeared in none of the southern tunebooks checked.

The melody of Putney is unusual in that its fourth and final phrase closely resembles the third, producing the form ABCC^1. The tune is dominated by the rhythmic figure introduced in m. 1 of the tenor and appearing in all subsequent phrases—the same figure that dominates Billings's Brookfield, for which Putney may have been a model. (Cf. mm. 12–16 in the two tunes.) The congregation at Harwinton, Connecticut, voted on 4 June 1776 to make it 1 of the 22 tunes sung there in public worship.

Additional References

1. Alderdice, p. 95; Read, No. 212
2. Hall

Cross-Reference

See entry on St. Martin's.

[74.] Rainbow, by Timothy Swan

Text from Watts, Psalm 65, C.M., 2d Part. First published in Oliver Brownson, *Select Harmony* ([Connecticut, 1785]), or, perhaps, Daniel Bayley, *The Essex Harmony* (Newburyport, 1785). Worcester 1788, p. 86.

Rainbow, a C.M. fuging-tune, was printed 51 times. Composed to dramatize the present text's image of the calming sea, Rainbow was set to that text in all but one of the tunebooks that printed it.

First published in Connecticut (Brownson 1785f) or, possibly, Massachusetts (Bayley 1785), Rainbow received 57 percent of its printings in New England. The tune was accepted enthusiastically by compilers of the 1780s, but then it declined in circulation during the next two decades. Rainbow appeared in eight more collections before the decade of the 1780s was over: in Worcester 1786ff, Federal 1788–93 and Sacred 1788 in Massachusetts; in Law 1786ff and Langdon 1786 in Connecticut; in Selection 1788ff and Adgate 1789ff in Philadelphia; and in Amphion 1789 in New York City. In the 1790s only five new works picked it up: Holden 1793ff, Mann 1797, and Boston 1799 in Massachusetts; Shumway 1793f in Philadelphia; and Ely 1792 in Baltimore. Printings after 1800 were scattered between urban centers like Boston (Cooper 1804, Suffolk 1807) and Philadelphia (Sacred 1806, Blake 1810), the smaller New England town of Northampton (Swan 1801, Bushnell 1807), and remote outposts like Hagerstown, Maryland (Arnold 1803), and Hanover, Pennsylvania (Rothbaust 1807). RAINBOW dropped almost completely out of the repertory in the next decade, appearing in only two works from the years 1811–1820. It did, however, enjoy something of a comeback in retrospective northern collections, five of which carried it, though it was not picked up by any of the southern tunebooks.

RAINBOW, which sets just one stanza of text, contains one of the most unusual and expressive fuges in the entire repertory. Introduced in the treble voice, the subject moves downward until it reaches the bass; then, instead of launching the customary drive toward the final cadence, Swan takes voices away one by one as "tempests cease to roar," until only the bass, intoning a quiet low C, is left.

Additional References

1. Alderdice, p. 104
2. Hitchcock 96, (500)

[75.] ROCHESTER, by Israel Holdroyd
(St. MICHAEL'S)

Text from Watts, Psalm 73, C.M., 2d Part. First published in Israel Holdroyd, *The Spiritual-Man's Companion* (London, ca., 1724). First published in America in James Lyon, *Urania* (Philadelphia, 1761). Federal 1790, p. 86.

ROCHESTER, a C.M. major mode tune in duple time, received 83 printings. Many are textless, but of the dozen different texts with which ROCHESTER was printed, the present one was the most prevalent.

Introduced in Philadelphia (Lyon 1761f), ROCHESTER received only 46 percent of its printings in New England. Soon after its first appearance it moved into New England publications (Bayley 1764ff, Flagg 1764, Williams 1769ff, Stickney 1774ff in Massachusetts; Law 1779, Law 1781 and Jocelin 1782f in Connecticut), appearing after the war in such Massachusetts items as Bayley 1784, Mass 1784f, New 1784, Bayley 1785, Worcester 1786, Federal 1788–93, and Sacred 1788. Thereafter, New England printings of ROCHESTER were relatively few (Law 1791f, Holyoke 1803, Brown 1804, PSA 1804, and a group of reform items: Middlesex 1807f, Blanchard 1808, Deerfield 1808, Huntington 1809). In the meantime, ROCHESTER caught on outside New England. A steady succession of tunebooks from Philadelphia (Selection 1788ff, Adgate 1789ff, Shumway 1793f, Poor 1794, Little 1801, Sacred 1806, Woodward 1806ff, Chapin 1808f, Blake 1810) and rural Pennsylvania (Cumberland 1804, Rothbaust 1807, Wyeth 1810) carried it, as did Amphion 1789 in New York City, Ely 1792, Cole 1804f, and Cole 1808 from Baltimore; Pilsbury 1799 from Charleston; Huntington 1800 and Little 1805ff from the Hudson Valley; and Erben 1806, Erben 1808, and Seymour 1809 from New York City. Circulation remained strong in the years 1811–1820, with more than thirty appearances in books published during that decade. ROCHESTER appeared in two retrospective northern collections and in three southern tunebooks, as well.

More than any other C.M. tune in the Core Repertory, ROCHESTER is dominated by dactylic rhythm. (Cf. WELLS, also by Holdroyd, which is in L.M.) The tune also has a counter part that is unusually active, descending below the tenor in both the second and third phrases.

Additional References

1. Alderdice, p. 168; Read, No. 74
2. Hall (attributed to Williams)

[76.] RUSSIA, by Daniel Read

Text from Watts, Psalm 62, L.M., stanzas 3–6. First published in [Amos Doolittle and Daniel Read], *The American Musical Magazine* (New Haven, [1786–87]). Little 1801, p. 30.

RUSSIA, a L.M. fuging-tune in minor mode, was printed 68 times. The present text appears with almost all of them; single appearances of two other texts can also be found.

Introduced in Connecticut (Doolittle 1786), RUSSIA received 62 percent of its printings in New England. At first RUSSIA circulated only in Massachusetts and Connecticut (Read 1787ff, Federal 1788–93); but in the next decade it appeared both in central New England (Worcester 1792ff, French 1793, Holden 1793ff, Read 1794ff, Mann 1797, and Boston 1799) and in five other states as well: Pennsylvania (Shumway 1793f), New York (Atwill 1795f), New Hampshire (Village 1795ff), New Jersey (New Jersey 1797), and South Carolina (Pilsbury 1799). Later printings were concentrated chiefly in Pennsylvania (Little 1801, Sacred 1806, Woodward 1806ff, Rothbaust 1807, Chapin 1808f, Blake 1810, Wyeth 1810) and New York (Huntington 1800, Seymour 1803f, Atwill 1804, Little 1805ff, Seymour 1809), though they also include a Delaware compilation (Fobes 1809) and a scattering of New England works: Holden 1800, Holyoke 1804, Jenks 1804f, and J. Read 1808 in central New England and Maxim 1805f in the north. Modest circulation continued in the next decade with at least ten printings in collections from the years 1811–1820. Of the retrospective northern collections, four carried RUSSIA, as well as two of the southern items.

RUSSIA is a classic American fuging-tune, setting one stanza and fuging the third line of the four-line text. The parts are written in the middle register for each voice, the counter spanning only a fourth, the tenor and treble just a sixth, with only the bass being required to cover as much as an octave. Read's use of chords built on the fifth scale degree is consistent: cadential chords are major (mm. 3, 5, 13), while chords in mid-phrase are minor or lack a third (mm. 1, beat 4; m. 2, beat 2; m. 4, beat 1; m. 9, beat 4; m. 11, beat 1; m. 12, beat 3). Bushnell suggests that Read's choice of text may have been topical—referring to Andrew Law, with whom Read was engaged in a dispute over copyright at about the time RUSSIA appeared (Bushnell, p. 95). The tune is identified as a favorite of members of the choir in Atkinson, New Hampshire, who returned to singing it when a reform movement there lost steam (Memoirs, p. 89). As late as the 1880s, it was included on a list of five tunes by Read that were "in general use at the present day and are likely to live for a long time to come" (Jones, p. 143).

Additional References

1. Alderdice, p. 148
2. AH, p. 182; Hall; Hitchcock 174, 194, (454)

Cross-Reference

See entry on SHERBURNE.

[77.] ST. ANNE, by William Croft
(MALDEN, PRESERVATION, ST. ANN'S)

Text from Watts, Hymns II, no. 94. First published in Nicholas Brady & Nahum Tate, *A Supplement to the New Version*, 6th ed. (London, 1708). First published in America in William Dawson, *The Youths Entertaining Amusement* (Philadelphia, 1754). Wyeth 1810, p. 26.

ST. ANNE, a major-mode C.M. tune in duple time, received 88 printings. Many were textless. But of the thirteen texts with which the tune appeared, the present was by far the most frequent.

Introduced in Philadelphia (Dawson 1754), ST. ANNE received more than three-quarters of its printings in New England. Its circulation was more spotty than consistent. In Philadelphia it appeared next in Lyon 1761f and Hopkinson 1763, while it is also found in almost every Massachusetts tunebook of the 1760s (Johnston 1763, Flagg 1764, Bayley 1766f, Bayley 1767f, Tans'ur 1768, Williams 1769ff) and in several of the 1770s (Bayley 1770ff, New England 1771, Stickney 1774ff, Billings 1779) and 1780s (Bayley 1784, Mass 1784f, New 1784, Worcester 1786–92, Bayley 1788, Federal 1788ff, and Sacred 1788). But elsewhere it is only in two New-England tune supplements, Gilman 1771 and Law 1781, and Selection 1788 in Philadelphia. During the 1790s only two new tunebooks carried it; Adgate 1791ff, in Philadelphia, and Boston 1799, in New England. After the turn of the century, ST. ANNE made a strong comeback, appearing in Worcester 1803 and fourteen new Massachusetts tunebooks, including both eclectic items (Brown 1802ff, Holyoke 1803, Cooper 1804, Boston First 1806, Mann 1807, Suffolk 1807) and reform works (Essex 1802, Law 1803, Salem 1805f, Middlesex 1807f, Deerfield 1808, Boston Brattle 1810, Boston West 1810, and Sacred 1810). A scattering of printings appeared elsewhere: Village 1800ff, Olmsted 1805, and Blanchard 1808 in New England; Jackson 1804 and Erben 1808 in New York City; Cole 1805 and Cole 1808 in Baltimore; Law 1807f, Blake 1810, and Wyeth 1810 in Pennsylvania; and Tomlins 1810 in Virginia. At least thirty collections of the next decade (1811–1820) printed ST. ANNE, which also appeared in a half-dozen northern retrospective collections but in none of the sample of southern tunebooks.

ST. ANNE's third phrase cadences on a major mediant triad (V/VI), making it the only four-line Core Repertory tune in major mode, except for CANTERBURY, to close a line on a level other than dominant or tonic. In view of that unusual touch, it seems a bit strange that the expected secondary dominant in m. 8 does not materialize, and that the counter moves so frequently in parallel octaves with the treble (mm. 4, 6–9, 15–16). Temperley praises ST. ANNE, together with PSALM 149: "They have a majestic dignity," he writes, marking them with "individual character" which makes them "miniature works of art" (Temperley, 1:124). "St. Anne" is the nickname given J.S. Bach's Prelude and Fugue in E-flat (BWV 552) from the *Clavier-Übung*, Part III (Leipzig, 1739), because the fugue subject closely resembles the first line of Croft's tune (see Scholes, p. 683).

Additional References

1. Alderdice, p. rr; Eckhard, No. 53; Read, No. 86
2. AMR 165; A&M 403; Hall; MinA, p. 39; Temperley, 2:ex. 83
3. Baptist; Congregational; Episcopal; Lutheran; Methodist; Presbyterian

Cross-References

See entries on CANTERBURY, PSALM 100 [OLD], ST. JAMES.

[78.] ST. DAVID'S
(ST. DAVID'S OLD)

Text from New Version, Psalm 27. First published in Thomas Ravenscroft, *The Whole Booke of Psalmes . . . Composed into 4. Parts by Sundry Authors* (London, 1621). First published in America in *The Psalms Hymns, and Spiritual Songs*, 9th ed. (Boston, 1698). Lyon 1761, p. 8.

ST. DAVID'S, a C.M. common tune in major mode, received 57 printings. Most were textless, and the tune was not closely linked with any single text; the present text, printed in Brady

1713, is assigned to it here in the belief that a pairing from the tune's early heyday is most suitable.

Introduced in Boston (Bay 1698ff), ST. DAVID'S received 88 percent of its printings in New England, most of them during the colonial period. The tune was a regular in pre-1760 Boston publications (Brady 1713f, Walter 1721ff, Tufts 1723ff, Turner 1752, Johnston 1755). In the 1750s and after, it also appeared in Philadelphia (Dawson 1754, Lyon 1761f, Hopkinson 1763), in several of Daniel Bayley's publications (Bayley 1764ff, Tans'ur 1767f, Tans'ur 1769ff, and Bayley 1770), and in New England 1771. After a break of some three decades, ST. DAVID'S reappeared in Massachusetts (Holyoke 1803, Middlesex 1808, Boston Brattle 1810, Boston West 1810) and elsewhere (Cole 1808 and Cole 1810 in Baltimore, and in one work compiled in a small town in Pennsylvania: Cumberland 1804). At least a dozen printings are found in collections from the decade 1811–1820. However, none of the northern retrospective collections nor any of the southern tunebooks examined carries ST. DAVID'S.

The most noteworthy trait of ST. DAVID'S, printed here in a setting with few harmonic irregularities, is the consistency of its disjunct motion: nearly two-thirds of its melodic intervals are skips. Samuel Sewall, a Boston precentor, recorded in his diary for 2 February 1718, that, to his dismay, the congregation had confused ST. DAVID'S with YORK, another similarly disjunct C.M. tune in the Core Repertory:

> In the morning I set York Tune, and in the 2d going over, the Gallery carried it irresistably to St. David's, which discouraged me very much (Sewall Diary, p. 881).

In a lively tract on regular singing, the Reverend Thomas Symmes, explaining the names of psalm tunes, had occasion to refer to ST. DAVID'S:

> And why may not a Tune be called St. Mary's as well as St. David's, and so one of our most celebrated Tunes is termed in our Psalm Books; unless you think with one, that said to me, He did not know but that Tune was made by King David, about 200 year ago. Commend me to that Man, however for a chronologer, if he's no Musician! (Symmes, p. 37)

Congregations in Weston (1724; 1 of 14 tunes) and Needham, Massachusetts (7 January 1729; 1 of 8 tunes), selected ST. DAVID'S for singing in public worship. In the Hutchinson Partbook (1763; probably copied in Pennsylvania), the following text was provided for a two-voice setting of ST. DAVID'S (here entitled "DAVID'S"):

> David he was a Shepherds Son
> When he went to the field
> And when that he had flung the stone
> He made Goliah yield[.]

Additional References

1. Eckhard, No. 64; Read, No. 7
2. AH, p. 87; Frost 235; Hitchcock 148, 175, 177, 194; Temperley, 2:ex. 19–22

Cross-References

See entries on PSALM 100 [OLD], YORK.

[79.] ST. GEORGE'S
(BRAY, DANVILLE, GEORGE'S, LEEDS)

Text from Watts, Hymns I, no. 20. First published in *Harmonia Sacra, or a Choice Collection of Psalm and Hymn Tunes* (London, [ca. 1760]), or before. First published in America in Josiah Flagg, *A Collection of the Best Psalm Tunes* (Boston, 1764). French 1802, p. 44, as BRAY.

ST. GEORGE'S, a major-mode C.M. tune-with-extension in

duple time, received 46 printings. Of the thirteen texts with which it was published, it appeared more frequently with the present one than any other.

Introduced in Boston (Flagg 1764), St. George's received 54 percent of its printings in New England. During the colonial period, the tune appeared in three of Daniel Bayley's publications (Tans'ur 1767f, Tans'ur 1769ff, Stickney 1774); but between that time and the turn of the century, only two Philadelphia items printed it: Shumway 1793f and Poor 1794. After 1800, twenty-seven tunebooks in seven states printed St. George's. New England publications include Jenks 1804f, Jenks 1805, Jenks 1805a, and Jenks 1810 in Connecticut; Village 1810 in New Hampshire; and French 1802, Holyoke 1803, Cooper 1804, Middlesex 1807f, Suffolk 1807, Deerfield 1808, Boston West 1810, and Brown 1810 in Massachusetts. St. George's also appeared in New York (Seymour 1803f, Erben 1806, Erben 1808, Evans 1808f, Little 1809f, Seymour 1809), in Pennsylvania (Cumberland 1804, Aitken 1806, Wyeth 1810), in Maryland (Arnold 1803, Cole 1804f, Cole 1808, Gillet 1809, and Cole 1810), and in Virginia (Tomlins 1810). St. George's maintained a healthy circulation in the decade 1811–1820, appearing in more than two-dozen collections. It was printed, however, in only one or two retrospective northern tunebooks and in only one of the southern collections canvassed.

St. George's is marked by several traits of the Methodist musical tradition that produced it: the first melodic phrase is repeated with the third line of text, the last phrase of text is repeated to new music for emphasis, and the basic beat is notated as a quarter-note rather than a half-note. The tune appears in a manuscript book for the fife compiled by Giles Gibbs, Jr., of Ellington, Connecticut—a collection of Revolutionary War times (1777) devoted almost entirely to secular music (Gibbs, p. 21).

Additional References

1. Alderdice, p. ppp; Read, No. 71
2. Hall (as Bray, attributed to Williams)

[80.] St. Helen's
(Jennings, Sunderland)

Text from Watts, Psalm 113, P.M. Probably first published shortly before its first known appearance in Aaron Williams, *The Universal Psalmodist* (London, 1763). First published in America in [Daniel Bayley], *A New and Compleat Introduction to the Grounds and Rules of Musick* (Newburyport, 1764). Village 1800, p. 53.

St. Helen's, a triple-time P.M. tune in major mode, received 71 printings. Of the eight texts with which it was published, it appeared most often with two: "I'll praise my Maker with my breath" (Watts, Psalm 146, P.M.) and the present one, chosen here because it appears in multi-edition works like Worcester 1786ff and Village 1796ff.

Introduced in Massachusetts (Bayley 1764ff), St. Helen's received some 93 percent of its printings in New England, a proportion surpassed by only one other Core Repertory piece. The tune was a special favorite in Massachusetts, where it appeared in a steady succession of collections from the 1760s (Flagg 1766, Tans'ur 1768, Williams 1769ff), the 1770s (Bayley 1770ff, New England 1771, Stickney 1774f, Billings 1779), the 1780s (Mass 1784f, New 1784, Worcester 1786ff, Bayley 1788, and Sacred 1788), and the 1790s (Federal 1794, Boston 1799), being carried also by three Connecticut items during that period (Law 1781, Jocelin 1782, and Law 1791f). The same pattern persisted after 1800. Olmsted 1805 and Gamut 1807, in Connecticut, and Village 1800ff and Blanchard 1808, in New Hampshire, included it; so did fifteen new Massachusetts tunebooks, both eclectic (Brown 1802ff, Holyoke 1803, Boston First 1806, Hun-

tington 1807a, Janes 1807, Mann 1807) and reform-minded (Essex 1802, Law 1803, Salem 1805f, Middlesex 1807f, Deerfield 1808, Shaw 1808, Boston Brattle 1810, Boston West 1810, and Sacred 1810). Outside New England only Pilsbury 1799, Erben 1806, Law 1807f, and Wyeth 1810 carried St. Helen's. It continued to circulate widely in the decade 1811–1820, when it appeared in at least thirty-five new collections. Later, four northern retrospective collections, but none of the southern tunebooks, carried it.

St. Helen's sets a stanza of six eight-syllable lines in consistent iambic rhythm, broken only in the last phrase (mm. 20ff), supplying new music for each line of text (ABCDEF). Congregations in Wilbraham, Massachusetts (22 October 1770; 1 of 23 tunes), and Harwinton, Connecticut (4 June 1776; 1 of 22 tunes), chose St. Helen's for singing in public worship. In the next decade, the difficulty that singers had with accurate performance of the secondary dominant in m. 7 was noted by the compiler of *The Massachusetts Harmony*:

> I wish Masters in particular would attend to such persons, and choirs as they instruct, and observe that they give the right sound to Mi, in a natural sharp key; for 'tis very seldom that I hear St. Hellens or 34th Psalm, &c. sung right (Mass 1784, "Advertisement").

Additional References

1. Alderdice, p. dd; Read, No. 294
2. Hall (attributed to Jennings)

Cross-Reference

See entry on Psalm 46.

[81.] St. James, by Rafael Courteville
Text from New Version, Psalm 8. First published in *Select Psalms and Hymns for the Use of . . . St. James's Westminister* (London, 1697). First published in America in Thomas Walter, *The Grounds and Rules of Musick* (Boston, 1721). Deerfield 1808, p. 99.

St. James, a duple-time C.M. common tune in major mode, was printed 57 times. Most printings were textless, and only two of the thirteen texts with which St. James appeared was printed with it more than once; the present text was one of them.

Introduced in Boston (Walter 1721ff), St. James received some 80 percent of its printings in New England, mostly before 1775 and after 1800. The tune appeared in many early New England supplements and tunebooks (Tufts 1723ff, Bay 1737f, Turner 1752, Johnston 1755f, Flagg 1764, Bayley 1767f, Williams 1769ff, Bayley 1770ff, Gilman 1771, New England 1771, Stickney 1774f) and in two early Philadelphia items as well (Dawson 1754, Hopkinson 1763). After only a scattering of appearances during the century's last quarter (Law 1783, Mass 1784f, Tunes 1786, Poor 1794), St. James made a comeback, first in Holyoke 1803, and then in a series of reform-minded collections in New England (Salem 1805f, Blanchard 1807, Middlesex 1807f, Deerfield 1808, Boston Brattle 1810, Village 1810), New York City (Jackson 1804), and Baltimore (Cole 1804f, Cole 1808, Cole 1810), and it also appeared in two Pennsylvania items (Cumberland 1804, Blake 1810). St. James appeared in nearly twenty more tunebooks from the decade 1811–1820. However, none of the retrospective northern collections or later southern tunebooks carried it.

St. James bears a close relationship to St. Anne, which it preceded into print by eleven years. Except for two notes (m. 1, beat 2; m. 11, beat 2), the melody of St. Anne could serve as a consonant counterpoint to St. James with almost no doubling.

Temperley provides some English background on ST. James, noting it as a "new tune in traditional style," appearing in 1697 in a book that represents "the first clear example of psalm tunes arranged for charity children alone, accompanied on the organ" (Temperley, 1:132). In 1724, the congregation at Weston, Massachusetts, chose ST. James for public singing (1 of 14 tunes).

Additional References

1. Eckhard, No. 37; Read, No. 11
2. AMR 199; A&M 344; Hall; Temperley, 2:ex. 23
3. Congregational; Episcopal; Presbyterian

[82.] ST. Martin's, by William Tans'ur
(Gainsborough, Norfolk)

Text from Watts, Hymns I, no. 1. First published in William Tans'ur, *A Compleat Melody*, 2d ed. (London, 1735). First published in America in Thomas Walter, *The Grounds and Rules of Musick*, [7th ed.] (Boston, 1760). Worcester 1786, p. 41.

ST. Martin's a major-mode C.M. tune in triple time, was printed 137 times. Most before the end of the 1780s were textless; yet in all, more than twenty different texts appeared with ST. Martin's—a sure sign that it was never identified with any one in particular. The present text, found in Worcester 1786, Adgate 1789ff, and later Philadelphia collections as well (Sacred 1806, Chapin 1808f), appeared with ST. Martin's as often as any other.

Introduced in Boston (Walter 1760f), ST. Martin's received 61 percent of its printings in New England. During the colonial period and thereafter, the tune established itself solidly in New England (Johnston 1763, Flagg 1764, Gilman 1771, New England 1771, Billings 1779, Jocelin 1782f, Law 1783ff, Mass 1784f, New 1784, Worcester 1786, Sacred 1788, and seven of Daniel Bayley's publications, 1764–88) before its first publication outside (Selection 1788ff and Adgate 1789ff in Philadelphia). Between 1790 and 1810, ST. Martin's appeared in fifty-three new collections, a total exceeded by only two other Core Repertory pieces. Outside New England, Pennsylvania collections accounted for eleven of those appearances (including Shumway 1793f, Stammers 1803, Aitken 1806, Addington 1808, among others), New York for eight more (Atwill 1795f, Huntington 1800, Atwill 1804, Little 1805ff, Erben 1806, Erben 1808, Evans 1808f, Seymour 1809), Maryland for three (Ely 1792, Cole 1805, Cole 1810), Virginia for two (Sandford 1793, Tomlins 1810), and South Carolina and New Jersey one each (Pilsbury 1799, Smith 1803f). Inside New England the roster includes sixteen collections from Massachusetts, six from Connecticut, and one from New Hampshire, among which are both eclectic works (Federal 1790–93, Law 1794f, Village 1795ff, Griswold 1798, Cooper 1804, PSA 1804, Boston First 1806, Griswold 1807, Read 1807f) and reform-minded items (Law 1803, Salem 1805f, Middlesex 1807f, Deerfield 1808, Sacred 1810). ST. Martin's remained one of the most widely circulated tunes of the perod 1811–1820, appearing in at least forty-eight collections from those years. It was also carried in seven of the northern retrospective collections and in two of the southern tunebooks examined.

ST. Martin's decorates its iambic rhythm by dissolving the downbeats of all but cadential measures. (M. 8 is an exception, and there the bass moves as the tenor sustains a whole-note.) Like Putney, ST. Martin's introduces the pattern ♩ ♪♩ in every phrase. Congregations in Wilbraham, Massachusetts (22 October 1770; 1 of 23 tunes), and Harwinton, Connecticut (4 June 1776; 1 of 22 tunes), chose it for singing in public worship. After the turn of the century, when reform was effected in Atkinson, New Hampshire, ST. Martin's was one of the first tunes sung by the choir (Memoirs, p. 84).

Additional References

1. Alderdice, p. 202; Read, No. 16
2. AH, p. 151; Hall; MinA, p. 57
3. Methodist

Cross-References

See entries on Morning Hymn, New Jerusalem, Psalm 100 [Old].

[83.] ST. Thomas, by Aaron Williams
(Beverley)

Text from Watts, Psalm 148, S.M. First published in Aaron Williams, *The New Universal Psalmodist*, 5th ed. (London, 1770). First published in America in Andrew Law, *Select Harmony* (Cheshire, Connecticut, 1778). Adgate 1789, p. 2.

ST. Thomas, a duple-time S.M. tune in major mode, was printed 51 times. Never linked closely with any single text, it appeared with at least thirteen different ones, the present choice more frequently than any other.

Introduced in Connecticut (Law 1778f), ST. Thomas received approximately half of its printings in New England. Circulation was slow in the first two decades after its introduction. Before 1800 ST. Thomas appeared in only a scattering of new works: three in Connecticut (Law 1781, Jocelin 1782, Law 1791f), three more in Massachusetts (Worcester 1786f, Sacred 1788, Boston 1799), and a pair in Philadelphia (Adgate 1789ff, Selection 1790ff). After 1800, however, ST. Thomas won a secure place in the repertory, being picked up in New England by fourteen new collections, from eclectic works (Brown 1802ff, Holyoke 1803, Boston First 1806, Mann 1807, Suffolk 1807, Sanger 1808) to reform-minded items (Essex 1802, Law 1803, Middlesex 1807f, Deerfield 1808, Huntington 1809, Boston West 1810, Sacred 1810, Village 1810). To the south, ST. Thomas was printed in New York City (Erben 1806, Erben 1808), Baltimore (Cole 1804f, Cole 1808), and Pennsylvania (Cumberland 1804, Woodward 1806ff, Law 1807f, Blake 1810, and Wyeth 1810). It held its place in the next decade, appearing in more than forty tunebooks from the years 1811–1820. All eight of the retrospective northern collections carried ST. Thomas, which is found also in two of the southern tunebooks. Jackson lists it as one of the most popular "standard hymns" in tunebooks of the south (Jackson, p. 130).

The rhythm of this setting of ST. Thomas separates the first two phrases and joins the next two, thus helping to support the tune's graceful, disjunct arc and high-note climax in the third and fourth phrases. Temperley mentions ST. Thomas and others (Burford, Bedford, All Saints) as "country psalm tunes . . . with a tendency to elaboration . . . [showing] the country psalmodist's grasp of simple melody" (Temperley, 1:176).

Additional References

1. Read, No. 240
2. AH, p. 448; AMR 48; Hall; Hitchcock 119; MinA, p. 58
3. Baptist; Congregational; Episcopal; Lutheran; Methodist; Presbyterian

[84.] Sherburne, by Daniel Read

Text from Hymns, no. XXVI, p. 243; written by Nahum Tate (see Julian, p. 1275). First published in Daniel Read, *The American Singing Book* (New Haven, 1785). Read 1785, p. 53.

Sherburne, a C.M. fuging-tune, was printed 79 times. It was closely linked with the present text, although it was also printed with others.

Introduced in Connecticut (Read 1785ff), Sherburne received half of its printings in New England. It won quick acceptance into the repertory. Between 1786 and the end of 1790

SHERBURNE had appeared in nine more tunebooks: in Connecticut, Doolittle 1786 and Law 1786; in Massachusetts, Worcester 1786ff, Bayley 1788a, Federal 1788f, and Sacred 1788a; in New York City, Amphion 1789; and in Philadelphia, Adgate 1789ff and Selection 1789ff. In the next decade circulation broadened to include Maryland (Ely 1792), Virginia (Sandford 1793), New York (Atwill 1795f), New Hampshire (Village 1795ff), and South Carolina (Pilsbury 1799). At the same time, SHERBURNE continued to appear in New England (Brownson 1791, French 1793, Read 1794ff, Holden 1796f, Boston 1799), though less often after 1800 (Holden 1800, Robbins 1805, J. Read 1808). It remained a favorite, however, in Pennsylvania (Shumway 1793f, Little 1801, Cumberland 1804, Sacred 1806, Rothbaust 1807, Chapin 1808f, Blake 1810, Wyeth 1810) and New York (Huntington 1800, Atwill 1804, Little 1805ff, Erben 1806, Seymour 1809). Circulation fell off in the next decade, as fewer than ten collections in the sample from 1811–1820 carried it. However, SHERBURNE appears in seven of the northern retrospective collections, and it is found in three of the southern tunebooks.

SHERBURNE fuges the third and fourth lines of its text. The fuge lasts three times as long as the opening section, sung in block chords; it also sustains quarter-note motion for fifty beats and verbal conflict for eleven consecutive measures (mm. 7–17). By early in the nineteenth century, SHERBURNE had come to be identified with old-fashionedness in music. One source names "old Sherburne" as a favorite tune of "old folks" in Rockingham County, New York (Memoirs, p. 113). In the 1830s, the *Boston Musical Gazette* carried some articles on earlier New England psalmody; a letter from "A Country Clergyman" recounts two incidents that relate to Read's composition:

> The tune called SHERBURNE was sung about every other Sabbath, without regard to any thing in the psalm or hymn given out, except its metre; and even in this particular the thoughtless leader, so anxious for his favorite air, once made a wretched mistake, and set it to a long metre hymn, which, nevertheless, was sung through, from beginning to end, making puerility and folly more ridiculous, and blasphemy more shocking . . . [But SHERBURNE] had its sure death-blow on a certain evening, when the teacher, according to his custom, admitted spectators into the singing hall to hear the performances. One of the visitors, inclined somewhat to be officious, requested that SHERBURNE might be sung, alledging it to be his peculiar favorite. The master, a little piqued at the interference, observed that his school had not learned it, and therefore could not perform it, but, to gratify the solicitous gentleman, he would sing it himself, alone, to words which he thought highly fit and appropriate to the air, and exceedingly well adapted, and therefore would answer as a good illustration how sound and sense might be made to correspond; and, accordingly, he sang it to the following verse, as near as I can recollect it:

> They took the loafer by the nose,
> And thus, through thick and thin,
> They led him to the saw-mill brook,
> And there they sous'd him in!

(Quoted from Bushnell, p. 452)

Near the end of the century, S. P. Cheney, writing about William Billings's skill as a composer, noted: "In the fugue style, Daniel Read of Conn. equals him in 'Sherburne' " (Cheney, p. 169). A few years later, F. O. Jones named SHERBURNE, together with several other Core Repertory tunes by Read, as being "in general use at the present day and are likely to live for a long time to come. Windham, Sherburne, Russia, Stafford, and Lisbon are known to almost every church singer" (Jones, p. 143).

Additional References

1. Alderdice, p. 52
2. Hall; Hitchcock 73, 151, 162, (455)

Cross-Reference

See entry on STAFFORD.

[85.] SOUTHWELL
(CAMBRIDGE SHORT)

Text from Watts, Psalm 36, S.M. First published in William Damon, *The Psalms of David in English Meter* (London, 1579). First published in America in *The Psalms Hymns, and Spiritual Songs*, 9th ed. (Boston, 1698). Lyon 1761, p. 28.

SOUTHWELL, a duple-time S.M. common tune in minor mode, was printed 51 times. Most were textless, including Lyon 1761f, the musical source chosen here. The present text, printed in Tunes 1763, published in Philadelphia only two years after Lyon, is one of at least six texts with which SOUTHWELL appeared.

Introduced in Boston (Bay 1698ff), SOUTHWELL received 86 percent of its printings in New England, all but a few before 1775. The tune appeared in many of the tunebooks and supplements of the colonial period, both in New England (Brady 1713f, Walter 1721ff, Tufts 1723ff, Turner 1752, Johnston 1755f, Bayley 1764ff, Flagg 1764, Bayley 1767f, Gilman 1771) and Philadelphia (Dawson 1754, Lyon 1761f, Hopkinson 1763, Tunes 1763f). After a break of three decades, SOUTHWELL was reintroduced in New England by Holyoke 1803 and was then picked up by Blanchard 1807, Griswold 1807, and, in Baltimore, Cole 1808 and Cole 1810. It received some half-a-dozen printings in collections from the period 1811–1820. SOUTHWELL is not found in any of the retrospective northern tunebooks, nor does it appear in any of the southern collections that were canvassed.

In the present setting SOUTHWELL is kept free of all melodic decoration, its austerity further emphasized by the open sonorities that conclude three of the four phrases. In midphrase, however, the harmony consists of full triads, handled for the most part in an orthodox way. (M. 2, beat 2, is an exception.) Temperley notes a late seventeenth-century English publication that first prints a plain version of SOUTHWELL, and then adds: "The notes of the foregoing tune are usually broken or divided; and they are better so sung, as is here pricked." There follows an ornamented version of the tune—one reproduced in Stevenson, p. 27. (See Temperley, 1:94.) In the colonies, SOUTHWELL is recorded as being one of the tunes commonly sung in Farmington, Connecticut, before 1725. Congregations in three Massachusetts towns chose SOUTHWELL for singing in public worship: Weston (1724; 1 of 14 tunes), Needham (7 January 1729; 1 of 8 tunes), and Wilbraham (22 October 1770; 1 of 23 tunes).

Additional References

1. Read, No. 266
2. AH, p. 125; Frost 45; Temperley, 2:ex. 16
3. Congregational; Lutheran; Methodist; Presbyterian

Cross-Reference

See entry on PSALM 100 [OLD].

[86.] STAFFORD, by Daniel Read

Text from Watts, Psalm 118, S.M. First published in [Simeon Jocelin], *The Chorister's Companion* (New Haven, 1782). Little 1801, p. 87.

STAFFORD, a S.M. fuging-tune, was printed 85 times, making it, together with GREENWICH, Read's most widely published piece in his own time. Closely identified with the present text, it also appeared with at least five others.

Introduced in Connecticut (Jocelin 1782f), STAFFORD received 61 percent of its printings in New England. Within a few years of its publication, the tune had caught on in Connecticut (Read 1785ff, Langdon 1786, Law 1786), Massachusetts (Bayley 1785, Worcester 1786ff, Federal 1788ff, Sacred 1788), New York City (Amphion 1789), and Philadelphia (Selection 1788ff, Adgate 1789ff). Continuing in print in these four states during the 1790s (Read 1794ff; French 1793, Holdon 1793f, Mann 1797, Boston 1799; Atwill 1795f; Shumway 1793f), STAFFORD broadened its circulation to include eight states in all, adding Maryland (Ely 1792), Virginia (Sandford 1793), New Hampshire (Village 1795ff), and South Carolina (Pilsbury 1799) to the previous list. Unlike some other fuging-tunes, STAFFORD maintained some popularity in New England after 1800, appearing in eclectic works like Holyoke 1803, Holyoke 1804, Robbins 1805, Boston First 1806, Griswold 1807, Huntington 1807, Janes 1807 and J. Read 1808. It also held a place in tunebooks from Pennsylvania (Little 1801, Sacred 1806, Blake 1810, Wyeth 1810) and New York (Atwill 1804, Little 1805–08, Seymour 1809, Evans 1810). Circulation fell off in the next decade, as STAFFORD appeared in fewer than ten collections from the years 1811–1820. Later, however, it was printed in five retrospective northern collections, though none of the southern tunebooks examined included it.

STAFFORD lacks the kind of momentum generated by some of Read's other fuging-tunes—SHERBURNE or GREENWICH, for example—because only between the second and third phrases does the tune move ahead without a long pause. An unusual unifying element in STAFFORD is the II/V cadence that resolves to tonic in mm. 3–4 and mm. 18–19, and that stays on the dominant in mm. 7–8; moreover, the fourth phrase is a recomposed, altered version of the second. In 1818, Read himself published a version of STAFFORD "corrected by the author" (*The New Haven Collection* [New Haven]). Two decades later, Thomas Hastings, usually critical of the work of earlier American psalmodists, found Read worthy of praise: "Reed's compositions manifested some traits of genius. His Stafford was comparatively of a chaste and durable character" (Musical Magazine I; quoted in Bushnell, p. 460). Near the end of the century, STAFFORD was named as one of several Core Repertory pieces by Read "in general use at the present day and . . . likely to live for a long time to come" (Jones, p. 143; see SHERBURNE, above, for full quotation).

Additional References

1. Alderdice, p. 64
2. Hall

Cross-Reference

See entries on SHERBURNE and GREENWICH.

[87.] STANDISH
(BEDFORD, WENDOVER)

Text from Watts, Psalm 119, C.M., 4th Part. First published in *The Psalm-Singer's Necessary Companion* (London, 1700). First published in America in John Tufts, *An Introduction to the Art of Singing Psalm-Tunes*, 3d ed. (Boston, 1723). Adgate 1789, p. 3.

STANDISH, a C.M. piece in traditional common tune style, was printed 56 times. Most were textless, and STANDISH was never closely linked with any of the five texts with which it was published.

Introduced in Boston (Tufts 1723ff), STANDISH received 64 percent of its printings in New England, most of them in Massachusetts. The tune appeared in a succession of works in colo-

nial New England (Bay 1737f, Walter 1740, Turner 1752, Johnston 1755f, Walter 1760f, Bayley 1764ff, Flagg 1764, Bayley 1767f, Bayley 1770ff, Gilman 1771, New England 1771) and Philadelphia (Dawson 1754, Lyon 1761f, Hopkinson 1763). Printings thereafter were scattered chronologically and geographically among Connecticut (Law 1783, Benham 1790ff), Pennsylvania (Selection 1788ff, Adgate 1789ff, Cumberland 1804), Maryland (Arnold 1803), and Massachusetts (Middlesex 1807f). At least ten printings can be found from the decade 1811–1820. But STANDISH appeared in none of the northern retrospective collections or southern tunebooks that were canvassed.

STANDISH is another psalm tune that creates a satisfying shape with simple means. Unadorned until the last phrase, the melody moves within the range of a fifth, managing to touch the tonic only at the beginning and the end, but still sustaining interest by playing with the fifth and the second. In 1723, the Reverend Thomas Symmes reported that STANDISH "has been sung for many years (as I am inform'd) in the church of N[orth] Hampton, [Massachusetts]" (Symmes, p. 25). Three New England congregations voted to approve the tune for performing in public worship, Weston (1724; 1 of 14 tunes) and Wilbraham, Massachusetts (22 October 1770; 1 of 23 tunes), and Harwinton, Connecticut (4 June 1776; 1 of 22 tunes).

Additional References

1. Alderdice, p. 87; Read, No. 94
2. AH, p. 166

Cross-Reference

See entry on LEBANON.

[88.] SUFFIELD, by Oliver King

Text from Watts, Psalm 39, C.M., 2d Part. First published in Andrew Law, *Select Harmony* ([Cheshire, Connecticut], 1779). Law 1792, p. 48.

SUFFIELD, a C.M. tune in minor mode, was printed 61 times. It was closely identified with the present text, appearing with only one other, and that in only a single tunebook.

Introduced in Connecticut (Law 1779f), SUFFIELD received 52 percent of its printings in New England. In the decade after its first publication, SUFFIELD was reprinted in ten new collections: seven in Massachusetts (Bayley 1784, Mass 1784f, New 1784, Worcester 1786–97, Bayley 1788, Federal 1788ff, Sacred 1788) and the others in Connecticut (Jocelin 1782) and Philadelphia (Selection 1788ff, Adgate 1789ff). Thereafter, its popularity in New England waned, with Law 1791f, Village 1796ff, Boston 1799, and Robbins 1805 the only works there to print it. In the meantime, however, SUFFIELD had also appeared in Maryland (Ely 1792), New Jersey (New Jersey 1797), and South Carolina (Pilsbury 1799), as well as in Philadelphia (Shumway 1793f, Poor 1794). Printings after 1800 were centered in Pennsylvania (Cumberland 1804, Sacred 1806, Woodward 1806ff, Rothbaust 1807, Blake 1810, Wyeth 1810), but Arnold 1803 (Hagerstown, Maryland) also included it. Moderate circulation continued in the next decade, with at least ten printings found in the period 1811–1820. None of the later northern retrospective collections carried SUFFIELD, but it was a favorite in the south, appearing in four of the five tunebooks canvassed.

SUFFIELD moves in spurts of quarter-note motion. The melody is often decorated and is divided by whole-note cadences, except for the fourth phrase, which leads back to a repeat of the last two phrases. Frequent open intervals (mm. 1, 2, 3, 9, 11), parallel motion (mm. 2, 5, 7), and harmonic clashes (m. 3, beats 1 and 2; m. 5, beat 1; m. 11, beats 1 and 2) create an environment within which a full triad like the one in m. 6—to which an enriching fifth voice has been added—sounds especially ravishing. The attribution to King is explained in Crawford MM.

Additional Reference

1. Alderdice, p. 49

[89.] SUTTON
(OLD SUTTON)

Text from Watts, Psalm 19, S.M., 1st Part. First published in *Harmonia Sacra, or a Choice Collection of Psalm and Hymn Tunes* (London, ca. 1760), or before. First published in America in Josiah Flagg, *A Collection of the Best Psalm Tunes* (Boston, 1764). Deerfield 1808, p. 111.

SUTTON, a major-mode S.M. tune in triple time, was printed 61 times. Of the ten texts with which it appeared, SUTTON was more closely identified with the present one than with any other.

Introduced in Boston (Flagg 1764), SUTTON received 95 percent of its printings in New England, the highest proportion of any Core Repertory piece. Most occurred in Massachusetts publications. During the colonial period, SUTTON was picked up by such Massachusetts imprints as Williams 1769ff, Bayley 1770ff, New England 1771, and Stickney 1774ff. In the century's last two decades, Law 1781, Jocelin 1782, and Law 1791f in Connecticut printed it, as did a succession of Massachusetts items: Bayley 1784, Mass 1784f, New 1784, Worcester 1786–92, Bayley 1788, Sacred 1788, Federal 1790–93, and Boston 1799. The turn of the century brought appearances in New Hampshire (Village 1800ff, Blanchard 1808) and Connecticut (Griswold 1807, Jenks 1810); but it was also printed in fifteen new Massachusetts tunebooks, both eclectic—Brown 1802ff, French 1802, Holyoke 1803, Cooper 1804, Holyoke 1804, Boston First 1806, Mann 1807—and reform-minded—Essex 1802, Law 1803, Salem 1805f, Middlesex 1807f, Deerfield 1808, Boston Brattle 1810, Boston West 1810, Sacred 1810. Outside New England, SUTTON appeared only in Law 1807f and Wyeth 1810, both published in Pennsylvania. Wide circulation continued in the next decade as SUTTON appeared in more than thirty collections from the years 1811–1820. It was included in two of the later retrospective northern collections but in none of the southern items.

SUTTON, the only major-mode S.M. tune in triple time, begins with a bold, disjunct ascent that supports the declamation and meaning of the present text admirably. In later phrases, decoration softens the melodic profile, which proceeds mostly in stepwise motion.

Additional References

1. Alderdice, p. uu; Read, No. 232
2. AH, p. 171; Hall (no attribution; may be other SUTTON)

[90.] SUTTON, by Ezra Goff
(SUTTON NEW)

Text from Watts, Psalm 69, C.M., 1st Part. First published in Jacob French, *The Psalmodist's Companion* (Worcester, 1793) or Nehemiah Shumway, *The American Harmony* (Philadelphia, 1793). Chapin 1808, p. 41.

SUTTON, a duple-time C.M. fuging-tune in minor mode, was printed 45 times. It was closely identified with the present text, and only one alternative text, appearing in just a single tunebook, has been found.

Introduced in the same year by collections in Massachusetts (French 1793) and Pennsylvania (Shumway 1793f), SUTTON received about half of its printings in New England. Within a short time of its first publication, SUTTON, though appearing in few collections, had achieved wide geographical dispersion, to

New Hampshire (Village 1795ff), Connecticut (Griswold 1796f), and New Jersey (New Jersey 1797); after 1800, circulation broadened further to include New York (Little 1805–08, Erben 1806, Seymour 1809) and Delaware (Fobes 1809) as well. In the meantime, appearances in non-reform New England tunebooks (Jenks 1801, Read 1804ff, Maxim 1805f, Belknap 1806f, J. Read 1808, Sanger 1808) balanced a run of printings in Pennsylvania (Little 1801, Aitken 1806, Sacred 1806, Woodward 1806ff, Chapin 1808f, Blake 1810, Wyeth 1810) and New Jersey (Smith 1803f). Circulation slowed in the next decade with fewer than ten printings appearing in collections from the years 1811–1820. SUTTON is also found in two of the retrospective northern collections and in one of the southern tunebooks that have been canvassed.

SUTTON, a standard four-line fuging-tune with the third and fourth lines fuged, is the only Core Repertory fuging-tune to present its first two lines in continuous quarter-note declamation, with no cadence separating them. The fuging section then follows the same technique, which it sustains exactly twice as long as the opening: 26 beats to 13.

Additional References

1. Alderdice, p. 124
2. Hall (no attribution; may be other SUTTON)

[91.] VIRGINIA, by Oliver Brownson
Text from Watts, Psalm 89, C.M., 2d Part, stanzas 4–6. First published in [Simeon Jocelin], *The Chorister's Companion* (New Haven, 1782). Worcester 1788, p. 55.

VIRGINIA, a duple-time C.M. tune-with-extension, was printed 92 times. It was closely identified with the present text, with which it was linked in almost all appearances.

Introduced in Connecticut (Jocelin 1782f), VIRGINIA received 51 percent of its printings in New England. The tune quickly established itself in Connecticut (Brownson 1783ff, Langdon 1786, Law 1786, Read 1787ff) and also in Massachusetts (Bayley 1785a, Worcester 1786ff, Bayley 1788, Sacred 1788), New York City (Amphion 1789), and Philadelphia (Selection 1788ff, Adgate 1789ff). In the 1790s, printings reached eight states: Maryland (Ely 1792), Virginia (Sandford 1793), New Hampshire (Village 1795ff), and South Carolina (Pilsbury 1799), as well as Connecticut (Read 1794ff), Massachusetts (Federal 1790–93, Holden 1793f, Mann 1797, Boston 1799), New York (Atwill 1795f), and Pennsylvania (Shumway 1793f, Poor 1794). New England printings dropped off in the last decade (Holden 1800, Robbins 1805, Bushnell 1807, Janes 1807, J. Read 1808). But compilers in New York (Seymour 1803f, Atwill 1804, Little 1805ff, Erben 1806, Seymour 1809) and Pennsylvania (Little 1801, Cumberland 1804, Sacred 1806, Woodward 1806ff, Rothbaust 1807, Chapin 1808f, Blake 1810, Wyeth 1810) continued to print it. Circulation declined even further in the next decade, as VIRGINIA appeared in only about a dozen collections in the years 1811–1820. The tune was included in five later retrospective northern collections and two southern tunebooks.

Flexible text declamation is a notable feature of VIRGINIA. Each of the tune's four phrases has its own rhythmic organization, and the fourth, marked with descriptive melismas on "rolling," is repeated to new music as well as being included in a repetition of the piece's second half. Harmonically, the chord built on the fifth scale degree is either minor or open in all appearances (mm. 2, 4, 6, 12) except its last (m. 15), where the D-sharp turns it into a true dominant. The author of an account describing psalmody in early nineteenth-century New Hampshire refers to VIRGINIA as a piece "of rapid and animated movement in which all the parts continued uninterrupted to the close" (Memoirs, p. 96).

Additional References

1. Alderdice, p. 293
2. Hall

[92.] WALSALL
(DURHAM)

Text from Watts, Psalm 5, C.M. First published in *A Choice Collection of Psalm-Tunes, Hymns and Anthems. Taught by William Anchors* (London, ca. 1726?). First published in America by James Lyon, *Urania* (Philadelphia, 1761). Bayley 1784, p. 182.

WALSALL, a duple-time C.M. tune in minor mode, was printed 58 times. It was not closely associated with any of the dozen texts with which it appeared, and it was often printed without any text at all.

Introduced in Philadelphia (Lyon 1761f), WALSALL received 62 percent of its printings in New England. Its printing history before 1800 was spotty: a flurry of Massachusetts items of the late colonial years carried it (Tans'ur 1767f, Tans'ur 1769ff, Williams 1769ff, Stickney 1774f), as did three New England works of the 1780s (Law 1783, Bayley 1784, Jocelin 1788) and one Philadelphia tunebook from the 1790s (Adgate 1791ff). After 1800, WALSALL caught on. Several New England reform collections picked it up (Essex 1802, Law 1803, Salem 1805f, Middlesex 1807f, Blanchard 1808, Wood 1810) and so did some more eclectic ones (Brown 1802f, Holyoke 1803, Boston First 1806, Village 1806, Mann 1807, Read 1807f, Village 1808f). To the south, WALSALL appeared in five new Pennsylvania collections (Cumberland 1804, Woodward 1806ff, Law 1807f, Chapin 1808f, Blake 1810) and four from Maryland (Cole 1805, Cole 1808, Gillet 1809, Cole 1810). Circulation continued strong in the decade 1811–1820, as WALSALL appeared in more than twenty-five different collections from that period. However, only one later retrospective northern collection, and none of the southern tunebooks, carried it.

WALSALL demonstrates the kind of melodic decoration that began to appear in English psalmody during the first half of the eighteenth century. The pitches sung on the first and third beats of each measure in the tenor form the tune's basic structure; the rest are passing or embellishmental tones, introduced to smooth its rather angular contour. This process is extended to the other voice-parts as well.

Additional References

1. Read, No. 98
2. AMR 56; Hall (attributed to Madan)
3. Congregational; Episcopal; Presbyterian

[93.] WANTAGE

Text from Watts, Psalm 89, C.M., 2d Part. Probably first published shortly before its first known appearance in Aaron Williams, *The Universal Psalmodist* (London, 1763). First published in America in Josiah Flagg, *A Collection of the Best Psalm Tunes* (Boston, 1764). Selection 1788, p. 76.

WANTAGE, a triple-time C.M. tune in minor mode, was printed 68 times. All printings before 1788 were textless, and WANTAGE was never closely identified with any single text, though it did appear with the present one more often than with any other.

Introduced in Massachusetts (Flagg 1764), WANTAGE received 72 percent of its printings in New England. As many as seven of Daniel Bayley's publications (from Bayley 1766 to Bayley 1788) carried it, as did New England 1771, Mass 1784f, New 1784, and Sacred 1788, all from Massachusetts, and Law 1781, Jocelin 1782f, and Langdon 1786 from Connecticut. WANTAGE was introduced in Philadelphia by Selection 1788, followed by Adgate 1789ff and Shumway 1793f. Other printings in the

1790s were scattered between New England (Read 1794, Boston 1799) and New York State (Atwill 1795f). After 1800 WANTAGE was picked up in New England both by reform collections (Salem 1806, Middlesex 1807f, Blanchard 1808, Deerfield 1808, Boston West 1810) and by more eclectic tunebooks (Brown 1802ff, Holyoke 1803, Village 1803ff, Collection 1804, Boston First 1806, Huntington 1807, Mann 1807). It also appeared in Albany (Atwill 1804), Pennsylvania (Sacred 1806, Wyeth 1810) and Baltimore (Gillet 1809). The tune appeared in at least twenty-seven collections from the years 1811–1820. It was also picked up by two of the later retrospective northern collections, though none of the southern tunebooks carried it.

WANTAGE, the only four-line Core Repertory composition whose phrases all end on the tonic, shows special eccentricity in its cadence-practice (mm. 3, 6, 10), only once (m. 13) reaching the tonic through a dominant in root position, albeit a thirdless dominant. WANTAGE was chosen for singing in public worship by congregations in Wilbraham, Massachusetts (22 October 1770; 1 of 23 tunes), and Harwinton, Connecticut (4 June 1776; 1 of 22 tunes). Early in the nineteenth century, compiler Jonathan Huntington cited it, apparently as an example of dignified solemnity. "By long experience," he wrote, "I find that there is as many different tastes for Music, as other things. Some will be pleased with Old Hundred, Bath, Plymouth, Wantage &c. Others would prefer light and airy tunes" (Huntington 1807).

Additional References

1. Read, No. 117
2. Hall (attributed to Tans'ur); Hitchcock 174

[94.] WELLS, by Israel Holdroyd
(RUGBY)

Text from Watts, Hymns I, no. 88. First published in Israel Holdroyd, *The Spiritual-Man's Companion* (London, ca. 1724). First published in America in James Lyon, *Urania* (Philadelphia, 1761). Shumway 1793, p. 24.

WELLS, a duple-time L.M. tune in major mode, was printed 160 times—second only to PSALM 100 [OLD] in total number of printings. All appearances before 1786 were textless; thereafter, WELLS was published with at least twenty-two different texts, though the present one appeared with it more often than any other.

From the time of its introduction in Philadelphia (Lyon 1761f), WELLS was a favorite at all times and in all places, with New England collections accounting for two-thirds of its printings. By 1790 WELLS had appeared in fifteen different collections in Massachusetts (from Johnston 1763 to Sacred 1788, and including seven of Daniel Bayley's publications). It was also established in New Hampshire (Gilman 1771), Connecticut (Law 1779, Law 1781, Jocelin 1782f), and Philadelphia (Selection 1788ff, Adgate 1789ff). Within the next decade WELLS appeared in nine states, including Maryland (Ely 1792, Cole 1799), Virginia (Sandford 1793), New Hampshire (Village 1795ff), New York (Atwill 1795f), New Jersey (New Jersey 1797), and South Carolina (Pilsbury 1799) as well as Massachusetts (Holden 1793ff, Boston 1799), Connecticut (Benham 1790ff, Law 1791f, Law 1794f, Read 1794ff, Bull 1795), and Pennsylvania (Shumway 1793f, Poor 1794). After 1800, forty-five new collections printed WELLS—a total exceeded only by OLD HUNDRED—including twenty-three in Massachusetts, nine in Pennsylvania, and seven in New York, as well as a scattering elsewhere, and also including works of every stylistic persuasion. Circulation continued unabated in the next decade, with more than forty-five printings in tunebooks from the period 1811–1820. WELLS also appeared in seven later retrospective northern collections and four southern tunebooks. Jackson named it as one of the most popular "standard hymns" in the south (Jackson, p. 130).

Each of the four phrases of WELLS follows the same rhythm, involving pairs of dactyls. Melodic integration unifies the piece even more closely: the cadential figure in mm. 3–4 is also used to end the third phrase at the same pitch (mm. 11–12); transposed down a fifth, it ends the second and fourth phrases, too. And the fourth phrase begins (mm. 13–14) as a downward transposition of the beginning of the third (mm. 9–10). When musical reform was launched early in the nineteenth century in the town of Atkinson, New Hampshire, the new musical director chose WELLS as the first piece for the "reformed" choir to sing (Memoirs, p. 10; see also p. 96).

Additional References

1. Alderdice, p. 65; Eckhard, No. 0.2; Read, No. 191
2. Hall; Hitchcock 174

Cross-References

See entries on PSALM 100 [OLD], ROCHESTER, WINDHAM.

[95.] WESTON FAVEL, by William Knapp
(WESTON FLAVEL)

Text from Watts, Hymns I, no. 62. First published in William Knapp, *A Sett of New Psalm-Tunes and Anthems* (London, 1738). First published in America in Josiah Flagg, *A Collection of the Best Psalm Tunes* (Boston, 1764) or [Daniel Bayley], *A New and Compleat Introduction to the Grounds and Rules of Musick* (Newburyport, 1764). Cooper 1804, p. 79.

WESTON FAVEL, a triple-time tune-with-extension in C.M., was printed 46 times. It was usually set to the present text, though it sometimes appeared textless, and printings with at least four other texts have also been found.

Introduced in Boston (Bayley 1764ff or Flagg 1764), WESTON FAVEL received less than half of its printings in New England (43 percent). Printed during the colonial period also by Walter 1764a, Williams 1769ff, and Stickney 1774f in Massachusetts and Gilman 1771 in New Hampshire, WESTON FAVEL next appeared in Philadelphia (Selection 1788ff, Adgate 1791ff, Poor 1794). Later printings were scattered among Massachusetts (Holden II 1793, Holden 1800, Law 1803, Cooper 1804, Middlesex 1807f), Pennsylvania (Cumberland 1804, Aitken 1806, Woodward 1806ff, Law H 1810, Blake 1810), New York City (Erben 1806, Erben 1808, Evans 1808f), Baltimore (Cole 1808), and Virginia (Tomlins 1810). Circulation dropped off in the next decade, and only seven printings have been found in collections from the years 1811–1820. WESTON FAVEL appears in none of the later retrospective collections from the north, nor in any southern tunebooks.

WESTON FAVEL, perhaps the sprightliest of the iambic Core Repertory tunes, is called by Routley "a musical herald of the evangelical Revival" whose "exuberant melody is the natural accompaniment and expression of that ecstatic individualism" brought into English Protestantism by the Wesleyan Methodists. Routley also notes WESTON FAVEL's "repeat of the words for the sake of the tune" (Routley 1957, pp. 89, 91–92). See also the Preface, above, p. xiii.

Additional Reference

1. Read, No. 59

[96.] WINCHESTER
(HARLEM)

Text from Watts, Psalm 141, L.M. First published in *Musicalisch Hand-Buch* (Hamburg, 1690). First published in America in A. Williams, *The American Harmony, or Universal Psalmodist*, vol.

II of Daniel Bayley, *The American Harmony*, 5th ed. (Newburyport, 1769). Deerfield 1808, p. 132.

WINCHESTER, a triple-time L.M. tune in major mode, was printed 52 times. It appeared most often with the present text, though at least ten others were printed with it, and some printings were textless.

Introduced in Massachusetts (Williams 1769ff), WINCHESTER received 85 percent of its printings in New England collections, most of them in the last three decades of the period. Except for Williams, only Stickney 1774f carried it during the colonial era. After the war, Jocelin 1782 and Law 1783 printed it in Connecticut, followed by Mass 1784f, Worcester 1786–92, Federal 1788–93, and Sacred 1788 in Massachusetts. In the next decade WINCHESTER was picked up in New York (Atwill 1795f) and South Carolina (Pilsbury 1799), appearing also in three new Massachusetts works (Holden 1793f, Gram 1795, Boston 1799). After 1800 WINCHESTER appeared in a few eclectic tunebooks in various locales (Holyoke 1803, Village 1803ff, Atwill 1804, Cooper 1804, Boston First 1806, Gamut 1807, Suffolk 1807, Blake 1810), but reform-minded works were more apt to carry it (Essex 1802, Cole 1805, Olmsted 1805, Salem 1805f, Erben 1806, Erben 1808, Middlesex 1807f, Deerfield 1808, Boston Brattle 1810, Boston West 1810, Brown 1810). Circulation remained vigorous in the next decade, as more than thirty collections from the years 1811–1820 included it. WINCHESTER also appeared in six later retrospective northern collections and in one southern tunebook.

WINCHESTER stands out among Core Repertory pieces for its wide melodic range of an eleventh and its frequent use of chords on the supertonic (mm. 2–3, 5, 9, 11), including a startling secondary dominant (m. 13) that requires the counter to sing an unusual chromatic alteration: F/F-sharp/G.

Additional References

1. Eckhard, No. 17; Read, No. 173
2. AMR 2; Hall (attributed to Williams)
3. Congregational; Episcopal; Methodist; Presbyterian

[97.] WINDHAM, by Daniel Read
(WINDSOR)

Text from Watts, Hymns II, no. 158. First published in Daniel Read, *The American Singing Book* (New Haven, 1785). Village 1800, p. 17.

WINDHAM, a minor-mode L.M. tune in duple time, was printed 65 times. Closely identified with the present text, it nevertheless received isolated printings with four others, and a few textless printings also occurred.

Introduced in Connecticut (Read 1785ff), WINDHAM received 69 percent of its printings in New England. Picked up by several Massachusetts collections of the later 1780s and 1790s—Bayley 1788a, Federal 1788ff, Worcester 1792ff, Holden 1793ff, Mann 1797f, Boston 1799—WINDHAM also appeared in Village 1795ff and Merrill 1799, and, outside New England, in Atwill 1795f (New York State) and Pilsbury 1799 (Charleston, South Carolina). After the turn of the century, circulation broadened to touch nine states in all—including New Jersey (Smith 1803f), Maryland (Cole 1804f, Gillet 1809), Delaware (Fobes 1809), and Pennsylvania (Peck 1810, Wyeth 1810). At the same time, it continued strong in New York State and City (Huntington 1800, Edson 1801f, Atwill 1804, Erben 1806, Erben 1808, Little 1809f, Seymour 1809) and in New England collections, most of them eclectic: Read 1804ff, Albee 1805, Robbins 1805, Boston First 1806, Jenks 1806, Mann 1807, Suffolk 1807, Maxim 1808, Peck 1808, J. Read 1808, and Jenks 1810. In the next decade, 1811–1820, WINDHAM appeared in twenty-five more collections, topping all other American-composed Core Repertory tunes except, perhaps, BROOKFIELD. It also was published in six later retrospective northern collections and in all five of the southern tunebooks canvassed. Jackson names it as one of the most popular "standard hymns" in southern tunebooks (Jackson, p. 130).

For its first three phrases WINDHAM is a direct rhythmic copy of WELLS (see p. 154). Then, however, it abandons its paired dactyls and moves purposefully in quarter-notes to a final cadence. Although it was not published until 1785, WINDHAM may have been composed as early as 1775, the date of a manuscript tunebook by Read in which it appears. Bushnell includes that version side by side with two others: the 1785 printing and one from "Musica Ecclesia," a manuscript that Read worked on in the 1820s and 1830s (see Bushnell, pp. 479ff). WINDHAM was one of very few early American tunes to win any praise from nineteenth-century American musicians. Thomas Hastings noted in the 1830s: "Windham is yet in favor, and has been on the whole a very useful tune" (Musical Magazine I; quoted in Bushnell, p. 460). A few years later, an unidentified correspondent to the *Boston Musical Gazette* reported:

> The writer is not among those who would reject every piece of music composed by our American authors of former days. Jordan and Brookfield, by Billings, Windham, by Read . . . and Coronation by Holden, are excellent, and not discreditable to musical genius, and their insertion in the Boston publications is honorable to the compilers (ca. 1838; quoted in Bushnell, p. 457).

Nearly half-a-century later, WINDHAM was still holding its own, being named as one of Read's tunes "still in general use at the present day and . . . likely to live for a long time to come" (Jones, p. 143). S. P. Cheney printed the following statement from a pioneer historian of music in New England: "Lisbon and Windham have embalmed the memory of the good man [Read] for generations to come. [signed:] Geo. Hood. White Lake, Sull. Co., N.Y. June 25, 1878." Cheney added his own postscript to Hood's endorsement, however: "There is doubt about [Read's] being the author of Windham. [Charles] Zeuner says he took it from Luther's choral, and if you will examine that tune in this book you may agree with him" (Cheney, p. 173).

The question of Read's authorship of WINDHAM was not new in the 1870s. In fact, it had been addressed at length by the scholarly Lowell Mason in the Musical Magazine III (1841–42). In view of Mason's well-known disaffection with the music of his American predecessors, his comments on the subject deserve to be quoted at length.

> I observe that in your last number [LXII], p. 157, you ascribe the psalm tune *Windham,* which is found in all our books of Church music, to Luther. In speaking of a certain monotony of rhythmical arrangement, your words are, "and even one of Luther's chorals is arranged that way—Windham, L.M." Now, sir, with all due respect for the excellent Editor of the Musical Magazine, and for the accuracy which in general characterizes that work, I beg leave to say that he has fallen into an error here. The tune *Windham,* is an original composition of the late Daniel Read of New Haven, Conn., and was first published in one of his books 40 or 50 years ago. I have taken particular pains to ascertain the facts in this matter, (the tune having been called a German Choral in one of the collections of psalmody published in Boston some six or eight years since,) and I am entirely satisfied that to our own countryman belongs the credit of this popular tune. . . . And it is a fine tune we may well be proud of; it has been sung for half a century, and it will probably continue to be sung longer than any other piece of music that has ever yet been composed on this side the Atlantic. . . . *Windham is an American tune,* and since it is one of the very few worth hav-

ing, I beg you will not try to take it from us (Quoted in Bushnell, pp. 458–59).

Additional References

1. Alderdice, p. 350; Read, No. 214
2. AH, p. 223; Hall; Hitchcock 119, 175, (458); MinA, p. 126
3. Lutheran; Methodist

Cross-References

See entries on CORONATION, LISBON, SHERBURNE.

[98.] WINDSOR
(OLD WINDSOR)

Text from Watts, Hymns II, no. 107. First published in William Damon, *The Former Booke of the Musicke of M. William Damon* ([London], 1591). First published in America in *The Psalms Hymns, and Spiritual Songs,* 9th ed. (Boston, 1698). Village 1800, p. 23.

WINDSOR, a duple-time C.M. common tune in minor mode, was printed 119 times. Many printings were textless, and WINDSOR appeared with more than twenty different texts in all, though the present stanzas were more frequently linked with it than any other.

Introduced in Boston (Bay 1698ff), WINDSOR received more than 80 percent of its printings in New England. A standard in New England colonial collections (Brady 1713f, Walter 1721ff, Tufts 1723ff, Turner 1752, Johnston 1755f, Bayley 1764ff, Flagg 1764, Bayley 1767f, Tans'ur 1767f, Tans'ur 1769ff, Bayley 1770f, Gilman 1771, New England 1771, Stickney 1774), WINDSOR appeared also in colonial Philadelphia (Dawson 1754, Lyon 1761f). During the 1780s and 1790s, printings continued in Massachusetts (Mass 1784f, New 1784, Worcester 1786, Sacred 1788, Federal 1790–93, Gram 1795, Holden 1796, Boston 1799), Connecticut (Jocelin 1788, Read 1794f, Bull 1795), New York City (Amphion 1789), and Philadelphia (Shumway 1793f), extending southward as well into Virginia (Sandford 1793) and South Carolina (Pilsbury 1799). After 1800, WINDSOR appeared in a half-dozen new New York tunebooks (Huntington 1800, Jackson 1804, Atwill 1806, Erben 1806, Erben 1808, Evans 1808f) as well as in three in Philadelphia (Aitken 1806, Sacred 1806, Law 1807f), pairs in Baltimore (Cole 1808, Cole 1810) and New Hampshire (Village 1800ff, Blanchard 1808), and one in Connecticut (Read 1807f). Its most enthusiastic acceptance, however, came in Massachusetts, where seventeen new tunebooks carried it, including a few eclectic items (Brown 1802ff, Cooper 1804, Hill 1806, Mann 1807) and a long roster of reform collections: Law 1803, Salem 1805f, Middlesex 1807f, and Boston West 1810, as well as many others. Circulation continued widespread in the next decade, as WINDSOR appeared in more than thirty-five different collections from the years 1811–1820. Every one of the later retrospective northern collections (eight) carries WINDSOR, which also appears in one of the southern items examined.

The link between WINDSOR and COLESHILL has already been shown (see entry on COLESHILL, above). The melodic structure of WINDSOR deserves comment as well: its third phrase (mm. 9–13) is built from parts of its second (cf. mm. 5–7 and mm. 9–11) and first phrases (cf. mm. 3–4 and mm. 12–13); and the first five notes of its fourth phrase repeat the ends of the first (mm. 2–4) and third phrases (mm. 11–13). WINDSOR was being sung in the colonies before it was printed on this side of the Atlantic. Samuel Sewall recorded in his diary that in his post as precentor of the South Church in Boston, he "sung the 27 Ps. 7–10. I set Windsor Tune and burst so into Tears that I could scarce continue singing" (Sewall Diary, 13 August 1695, p. 337). Some years later, when requested to "set the tune" by the preacher, he "intended Windsor, and fell into High-Dutch, and then essaying to set another tune, went into a Key much too high" (Sewall Diary, 28 December 1705, p. 538). In the 1720s, the congregation at Weston, Massachusetts, chose WINDSOR for singing in public worship (1724; 1 of 14 tunes), while, nearly half a century later, the congregation at Wilbraham, Massachusetts, did the same (22 October 1770; 1 of 23 tunes). WINDSOR was reported also as 1 of 5 tunes sung on 19 October 1781 at a service of worship in Brimfield, Massachusetts. In the Hutchinson Partbook (1763; probably copied in Pennsylvania), the following text was provided for a two-voice setting of WINDSOR (here entitled DUNDEE):

> This Dundee is a famous Place
> Surrounded with a Wall
> Where brave Argile the Battle won
> With powder and with ball.

By the turn of the century, WINDSOR, now more than two centuries old, was being held up by some American psalmodists as the epitome of sacred music:

> None will object, that the Music is too dull and antiquated; for, after passing through all the grades of improvement, men will at last come to admire the old slow church Music; and will consider the use of Old Hundred and Windsor, as evidence of a correct taste (Brown 1802).

Additional References

1. Eckhard, No. 41; Read, No. 97
2. AH, p. 55; Fisher, p. 1; Frost 129; Hall (attributed to Kirby); Hitchcock 148, 158, 175, 192, (20); Temperley, 2:ex. 15a, 18
3. Congregational; Episcopal; Lutheran; Methodist

Cross-References

See entries on BANGOR, COLESHILL, LEBANON, PSALM 100 [OLD].

[99.] WINTER, by Daniel Read

Text from Watts, Psalm 147, C.M., stanzas 5-8. First published in Daniel Read, *The American Singing Book* (New Haven, 1785). Worcester 1797, p. 63.

WINTER, a major-mode C.M. tune in duple time, was printed 52 times. It was closely identified with the present text, though two others, both on wintry subjects, also appeared with it.

WINTER received 85 percent of its printings in New England. Introduced in Connecticut (Read 1785ff), it was published there only by its composer (Read 1794ff) and, much later, Jenks 1810. Its acceptance in Massachusetts was swift, including five new collections in three years' time—Worcester 1786ff, Bayley 1788, Federal 1788-93, Sacred 1788, Federal 1792f—but then leveling off to only eight in the next twenty-two: Holden 1793ff, Mann 1797, Boston 1799, Holden 1800, Holyoke 1804, Holyoke 1807, Janes 1807, and J. Read 1808. Village 1795ff and Merrill 1799 made it available to singers in the north. Outside New England, circulation was widely dispersed but sparse, including appearances in Pennsylvania (Shumway 1793f, Sacred 1806, Wyeth 1810), the Hudson Valley (N. Billings 1795), South Carolina (Pilsbury 1799), and Delaware (Fobes 1809). Substantial circulation continued in the next decade, with appearances in at least fourteen collections from the years 1811-1820. WINTER also appeared in six retrospective northern collections and in four southern tunebooks.

WINTER shows Daniel Read working in a style closer than any of his other Core Repertory pieces to that of the Methodists. Especially noteworthy is the ornamentation of the melodic line in the second half. This seems to invite a lighter, more flexible kind of singing than is called for in the fuging-tunes, with their frequent repeated notes and spurts of quarter-note declamation. *The New Haven Collection* (New Haven, 1818) carries a version of WINTER "corrected by the author."

Additional References

1. Alderdice, p. 44; Read, No. 19
2. Hall

[100.] WORCESTER, by Abraham Wood

Text from Watts, Hymns I, no. 10. First published in Andrew Law, *Select Harmony* (Cheshire, Connecticut, 1778). Selection 1788, p. 54.

WORCESTER, a S.M. fuging-tune that sets two stanzas of text, was printed 61 times. All printings examined set the present text.

WORCESTER received 59 percent of its printings in New England. Introduced in Connecticut (Law 1778f), the tune enjoyed its heyday in the next two decades, appearing in tunebooks in Massachusetts (Stickney 1783, Bayley 1784, Bayley 1785, Worcester 1786ff, Bayley 1788, Federal 1788-93, Holden 1793ff, Stone 1793, Mann 1797, Boston 1799), Pennsylvania (Selection 1788ff, Adgate 1789ff, Shumway 1793f), Connecticut (Law 1791f), Maryland (Ely 1792), New York (Amphion 1789, Atwill 1795f), New Hampshire (Village 1795ff), and South Carolina (Pilsbury 1799). In the decade following the turn of the century, circulation dropped to a scattering of only five new tunebooks: Holden 1800, Atwill 1804, Sacred 1806, Rothbaust 1807, Blake 1810. Circulation came nearly to a halt in the next decade, with only two printings found in collections from the period 1811-1820. WORCESTER appears, however, in seven northern retrospective collections and in two southern tunebooks.

WORCESTER is unique among Core Repertory fuging-tunes for its long opening antiphonal section, for the varied ways in which it repeats the last two lines in each stanza of text, and for its fuge's carrying out of strict imitation for two full measures in each voice. Toward the end of the nineteenth century, S. P. Cheney, looking back at American psalmody a hundred years earlier, proclaimed WORCESTER "excellent," calling it one of the outstanding compositions of that age (p. 169).

Additional References

1. Alderdice, p. 170
2. Hitchcock 119, 122, (533); MinA, p. 138

[101.] YORK
(STILT)

Text from Watts, Hymns I, no. 95. First published in *The CL. Psalmes of David, in Scottish Meter* (Edinburgh, 1615). First published in America in *The Psalms Hymns, and Spiritual Songs*, 9th ed. (Boston, 1698). Deerfield 1808, p. 135.

YORK, a duple-time C.M. common tune in major mode, was printed 57 times. Most appearances were textless, and the tune was linked closely to none of the seven different texts with which it appeared.

More than 90 percent of the printings of YORK occurred in New England, most of them in Massachusetts during the colonial period. Introduced in Boston (Bay 1698ff), YORK appeared in most early New England supplements and tunebooks (Brady 1713f, Walter 1721ff, Tufts 1723ff, Turner 1752, Johnston 1755f, Bayley 1764ff, Flagg 1764, Bayley 1767f, Bayley 1770ff, Gilman 1771, and New England 1771) and in Philadelphia as well (Dawson 1754, Hopkinson 1763). Its only printing in the century's last two decades was Law 1783. But after 1800 it made a comeback in Massachusetts, mostly in reform collections (Holyoke 1803, Salem 1805f, Middlesex 1807f, Deerfield 1808, Boston West 1810, Brown 1810), and Baltimore (Cole 1805, Cole 1810).

Circulation continued in the next decade, with appearances in twenty-one collections from the years 1811–1820. Only one retrospective northern collection and one southern tunebook carried YORK.

The third phrase of the melody of YORK is a direct repetition of the first, producing the melodic form ABAC, rare among common tunes from the British Isles. Also unusual is the range of the treble, seemingly written an octave above the normal counter range, though the source gives no indication that it should be sung lower. Temperley notes than in 1733 Robert Barber printed a "florid version" of YORK, "which he headed 'Psalm IV, called the old way of singing'" (Temperley, 1:94). In the colonies, Samuel Sewall recorded in his diary for 2 February 1718 that he began to sing YORK, but "the Gallery" shifted the tune to ST. DAVID's. (See entry on ST. DAVID's, above, for the complete quotation.) YORK was chosen for singing in public worship by congregations at Weston (1724; 1 of 14 tunes) and Needham (7 January 1729; 1 of 8 tunes), Massachusetts; and it was 1 of 5 tunes sung at a service in Brimfield on 19 October 1781. In the Hutchinson Partbook (1763; probably copied in Pennsylvania), the following text was provided for a two-voice setting:

> I wish I was in old England
> As poor then as I am
> I'd soon get cloaths and go as fine
> As any in the Land.

H. W. Foote, writing in 1940, recalled the singing of YORK at the Harvard University Tercentenary celebration: "the old tune had a simple dignity and austere beauty all its own" (quoted in Stevenson, p. 20n).

Additional References

1. Read, No. 72
2. AH, p. 54; Fisher, p. 3; Frost 205; Hall (attributed to Ravenscroft); Hitchcock 122, 148, 158, 163, 175, 184, 192, (20); MinA, p. 29; Temperley, 2:ex. 17
3. Congregational; Episcopal

Cross-Reference

See entry on ST. DAVID's.

References for Appendix I

Literary Sources

AH — Christ-Janer, Albert, Charles Hughes, and Carleton Sprague Smith. *American Hymns Old and New*. New York: Columbia University Press, 1980.

Bentley Diary — *The Diary of William Bentley, D.D., Pastor of East Church, Salem, Massachusetts*. 4 vols. Salem: Essex Institute, 1905–14.

Boston Musical Gazette — *Boston Musical Gazette, a Semi-Monthly Journal, Devoted to the Science of Music*. Boston, 1838–39.

Brimfield, Mass. — *Historical Celebration of the Town of Brimfield*. Springfield: C.W. Bryan and Co., 1879, p. 128.

Brown 1802 — See Appendix II.

Bull 1795 — See Appendix II.

Bushnell — Bushnell, Vinson C. "Daniel Read of New Haven (1757–1836): The Man and His Musical Activities." Ph.D. diss. Harvard University, 1978.

Camus — Camus, Raoul F. *Military Music of the American Revolution*. Chapel Hill: University of North Carolina Press, 1976.

Canton, Mass. — Huntoon, Daniel T. V. *History of the Town of Canton*. Cambridge: John Wilson and Son, 1893, p. 312.

Carr — Carr, Bruce Alan. "Vital Spark, or The Dying Christian: A Study of the Musical Settings of Pope's Ode as They Appeared in Selected Early American Tune-books." Master's thesis, State University of New York at Buffalo, 1967.

Chase — Chase, Gilbert. *America's Music*. New York: McGraw-Hill, 1955.

Cheney — Cheney, Simeon Pease. *The American Singing Book*. Boston: White, Smith and Company, 1879. Reprint, with an introduction by Karl Kroeger. New York: Da Capo Press, 1980.

Columbian Centinel — *Columbian Centinel*. Boston, 5 January 1811.

Connecticut Journal — *The Connecticut Journal*. New Haven, 19 September 1782.

Crawford — Crawford, Richard A. *Andrew Law, American Psalmodist*. Evanston: Northwestern University Press, 1968.

Crawford, Lyon — Lyon, James. *Urania*. Reprint, with new preface by Richard Crawford. New York: Da Capo Press, 1974.

Crawford MM — Crawford, Richard. "Massachusetts Musicians and the Core Repertory of Early American Psalmody." In *Music in Colonial Massachusetts, 1630–1820*, vol. 2. Boston: The Colonial Society of Massachusetts, forthcoming.

Farmington, Conn. — Gay, Julius. *Church Music in Farmington in the Olden Time*. Hartford, Conn.: the Case, Lockwood & Brainard Company, 1891, p. 18.

Gibbs — *Giles Gibbs Jr., His Book for the Fife*. Edited by Kate Van Winkle Keller. Hartford: Connecticut Historical Society, 1974.

Goodrich — Goodrich, Samuel Griswold. *Recollections of a Lifetime*. Vol. I. New York, n.d. [ca. 1804?], pp. 72–73.

Harwinton, Conn. — Chipman, R. Manning. *The History of Harwinton*. Hartford: Williams, Wiley & Turner, 1860, p. 113.

Hastings, Dissertation — Hastings, Thomas. *A Dissertation on Musical Taste*. Albany: Websters and Skinners, 1822. Reprint, with an introduction by James E. Dooley. New York: Da Capo Press, 1974.

Huckleberry Finn — Twain, Mark. *Adventures of Huckleberry Finn*. New York: C. L. Webster, 1885. Reprint. New York: Bantam Classic edition, 1981.

Huntington 1807 — See Appendix II.

Hutchinson Partbook — Untitled manuscript hymnal signed "John Hutchinson" and dated 12 April 1763, reportedly from the Ephrata Cloister in Pennsylvania. Franklin and Marshall College Library.

Independent Chronicle	*The Independent Chronicle.* Boston, 3 April 1797, and 26 November 1795.
Jackson	Jackson, George Pullen. *White Spirituals in the Southern Uplands.* Chapel Hill: University of North Carolina Press, 1933. Reprint. New York: Dover, 1965.
Jones	Jones, F. O. *A Handbook of American Music and Musicians.* Canaseraga, N.Y.: F. O. Jones, 1886. Reprint. New York: Da Capo Press, 1971.
Julian	Julian, John. *A Dictionary of Hymnology.* 2d revised edition, with new supplement. 2 vols. London: Murray, 1907. Reprint. New York: Dover, 1957.
Kemp	Kemp, Robert. *Father Kemp and His Old Folks.* Boston: Robert Kemp, 1868. Reprint, with a new introduction by Richard Crawford, New York: Da Capo Press, 1984.
Kroeger 1973	Kroeger, Karl. "Moravian Music in 19th-Century American Tunebooks." *The Moravian Music Foundation Bulletin* 28 (Spring–Summer 1973): 1, 3n.
Kroeger 1976	Kroeger, Karl D. "The Worcester Collection of Sacred Harmony and Sacred Music in America, 1786–1803." Ph.D. diss., Brown University, 1976.
Law Essays	Law, Andrew. *Essays on Music.* Philadelphia: printed for the author, 1814.
Lowens	Lowens, Irving. *Music and Musicians in Early America.* New York: Norton, 1964.
Mass 1784	See Appendix II.
McKay & Crawford	McKay, David P. and Richard Crawford. *William Billings of Boston: Eighteenth-Century Composer.* Princeton: Princeton University Press, 1975.
Memoirs	Gilman, Samuel. *Memoirs of a New England Village Choir.* By a member. Boston: S. G. Goodrich, 1829.
Moby Dick	Melville, Herman. *Moby-Dick; or The Whale.* New York: Harper & brothers, 1851. Reprint. New York: Norton, 1976.
Murray	Murray, Sterling E. "Timothy Swan and Yankee Psalmody." *Musical Quarterly* 61 (July 1975): 433–63.
Musical Magazine I	*The Musical Magazine.* Vol. I. New York, July 1835.
Musical Magazine III	*The Musical Magazine; or, Repository of Musical Science, Literature and Intelligence.* Vol. III. Boston, 1841–42.
Needham, Mass.	Clarke, George Kuhn. *History of Needham, Massachusetts, 1711–1911.* [Cambridge:] priv. print. at the University Press, [1912], p. 308.
Parkman Diary	*The Diary of Ebenezer Parkman 1703–1782.* First Part. Edited by Francis G. Walett. Worcester: American Antiquarian Society, 1974.
Philadelphia Repository	*Philadelphia Repository and Weekly Register.* Vol. I. Philadelphia, 20 September 1801.
Randolph	*Ozark Folksongs.* Vol. IV, *Religious Songs and Other Items.* Collected and edited by Vance Randolph. Columbia: State Historical Society of Missouri, 1946–50. Reprint. Columbia: University of Missouri Press, 1980.
Routley 1957	Routley, Erik. *The Music of Christian Hymnody.* London: Independent Press, 1957.
Routley 1959	Routley, Erik. *The English Carol.* New York: Oxford University Press, 1959.
Scholes	Scholes, Percy A. *The Oxford Companion to Music.* 9th ed. New York: Oxford University Press, 1955.
Sewall Diary	*The Diary of Samuel Sewall, 1674–1729.* 2 vols. Edited by M. Halsey Thomas. New York: Farrar, Straus, and Giroux, 1973.
Song Messenger	*The Song Messenger of the North-West.* Chicago, July, 1865.
Steel	Steel, David Warren. "Stephen Jenks (1772–1856): American Composer and Tunebook Compiler." Ph. D. diss. University of Michigan, 1982.
Stevenson	Stevenson, Robert. *Protestant Church Music in America.* New York: Norton, 1966.
Stiles Diary	*The Literary Diary of Ezra Stiles.* 3 vols. Edited by Franklin B. Dexter. New York: Scribner's 1901.
Sutton	Sutton, Brett. "Shape-Note Tune Books and Primitive Hymns." *Ethnomusicology* 26 (January 1982): 11–26.
Swan	Manuscript notes written by Emily C. Swan, as dictated by her father, Timothy Swan, March–August 1842. Swan Papers, American Antiquarian Society, Worcester, Massachusetts.
Symmes	Symmes, Thomas. *Utile Dulci. Or, A Joco-Serious Dialogue, Concerning Regular Singing.* Boston: B. Green for Samuel Gerrish, 1723.
Temperley	Temperley, Nicholas. *The Music of the English Parish Church.* 2 vols. Cambridge: Cambridge University Press, 1979.
Thayer	Thayer, Alexander. "Mr. Thayer's Catalogue Continued." *The World of Music* IV (15 May 1847): 43.
Upton	Upton, William Treat. *William Henry Fry, American Journalist and Composer-Critic.* New York: Crowell, 1954.
Walter 1721	See Appendix II.
Westfield, Mass.	Lockwood, Rev. John H. *Westfield and its Historic Influences, 1669–1919.* Westfield: the author, 1922, p. 427.
Weston, Mass.	*Town of Weston. Births, Deaths and Marriages, 1707–1850. . . . Church Records, 1709–1825.* Boston: McIndoe Bros., 1901, p. 529.
Wilbraham, Mass.	Stebbins, Rufus P. *An Historical Address, Delivered at the Centennial Celebration of the Incorporation of the Town of Wilbraham.* Boston: G. C. Rand & Avery, 1864, p. 86.
Wienandt & Young	Wienandt, Elwyn A., and Robert H. Young. *The Anthem in England and America.* New York: The Free Press, 1970.
Wolfe	Wolfe, Richard J. *Secular Music in America, 1801–1825.* 3 vols. New York: The New York Public Library, 1964.

Sources for Underlaid Texts

Arnold	Arnold, John. *The Complete Psalmodist.* 7th ed. London, 1779.

Bay Psalm Book	*The Psalms, Hymns and Spiritual Songs of the Old and New Testament.* 21st ed. Boston, 1726. E2729.	New Version	Brady, N., and N. Tate. *A New Version of the Psalms of David.* Boston, 1793. E25176.
Belknap	Belknap, Jeremy. *Sacred Poetry.* Boston, 1795. E28258.	Rippon	Rippon, John. *A Selection of Hymns . . . First American Edition.* New York, 1792. E24749.
Boston West	*A Collection of Hymns . . . for the Use of the West Society.* Boston, 1783. E17848.	Rowe	*The Miscellaneous Works . . . of Mrs. Elizabeth Rowe.* 5th ed. 2 vols. London, 1772.
Common Prayer	*The Book of Common Prayer.* Cambridge, England, 1762.	Smith	Smith, Joshua. *Divine Hymns, or Spiritual Songs.* New London, 1800. E38522.
Hymns	*Hymns. Collected Chiefly from Dr. Watts's Hymns.* This is the last part (pp. 228–94) of the 1793 edition of Brady and Tate's *New Version.* E25176.	Watts, Horae	Watts, Isaac. *Horae lyricae.* 12th ed. Boston, 1772. E12604.
		Watts, Hymns	Watts, Isaac. *Hymns and Spiritual Songs in Three Books.* Norwich, [1793]. Part of E25184.
Hymns & Songs	*Hymns and Spiritual Songs, Collected from the Works of Several Authors.* Newport, 1766. E10233.	Watts, Psalm 00	Watts, Isaac. *The Psalms of David Imitated in the Language of the New Testament.* Norwich, [1793]. E25184.
Law CH	Law, Andrew. *The Christian Harmony.* Part II of *The Art of Singing.* Cheshire, Connecticut, 1794. E27205.	Whitefield	Whitefield, George. *A Collection of Hymns.* 13th ed. Philadelphia, 1768. E41900.
Law Collection	Law, Andrew. *A Collection of Hymns for Social Worship.* [Cheshire, 1783]. E17996.	Young	Young, Edward. *The Complaint: or, Night-Thoughts.* Philadelphia, 1798. E35067.

Appendix II: Collections Containing Core Repertory Compositions

Elsewhere in the present edition, and especially in Appendix I, collections of sacred music published in America before 1811 are referred to by sigla. Here those sigla are identified. The number of Core Repertory compositions in each collection is reported in parentheses. Collections reproduced in the Readex Microprint Early American Imprints series are also cited by Evans number (e.g., E5000) or Shaw-Shoemaker number (e.g., S1234). Those numbers refer to the following bibliographical works:

Evans, Charles. *American Bibliography.* 14 vols. Chicago: Blakely Press; Worcester: American Antiquarian Society, 1903–59. [Evans lists American imprints through 1800.]

Shaw, Ralph R., and Richard H. Shoemaker. *American Bibliography: a Preliminary Checklist, 1801–19.* 20 vols. New York: Scarecrow Press, 1958–65. [Shaw-Shoemaker lists American imprints after 1800.]

Shipton, Clifford K., and James E. Mooney. *National Index of American Imprints through 1800: The Short-Title Evans.* Barre, Massachusetts: American Antiquarian Society and Barre Publishers, 1969. [Shipton-Mooney is an update of Evans.]

"Later ed." refers to later editions of the work containing the same Core Repertory pieces, sometimes with additions, which are indicated by changed numbers. Wherever the word "see" precedes the Evans or Shaw-Shoemaker number, it signals that, although discrepancies exist between the citations in these bibliographies and the copies reproduced on microprint, the copies referred to here are ones from which the tabulations in the present appendix were made. For Sacred 1803 (see p. lxxv below), Richard J. Wolfe's bibliography is cited; although *Sacred Harmony* does not appear in Evans, Shaw-Shoemaker, or Shipton-Mooney, it is listed by Wolfe (see References for Appendix I). Collections not reproduced on Readex Microprint are not listed by number here, even if they do appear in one of the bibliographies mentioned above.

Addington 1808	Addington, Stephen. *A Valuable Selection of Psalm and Hymn Tunes.* Philadelphia: M. Carey, 1808. (9)
Adgate 1789	Adgate, [Andrew], and [Ishmael] Spicer. *Philadelphia Harmony.* Philadelphia: for the authors, [1789]. (48) E21629 Later eds.: 1790, 1791, 1796, 1797, 1799, 1801, 1803, 1807, 1808.
Adgate 1791	Adgate, A[ndrew]. *Philadelphia Harmony.* [4th ed.]. With *Philadelphia Harmony, Part II.* Philadelphia: for the author, [1791]. (58) E46110 Later eds.: 1796, 1797, 1799, 1801, 1803, 1807, 1808.
Aitken 1806	[Aitken, John]. *Aitken's Collection of Divine Music.* Philadelphia: John Aitken, [1806]. (13)
Albee 1805	Albee, Amos. *The Norfolk Collection of Sacred Harmony.* Dedham: H. Mann, 1805. (24) S7845
AMM 1800	*The American Musical Magazine,* vol. 1, nos. 1–4. Northampton: Hampshire Musical Society, printed by Andrew Wright, 1800–01. (2)
Amphion 1789	*Amphion or the Chorister's Delight.* New York: John Burger Jr. and Cornelius Tiebout, [ca. 1789]. (25)
Arnold 1803	Arnold, Adam. *Geistliche Ton-Kunst.* Hagerstown, Maryland: Johann Gruber, 1803. (13)
Atwill 1795	Atwill, Thomas H. *The New-York Collection of Sacred Harmony.* Lansingburg: for the editor, 1795. (41) E28216 Later ed.: 1802.
Atwill 1804	Atwill, Thomas H. *The New York & Vermont Collection of Sacred Harmony.* 2d ed. Albany: B. Buckley, [1804]. (39) S5741 Later eds.: 1805, 1806.
Atwill 1806	Atwill, Thomas H. *The New York & Vermont Collection of Select Music.* 3d ed. New York, [1806–14?]. (12)
Bay 1698	*The Psalms Hymns, and Spiritual Songs, of the Old & New-Testament.* 9th ed. Boston: B. Green, and J. Allen, for Michael Perry, 1698. (7) E817 Later eds.: 1702, 1705, 1706, 1709, 1711, 1713, 1716, 1718, 1720, 1726, 1729, 1730, 1737, 1742, 1744.
Bay 1737	*The Psalms, Hymns, and Spiritual Songs.* 24th ed. Boston: S. Kneeland & T. Green, for the booksellers, 1737. (15) E4115 Later eds.: 1742, 1744.
Bayley 1764	[Bayley, Daniel]. *A New and Compleat Introduction to the Grounds and Rules of Musick.* Newbury-port: printed for and sold by Bulkeley Emerson, 1764. (24) E9598 Later eds.: 1764, 1765, 1766, 1768.
Bayley 1766	[Bayley, Daniel]. *A New and Compleat Introduction to the Grounds and Rules of Musick.* [4th ed.]. Boston: Thomas Johnston, 1766. (27) Later ed.: 1768.
Bayley 1767	Bayley, Daniel. *The Psalm-Singer's Assistant.* Boston: W. M'Alpine, for the author in Newbury-port, 1767. (27) E41691 Other ed.: ca. 1764.

Bayley 1768   Bayley, Daniel. *A New and Complete Introduction to the Grounds and Rules of Music*. [5th ed.]. Newbury Port: Daniel Bayley, [1768]. (29) E10829

Bayley 1770   Bayley, Daniel. *The Essex Harmony*. Newbury Port: the author, 1770. (35) see E11560
Later eds.: 1771, 1772.

Bayley 1771   Bayley, Daniel. *The Essex Harmony*. [2d ed.]. Newbury Port: the author, 1771. (33) E11969
Later ed.: 1772.

Bayley 1784   [Bayley, Daniel]. *Select Harmony, Containing . . . the Rules of Singing Chiefly by Andrew Law, A.B.* Newbury-port: Daniel Bayley, [1784]. (37) E18553

Bayley 1785   Bayley, Daniel. *The Essex Harmony, or Musical Miscellany*. Newburyport: the author and son, 1785. (30) E18925

Bayley 1785a   Bayley, Daniel. *The Essex Harmony, or Musical Miscellany*. Newburyport: the author and son, 1785. (33) [This issue has 48 pp., while Bayley 1785 has 40 pp.]

Bayley 1788   Bayley, Daniel, Sr. *The New Harmony of Zion*. Newbury-port: the publisher, 1788. (44) see E20956

Bayley 1788a   Bayley, Daniel, Sr. *The New Harmony of Zion*. Newbury-port: the publisher, 1788. (49) [This issue has 112 pp., while Bayley 1788 has 96 pp.]

Belknap 1800   Belknap, Daniel. *The Evangelical Harmony*. Boston: Isaiah Thomas and Ebenezer T. Andrews, for the author, 1800. (1) E36939

Belknap 1802   Belknap, Daniel. *The Middlesex Collection of Sacred Harmony*. Boston: Isaiah Thomas and Ebenezer T. Andrews, for the author, 1802. (5) S1857

Belknap 1806   Belknap, Daniel. *The Village Compilation of Sacred Musick*. Boston: J. T. Buckingham, for the author, 1806. (6) S9953
Later ed.: 1806.

Benham 1790   Benham, Asahel. *Federal Harmony*. New-Haven: A. Morse, 1790. (8) E22340
Later eds.: 1792, ca. 1793, ca.1794, ca.1795, ca. 1796.

Benham 1792   Benham, Asahel. *Federal Harmony*. 2d ed. New-Haven: A. Morse, 1792. (9) E24092
Later eds.: ca. 1793, ca. 1794, ca. 1795, ca. 1796.

Benjamin 1799   Benjamin, Jonathan. *Harmonia Coelestis*. Northampton: Andrew Wright, for Oliver D. & I. Cooke, Hartford, 1799. [Compiled in Hartford, Connecticut]. (3) E25179

N. Billings 1795   Billings, Nathaniel. *The Republican Harmony*. Lansingburgh, New York: Silvester Tiffany, for the publisher, 1795. (5)

Billings 1770   Billings, William. *The New-England Psalm-Singer*. Boston: Edes and Gill, [1770]. (4) E11572

Billings 1778   Billings, William. *The Singing Master's Assistant*. Boston: Draper and Folsom, 1778. (6) E43416
Later eds: ca. 1779, 1781, ca. 1786.

Billings 1779   Billings, W[illiam]. *Music in Miniature*. Boston: the author, 1779. (15) E16205

Billings 1786   Billings, William. *The Suffolk Harmony*. Boston: J. Norman, for the author, 1786. (1) see E19512

Billings 1787   Billings, W[illia]m. *An Anthem for Easter*. [Boston, 1787]. (1) see E19512

Blake 1810   Blake, G E. *Vocal Harmony*. Philadelphia: G. E. Blake, [1810?]. (55) S8041

Blanchard 1807   [Blanchard, Amos]. *The Newburyport Collection of Sacred, European Musick*. Exeter: Ranlet & Norris, 1807. [Perhaps compiled in Massachusetts]. (3) S12167

Blanchard 1808   Blanchard, Amos. *The American Musical Primer*. Exeter: Norris & Sawyer, 1808. (26) S14537

Boston 1799   *The Boston Collection*. Boston: William Norman, [ca. 1799]. (62) E48377

Boston Brattle 1810   *LXXX Psalm and Hymn Tunes, for Public Worship*. Boston: Manning & Loring, 1810. (29) S20039

Boston First 1805   *The First Church Collection of Sacred Musick*. Boston: J. T. Buckingham, 1805. (3) S8443
Later ed.: 1806.

Boston First 1806   *The First Church Collection of Sacred Musick*, 2d ed. Boston: Thomas & Andrews, for the First Church Singers, 1806. (52)

Boston Hymns 1808   *The Boston Collection of Sacred and Devotional Hymns*. Boston: Manning and Loring, 1808. (1) S14553

Boston Trinity 1808   *Hymns, Selected from the Most Approved Authors, for the Use of Trinity Church, Boston*. Boston: Munroe, Francis, & Parker, 1808. (1) S15290

Boston West 1810   *A Collection of Sacred Musick . . . Designed for the Use of the West Church in Boston*. Boston: Buckingham & Titcomb, 1810. (30)
Later ed.: 1810.

Boston West 1810a   *A Collection of Sacred Musick . . . Designed for the Use of the West Church in Boston*. Boston: Buckingham & Titcomb, 1810. (37)

Brady 1713   Brady, N., & N. Tate. *A New Version of the Psalms of David*. Boston: J. Allen, for Nicholas Boone, 1713. (5)
Later ed.: 1720.

Brady 1720   Brady, N., & N. Tate. *A New Version of the Psalms of David*. Boston: J. Allen, for Benjamin Elliot, 1720. (6) E2094

Brown 1802   Brown, Bartholomew, and others. *Columbian and European Harmony: or, Bridgewater Collection of Sacred Music*. Boston: Isaiah Thomas and Ebenezer T. Andrews, 1802. (38) S1951
Later eds.: 1804, 1810.

Brown 1804   Brown, Bartholomew, and others. *Columbian and European Harmony: or, Bridgewater Collection of Sacred Music*. 2d ed. Boston: Isaiah Thomas and Ebenezer T. Andrews, 1804. (40) S5914
Later ed.: 1810.

Brown 1810   Brown, Bartholomew, and others. *Bridgewater Collection of Sacred Musick*. 3d ed. Boston: Thomas & Andrews and J. West & Co., J. T. Buckingham, printer, 1810. (47) S19644

Brownson 1783   Brownson, Oliver. *Select Harmony*. [Connecticut], 1783. (11)
Later eds.: 1785, ca. 1791.

Brownson 1785 Brownson, Oliver. *Select Harmony.* [Connecticut], 1783 [i.e., 1785]. (14) Later ed., ca. 1791.

Brownson 1791 Brownson, Oliver. *Select Harmony.* [Connecticut], 1783 [i.e., 1789–91]. (15) E23227

Brownson 1797 Brownson, Oliver. *A New Collection of Sacred Harmony.* Simsbury, Connecticut: the author, 1797. (6) E31884

Bull 1795 Bull, Amos. *The Responsary.* Worcester: Isaiah Thomas; sold by the editor in Hartford, Connecticut, 1795. (14) E28370

Bushnell 1807 Bushnell, John. *The Musical Synopsis.* Northampton: Graves & Clap, for the compiler, 1807. (10) S12255

Carr 1805 Carr, Benjamin. *Masses, Vespers, Litanies, Hymns, Psalms, Anthems & Motetts.* [Philadelphia, 1805]. (3) S8141

Chapin 1808 Chapin, Nathan, and Joseph L. Dickerson. *The Musical Instructor.* Philadelphia: W. M'Culloch, 1808. (28) S14673 Later ed.: 1810.

Child 1804 Child, Ebenezer. *The Sacred Musician.* Boston: Manning & Loring, for the author, 1804. [Compiled in Brandon, Vermont]. (2) S6011

Cole 1799 Cole, John. *Sacred Harmony.* 2d ed. With *Sacred Harmony, Part the Second.* Baltimore: printed for, and sold . . . by J. Carr, B. Carr, Philadelphia, and J. Hewitt, New-York, [1799–1802]. (10)

Cole 1803 Cole, John. *A Collection of Psalm Tunes and Anthems.* Boston: Isaiah Thomas and Ebenezer T. Andrews, 1803. [Compiled in Baltimore, Maryland]. (1)

Cole S 1803 Cole, S[amuel] and J[ohn]. *Sacred Music.* Baltimore, [1803]. (1) S3981

Cole 1804 [Cole, John, et. al.?]. *The Beauties of Psalmody.* Baltimore: Sower and Cole, 1804. (21) S6039 Later ed.: 1805.

Cole 1805 Cole, John. *The Beauties of Psalmody.* 2d ed. Baltimore: Cole & Hewes, 1805. (22) S8206

Cole 1808 Cole, John. *The Divine Harmonist.* [Baltimore: John Cole, 1808]. (21) S14723

Cole 1810 Cole, John. *Ecclesiastical Harmony.* Baltimore: G. Dobbin & Murphy for the author, [1810?]. (23) S19795

Collection 1774 *A Collection of the Psalm and Hymn Tunes, Used by the Reformed Protestant Dutch Church of the City of New-York.* New York: Hodge and Shober, 1774. (3) E42655

Collection 1804 *A Collection of Sacred Vocal Music.* Northampton: Andrew Wright, 1804. (5)

Cooper 1804 Cooper, William. *The Beauties of Church Music.* Boston: Manning & Loring, [1804]. (38) S6079

Cumberland 1804 *The Cumberland Melodist.* Philadelphia: William M'Culloch, for John M'Carrell, Shippensburg, 1804. (31)

Dawson 1754 Dawson, W. *The Youths Entertaining Amusement, or A Plain Guide to Psalmody.* Philadelphia: printed at the German printing-office . . . and sold by the author, 1754. (18)

Dearborn 1785 Dearborn, Benjamin. *A Scheme, for Reducing the Science of Music to a More Simple State.* Portsmouth, New-Hampshire, 1785. (6) E44674

Deerfield 1808 *Deerfield Collection of Sacred Music.* Northampton: Graves and Clap for S. & E. Butler, [1808]. (40) S12410

Doll 1810 Doll, Joseph. *Der leichte Unterricht, von der Vocal Musik.* Harrisburg: Johan Wyeth, 1810. (6) S19986

Doolittle 1786 [Doolittle, Amos, and Daniel Read]. *The American Musical Magazine,* vol. I. New-Haven: Amos Doolittle & Daniel Read, [1786–87]. (2)

Edson 1801 Edson, Lewis, Jr. *The Social Harmonist.* 2d ed. New York, 1801. (7) S433 Later ed.: 1803.

Ely 1792 Ely, Alexander. *The Baltimore Collection of Church Music.* Baltimore: printed and sold by John Hagerty, 1792. (39)

Erben 1806 Erben, P. *A Selection of the Psalm and Hymn Tunes, for the Use of the Dutch Reformed Churches in the City of New-York.* New-York: published and sold by P. Erben, J. C. Totten, printer, 1806. (36)

Erben 1808 Erben, Peter. *Sacred Music in Two, Three, and Four Parts.* [New York, 1808]. (30)

Essex 1802 *The Essex Harmony, Part II.* Salem: printed by Joshua Cushing, and sold by Cushing & Appleton, 1802. (20) S2196

Evans 1808 Evans, J. *David's Companion.* New York: J. Evans, 1808. (23) S14970 Later ed.: 1810.

Evans 1810 Evans, James. *David's Companion, or, The Methodist Standard.* [2d ed.]. [New York: James Evans, 1810]. (28) S20069

Federal 1788 *The Federal Harmony.* Boston: for the editor, [1788]. (41) E21485 Later eds.: 1790, ca. 1791, 1792, 1793, 1794.

Federal 1790 *The Federal Harmony.* Boston: John Norman, 1790. (47) E22919 Later eds., ca. 1791, 1792, 1793, 1794.

Federal 1791 *The Federal Harmony.* Boston: John Norman, 1790 [i.e., ca. 1791]. (54) Later eds.: 1792, 1793, 1794.

Federal 1792 *The Federal Harmony.* Boston: John Norman, 1792. (52) E24831 Later eds.: 1793, 1794.

Federal 1794 *The Federal Harmony.* 8th ed. Boston: William Norman, 1794. (32)

Flagg 1764 Flagg, Josiah. *A Collection of the Best Psalm Tunes.* Boston: Paul Revere and Josiah Flagg, 1764. (36) E9659

Flagg 1766 [Flagg, Josiah]. *Sixteen Anthems.* Boston: Josiah Flagg, [1766]. (3) E41612

Fobes 1809 Fobes, Azariah. *The Delaware Harmony.* Philadelphia: W. M'Culloch; sold also by the publisher, Wilmington, 1809. (13)

French 1793 French, Jacob. *The Psalmodist's Companion.* Worcester: Leonard Worcester, for Isaiah Thomas, 1793. (15) E25513

French 1802 French, Jacob. *Harmony of Harmony.* Northampton: Andrew Wright, for the compiler, 1802. (11) S2277

Gamut 1807 — *A Gamut, or Scale of Music.* Hartford: Oliver D. Cooke; Graves and Clap, printers, Northampton, 1807. (15) S12642

Gillet 1809 — Gillet, Wheeler, and Co. *The Maryland Selection of Sacred Music.* Baltimore: printed by Henry S. Keatinge, 1809. (17) S18006

Gilman 1771 — [Gilman, John Wd.]. *A New Introduction to Psalmody.* Exeter: engrav'd printed & sold by John Wd. Gilman, 1771. (29) E42240

Gram 1795 — [Gram, Hans, Samuel Holyoke, and Oliver Holden]. *The Massachusetts Compiler of Theoretical and Practical Elements of Sacred Vocal Music.* Boston: Isaiah Thomas and Ebenezer T. Andrews, [1795]. (5) E28848

Graupner 1806 — [Graupner, G.]. *The Monitor, or Celestial Melody.* Boston: G. Graupner, [1806]. (8) S29186

Griswold 1796 — Griswold, Elijah, and Thomas Skinner. *Connecticut Harmony.* [Connecticut, ca. 1796]. (4) Later ed.: ca. 1798.

Griswold 1798 — Griswold, Elijah, and Thomas Skinner. *Connecticut Harmony.* [Connecticut, ca. 1798]. (7) E30521

Griswold 1807 — Griswold, Elijah, Stephen Jenks, and John C. Frisbie. *The Hartford Collection of Sacred Harmony.* Hartford: Lincoln and Gleason, 1807. (16) S12698

Hill 1801 — Hill, Uri K. *The Vermont Harmony*, vol 1. Northampton: Andrew Wright, for the compiler, 1801. (9) S653

Hill 1806 — Hill, Uri K. *The Sacred Minstrel*, no. 1. Boston: Manning & Loring, 1806. (5) S10577

Holden 1793 — Holden, Oliver. *The Union Harmony*, vol. I. Boston: Isaiah Thomas and Ebenezer T. Andrews, 1793. (40) E25619
Later eds.: 1796, 1801.

Holden II 1793 — Holden, Oliver. *The Union Harmony*, vol. II. Boston: Isaiah Thomas and Ebenezer T. Andrews, 1793. (24) E25619

Holden 1796 — Holden, Oliver. *The Union Harmony.* 2d ed. Boston: Isaiah Thomas and Ebenezer T. Andrews, 1796. (40) E30573
Later ed.: 1801.

Holden 1800 — [Holden, Oliver]. *The Modern Collection of Sacred Music.* Boston: Isaiah Thomas and Ebenezer T. Andrews, 1800. (29) E37980

Holden 1801 — Holden, Oliver. *The Union Harmony.* 3d ed. Boston: Isaiah Thomas and Ebenezer T. Andrews, 1801. (33) S662

Holt 1803 — Holt, Benjamin, Jr. *The New-England Sacred Harmony.* Boston: Isaiah Thomas and Ebenezer T. Andrews, 1803. (1)

Holyoke 1803 — Holyoke, Samuel. *The Columbian Repository of Sacred Harmony.* Exeter: Henry Ranlet, [1803]. [Probably compiled in Massachusetts]. (42) S2421

Holyoke 1804 — Holyoke, Samuel. *The Christian Harmonist.* Salem: Joshua Cushing, 1804. (26) S6492

Holyoke 1807 — Holyoke, Samuel. *The Vocal Companion.* Exeter: Norris & Sawyer, 1807. [Probably compiled in Massachusetts]. (20) S12776

Hopkinson 1763 — [Hopkinson, Francis]. *A Collection of Psalm Tunes, with a Few Anthems and Hymns . . . for the Use of the United Churches of Christ Church and St. Peter's Church in Philadelphia.* [Philadelphia], 1763. (16) E9406

Huntington 1800 — Huntington, Jonathan. *The Albany Collection of Sacred Harmony.* Northampton: Andrew Wright, for Daniel Steel, Albany, 1800. (34) E37667

Huntington 1807 — Huntington, Jonathan. *The Apollo Harmony.* Northampton: Horace Graves, 1807. (22) S12796
Later ed.: 1807a, which has 148 pp., while 1807 has 127, [1].

Huntington 1807a — Huntington, Jonathan. *The Apollo Harmony.* Northampton: Horace Graves, 1807. (27)

Huntington 1809 — Huntington, J[onathan]. *The English Extracts, or Hampshire Musical Magazine*, no. 1. Northampton: for the compiler, 1809. (13)

Ingalls 1805 — Ingalls, Jeremiah. *The Christian Harmony; or, Songster's Companion.* Exeter: Henry Ranlet, for the compiler, 1805. (1) S8680

Jackson 1804 — Jackson, Dr. [George K.]. *David's Psalms.* [New York], 1804. (4)

Janes 1807 — Janes, Walter. *The Harmonic Minstrelsey.* Dedham: H. Mann, 1807. (8) S12824

Jenks 1801 — Jenks, Stephen. *The New-England Harmonist,* with *The Musical Harmonist.* Danbury: Douglas & Nichols for the author, [1800 or later]. (4) E37707

Jenks 1803 — Jenks, Stephen, and Elijah Griswold. *The American Compiler of Sacred Harmony*, no. 1. Northampton: for the compilers, 1803. [Probably compiled in Connecticut]. (6) S4449

Jenks 1804 — Jenks, Stephen. *The Delights of Harmony.* New-Haven: for the editor, 1804. (9) S6554
Later ed.: (S8701), undated but published after 1804, is paged 8, 17–59, [1], while the issue dated 1804 is paged 8, [4], 17–68.

Jenks 1805 — Jenks, Stephen. *The Delights of Harmony; or, Norfolk Compiler.* Dedham: H. Mann, for the author, 1805. [Probably compiled in Connecticut]. (3) S8699
Later ed.: 1805a, has 112 pp., while this one has 95, [1].

Jenks 1805a — Jenks, Stephen. *The Delights of Harmony; or, Norfolk Compiler*, with *Additional Music.* Dedham: H. Mann, for the author, 1805. (4)

Jenks 1806 — Jenks, Stephen. *The Delights of Harmony; or Union Compiler*, no. II. Dedham: H. Mann, for the author, 1806. [Probably compiled in Connecticut]. (6) S10635

Jenks 1810 — Jenks, S[tephen]. *The Royal Harmony of Zion Complete.* Dedham: H. Mann, for the author, 1810. [Probably compiled in Connecticut]. (13) S20448

Jocelin 1782 — [Jocelin, Simeon]. *The Chorister's Companion: or Church Music Revised.* New Haven: Simeon Jocelin and Amos Doolittle, [1782]. (38) see E17567
Later ed.: 1788.

Jocelin 1783 — [Jocelin, Simeon]. *The Chorister's Companion: or Church Music Revised,* with *The Chorister's Companion, Part third.* New Haven: Simeon Jocelin and Amos Doolittle, [1783]. (41) E17567
Later ed.: 1788.

Jocelin 1788   [Jocelin, Simeon]. *The Chorister's Companion.* 2d ed. New Haven: Simeon Jocelin, 1788. (37) E21177

Johnston 1755   [*Collection of Psalm Tunes, with an Introduction "To Learn to Sing"*]. Boston: engrav'd printed & sold by Thomas Johnston, 1755. (16) see E7442
Later ed.: 1763, has 22 pp., while this one has 16.

Johnston 1763   [*Collection of Psalm Tunes, with an Introduction "To Learn to Sing"*]. Boston: engrav'd printed & sold by Thomas Johnston, 1755 [i.e., 1763–67]. (25) see E10558

Langdon 1786   [Langdon, Chauncey]. *Beauties of Psalmody . . . by a Member of the Musical Society of Yale College.* [New Haven, 1786]. (14) E19749

Law 1778   Law, Andrew. *Select Harmony.* Cheshire, [Connecticut], 1778. (19)
Later eds.: 1779, 1782. (This issue, with 44 pp., is an unfinished version of 1779.)

Law 1779   Law, Andrew. *Select Harmony.* Farmington [i.e., Cheshire, Connecticut], 1779. (23) E16318
Later ed.: 1782.

Law 1781   Law, Andrew. *A Select Number of Plain Tunes Adapted to Congregational Worship.* [Cheshire, Connecticut, 1781]. (22) see E17098

Law 1782   Law, Andrew. *Select Harmony.* [Cheshire, Connecticut, 1781–82]. (12) E23492

Law C 1783   Law, Andrew. *A Collection of Hymn Tunes.* Cheshire: William Law, [1783]. (5) see E17571

Law 1783   Law, Andrew. *The Rudiments of Music.* [Cheshire, Connecticut], 1783. (13) E17997
Later eds.: 1786, 1791, 1792.

Law 1786   Law, Andrew. *The Rudiments of Music.* 2d ed. [Cheshire, Connecticut, 1786]. (19) E19057
Later eds.: 1791, 1792.

Law 1787   Law, Andrew. *The Rudiments of Music.* 2d ed. [Cheshire, Connecticut, 1787–90]. (23) (This is a variant issue of Law 1786.)

Law 1791   Law, Andrew. *The Rudiments of Music.* 3d ed. [Cheshire, Connecticut, 1791]. (41) E23491
Later ed.: 1792.

Law 1792   Law, Andrew. *The Rudiments of Music.* 4th ed. Cheshire, Connecticut: William Law, 1792. (42) E24466

Law 1793   Law, Andrew. *The Musical Primer.* Cheshire, Connecticut: William Law, 1793. (1) E24709
Later eds.: 1794, 1800.

Law M 1793   Law, Andrew. *The Musical Magazine,* no. 2. Cheshire, Connecticut: William Law, 1793. (1) E25708
Later ed.: 1800.

Law M 1794   Law, Andrew. *The Musical Magazine,* no. 3. Cheshire, Connecticut, [1794]. (1)

Law P 1794   Law, Andrew. *The Art of Singing, Part I: The Musical Primer.* Cheshire, Connecticut: William Law, 1794. (1) see 27204
Later eds.: 1800, 1803, 1810.

Law 1794   Law, Andrew. *The Art of Singing, Part II: The Christian Harmony,* vol. I. Cheshire, Connecticut: William Law, 1794. (16) E27205
Later eds.: 1800, 1805.

Law 1796   Law, Andrew. *The Art of Singing, Part II: The Christian Harmony,* vol. II. Cheshire, Connecticut: William Law, 1794 [i.e., 1796]. (1) E30680

Law 1800   Law, Andrew. *The Art of Singing, Parts I, II, & III: The Musical Primer, The Christian Harmony, The Musical Magazine.* 3d [i.e., 2d] ed. [Cheshire, Connecticut, 1800]. (20) see E49106

Law 1801   Law, Andrew. *The Musical Magazine,* no. 6. [Philadelphia], 1801. (1) see E37787

Law 1803   Law, Andrew. *The Art of Singing,* 4th [i.e., 3d] ed. *Part I: The Musical Primer.* Cambridge: W. Hilliard, 1803. (31) S4509
Later ed.: 1810.

Law 1804   Law, Andrew. *The Art of Singing,* 4th [i.e. 3d] ed. *Part III: The Musical Magazine.* Boston: E. Lincoln, for the author, 1805 [i.e., 1804]. (2) see S8764

Law 1805   Law, Andrew. *The Art of Singing,* 4th [i.e., 3d] ed. *Part II: The Christian Harmony.* Windsor, Vermont: Nahum Mower, 1805. [Probably compiled in Connecticut]. (5) see S8763

Law 1807   Law, Andrew. *Harmonic Companion.* Philadelphia: the author, and David Hogan; from the press of Thomas T. Stiles, [1807]. (32) see S12895
Later ed.: 1810.

Law 1810   Law, Andrew. *The Musical Primer.* [2d ed.]. Philadelphia: Robert and William Carr, for the author, [1810]. (2)

Law H 1810   Law, Andrew. *Harmonic Companion.* Philadelphia: the author, and David Hogan; from the press of Thomas T. Stiles, [1809–10]. (33) S12895

Little 1801   Little, William, and William Smith. *The Easy Instructor.* [Philadelphia?, 1801?]. (27) S2545
Later eds.: ca. 1802, 1805, 1806, 1807, 1808, ca. 1809, ca. 1810.

Little 1805   Little, William, and William Smith. *The Easy Instructor.* Albany: printed by Charles R. and George Webster, and Daniel Steele, 1805. (34) S8794
Later eds.: 1805, 1806, 1807, 1808, ca. 1809, ca. 1810.

Little 1807   Little, William, and William Smith. *The Easy Instructor.* Albany: printed by Websters & Skinner, and Daniel Steele, 1807. (34) S12933
Later eds.: 1808, ca. 1809, ca. 1810.

Little 1809   Little, William, and William Smith. *The Easy Instructor.* Albany: Websters & Skinner and Daniel Steele, [1808–1810]. (41) S17921
Later ed.: ca. 1810.

Lyon 1761   Lyon, James. *Urania, or a Choice Collection of Psalm-tunes, Anthems, and Hymns.* Philadelphia, 1761. (27) E8908
Later ed.: [1767].

Madan 1809   *The Collection of Psalm and Hymn Tunes Sung at the Chapel of the Lock Hospital.* [Boston]: West & Blake, and Manning & Loring, [1809]. (4) S17967
(This work was first published in London in 1769, signed by Martin Madan as compiler.)

Mann 1797   Mann, Elias. *The Northampton Collection of Sacred Harmony*. Northampton: Daniel Wright & Co., 1797. (38) E32416
Later ed.: 1802.

Mann 1802   Mann, Elias. *The Northampton Collection of Sacred Harmony*. [2d ed.]. Northampton: Andrew Wright, for Daniel Wright, 1802. (21) S2582

Mann 1807   Mann, Elias. *The Massachusetts Collection of Sacred Harmony*. Boston: Manning and Loring, for the author, 1807. (40) S12981

Mass 1784   *The Massachusetts Harmony*. Boston: printed for, and sold by John Norman, [1784]. (45) see E18933
Later ed.: [1785].

Maxim 1805   Maxim, Abraham. *The Northern Harmony*. Exeter, New Hampshire: Henry Ranlet, for the compiler, 1805. [Compiled in Turner, Maine]. (13) S8882
Later ed.: 1808.

Maxim 1808   Maxim, Abraham. *The Northern Harmony*. 2d ed. Exeter, New Hampshire: Norris & Sawyer, 1808. [Compiled in Turner, Maine]. (16) S15568

Mennonite 1803   [Mennonite Congregations]. *Die kleine geistliche Harfe*, 1st ed. Germantaun, [Pennsylvania]: Michael Billmeyer, 1803. (2) S4485

Mennonite 1804   [Mennonite Congregations]. *Ein unpartheyisches Gesang-Buch*. Lancaster, [Pennsylvania]: Johann Albrecht, 1804. (2) S6767
Later ed.: 1808.

Merrill 1799   Merrill, David. *The Psalmodist's Best Companion*. Exeter, New Hampshire: Henry Ranlet for the author, 1799. (10)

Middlesex 1807   *The Middlesex Collection of Church Music*. Boston: Manning & Loring, 1807. (45) S13079
Later ed.: 1808.

Middlesex 1808   *The Middlesex Collection of Church Music*. 2d ed. Boston: Manning & Loring, 1808. (50) S15600

Neu 1753   [German Reformed Church in the U. S.]. *Neu-vermehrt-und vollständiges Gesang-Buch*. Germantown, [Pennsylvania]: Christoph Saur, 1753. (2) see E9495
Later eds.: 1763, 1772, 1774.

Neue 1797   [German Reformed Church in the U. S.]. *Das neue und verbesserte Gesang-Buch*. Philadelphia: Steiner und Kammerer, und H. Kammerer, Jr., 1797. (2) E32100
Later eds.: 1799, 1807.

New 1784   *A New Collection of Psalm Tunes Adapted to Congregational Worship*. [Boston, 1784]. (35) see E18930

New England 1771   *The New-England Harmony*. Boston: John Fleeming, 1771. (36)

New Jersey 1797   *New-Jersey Harmony*. Philadelphia: John M'Culloch, 1797. (13) E32547

New York 1803   [Collection of sacred vocal music, bound with New York Musical Society, *Constitution and Bye-Laws*]. New York: Sage and Clough, 1803. (1)

Olmsted 1805   Olmsted, T[imothy]. *The Musical Olio*. Northampton: Andrew Wright, 1805. [Compiled in Connecticut]. (12) S9062

Peck 1808   Peck, Daniel L. *The Musical Medley*. Dedham: H. Mann, for the author, 1808. [Compiled in Bridgeport, Connecticut]. (2) S15859

Peck 1810   Peck, Daniel L. *A Valuable Selection of Sacred Music*. Philadelphia: W. M'Culloch, for the compiler, 1810. (6) S21007

Pilsbury 1799   Pilsbury, Amos. *The United States' Sacred Harmony*. Boston: Isaiah Thomas and Ebenezer T. Andrews, sold by them . . . and by the compiler, in Charleston, (South Carolina), 1799. (64) E36119

Poor 1794   Poor, John. *A Collection of Psalms and Hymns, with Tunes Affixed*. Philadelphia: John M'Culloch, 1794. (16) E27533

Psalms 1767   [New York Reformed Protestant Dutch Church]. *The Psalms of David*. New-York: James Parker, 1767. (3) E10561

PSA 1804   *The Psalm-Singer's Amusement*. [Greenwich, Mass.: John Howe?, 1804–10]. (7)

Read 1785   Read, Daniel. *The American Singing Book*. New-Haven: printed for and sold by the author, 1785. (7) E19213
Later eds.: 1786, 1787, 1793, 1796.

Read 1787   Read, Daniel. *The American Singing Book*. With *Supplement to the American Singing Book*. New Haven: printed for, and sold by the author, 1787. (25) E20673
Later eds.: 1793, 1796.

Read 1794   Read, Daniel. *The Columbian Harmonist*, no. 2. New Haven: printed for & sold by the editor, [1794]. (32) see E29390
Later eds.: 1798, 1804, 1807, 1810.

Read 1795   Read, Daniel. *The Columbian Harmonist*, no. 3. New Haven: D. Read, [1795]. (1) E29391

Read 1797   Read, Daniel. *The Columbian Harmonist*, no. 1 [with nos. 2 and 3]. New Haven: printed for & sold by the editor, [1797]. (33) E29389

Read 1798   Read, Daniel. *The Columbian Harmonist*, no. 2. New Haven: printed for & sold by the editor, [1798]. (33)
Later eds.: 1804, 1807, 1810.

Read 1804   Read, Daniel. *The Columbian Harmonist*. 2d ed. Dedham: H. Mann, 1804 [i.e., 1805]. [Compiled in New Haven, Connecticut]. (26) see S7155
Later eds.: 1806, 1807, 1810.

Read 1806   Read, Daniel. *The Columbian Harmonist*. 3d ed. With *Supplement*. Dedham: H. Mann, 1806. (26) S11251

Read 1807   Read, Daniel. *The Columbian Harmonist*. 3d ed. Boston: Manning and Loring, 1807. [Compiled in New Haven, Connecticut]. (40) S13464
Later ed.: 1810.

Read 1810   Read, Daniel. *The Columbian Harmonist*. 4th ed. Boston: Manning and Loring, 1810. [Compiled in New Haven, Connecticut]. (42) S21176

J. Read 1808   Read, Joel. *The New-England Selection: or Plain Psalmodist*. Boston: J. T. Buckingham, for the author, 1808. (26)

Robbins 1805   Robbins, Charles. *The Columbian Harmony; or Maine Collection of Church Music*. Exeter, New

Hampshire: Henry Ranlet, 1805. [Compiled in Winthrop, Maine]. (30)

Rothbaust 1807 — Rothbaust, Johannes. *Geistliche Ton-Kunst.* Hannover, [Pennsylvania]: Wilhelm D. Lepper, 1807. (16)

Sacred 1788 — *Sacred Harmony or A Collection of Psalm Tunes, Ancient and Modern.* Boston: C. Cambridge, [1786–88]. (54) E22615

Sacred 1803 — *Sacred Harmony.* Philadelphia: Carr & Schetky, [1803–04]. (5) Wolfe 7722

Sacred 1806 — *Sacred Harmony.* Philadelphia: John M'Culloch, 1806. (43) S11314

Sacred 1810 — *Sacred Psalmody, Selected for the Church in Federal-Street.* [Boston, 1810?]. (27) S21258

Salem 1805 — *The Salem Collection of Classical Sacred Musick.* Salem: Joshua Cushing, 1805. (39) S9302
Later ed.: 1806.

Salem 1806 — *The Salem Collection of Classical Sacred Musick.* 2d ed. Boston: Manning & Loring, for Cushing & Appleton, 1806. (41) S11320

Sandford 1793 — Sandford, E., and J[ohn] Rhea. *Columbian Harmony.* Baltimore: Samuel & John Adams, [1793]. [Compiled in Alexandria, Virginia]. (29)

Sanger 1808 — Sanger, Zedekiah, and others. *The Meridian Harmony.* Dedham: H. Mann, for the author, 1808. (21) S16139

Sanno 1807 — Sanno, F[riedrich]. *Sammlung Geistlicher Lieder.* Carlisle, Pennsylvania: F. Sanno, [1807]. (2)

Selection 1788 — *A Selection of Sacred Harmony.* Philadelphia: W. Young, 1788. (40) S45213
Later eds.: 1789, 1790, 1794, 1797.

Selection 1789 — *A Selection of Sacred Harmony.* [2d ed.]. Philadelphia: John M'Culloch, for W. Young, 1789. (42)
Later eds.: 1790, 1794, 1797.

Selection 1790 — *A Selection of Sacred Harmony.* 3d ed. Philadelphia: John M'Culloch, for William Young, 1790. (48) S22884
Later eds.: 1794, 1797.

Selection 1794 — *A Selection of Sacred Harmony.* 4th ed. Philadelphia: John M'Culloch, for William Young, 1794. (50) E47212
Later ed.: 1797.

Seymour 1803 — Seymour, Lewis and Thaddeus. *The Musical Instructor.* New York: John C. Totten, 1803. (14) S5038
Later ed.: 1808.

Seymour 1809 — Seymour, Lewis and Thaddeus. *The New-York Selection of Sacred Music.* New York: the compilers and J. C. Totten, 1809. (31) S18592

Shaw 1808 — Shaw, O[liver], A[mos] Albee, and H[erman] Mann. *The Columbian Sacred Harmonist: or, Collection of Grammatical Music.* Dedham: H. Mann, 1808. (8) S16181

Shumway 1793 — Shumway, Nehemiah. *The American Harmony.* Philadelphia: John M'Culloch, 1793. (47) E26162
Later ed.: 1801.

Shumway 1801 — Shumway, Nehemiah. *The American Harmony.* 2d ed. Philadelphia: John M'Culloch, 1801. (52) S1321

Smith 1803 — Smith, William & Co. *The Easy Instructor . . . Part II.* [Hopewell, New Jersey, 1803]. (12) see S11387
Later ed.: 1806.

Stammers 1803 — Stammers, Edward. *Philadelphia Chorister.* Philadelphia: John M'Culloch, 1803. (9) S5093

Stickney 1774 — Stickney, John. *The Gentleman and Lady's Musical Companion.* Newbury-port: Daniel Bayley, 1774. (40) E13642
Later ed.: ca. 1780, 1783.

Stickney 1783 — Stickney, John. *The Gentleman and Lady's Musical Companion.* Newbury-port: Daniel Bayley, [1783]. (23)

Stone 1793 — Stone, Joseph, and Abraham Wood. *The Columbian Harmony.* [Massachusetts, 1793]. (2) E26215

Suffolk 1807 — *The Suffolk Selection of Church Musick.* Boston: Thomas & Andrews, J. T. Buckingham, printer, 1807. (28) S13695

Swan 1801 — Swan, Timothy. *New England Harmony.* Northampton: Andrew Wright, 1801. [Compiled in Suffield, Connecticut]. (3) S1378

Tans'ur 1767 — Tans'ur, William. *The Royal Melody Complete.* 3d ed. Boston: W. M'Alpine; also sold by D. Bayley, Newburyport, and M. Williams, Salem, 1767. (21) E10782
Later ed.: 1768.

Tans'ur 1768 — Tans'ur, William. *The Royal Melody Compleat.* 4th ed. [Newburyport]: printed for and sold by Daniel Bayley, 1768. (24) E11085

Tans'ur 1769 — Tans'ur, William. *The American Harmony: or, Royal Melody Complete.* Vol. I of [Daniel Bayley]. *The American Harmony.* 5th ed. Newbury-port: Daniel Bayley, 1769. (17) see E11489
Later eds.: 1771, 1771, 1773, 1774.

Terril 1800 — Terril, Israel. *The Episcopal Harmony.* New Haven: engrav'd, printed and sold by the author, [1803 or earlier]. (3)

Tomlins 1810 — Tomlins, James. *Sacred Musick.* Boston: J. T. Buckingham, for the compiler, 1810. [Compiled in Virginia]. (9)

Tufts 1723 — Tufts, [John]. *An Introduction to the Art of Singing Psalm-Tunes.* 3d ed. Boston: T. Fleet, for Samuel Gerrish, 1723. (11)
Later eds.: 1726, 1728, 1731, 1736, 1738, 1744.

Tufts 1726 — Tufts, [John]. *An Introduction to the Singing of Psalm-Tunes,* 5th ed. Boston: for Samuel Gerrish, 1726. (14) E39856
Later eds.: 1728, 1731, 1736, 1738, 1744.

Tunes 1763 — *Tunes in Three Parts.* Philadelphia: Anthony Armbruster, 1763. (12) E9526
Later ed.: 1764.

Tunes 1786 — [Protestant Episcopal Church]. *Tunes Suited to the Psalms and Hymns of the Book of Common Prayer.* [Philadelphia: Hall and Sellers, 1786]. (10) E19940

Turner 1752 — [*A Collection of Psalm Tunes, with an Introduction "To Learn to Sing"*]. Boston: engrav'd printed & sold by James A. Turner, 1752. (15) E6820

Village 1795 — *The Village Harmony, or Youth's Assistant to Sacred Musick.* Exeter, New Hampshire: Henry

Ranlet, 1795. (41)
Later eds.: 1796, 1797, 1798, 1800, 1803, 1806, 1807, 1808, 1810.

Village 1796   *The Village Harmony.* 2d ed. Exeter: Henry Ranlet, 1796. (49) E31494
Later eds.: 1797, 1798, 1800, 1803, 1806, 1807, 1808, 1810.

Village 1798   *The Village Harmony.* 4th ed. Exeter: Henry Ranlet, 1798. (52) E34930
Later eds.: 1800, 1803, 1806, 1807, 1808, 1810.

Village 1800   *The Village Harmony.* 5th ed. Exeter: Henry Ranlet, 1800. (60) E38938
Later eds.: 1803, 1806, 1807, 1808, 1810.

Village 1803   *The Village Harmony.* 6th ed. Exeter: Henry Ranlet, 1803. (62) S5506
Later eds.: 1806, 1807, 1808, 1810.

Village 1806   *The Village Harmony.* 7th ed. Exeter: Ranlet & Norris, 1806. (62) S11769
Later eds.: 1807, 1808, 1810.

Village 1807   *The Village Harmony.* 8th ed. Exeter: Norris & Sawyer, 1807. (63) S14125
Later eds.: 1808, 1810.

Village 1808   *The Village Harmony.* 9th ed. Exeter: Norris & Sawyer, 1808. (66) S16636
Later ed.: 1810.

Village 1810   *The Village Harmony.* 10th ed. Exeter: C. Norris & Co., [1810]. (75) S19115

Walter 1721   Walter, Thomas. *The Grounds and Rules of Musick.* Boston: J. Franklin, for S. Gerrish, 1721. (9) E2303
Later eds.: 1723, 1740, 1746, 1759, 1760, 1764, 1764a.

Walter 1740   Walter, Thomas. *The Grounds and Rules of Musick.* 3d ed. Boston: J. Draper for S. Gerrish, 1740. (11) E4622
Later eds.: 1746, 1759, 1760, 1764, 1764a.

Walter 1759   Walter, Thomas. *The Grounds and Rules of Musick.* Boston: Benjamin Mecom, for Thomas Johnston, [1759?]. (12)
Later eds.: 1760, 1764, 1764a.

Walter 1760   Walter, Thomas. *The Grounds and Rules of Musick.* Boston: Benjamin Mecom, 1760. (17)
Later eds.: 1764, 1764a.

Walter, 1764   Walter, Thomas. *The Grounds and Rules of Musick.* Boston: for Thomas Johnston, 1764, 1764a. (21)

Walter 1764a   Walter, Thomas. *The Grounds and Rules of Musick.* Boston: for Thomas Johnston, 1764. (26)

West 1802   West, Elisha. *The Musical Concert.* Northampton: Andrew Wright, for Elisha West and John Billings, Jr., 1802. [Compiled in Woodstock, Vermont]. (3) S3532
Later ed.: 1807.

Willard 1796   *Sacred Harmony.* [Connecticut]: published by Daniel Williard and Thomas Lee Jr., [ca. 1791–96]. (1)

Williams 1769   Williams, A. *The American Harmony, or Universal Psalmodist.* Vol. II of [Daniel Bayley].

The American Harmony. 5th ed. Newburyport, 1769. (25) see E11489
Later eds.: 1771, 1771, 1773, 1774.

Williams 1771   Williams, A. *The American Harmony, or Universal Psalmodist.* Vol. II of [Daniel Bayley]. *The American Harmony.* 6th ed. Newburyport, 1771. (25) E12240
Later eds.: 1771, 1773, 1774.

Wood 1810   Wood, William. *Harmonia Evangelica.* Exeter: C. Norris & Co., [1810]. [Compiled in Massachusetts]. (2) S22081

Woodward 1806   Woodward, [Charles], and [John] Aitken. *Ecclesia Harmonia.* Philadelphia, [1806]. (37)
Later eds.: 1807, 1809.

Woodward 1809   Woodward, Charles. *Ecclesiae Harmonia.* 2d ed. Philadelphia: Sold by W. W. Woodward . . . and by the editor, [1809]. (38) S19262

Worcester 1786   *The Worcester Collection of Sacred Harmony.* Worcester: Isaiah Thomas, 1786. (49) see E19752
Later eds.: 1788, 1791, 1792, 1794, 1797, 1800, 1803.

Worcester 1786 III   *The Worcester Collection of Sacred Harmony,* pt. 3. Worcester: Isaiah Thomas, [1786]. (2) see E19752

Worcester 1788   *The Worcester Collection of Sacred Harmony.* 2d ed. Worcester: Isaiah Thomas, 1788. (49) E21193
Later eds.: 1791, 1792, 1794, 1797, 1800, 1803.

Worcester 1791   *The Worcester Collection of Sacred Harmony.* 3d ed. Boston: Isaiah Thomas and Ebenezer T. Andrews, 1791. (43) E23490
Later eds.: 1792, 1794, 1797, 1800, 1803.

Worcester 1792   *The Worcester Collection of Sacred Harmony.* 4th ed. Boston: Isaiah Thomas and Ebenezer T. Andrews, 1792. (46) E24461
Later eds.: 1794, 1797, 1800, 1803.

Worcester 1794   *The Worcester Collection of Sacred Harmony.* 5th ed. Boston: Isaiah Thomas and Ebenezer T. Andrews, 1794. (45) E27202
Later eds.: 1797, 1800, 1803.

Worcester 1797   [Holden, Oliver]. *The Worcester Collection of Sacred Harmony.* 6th ed. Boston: Isaiah Thomas and Ebenezer T. Andrews, 1797. (46) E32363
Later eds.: 1800, 1803.

Worcester 1800   [Holden, Oliver]. *The Worcester Collection of Sacred Harmony.* 7th ed. Boston: Isaiah Thomas and Ebenezer T. Andrews, 1800. (39) E37786
Later ed.: 1803.

Worcester 1803   [Holden, Oliver]. *The Worcester Collection of Sacred Harmony.* 8th ed. Boston: Isaiah Thomas and Ebenezer T. Andrews, 1803. (39) S4892

Wyeth 1810   Wyeth, John. *Wyeth's Repository of Sacred Music.* Harrisburgh: John Wyeth, 1810. (62) S22116

Appendix III: Tables

Table 1. Core Repertory Compositions: First American Printings

Year	Title(s)
1698	CANTERBURY, PSALM 100 [OLD], PSALM 148, ST. DAVID'S, SOUTHWELL, WINDSOR, YORK
1721	LONDON NEW, ST. JAMES
1723	PSALM 100 [NEW], STANDISH
1726	ISLE OF WIGHT, PSALM 149, PORTSMOUTH (English, 1711)
1737	MEAR
1753	LANDAFF
1754	COLESHILL, ST. ANNE
1755	BATH
ca. 1759	BURFORD
1760	BROMSGROVE, COLCHESTER, ST. MARTIN'S
1761	ANGELS HYMN, AYLESBURY, BEDFORD, MORNING HYMN, NEWBURY, PSALM 33, ROCHESTER, WALSALL, WELLS
1764	ALL SAINTS, AMSTERDAM, BANGOR, DALSTON, FUNERAL THOUGHT, IRISH, KINGSBRIDGE, LITTLE MARLBOROUGH, PLYMOUTH, ST. GEORGE'S, ST. HELEN'S, SUTTON (English, ca. 1760), WANTAGE, WESTON FAVEL
1766	PSALM 34
1767	PUTNEY
1769	BETHESDA, BUCKINGHAM, WINCHESTER
1770	AMHERST, BROOKFIELD, CHESTER, LEBANON
1778	MAJESTY, MARYLAND, PSALM 136, ST. THOMAS, WORCESTER
1779	HARTFORD, MIDDLETOWN, MILFORD, NORWICH, PSALM 25, SUFFIELD
1782	BRIDGEWATER, DENMARK, GREENFIELD, LENOX, STAFFORD, VIRGINIA
1783	CHRISTMAS, DUNSTAN, HABAKKUK, HOTHAM, MONTAGUE, PORTSMOUTH (English, ca. 1760 or before)
1784	PSALM 46
1785	BRISTOL, CALVARY, ENFIELD, JUDGMENT, LISBON, RAINBOW, SHERBURNE, WINDHAM, WINTER
1786	THE DYING CHRISTIAN, GREENWICH, JORDAN, RUSSIA
1787	ANTHEM FOR EASTER
ca. 1787	OCEAN
1788	NEWTON
1790	MONTGOMERY
1793	CORONATION, SUTTON (Ezra Goff, 1793)
1795	PORTUGAL
1796	NEW JERUSALEM
1801	ADESTE FIDELES

Table 2. Core Repertory Compositions: Number of Printings (1698–1810)

Printings	Title(s)
226	PSALM 100 [OLD]
160	WELLS
137	ST. MARTIN'S
135	LITTLE MARLBOROUGH
130	AYLESBURY
121	MEAR, PSALM 149
119	WINDSOR
115	PSALM 34
110	BANGOR
105	LENOX
103	GREENFIELD
100	PLYMOUTH
99	BRIDGEWATER
96	COLCHESTER
95	FUNERAL THOUGHT
93	DENMARK
92	VIRGINIA
90	BATH, CANTERBURY
88	BROOKFIELD, ST. ANNE
85	NORWICH, STAFFORD
84	LANDAFF
83	BEDFORD, ROCHESTER
82	GREENWICH, IRISH
79	BRISTOL, SHERBURNE
76	OCEAN
75	MAJESTY
74	AMHERST, BUCKINGHAM
73	ANGELS HYMN
71	DALSTON, JORDAN, ST. HELEN'S
69	PUTNEY
68	MILFORD, RUSSIA, WANTAGE
65	LISBON, WINDHAM
64	MIDDLETOWN
62	ISLE OF WIGHT
61	BROMSGROVE, NEWTON, SUFFIELD, SUTTON (English, ca. 1760), WORCESTER
60	MARYLAND, MONTAGUE
59	HOTHAM
58	ALL SAINTS, WALSALL
57	ENFIELD, ST. DAVID'S, ST. JAMES, YORK
56	CHESTER, STANDISH
55	HABAKKUK, MONTGOMERY
54	DUNSTAN, PORTUGAL
53	NEWBURY, PORTSMOUTH (English, 1711)

Printings	Title(s)
52	CHRISTMAS, LONDON NEW, NEW JERUSALEM, PSALM 100 [NEW], WINCHESTER, WINTER
51	KINGSBRIDGE, PSALM 148, RAINBOW, ST. THOMAS, SOUTHWELL
50	BETHESDA
49	PSALM 136
48	ADESTE FIDELES, AMSTERDAM, JUDGMENT, LEBANON
47	CORONATION, PORTSMOUTH (English, ca. 1760 or before)
46	ANTHEM FOR EASTER, CALVARY, THE DYING CHRISTIAN, HARTFORD, PSALM 25, ST. GEORGE'S, WESTON FAVEL
45	BURFORD, COLESHILL, MORNING HYMN, PSALM 33, SUTTON (Ezra Goff, 1793)
44	PSALM 46

Table 3. Core Repertory Compositions: Proportion of New England Printings

Percent	Title(s)
95	SUTTON (English, ca. 1760)
93	COLCHESTER, ST. HELEN'S, YORK
92	BUCKINGHAM, PSALM 148
90	BETHESDA, PORTSMOUTH (English, 1711)
88	CHESTER, ST. DAVID'S
87	PSALM 25
86	ALL SAINTS, CANTERBURY, SOUTHWELL
85	WINCHESTER, WINTER
83	DUNSTAN, JUDGMENT
82	BURFORD, WINDSOR
81	CORONATION, ST. JAMES
80	DALSTON
79	ENFIELD
78	MILFORD
77	BATH, BROMSGROVE, FUNERAL THOUGHT
76	KINGSBRIDGE, PLYMOUTH, ST. ANNE
75	LONDON NEW, PUTNEY
74	PSALM 149
73	HABAKKUK, LITTLE MARLBOROUGH
72	WANTAGE
70	ANTHEM FOR EASTER
69	LEBANON, NEW JERUSALEM, WINDHAM
67	BANGOR, THE DYING CHRISTIAN
66	WELLS
65	CALVARY, CHRISTMAS, IRISH, LISBON, PSALM 136
64	PSALM 100 [OLD], STANDISH
63	AMHERST, JORDAN, PSALM 34
62	LANDAFF, PSALM 33, RUSSIA, WALSALL
61	DENMARK, NEWTON, NORWICH, ST. MARTIN'S, STAFFORD
59	BRISTOL, BROOKFIELD, HOTHAM, WORCESTER
58	ISLE OF WIGHT, NEWBURY
57	GREENFIELD, MARYLAND, MONTAGUE, PSALM 46, RAINBOW
56	AMSTERDAM, AYLESBURY, MAJESTY, PSALM 100 [NEW]

Percent	Title(s)
55	GREENWICH, MEAR, OCEAN, PORTSMOUTH (English, ca. 1760 or before)
54	PORTUGAL, ST. GEORGE'S
53	MONTGOMERY, MORNING HYMN
52	SUFFIELD
51	ST. THOMAS, SHERBURNE, SUTTON (Ezra Goff, 1793), VIRGINIA
50	HARTFORD, LENOX, MIDDLETOWN
48	ADESTE FIDELES
46	BRIDGEWATER, ROCHESTER
43	BEDFORD, WESTON FAVEL
33	ANGELS HYMN
24	COLESHILL

Table 4. Tunebooks with 25 or More Core Repertory Compositions

Number of Tunes	Title(s)
75	Village 1810
66	Village 1808
64	Pilsbury 1799
63	Village 1807
62	Boston 1799, Village 1803, Village 1806, Wyeth 1810
60	Village 1800
58	Adgate 1791
55	Blake 1810
54	Federal 1791, Sacred 1788
52	Boston First 1806, Federal 1792, Shumway 1801, Village 1798
50	Middlesex 1808, Selection 1794
49	Bayley 1788a, Village 1796, Worcester 1786, Worcester 1788
48	Adgate 1789, Selection 1790
47	Brown 1810, Federal 1790, Shumway 1793
46	Worcester 1792, Worcester 1797
45	Mass 1784, Middlesex 1807, Worcester 1794
44	Bayley 1788
43	Sacred 1806, Worcester 1791
42	Holyoke 1803, Law 1792, Read 1810, Selection 1789
41	Atwill 1795, Federal 1788, Jocelin 1783, Law 1791, Little 1809, Salem 1806, Village 1795
40	Brown 1804, Deerfield 1808, Holden 1793, Holden 1796, Mann 1807, Read 1807, Selection 1788, Stickney 1774
39	Atwill 1804, Ely 1792, Salem 1805, Worcester 1800, Worcester 1803
38	Brown 1802, Cooper 1804, Jocelin 1782, Mann 1797, Woodward 1809
37	Bayley 1784, Boston West 1810a, Jocelin 1788, Woodward 1806
36	Erben 1806, Flagg 1764, New England 1771
35	Bayley 1770, New 1784
34	Huntington 1800, Little 1805, Little 1807
33	Bayley 1771, Bayley 1785a, Holden 1801, Law H 1810, Read 1797, Read 1798

Number of Tunes	Title(s)
32	Federal 1794, Law 1807, Read 1794
31	Cumberland 1804, Law 1803, Seymour 1809
30	Bayley 1785, Boston West 1810, Erben 1808, Robbins 1805
29	Bayley 1768, Boston Brattle 1810, Gilman 1771, Holden 1800, Sandford 1793
28	Chapin 1808, Evans 1810, Suffolk 1807

Number of Tunes	Title(s)
27	Bayley 1766, Bayley 1767, Huntington 1807a, Little 1801, Lyon 1761, Sacred 1810
26	Blanchard 1808, Holyoke 1804, Read 1804, Read 1806, J. Read 1808, Walter 1764a
25	Amphion 1789, Johnston 1763, Read 1787, Williams 1769

Critical Commentary

The following commentary covers editorial details in the music and additional stanzas. Citation of the primary sources for the music and underlaid text for each piece is made in the Tune Biographies given in Appendix I. However, when the primary musical source is textless or when it lacks coherent punctuation, the text and/or punctuation are supplied from the text source rather than from the musical source, and these instances are cited in the Critical Commentary. Moreover, if the underlaid text represents only a fragment of the text as it appears in the text source, this fragment is located within the whole text by means of a citation in the Critical Commentary.

In the Critical Commentary, the voice parts are given their eighteenth-century names: treble (soprano), counter (alto), tenor, and bass. Pieces not listed in this section are those in which there are no variations between the sources and the edition. Pitches are designated according to the usual system, wherein c′ = middle C, c″ = the C above middle C, and so forth.

[2.] ALL SAINTS
Capitalization of underlaid text in musical source not followed here. Upbeat, all voices, 2 beats of rest inserted before note. Period omitted at end of text.

[3.] AMHERST
M. 1, all voices, time signature is Ɔ, and a full measure of rest is inserted before m. 1 in all parts.

[4.] AMSTERDAM
Text taken in full from Law 1779, introduction, p. 6. M. 1, all parts, 2 mm. of rest inserted before m. 1. M. 25, note 1, underlaid text is "hast." M. 29, all parts, first and second endings are given here.

[5.] ANGELS HYMN
Punctuation supplied from New Version, Psalm 95. Upbeat, all parts, 2 beats of rest inserted at beginning of m.; counter written in octavating G clef. M. 16, all parts, note is a dotted whole-note.

[6.] ANTHEM FOR EASTER: THE LORD IS RISEN INDEED
Capitalization of underlaid text not followed in every detail here. M. 23, counter, note 2 is a quarter-note. M. 85, all parts, period omitted from text underlay. M. 96, comma omitted from text underlay.

[6a.] ANTHEM FOR EASTER, additional section
This section, added to the printing in Village 1800 between m. 66 and m. 67, is missing from most printings; it is provided here as an option. Text from Young, p. 57. M. 13, tenor, note 1 is a dotted quarter-note. M. 15, bass, note 2 is a sixteenth-note.

[7.] AYLESBURY
M. 1, all parts, time signature is Ɔ, and a full measure of rest is inserted before m. 1. Mm. 12–13, underlaid text is "be sides." M. 13, all parts, question mark omitted from text underlay.

[8.] BANGOR
M. 1, all parts, time signature is Ɔ, tempo is marked "slow," and the opening rest is omitted.

[9.] BATH
Stanza 3 in text source is in brackets. Music is printed in shape-notes. Upbeat, all parts, time signature omitted, and 2 beats of rest inserted before note. M. 16, all parts, note is a dotted whole-note.

[10.] BEDFORD
First line in text source reads, "O praise the Lord with hymns of joy." Upbeat, all parts, 2 beats of rest inserted before note. M. 14, all parts, note is a dotted whole-note. Additional stanza 12, line 1, penultimate word in text source spelled "fleccy."

[11.] BETHESDA
Punctuation supplied from Watts, Psalm 84. The text source indicates "pause" after stanza 4. Upbeat, all parts, time signature is C; counter written in octavating G clef. M. 13, all parts, quarter-rest omitted.

[12.] BRIDGEWATER
The text source indicates "pause" after stanzas 8, 12, and 20. M. 1, all parts, time signature is Ɔ. M. 7, all parts, repeat sign omitted, but since most printings, including Jocelin 1782, do repeat the fuging section, a repeat is introduced here and first and second endings manufactured to support it.

[13.] BRISTOL
The first 4 lines of the poem as printed in the text source read as follows:

The spacious firmament on high,
With all the blue ethereal sky,
And spangled heavens, a shining frame,
Their great original proclaim.

M. 1, all parts, time signature is ₵, and tempo is marked "brisk."

[14.] BROMSGROVE
Stanza 2 in text source is in brackets. Upbeat, all parts, 2 beats of rest inserted before note. M. 14, all parts, note is a dotted whole-note.

[15.] BROOKFIELD
M. 16, all parts, note is a dotted whole-note. The accidentals appear over the affected notes rather than next to them, apparently to save space rather than to designate them as optional.

[16.] BUCKINGHAM
Upbeat, counter written in octavating G clef. M. 14, all parts, note is a dotted whole-note.

[18.] CALVARY
Underlaid text, line 3, reads: "Where nature in all ruin lies." Punctuation supplied from Watts, Horae. Additional stanzas, capitalization in text source not followed. M. 1, all parts, time signature is Ɔ, and a full measure of rest is inserted before m. 1; tenor, text spelled "th'ots."

[19.] CANTERBURY
Punctuation supplied from Watts, Hymns II, no. 3. M. 1, all parts, time signature is ₵; counter written in octavating G clef.

[20.] CHESTER
M. 1, all parts, time signature is 𝄵.

[21.] CHRISTMAS
Upbeat, all parts, time signature is ↄ, tempo is marked "moderate," melody in top voice is marked "air," and this m. is occupied by half-note and quarter-rest; counter written in G clef. M. 20, all parts, note is a whole-note.

[22.] COLCHESTER
Upbeat, all parts, 2 beats of rest inserted before note. M. 1, all parts, note 1, apostrophe in underlaid text supplied by editor. M. 7, all parts, note 1, underlaid text, dash in source, replaced here with a colon. M. 14, all parts, note is a dotted whole-note.

[23.] COLESHILL
Text supplied from Watts, Psalm 144, since musical source is textless. M. 1, all parts, time signature is ¢; counter written in octavating G clef.

[24.] CORONATION
Upbeat, all parts, time signature is ↄ.

[25.] DALSTON
Punctuation supplied from Watts, Psalm 122. M. 1, all parts, time signature is 𝄵; counter written in octavating G clef.

[26.] DENMARK
M. 2, all parts, apostrophes in text are editorial. M. 32, treble, note 4 is a sixteenth-note. M. 48, all parts, text is spelled "heavn's." Dynamic markings in m. 90 and m. 94 are on the downbeat of m. 91 and m. 95.

[27.] DUNSTAN
Stanzas 2–3 and 7–8 in text source are in brackets. M. 1, all parts, time signature is 𝄵, tempo is marked "cheerful"; top voice sings melody, which is marked "air"; counter written in G clef.

[28.] THE DYING CHRISTIAN
M. 1, all parts, time signature is ↄ; top voice marked "air" to show that it carries the tune. Mm. 10 and 18, all parts, the indication is "slow and soft," here designated "p." M. 25, text, period supplied by editor. M. 80, all parts, the performance instruction is "lively and loud." "Marks of Distinction" in the bass, m. 37 and elsewhere, are described in the musical source, p. iii, as calling for notes so marked to be performed "plainly and distinctly." These marks are not retained in the present edition.

[29.] ENFIELD
Stanzas renumbered because setting covers 2 stanzas of text; since the source has 9 stanzas, the final one is omitted here. Punctuation and spelling supplied from Rowe. Upbeat, all parts, time signature is ¢, and 3 beats of rest are inserted before note 1. M. 16, all parts, note is a whole-note.

[30.] FUNERAL THOUGHT
Punctuation and capitalization supplied from Watts, Hymns II, no. 63. M. 1, all parts, time signature is ¢.

[31.] GREENFIELD
Punctuation supplied from New Version, Psalm 46. Music is printed in shape-notes. M. 1, all parts, time signature is ↄ, and a full measure of rest is inserted before m. 1. M. 10, tenor, quarter-rest omitted.

[32.] GREENWICH
Text supplied from Watts, Psalm 73, because musical source prints only its first line. Stanzas renumbered because setting covers 2 stanzas of text; since the source has 5 stanzas, the final one is omitted here. M. 1, all parts, time signature is ↄ.

[33.] HABAKKUK
Upbeat, all parts, time signature is C; middle voice (carrying melody), written in G clef and is meant to be sung by the tenor an octave below notated pitch. M. 23, beat 1, tenor, note 1 has no flat-sign.

[34.] HARTFORD
Stanzas renumbered because setting covers 2 stanzas of text; since the source has 7 stanzas, the final one is omitted here. Pause marked after stanza 2. M. 1, all parts, time signature is ↄ, and a full measure of rest is inserted before m. 1.

[35.] HOTHAM
Punctuation supplied from Law Collection. M. 1, all parts, time signature is C. M. 10, bass, beats 3 and 4 written as 2 tied quarter-notes.

[36.] IRISH
Stanza 5 in text source is in brackets. The first stanza of Watts's version reads as follows:

Blest morning, whose young dawning rays
Beheld our rising God;
Which saw him triumph o'er the dust,
And leave his last abode!

[37.] ISLE OF WIGHT
Text is stanzas 3–4 of Watts's original. M. 1, all parts, time signature is ¢. Mm. 16–17, treble, slur seems to shift last syllable of "prepare" to second beat of m. 17 and is adjusted here by the editor to agree with other voices.

[38.] JORDAN
Punctuation supplied from Watts, Hymns II, no. 66. The tune sets stanzas 1 and 3; here the editor has supplied two additional stanzas, the first made up of Watts's nos. 2 and 4, the second of Watts's 5 and 6. Stanzas 3 and 4 in text source are in brackets. Music is printed in shape-notes. Upbeat, all parts, time signature is ↄ. M. 16, all parts, repeat sign omitted; although musical source lacks this sign, most other printings carry it, including the tune's first in Billings 1786.

[39.] JUDGMENT
Text is stanzas 2–9 of Watts's original. M. 1, all parts, time signature is ↄ, and a full measure of rest is inserted before m. 1.

[40.] KINGSBRIDGE
Text alternatives are provided because musical source carries 2 stanzas, the first being stanza 5 of Watts, Psalm 24, L.M., and the second, stanza 1 of Watts, Psalm 107, L.M., 4th Part. Here the additional stanzas of Psalm 107 are given first, followed by stanzas 6–7 of Psalm 24 (renumbered). Punctuation supplied from Watts, Psalm 24 and Psalm 107. Upbeat, all parts, 2 beats of rest inserted before note. M. 16, all parts, note is a dotted half-note.

[41.] LANDAFF
Text supplied from Watts, Psalm 50, 2d Part, since musical source is textless. Text source indicates "pause" after stanzas 5, 10, and 14; last stanza labeled "Epiphonema." Stanza 8, line 4, punctuation illegible at end of line, and period supplied here. Stanza 15, line 4, "you" emended here as "your." M. 1, all parts, time signature is ¢; counter written in octavating G clef.

[42.] LEBANON
M. 1, all parts, time signature is 𝄵.

[43.] LENOX
Text source indicates "pause" after stanza 4. M. 1, all parts,

time signature is ꜱ, and a full measure of rest is inserted before m. 1. M. 10, all parts, note 1, period omitted from text underlay.

[44.] LISBON
M. 1, all parts, time signature is ꜱ.

[45.] LITTLE MARLBOROUGH
Upbeat, all parts, 2 beats of rest are inserted before note. M. 13, all parts, note is a dotted whole-note.

[46.] LONDON NEW
Text supplied from Watts, Psalm 145, 3d Part, because musical source is textless. Stanzas 6–7 in text source are in brackets. M. 1, all parts, time signature is 𝄵; counter written in octavating G clef.

[47.] MAJESTY
Text stanzas, renumbered here, omit verses 17–20 of Psalm 18, Part II. M. 1, all parts, time signature is ꜱ.

[48.] MARYLAND
M. 1, all parts, time signature is ꜱ.

[49.] MEAR
Upbeat, all parts, 2 beats of rest are inserted before note. M. 14, all parts, note is a dotted whole-note.

[50.] MIDDLETOWN
Punctuation supplied from Whitefield, pp. 35f. Capitalization of underlaid text and additional stanzas in text source not followed here. M. 1, all parts, 2 full measures of rest are inserted before m. 1.

[51.] MILFORD
Punctuation supplied from Arnold. M. 1, all parts, time signature is ꜱ, and a full measure of rest is inserted before m. 1.

[52.] MONTAGUE
M. 1, all parts, time signature is 𝄵. M. 26b, all parts, note is a half-note.

[53.] MONTGOMERY
M. 1, all parts, time signature is ꜱ, and a full measure of rest is inserted before m. 1. M. 11, all parts, source has no repeat sign; sign placed in m. 11 in accord with Village 1795 and other printings. M. 18, all parts, repeat sign.

[54.] MORNING HYMN
Punctuation supplied from Hymns and Songs, p. 183. Note that stanza 4, line 3, is short a syllable; in Flatman's original the word "given" is used instead of "kept."

[55.] NEW JERUSALEM
Text is stanzas 2–6 of Watts's original. M. 1, all parts, time signature is ꜱ; middle voice (tenor), labeled "air." M. 5, all parts, no repeat sign; supplied here in accord with other printings, including Ingalls 1805.

[56.] NEWBURY
Stanzas 8–10 in text source are in brackets. M. 1, all parts, time signature is ꜱ, and a full measure of rest is inserted before m. 1. M. 3, all parts, apostrophe in "chast'ning" supplied by the editor.

[57.] NEWTON
M. 1, all parts, time signature ꜱ, and a full measure of rest is inserted before m. 1.

[58.] NORWICH
The attribution in the text source reads: "Watts, abbreviated and altered." The first stanza is stanza 3 of a poem in Watts, Horae, p. 48, and 2 more stanzas of Belknap's version also come from Watts's 17-stanza poem. The source of the rest has not been identified. Punctuation supplied from text source. M. 1, all parts, time signature is ꜱ.

[59.] OCEAN
Stanzas are renumbered because the setting covers 2 stanzas of text. Stanza 2 in text source is in brackets. The first 4 lines of Watts's text read as follows:

Thy works of glory, mighty Lord,
Thy wonders in the deeps,
The sons of courage shall record;
Where rolling ocean sleeps.

M. 1, all parts, time signature is ꜱ.

[60.] PLYMOUTH
Punctuation supplied from Watts, Psalm 51, 2d Part. Upbeat, all parts, 2 beats of rest are inserted before note. M. 1, bass, note 1 is a half-note. M. 8. all parts, text source has "the" instead of "this." M. 14, all parts, note is a dotted whole-note.

[61.] PORTSMOUTH
Text source indicates "pause" after stanza 3. Upbeat, all parts, counter written in octavating G clef. M. 14, all parts, note is a dotted whole-note.

[62.] PORTSMOUTH
M. 1, all parts, tempo marked "slow."

[63.] PORTUGAL
Editor has added period at end of stanza 3. Stanza 7, line 4, first word of text in source has typographical error, "Hnd"; corrected here.

[64.] PSALM 25
M. 1, all parts, time signature is ꜱ.

[65.] PSALM 33
Stanzas renumbered because setting covers 2 stanzas of text. M. 1, all parts, tempo marked "largo," and 2 full measures of rest are inserted before m. 1.

[66.] PSALM 34
M. 1, all parts, time signature is ꜱ, and a full measure of rest is inserted before m. 1.

[67.] PSALM 46
Text is supplied from Watts, Psalm 146, because the musical source prints only the first line. M. 1, all parts, time signature is ꜱ.

[68.] PSALM 100 [OLD]
M. 1, all parts, time signature is ꜱ, and tempo is marked "slow."

[69.] PSALM 100 [NEW]
Punctuation supplied from Watts, Psalm 90. Stanzas 2–3 in text source are in brackets. M. 16, bass, note is a dotted whole-note.

[70.] PSALM 136
Since the text that is set is the final stanza in the text source (Watts, Psalm 121), no additional stanzas are here supplied. M. 1, all parts, time signature is ꜱ, and a full measure of rest is inserted before m. 1.

[71.] PSALM 148
Text supplied from Bay 1698 because musical source is textless. M. 1, all parts, time signature is 𝄵; counter written in octavating G clef.

[72.] PSALM 149
First stanza in text source differs from that set in Worcester 1788, reading as follows from the 5th line on:

In our great Creator
Let Israel rejoice;
And children of Sion
Be glad in their King.

Upbeat, all parts, 2 beats of rest inserted before note. M. 16, all parts, note is a dotted half-note.

[73.] Putney

Heavy bars between phrases in musical source suggest pauses longer than the notation indicates. Upbeat, all parts, 2 beats of rest are inserted before note; counter written in octavating G clef. M. 8, all parts, note 2, the word is spelled "tost" in musical source. M. 16, all parts, note is a dotted whole-note.

[74.] Rainbow

M. 1, all parts, time signature is ɔ. M. 21b, all parts, second ending comprised of 2 tied whole-notes.

[75.] Rochester

Punctuation supplied from Watts, Psalm 73. M. 1, all parts, time signature is ɔ, and a full measure of rest is inserted before m. 1. Stanza 2, line 4, ends with comma.

[76.] Russia

Music printed in shape-notes. M. 1, all parts, time signature is ɔ. M. 4, treble, note 1 has no natural sign. M. 6, underlaid text has no punctuation. Mm. 7–10, the word "a" in the musical source ("Laid in a balance") is changed to "the" to agree with the text sources.

[77.] St. Anne

Stanzas 2–4 in text source are in brackets. Music printed in shape-notes. M. 1, all parts, time signature is ¢.

[78.] St. David's

Text supplied from New Version, since musical source is textless. M. 1, all parts, time signature is ¢; counter written in octavating G clef.

[79.] St. George's

Upbeat, all parts, time signature is ¢, and 3 beats of rest inserted before note. M. 10, all parts, note is a whole-note.

[80.] St. Helen's

Upbeat, all parts, 2 beats of rest are inserted before note. M. 24, all parts, note is a dotted half-note.

[81.] St. James

M. 1, all parts, time signature is ¢, and half-rest is omitted; counter written in octavating G clef.

[82.] St. Martin's

Stanzas 4–5 in text source are in brackets. Upbeat, all parts, 2 beats of rest inserted before note. M. 14, all parts, note is a dotted whole-note; bass, note is c-sharp.

[83.] St. Thomas

Text source indicates "pause" after stanzas 6 and 12. M. 1, all parts, time signature is ɔ, and a full measure of rest is inserted before note. M. 16, all parts, underlaid text has no period.

[84.] Sherburne

M. 1, all parts, time signature is ɔ, and a full measure of rest is inserted before first note.

[85.] Southwell

Text supplied from Watts, Psalm 36, because musical source is textless. Stanza 2 in text source is in brackets. M. 1, all parts, time signature is ¢.

[86.] Stafford

Music is printed in shape-notes. M. 1, all parts, time signa-ture is ɔ. M. 8, all parts, repeat sign omitted; sign supplied here because first and second endings are printed at the end of the piece in the source, and most printings, including Read 1785, show the fuging section repeated from m. 8. M. 18, all parts, underlaid text spelled "env'ous."

[87.] Standish

Stanzas 6–7 in text source are in brackets. Punctuation sup-plied from Watts, Psalm 119. M. 1, all parts, time signature is ¢.

[88.] Suffield

Punctuation supplied from Watts, Psalm 39. M. 1, all parts, time signature is ɔ, and a full measure of rest is inserted before m. 1. M. 7, all parts, repeat sign omitted; supplied here from Adgate 1789 and is present in many other printings; first and second endings (mm. 11, 11b, 11c) are editorially added to sup-port the repeat.

[89.] Sutton

Stanzas 7–8 in text source are in brackets. Upbeat, all parts, 2 beats of rest inserted before note; counter written in octavating G clef. M. 12, all parts, underlaid text spelled "power." M. 13, all parts, note is a dotted whole-note.

[90.] Sutton

Music is printed in shape-notes. M. 1, all parts, time signa-ture is ɔ, and a full measure of rest inserted before first note. Mm. 1 and 13, all parts, quotation marks supplied from text source. Mm. 6ff, all parts, underlaid text spelled "sorrow's."

[91.] Virginia

M. 1, all parts, time signature is ɔ, and a full measure of rest is inserted before m. 1. Mm. 3–4, all parts, underlaid text is "controul." M. 5, tenor, note 4 is b.

[92.] Walsall

Pause marked after stanza 5 in text source. Punctuation sup-plied from Watts, Psalm 5. M. 1, all parts, time signature is ¢; counter written in octavating G clef. Mm. 5, 9, and 14, all parts, phrase endings at ends of these mm. marked with heavy bars; rests supplied by editor in mm. 6, 10, and 15 because these mea-sures contain only one half-note. M. 9, treble, note is a half-note. M. 11, all parts, note 1, underlaid text is "the." M. 15, tenor and bass, note is a whole-note. M. 16, treble, slur covers notes 1–3; corrected here by analogy with the other 3 voices; bass, note 1 is indistinctly engraved and could be F or G.

[93.] Wantage

Punctuation supplied from Watts, Psalm 89. Upbeat, all parts, 2 beats of rest inserted before note. M. 13, bass, note 2 is a half-note. M. 14, all parts, note is a dotted whole-note.

[94.] Wells

Stanzas 2 and 4 in text source are in brackets. M. 1, all parts, time signature is ɔ, and a full measure of rest is inserted before m. 1.

[95.] Weston Favel

Upbeat, counter written in octavating G clef. M. 6, tenor, note 1 is a half-note. M. 19, all parts, comma in underlaid text supplied by editor.

[96.] Winchester

Upbeat, all parts, dynamic level marked "very soft," and 2 beats of rest are inserted before note; counter, written in oc-tavating G clef. M. 16, all parts, note is a dotted whole-note.

[97.] Windham

M. 1, all parts, time signature is ɔ, and tempo marked "slow."

[98.] WINDSOR

Stanzas 3, 4–8 in text source are in brackets. Upbeat, all parts, time signature is Ɔ, and tempo marked "slow." Heavy bars between phrases suggest longer pauses than the notation calls for.

[99.] WINTER

M. 1, all parts, time signature is ₵.

[100.] WORCESTER

Punctuation supplied from Watts, Hymns I. M. 1, all parts, time signature is Ɔ, and a full measure of rest is inserted before m. 1. Mm. 22ff, all parts, underlaid text spells "saviour" as "sav'our."

[101.] YORK

Upbeat, all parts, time signature is ₵. Mm. 4, 7, and 11, all parts, heavy bars between phrases suggest pauses, here marked by the editor as fermatas.

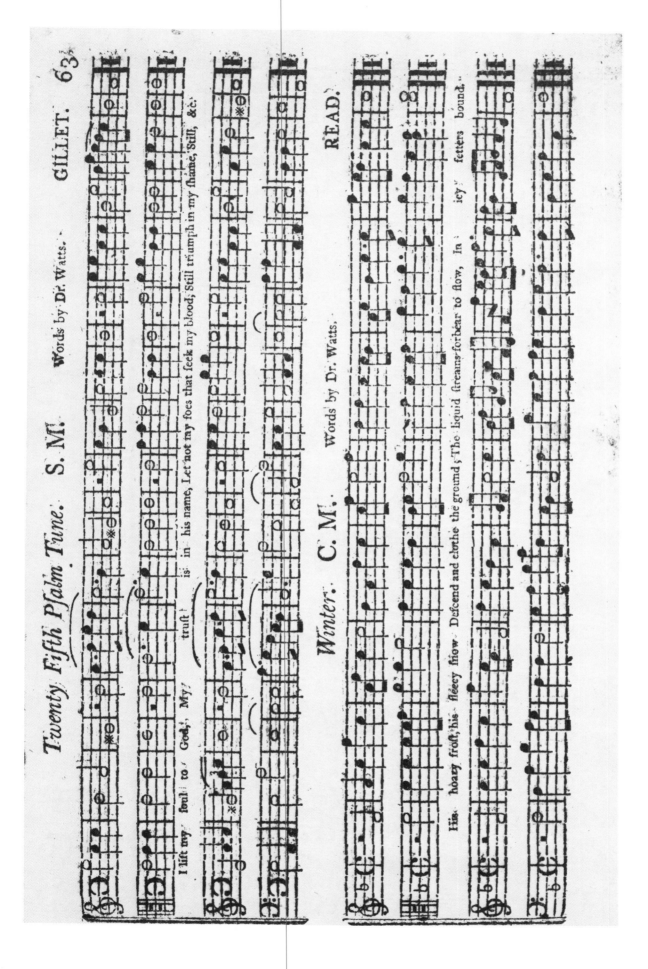

Plate I. Psalm 25 by Alexander Gillet and Winter by Daniel Read, two Core Repertory tunes, as printed typographically in Oliver Holden, *The Worcester Collection of Sacred Harmony*, 6th ed. (Boston: Isaiah Thomas and Ebenezer T. Andrews, 1797), p. 63. (Photograph courtesy of William L. Clements Library, University of Michigan)

THE CORE REPERTORY
OF
EARLY AMERICAN
PSALMODY

[1.] Adeste Fideles

English, 1782

2

2. There grow thy saints in faith and love
Blest with thy infl'ence from above;
Not Lebanon, with all its trees,
Yields such a comely sight as these.

3. The plants of grace shall ever live:
(Nature decays, but grace must thrive)
Time, which doth all things else impair,
Still makes them flourish strong and fair.

4. Laden with fruits of age, they show
The Lord is holy, just and true:
None who attend his gates shall find
A God unfaithful or unkind.

[2.] All Saints

William Knapp, 1738

The heav'ns de- clare thy glo- ry Lord, In ev- 'ry star thy wis- dom

shines, But when our eyes be- hold thy word, We read thy name in fair- er lines.

2. The rolling sun, the changing light,
   And nights, and days, thy pow'r confess;
   But the blest volume thou hast writ
   Reveals thy justice and thy grace.

3. Sun, moon and stars, convey thy praise
   Round the whole earth, and never stand:
   So when the truth began its race,
   It touch'd, it glanc'd on ev'ry land.

4. Nor shall thy spreading gospel rest,
   Till thro' the world thy truth has run;
   Till Christ has all the nations blest
   Which see the light, or feel the sun.

5. Great sun of right'ousness, arise!
   Bless the dark world with heav'nly light;
   Thy gospel makes the simple wise;
   Thy laws are pure, thy judgments right.

6. Thy noblest wonders here we view,
   In souls renew'd, and sins forgiv'n:
   Lord, cleanse my sins, my soul renew,
   And make thy word my guide to heav'n.

[3.] Amherst

William Billings, 1770

Ye bound-less realms of joy, Ex- alt your Mak- er's fame;

His praise your songs em- ploy A- bove the star- ry frame:

Your voic-es raise, Ye Cher-ub- im And Ser-a- phim,To sing his praise.

2. Thou moon, that rul'st the night,
   And sun, that guid'st the day,
   Ye glitt'ring stars of light,
   To him your homage pay:
   His praise declare,
   Ye heav'ns above,
   And clouds that move
   In liquid air.

3. Let them adore the Lord,
   And praise his holy Name,
   By whose Almighty word
   They all from nothing came:
   And all shall last,
   From changes free;
   His firm decree
   Stands ever fast.

4. Let earth her tribute pay;
   Praise him, ye dreadful whales,
   And fish that through the sea
   Glide swift with glitt'ring scales;
   Fire, hail, and snow,
   And misty air,
   And winds that, where
   He bids them, blow.

5. By hills and mountains, all
   In grateful concert join'd;
   By cedars stately tall,
   And trees for fruit design'd;
   By ev'ry beast,
   And creeping thing,
   And fowl of wing,
   His Name be blest.

6. Let all of royal birth,
   With those of humbler frame,
   And judges of the earth,
   His matchless praise proclaim:
   In this design,
   Let youths with maids,
   And hoary heads
   With children join.

7. United zeal be shown,
   His wond'rous fame to raise,
   Whose glorious Name alone
   Deserves our endless praise:
   Earth's utmost ends
   His pow'r obey;
   His glorious sway
   The sky transcends.

8. His chosen saints to grace,
   He sets them up on high,
   And favours Israel's race,
   Who still to him are nigh:
   O therefore raise
   Your grateful voice,
   And still rejoice
   The Lord to praise.

[4.] Amsterdam

English, 1742

Rise, my soul, and stretch thy wings,—Thy bet - ter por - tion trace,

Rise, my soul, and stretch thy wings,—Thy bet - ter___ por - tion trace,

Rise, my soul,___ and stretch thy wings,—Thy bet - ter por - tion trace,

Rise, my soul, and stretch thy wings,—Thy bet - ter por - tion trace,

Rise from tran - si - to - ry things,—Tow'rds heav'n thy na - tive place.

Rise from tran - si - to - ry things,—Tow'rds heav'n_ thy___ na - tive place.

Rise from tran - si - to - ry things,—Tow'rds heav'n thy na - tive place.

Rise from tran - si - to - ry things,—Tow'rds heav'n thy na - tive place.

Sun, and moon and stars_ de - cay, Time shall soon_ this_ earth_ re - move,

Sun, and moon and stars de - cay, Time shall soon this earth re - move,

Sun, and moon and stars_ de - cay, Time shall_ soon this earth_ re - move,

Sun, and moon and stars_ de - cay, Time shall soon this earth_ re - move,

6

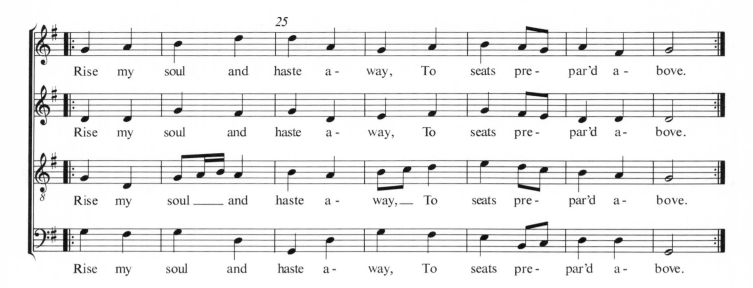

Rise my soul and haste a-way, To seats pre-par'd a-bove.

2. Rivers to the ocean run,
   Nor stay in all their course;
   Fire ascending seeks the sun,
   Both speed them to their source;
   So a soul that's born of God,
   Pants to view his glorious face;
   Upwards tends to his abode,
   To rest in his embrace.

3. Fly me riches, fly me cares,
   While I that coast explore;
   Flatt'ring world, with all thy snares,
   Sollicit me no more.
   Pilgrims fix not here their home:
   Strangers tarry but a night,
   When the last dear morn is come,
   They'll rise to joyful light.

4. Cease ye pilgrims, cease to mourn,
   Press onward to the prize:
   Soon our Saviour will return
   Triumphant in the skies:
   Yet a season and you know
   Happy entrance will be given,
   All our sorrows cast below,
   And earth exchang'd for heaven.

[5.] Angels Hymn

Orlando Gibbons, 1623

O come, loud an-thems let us sing, Loud thanks to our al-might-y

king; For we our voic - es high should raise, When our sal - va - tion's rock we praise.

king; For we our voic - es high should raise, When our sal - va - tion's_ rock we _ praise.

king; For we our voic - es high should raise, When our sal - va - tion's rock we praise.

king; For we our voic - es high _ should_ raise, When our sal - va - tion's rock we praise.

2. Into his presence let us haste,
   To thank him for his favours past;
   To him address, in joyful songs,
   The praise that to his Name belongs.

3. For God the Lord, enthron'd in state,
   Is, with unrivall'd glory, great:
   A King superior far to all,
   Whom gods the heathen falsely call.

4. The depths of earth are in his hand,
   Her secret wealth at his command,
   The strength of hills that reach the skies,
   Subjected to his empire lies.

5. The rolling ocean's vast abyss,
   By the same sov'reign right, is his;
   'Tis mov'd by his Almighty Hand,
   That form'd and fix'd the solid land.

6. O let us to his courts repair,
   And bow with adoration there;
   Down on our knees devoutly all
   Before the Lord, our Maker, fall.

7. For he's our God, our shepherd he,
   His flock and pasture sheep are we,
   If then you'll, like his flock, draw near,
   To-day if you his voice will hear,

8. Let not your harden'd hearts renew
   Your fathers' crimes and judgments too;
   Nor here provoke my wrath, as they
   In desert plains of Meribah.

9. When through the wilderness they mov'd,
   And me with fresh temptations prov'd,
   They still, through unbelief, rebell'd,
   Whilst they my wond'rous works beheld.

10. They forty years my patience griev'd,
    Though daily I their wants reliev'd.
    Then—'Tis a faithless race, I said,
    Whose heart from me has always stray'd.

11. They ne'er will tread my righteous path;
    Therefore to them, in settled wrath,
    Since they despis'd my rest, I sware,
    That they shall never enter there.

[6.] Anthem for Easter: The Lord Is Risen Indeed

William Billings, 1787

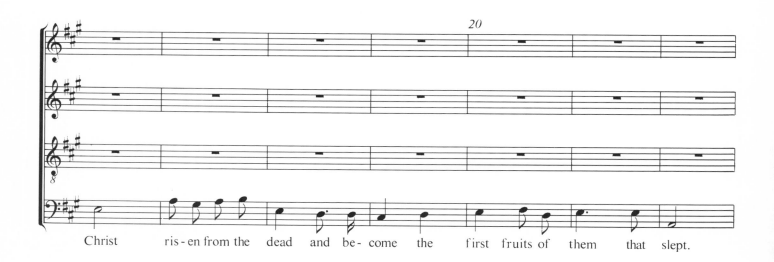

10

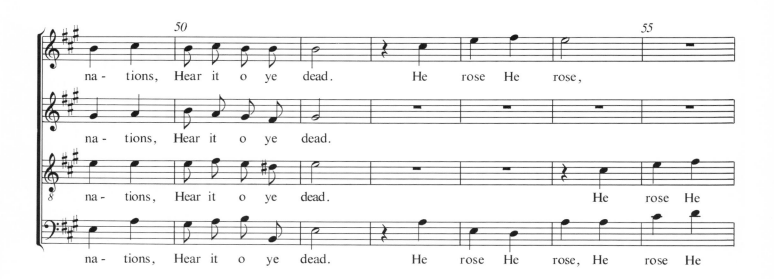

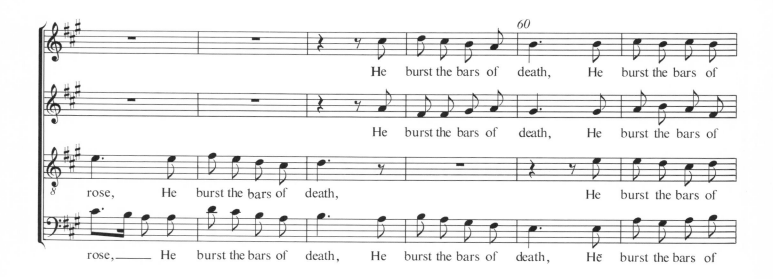

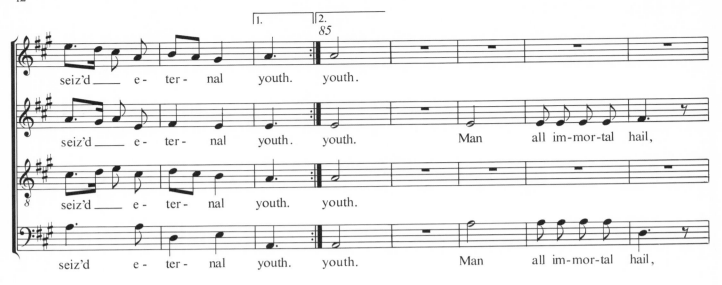

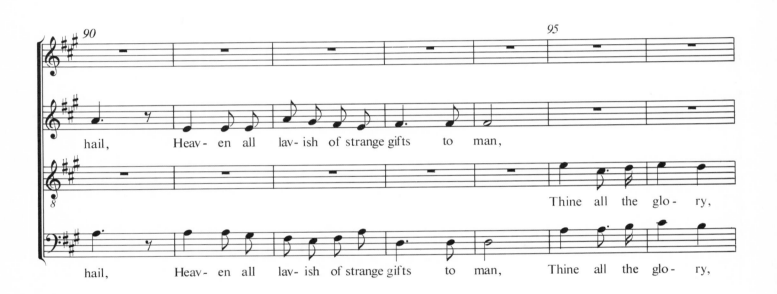

[6a.] Anthem for Easter, additional section*

William Billings, 1795

* This section, published after the "Anthem for Easter" (No. [6]) was already in circulation, can be sung between m. 66 and m. 67 of No. [6].

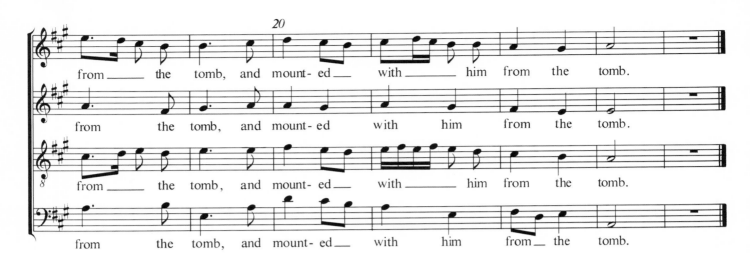

from _____ the tomb, and mount- ed _____ with _____ him from the tomb.

from the tomb, and mount- ed with him from the tomb.

from _____ the tomb, and mount- ed _____ with _____ him from the tomb.

from the tomb, and mount- ed _____ with him from ____ the tomb.

[7.] Aylesbury

English, 1718

The Lord my shep- herd is, I shall be well sup- plied

The Lord my shep- herd is, I shall be well sup- plied

The Lord my shep- herd is, I shall be well sup- plied

The Lord my shep- herd is, I shall be well sup- plied

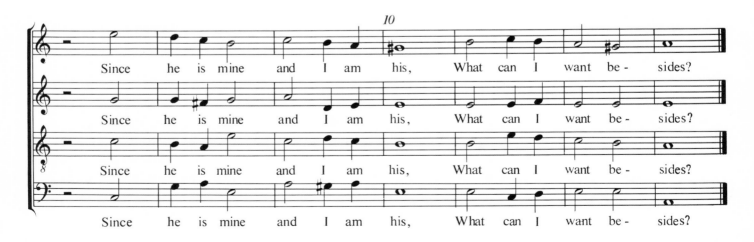

Since he is mine and I am his, What can I want be - sides?

Since he is mine and I am his, What can I want be - sides?

Since he is mine and I am his, What can I want be - sides?

Since he is mine and I am his, What can I want be - sides?

2. He leads me to the place
   Where heav'nly pasture grows,
   Where living waters gently pass,
   And full salvation flows.

3. If e'er I go astray,
   He doth my soul reclaim,
   And guides me in his own right way,
   For his most holy name.

4. While he affords his aid,
   I cannot yield to fear;
   Though I should walk through death's dark shade,
   My shepherd's with me there.

5. In spite of all my foes
   Thou dost my table spread;
   My cup with blessings overflows,
   And joy exalts my head.

6. The bounties of thy love
   Shall crown my foll'wing days:
   Nor from thy house will I remove,
   Nor cease to speak thy praise.

16

[8.] Bangor

William Tans'ur, 1735

Teach me the mea-sure of my days, Thou mak-er of my frame,

I would sur-vey life's nar-row space, And learn how frail I am.

2. A span is all which we can boast,
An inch or two of time:
Man is but vanity and dust,
In all his flow'r and prime.

3. See the vain race of mortals move,
Like shadows, o'er the plain,
They rage and strive, desire and love,
But all their noise is vain.

4. Some walk in honor's gaudy show;
Some dig for golden ore;
They toil for heirs, they know not who,
And straight are seen no more.

5. What could I wish or wait for then
From creatures, earth and dust?
They make our expectations vain,
And disappoint our trust.

6. Now I forbid my carnal hope,
My fond desires recall;
I give my mortal int'rest up,
And make my God my All.

[9.] Bath

English, 1713

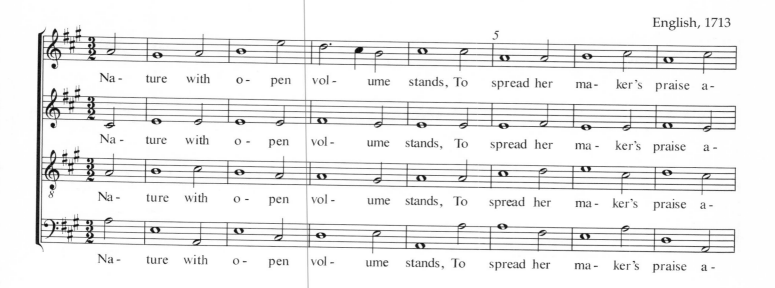

Nature with o - pen vol - ume stands, To spread her ma - ker's praise a -

Nature with o - pen vol - ume stands, To spread her ma - ker's praise a -

Nature with o - pen vol - ume stands, To spread her ma - ker's praise a -

Nature with o - pen vol - ume stands, To spread her ma - ker's praise a -

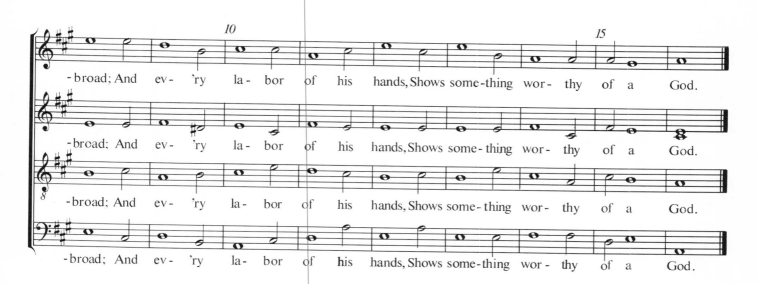

-broad; And ev - 'ry la - bor of his hands, Shows some-thing wor - thy of a God.

-broad; And ev - 'ry la - bor of his hands, Shows some-thing wor - thy of a God.

-broad; And ev - 'ry la - bor of his hands, Shows some-thing wor - thy of a God.

-broad; And ev - 'ry la - bor of his hands, Shows some-thing wor - thy of a God.

2. But in the grace which rescu'd man,
   His brightest form of glory shines:
   Here, on the cross, 'tis fairest drawn
   In precious blood, and crimson lines.

3. Here his whole name appears complete;
   Nor wit can guess, nor reason prove,
   Which of the letters best is writ,
   The pow'r, the widsom, or the love.

4. Here I behold his inmost heart,
   Where grace and vengeance strangely join;
   Piercing his Son with sharpest smart,
   To make the purchas'd pleasures mine.

5. Oh! the sweet wonders of that cross,
   Where God, the Saviour, lov'd and dy'd!
   Her noblest life my spirit draws
   From his dear wounds, and bleeding side.

6. I would for ever speak his name
   In sounds, to mortal ears unknown,
   With angels join to praise the Lamb,
   And worship at his Father's throne.

18

[10.] Bedford

William Wheall, ca. 1720

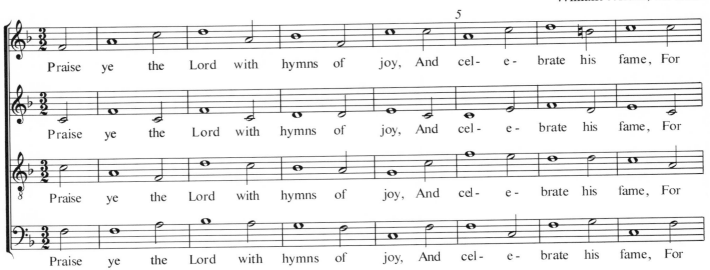

Praise ye the Lord with hymns of joy, And cel - e - brate his fame, For

Praise ye the Lord with hymns of joy, And cel - e - brate his fame, For

Praise ye the Lord with hymns of joy, And cel - e - brate his fame, For

Praise ye the Lord with hymns of joy, And cel - e - brate his fame, For

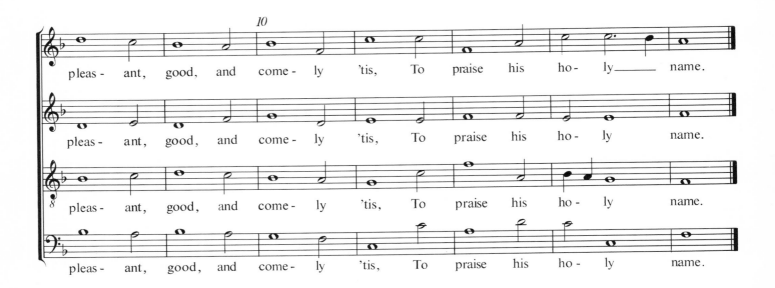

pleas - ant, good, and come - ly 'tis, To praise his ho - ly _____ name.

pleas - ant, good, and come - ly 'tis, To praise his ho - ly name.

pleas - ant, good, and come - ly 'tis, To praise his ho - ly name.

pleas - ant, good, and come - ly 'tis, To praise his ho - ly name.

2. His holy city God will build,
   Though levell'd with the ground;
   Bring back his people, though dispers'd
   Through all the nations round.

3. He kindly heals the broken hearts,
   And all their wounds does close;
   He tells the number of the stars,
   Their sev'ral names he knows.

4. Great is the Lord, and great his pow'r,
His wisdom has no bound;
The meek he raises, and throws down
The wicked to the ground.

5. To God, the Lord, a hymn of praise
With grateful voices sing;
To songs of triumph tune the harp,
And strike each warbling string.

6. He covers heav'n with clouds, and thence
Refreshing rain bestows;
Through him, on mountain-tops, the grass
With wond'rous plenty grows.

7. He savage beasts, that loosely range,
With timely food supplies;
He feeds the ravens' tender brood,
And stops their hungry cries.

8. He values not the warlike steed,
But does his strength disdain;
The nimble foot that swiftly runs
No prize from him can gain.

9. But he to him that fears his Name
His tender love extends;
To him that on his boundless grace
With stedfast hope depends.

10. Let Sion and Jerusalem
To God their praise address;
Who fenc'd their gates with massy bars,
And does their children bless.

11. Through all their borders he gives peace,
With finest wheat they're fed;
He speaks the word, and what he wills
Is done as soon as said.

12. Large flakes of snow, like fleecy wool,
Descend at his command;
And hoary frost, like ashes spread,
Is scatter'd o'er the land.

13. When, join'd to these, he does his hail
In little morsels break,
Who can against his piercing cold
Secure defences make?

14. He sends his word, which melts the ice;
He makes his wind to blow;
And soon the streams, congeal'd before,
In plenteous currents flow.

15. By him his statutes and decrees
To Jacob's sons were shown;
And still to Israel's chosen seed
His righteous laws are known.

16. No other nation this can boast;
Nor did he e'er afford
To heathen lands his oracles,
And knowledge of his word.

[11.] Bethesda

English, ca. 1760 or before

Lord of the worlds a - bove, How pleas - ant and how fair The

dwell - ings of thy love, Thy earth - ly tem - ples are! To

thine a - bode My heart as - pires, With warm de - sires, To see my God.

2. The sparrow for her young
   With pleasure seeks a nest:
   And wand'ring swallows long
   To find their wonted rest;
   My spirit faints
   With equal zeal,
   To rise and dwell
   Among thy saints.

3. O happy souls who pray
   Where God appoints to hear!
   O happy men who pay
   Their constant service there!
   They praise thee still;
   And happy they
   Who love the way
   To Sion's hill.

4. They go from strength to strength
   Through this dark vale of tears,
   Till each arrives at length,
   Till each in heaven appears:
   O glor'ous seat,
   When God our King
   Shall thither bring
   Our willing feet!

5. To spend one sacred day
   Where God and saints abide,
   Affords diviner joy
   Than thousand days beside:
   Where God resorts
   I love it more
   To keep the door
   Than shine in courts.

6. God is our sun and shield,
   Our light and our defence;
   With gifts his hands are fill'd,
   We draw our blessings thence:
   He shall bestow
   On Jacob's race
   Peculiar grace
   And glory too.

7. The Lord his people loves;
   His hand no good with-holds
   From those his heart approves,
   From pure and pious souls:
   Thrice happy he,
   O God of hosts,
   Whose spirit trusts
   Alone in thee.

22

[12.] Bridgewater

Lewis Edson, 1782

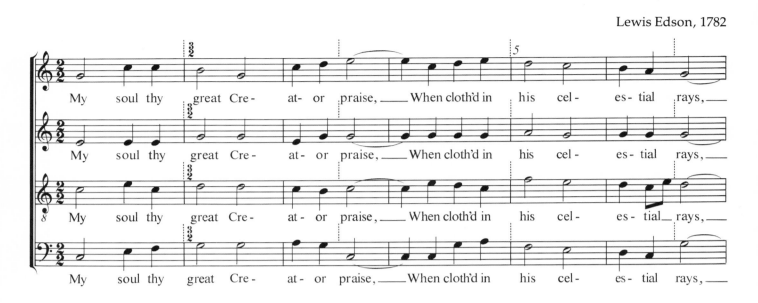

My soul thy great Cre - at - or praise, ___ When cloth'd in his cel - es - tial rays, ___

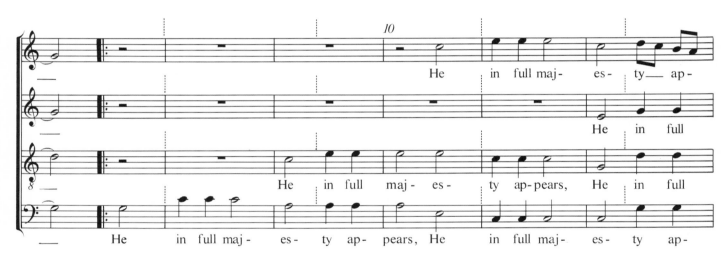

He in full maj - es - ty ___ ap -
He in full
He in full maj - es - ty ap - pears, He in full
He in full maj - es - ty ap - pears, He in full maj - es - ty ap -

-pears, And like ___ a robe ___ his glo - ry wears. wears.
maj - es - ty ap - pears, And like a robe his glo - ry wears. wears.
maj - es - ty ap - pears, And like a robe his glo - ry wears. wears.
-pears, And like a robe his glo - ry wears. wears.

2. The heav'ns are for his curtains spread;
   Th'unfathom'd deep he makes his bed,
   Clouds are his char'ot, when he flies
   On winged storms across the skies.

3. Angels, whom his own breath inspires,
   His ministers are flaming fires:
   And, swift as thought, their armies move,
   To bear his vengeance or his love.

4. The world's foundations, by his hand,
   Are pois'd, and shall forever stand;
   He binds the ocean in his chain,
   Lest it should drown the world again.

5. When earth was cover'd with the flood,
   Which high above the mountains stood,
   He thunder'd, and the ocean fled,
   Confin'd to its appointed bed.

6. The swelling billows know their bound,
   And in their channels walk their round;
   Yet thence convey'd by secret veins,
   They spring on hills, and drench the plains.

7. He bids the crystal fountains flow;
   And chear the vallies as they go;
   Tame heifers there their thirst allay,
   And for the stream wild asses bray.

8. From pleasant trees which shade the brink,
   The lark and linnet light to drink:
   Their songs the lark and linnet raise,
   And chide our silence in his praise.

9. God, from his cloudy cistern, pours,
   On the parch'd earth enriching show'rs;
   The grove, the garden, and the field,
   A thousand joyful blessings yield.

10. He makes the grassy food arise,
    And gives the cattle large supplies;
    With herbs for man of var'ous pow'r,
    To nourish nature, or to cure.

11. What noble fruit the vines produce?
    The olive yields a shining juice;
    Our hearts are cheer'd with gen'rous wine,
    With inward joy our faces shine.

12. O bless his name, ye nations fed
    With nature's chief supporter, bread:
    While bread your vital strength imparts,
    Serve him with vigor in your hearts.

13. Behold the stately cedar stands,
    Rais'd in the forest by his hands;
    Birds to the boughs for shelter fly,
    And build their nests secure on high.

14. To craggy hills ascends the goat;
    And at the airy mountain's foot,
    The feebler creatures make their cell;
    He gives them wisdom where to dwell.

15. He sets the sun his circling race,
    Appoints the moon to change her face;
    And when thick darkness veils the day,
    Calls out wild beasts to hunt their prey.

16. Fierce lions lead their young abroad,
    And, roaring, ask their meat from God;
    But when the morning beams arise,
    The savage beast to covert flies.

17. Then man to daily labor goes;
    The night was made for his repose:
    Sleep is thy gift, that sweet relief
    From tiresome toil and wasting grief.

18. How strange thy works! how great thy skill!
    And ev'ry land thy riches fill:
    Thy wisdom round the world we see,
    This spacious earth is full of thee.

19. Nor less thy glories in the deep,
    Where fish in millions swim and creep,
    With wond'rous motions swift or slow,
    Still wand'ring in the paths below.

20. There ships divide their wat'ry way,
    And flocks of scaly monsters play;
    There dwells the huge Leviathan,
    And foams and sports in spite of man.

21. Vast are thy works, almighty Lord!
    All nature rests upon thy word,
    And the whole race of creatures stand
    Waiting their portion from thy hand.

22. While each receives his diff'rent food,
    Their chearful looks pronounce it good:
    Eagles and bears, and whales and worms,
    Rejoice and praise in diff'rent forms.

23. But when thy face is hid, they mourn,
    And dying, to their dust return;
    Both man and beast their souls resign;
    Life, breath and spirit, all are thine.

24. Yet thou canst breathe on dust again,
    And fill the world with beasts and men;
    A word of thy creating breath
    Repairs the wastes of time and death.

25. His works, the wonders of his might,
    Are honor'd with his own delight:
    How awful are his glor'ous ways!
    The Lord is dreadful in his praise.

26. The earth stands trembling at thy stroke,
    And, at thy touch, the mountains smoke;
    Yet humble souls may see thy face,
    And tell their wants to sov'reign grace.

27. In thee my hopes and wishes meet,
    And make my meditation sweet:
    Thy praises shall my breath employ,
    Till it expires in endless joy.

28. While haughty sinners die accurst,
    Their glory bury'd with their dust,
    I to my God, my heav'nly King,
    Immortal hallelujahs sing.

[13.] Bristol

Timothy Swan, 1785

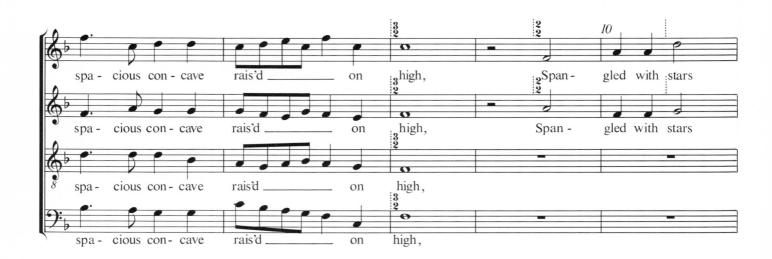

The lof - ty pil - lars of ___ the sky, And
The lof - ty pil - lars of the sky, And
The lof - ty pil - lars of ___ the sky, And
The lof - ty pil - lars of the sky, And

spa - cious con - cave rais'd ___ on high, Span - gled with stars
spa - cious con - cave rais'd ___ on high, Span - gled with stars
spa - cious con - cave rais'd ___ on high,
spa - cious con - cave rais'd ___ on high,

a shin - ing frame, ___ Their great ___ o - ri - gin - nal pro -
a shin - ing frame, ___ Their great o - ri - gin - nal ___ pro -
Their great o - ri - gin - nal ___ pro -
Their great o - ri - gin - nal pro -

2. Soon as the evening shades prevail,
   The Moon takes up the wond'rous tale,
   And nightly to the list'ning earth,
   Repeats the story of her birth:
   Whilst all the stars that round her burn,
   And all the planets in their turn,
   Confirm the tidings as they roll,
   And spread the truth from pole to pole.

3. What though, in solemn silence, all
   Move round the dark terrestrial ball?
   What though nor real voice nor sound
   Amid their radiant orbs be found?
   In reason's ear they all rejoice,
   And utter forth a glorious voice,
   For ever singing as they shine,
   "The Hand that made us is Divine."

[14.] Bromsgrove

English, ca. 1729

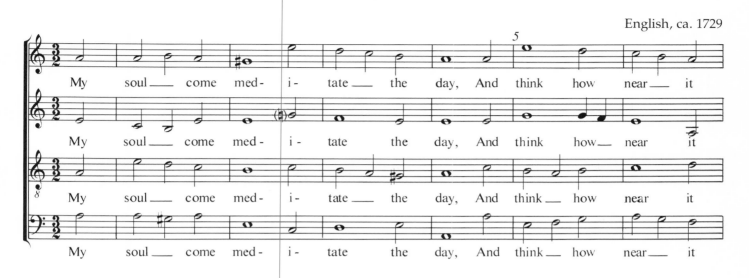

My soul come med-i-tate the day, And think how near it

My soul come med-i-tate the day, And think how near it

My soul come med-i-tate the day, And think how near it

My soul come med-i-tate the day, And think how near it

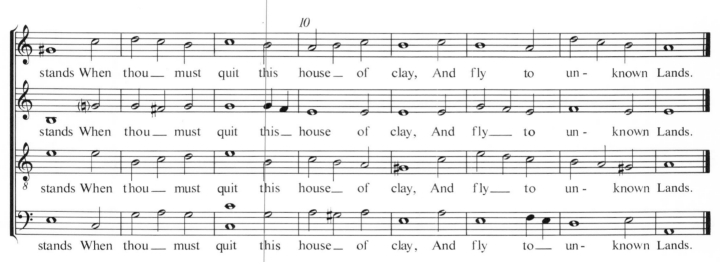

stands When thou must quit this house of clay, And fly to un-known Lands.

stands When thou must quit this house of clay, And fly to un-known Lands.

stands When thou must quit this house of clay, And fly to un-known Lands.

stands When thou must quit this house of clay, And fly to un-known Lands.

2. And you, mine eyes, look down and view
   The hollow gaping tomb;
   This gloomy prison waits for you,
   Whene'er the summons come.

3. Oh! could we die with those who die,
   And place us in their stead;
   Then would our spirits learn to fly,
   And converse with the dead.

4. Then should we see the saints above
   In their own glor'ous forms,
   And wonder why our souls should love
   To dwell with mortal worms!

5. How we should scorn these clothes of flesh,
   These fetters, and this load:
   And long for ev'ning, to undress,
   That we may rest with God.

6. We should almost forsake our clay
   Before the summons come;
   And pray, and wish our souls away
   To their eternal home.

[15.] Brookfield

William Billings, 1770

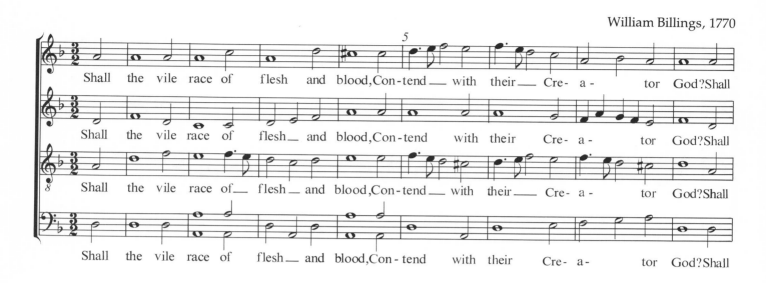

Shall the vile race of flesh and blood, Con-tend with their Cre-a-tor God? Shall

mor-tal worms pre-sume to be More ho-ly, wise, or just than He?

2. Behold, he puts his trust in none
Of all the spirits round his throne;
Their natures, when compar'd with his,
Are neither holy, just nor wise.

3. But how much meaner things are they
Who spring from dust, and dwell in clay!
Touch'd by the finger of thy wrath,
We faint and vanish like the moth.

4. From night to day, from day to night,
We die by thousands in thy sight;
Buri'd in dust, whole nations lie
Like a forgotten vanity.

5. Almighty Pow'r, to thee we bow;
How frail are we! how glor'ous thou!
No more the sons of earth shall dare
With an eternal God compare!

[16.] Buckingham

English, 1763 or before

Lord thou __ wilt hear __ me when __ I pray, I am for ev - er thine, I

Lord thou wilt hear me when __ I pray, I am for ev - er thine, I

Lord thou __ wilt hear me when __ I pray, I am for ev - er thine, I

Lord thou wilt hear me when __ I pray, I am for ev - er thine, I

fear __ be - fore __ thee __ all the __ day, Nor would __ I dare __ to sin.

fear be - fore thee all the day, Nor would __ I dare to sin.

fear __ be - fore __ thee all __ the day, Nor would __ I dare __ to sin.

fear __ be - fore thee all the day, Nor would __ I dare __ to sin.

2. And while I rest my weary head
From cares and bus'ness free,
'Tis sweet conversing on my bed
With my own heart and thee.

3. I pay this ev'ning sacrifice;
And when my work is done,
Great God, my faith and hope relies
Upon thy grace alone.

4. Thus, with my thoughts compos'd to peace,
I'll give mine eyes to sleep;
Thy hand in safety keeps my days.
And will my slumbers keep.

[17.] Burford

English, 1718

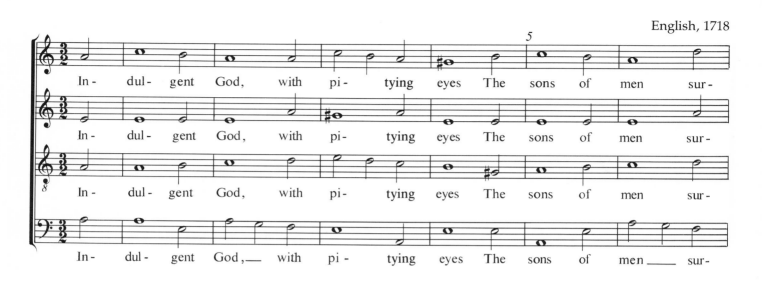

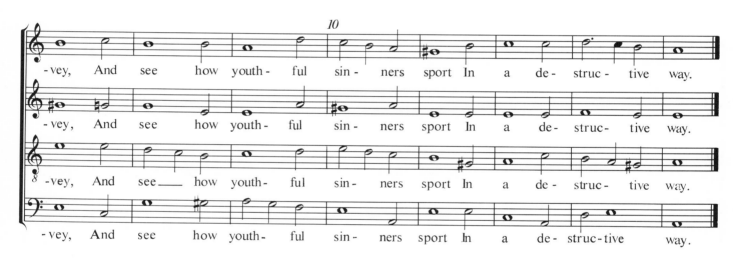

2. Ten thousand dangers lurk around,
   To bear them to the tomb;
   Each in an hour may plunge them down
   Where hope can never come.

3. Reduce, O Lord, their wand'ring minds,
   Amus'd with airy dreams,
   That heav'nly wisdom may dispel
   Their visionary schemes.

4. With holy caution may they walk,
   And be thy word their guide;
   Till each, the desert safely pass'd,
   On Sion's hill abide.

[18.] Calvary

Daniel Read, 1785

2. The tyrant, how he triumphs here!
   His trophies spread around!
   And heaps of dust and bones appear
   Thro' all the hollow ground.

3. These skulls, what ghastly figures now!
   How loathsome to the eyes?
   These are the heads we lately knew
   So beauteous and so wise.

4. But where the souls, those deathless things,
   That left his dying clay?
   My thoughts, now stretch out all your wings,
   And trace eternity.

5. O that unfathomable sea!
   Those deeps without a shore!
   Where living waters gently play,
   Or fiery billows roar.

6. Thus must we leave the banks of life,
   And try this doubtful sea,
   Vain are your groans, and dying strife,
   To gain a moment's stay.

7. There we shall swim in heav'nly bliss,
   Or sink in flaming waves,
   While the pale carcass thoughtless lies,
   Amongst the silent graves.

8. Some hearty friend shall drop his tear
   On our dry bones, and say,
   "These once was strong, as mine appear,
   And mine must be as they."

9. Thus shall our mould'ring members teach
   What now our senses learn:
   For dust and ashes loudest preach
   Man's infinite concern.

[19.] Canterbury

English, 1585

2. Are we not tending upward, too,
   As fast as time can move?
   Nor would we wish the hours more slow
   To keep us from our Love.

3. Why should we tremble to convey
   Their bodies to the tomb?
   There the dear flesh of Jesus lay,
   And left a long perfume.

4. The graves of all his saints he bless'd,
   And soft'ned ev'ry bed:
   Where should the dying members rest,
   But with the dying Head?

5. Thence he arose, ascending high,
   And show'd our feet the way:
   Up to the Lord our souls shall fly,
   At the great rising day.

6. Then let the last loud trumpet sound,
   And bid our kindred rise;
   Awake, ye nations, under ground;
   Ye saints, ascend the skies.

[20.] Chester

William Billings, 1770

Let the high heav'ns your songs ____ in - vite, Those spa - cious fields of bril - liant ____ light; Where sun, and moon, ____ and plan - ets roll, And stars that glow from pole ____ to pole.

Let the high heav'ns your songs in - vite, Those spa - cious fields of bril - liant light; Where sun, and moon, and ____ plan - ets roll, And stars that glow from pole ____ to pole.

Let the high heav'ns your songs ____ in - vite, Those spa - cious fields ____ of bril - liant light; Where sun, and moon, and ____ plan - ets roll, And ____ stars that glow ____ from pole ____ to pole.

Let the high heav'ns your songs ____ in - vite, Those spa - cious fields ____ of bril - liant light; Where sun, and moon, and ____ plan - ets roll, And stars that glow ____ from pole ____ to pole.

2. Sing earth, in verdant robes array'd,
   Its herbs and flow'rs, its fruit and shade;
   Peopl'd with life of various forms,
   Fishes, and fowls, and beasts, and worms.

3. View the broad sea's majestic plains,
   And think how wide its maker reigns;
   That band remotest nations join,
   And on each wave his goodness shines.

4. But, O that brighter world above,
   Where lives and reigns incarnate love;
   God's only Son in flesh array'd,
   For man a bleeding victim made.

5. Thither, my soul, with rapture soar;
   There in the land of praise adore:
   This theme demands an angel's tongue,
   Demands a never-ending song.

[21.] Christmas

Martin Madan, 1769

36

hour, Lo Je - sus the Sav- iour is born, Lo Je - sus the Sav- iour is born.

hour, Lo Je - sus the Sav- iour is born, Lo Je - sus the Sav- iour is born.

hour, Lo Je - sus the Sav- iour is born.

hour, Lo Je - sus the Sav- iour is born, Lo Je - sus the Sav- iour is born.

2. All glory be to God on high,
   To him all praise is due,
   The promise is seal'd,
   The Saviour's reveal'd
   And proves that the record is true.

3. Let joy around like rivers flow,
   Flow on, and still increase,
   Messiah is come
   To ransom his own,
   And heaven and earth are at peace.

4. Then let us join the heavens above,
   Where hymning seraphs sing,
   Join all the glad pow'rs,
   For their Lord is ours,
   Our prophet, our priest, and our king.

[22.] Colchester

William Tans'ur, 1735

O, 'twas ___ a joy- ful sound to hear, Our tribes de- vout- ly say: Up Is- rel to the tem- ple haste, And keep your fes- tal day.

2. At Salem's courts we must appear,
   With our assembled pow'rs,
   In strong and beauteous order rang'd,
   Like her united tow'rs.

3. 'Tis thither, by divine command,
   The tribes of God repair,
   Before his ark to celebrate
   His name with praise and pray'r.

4. Tribunals stand erected there,
   Where equity takes place:
   There stand the courts and palaces
   Of royal David's race.

5. O, pray we then for Salem's peace,
   For they shall prosp'rous be,
   Thou holy city of our God,
   Who bear true love to thee.

6. May peace within thy sacred walls
   A constant guest be found,
   With plenty and prosperity
   Thy palaces be crown'd.

7. For my dear brethren's sake, and friends
   No less than brethren dear,
   I'll pray—May peace in Salem's tow'rs
   A constant guest appear.

8. But most of all I'll seek thy good,
   And ever wish thee well,
   For Sion and the temple's sake,
   Where God vouchsafes to dwell.

[23.] Coleshill

English, 1644

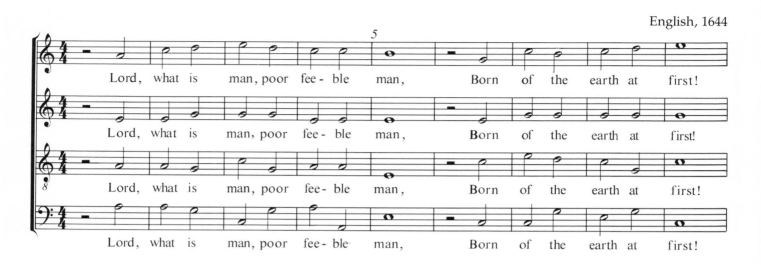

Lord, what is man, poor fee-ble man, Born of the earth at first!

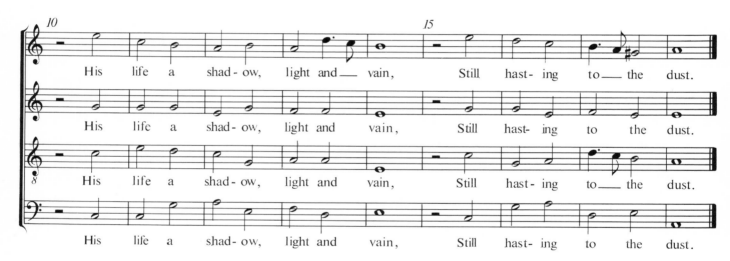

His life a shad-ow, light and — vain, Still hast-ing to — the dust.

2. O what is feeble dying man,
   Or any of his race,
   That God should make it his concern
   To visit him with grace?

3. That God, who darts his lightnings down;
   Who shakes the world above,
   And mountains tremble at his frown,
   How wond'rous is his love!

[24.] Coronation

Oliver Holden, 1793

2. Crown him ye martyrs of our God,
Who from the altar call,
Extol the stem of Jesse's rod,
And crown him Lord of all.

3. Ye chosen seed of Isr'els race,
A remnant weak and small,
Hail him who saves you by his grace,
And crown him Lord of all.

4. Ye gentile sinners, ne'er forget,
The wormwood and the gall,
Go spread your trophies at his feet,
And crown him Lord of all.

5. Babes, men and sires, who know his love,
Who feel your sin and thrall,
Now joy with all the host above,
And crown him Lord of all.

6. Let ev'ry kindred, ev'ry tongue,
On this terrestrial ball,
To him all majesty ascribe,
And crown him Lord of all.

7. O that with yonder sacred throng,
We at his feet may fall
We'll join the everlasting song,
And crown him Lord of all.

[25.] Dalston

English, 1763

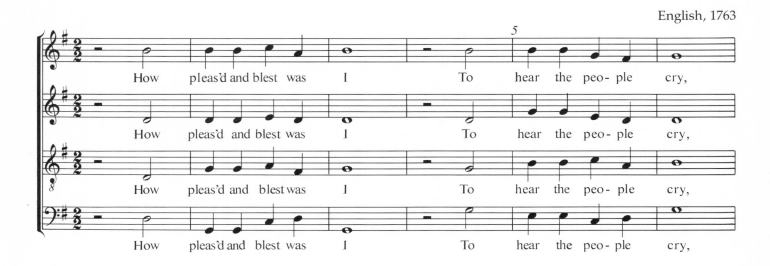

How pleas'd and blest was I To hear the peo- ple cry,
How pleas'd and blest was I To hear the peo- ple cry,
How pleas'd and blest was I To hear the peo- ple cry,
How pleas'd and blest was I To hear the peo- ple cry,

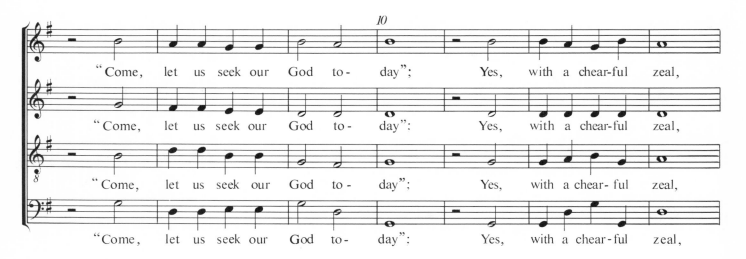

"Come, let us seek our God to- day"; Yes, with a chear-ful zeal,
"Come, let us seek our God to- day": Yes, with a chear-ful zeal,
"Come, let us seek our God to- day": Yes, with a chear-ful zeal,
"Come, let us seek our God to- day": Yes, with a chear-ful zeal,

2. Zion, thrice happy place!
   Adorn'd with wond'rous grace,
   And walls of strength embrace thee round;
   In thee our tribes appear,
   To pray and praise and hear
   The scared gospel's joyful sound.

3. There David's greater Son
   Has fix'd his royal throne;
   He sits for grace and judgment there;
   He bids the saint be glad,
   And makes the sinner sad,
   And humble souls rejoice with fear.

4. May peace attend thy gate,
   And joy within thee wait
   To bless the soul of ev'ry guest!
   The man who seeks thy peace,
   And wishes thine increase,
   A thousand blessings on him rest!

5. My tongue repeats her vows,
   "Peace to this sacred house!"
   For there my friends and kindred dwell;
   And, since my glor'ous God
   Makes thee his blest abode,
   My soul shall ever love thee well!

[26.] Denmark

Martin Madan, 1769

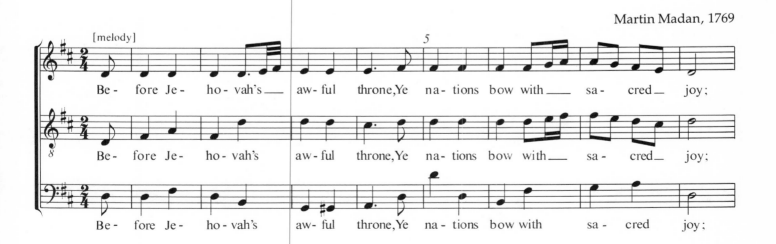

42

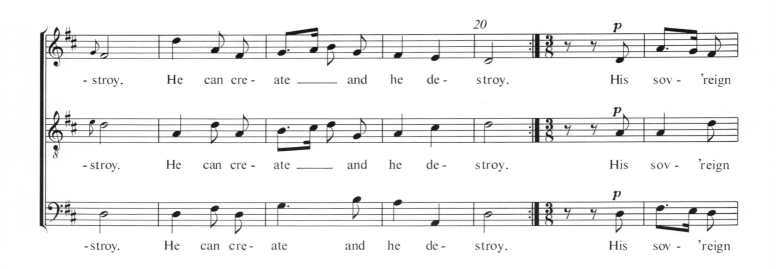

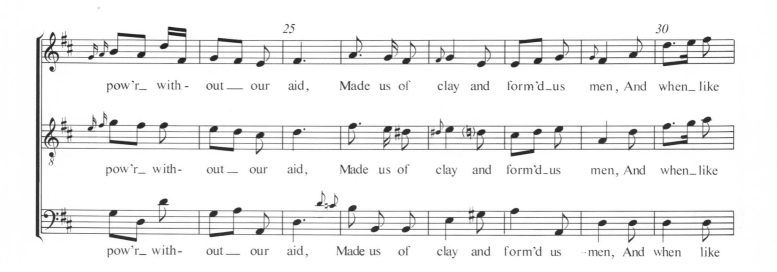

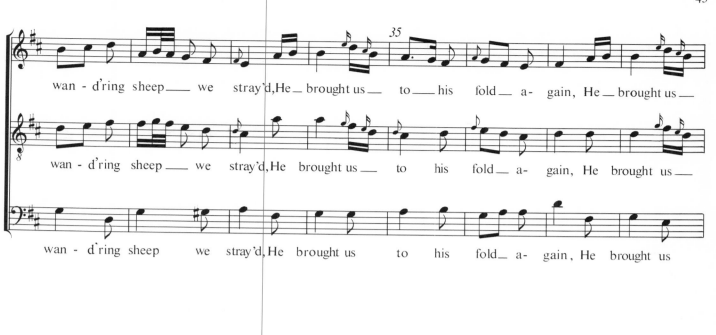

wan - d'ring sheep＿ we stray'd, He＿ brought us＿ to＿ his fold＿ a- gain, He＿ brought us＿

wan - d'ring sheep＿ we stray'd, He brought us＿ to his fold＿ a- gain, He brought us＿

wan - d'ring sheep we stray'd, He brought us to his fold＿ a- gain, He brought us

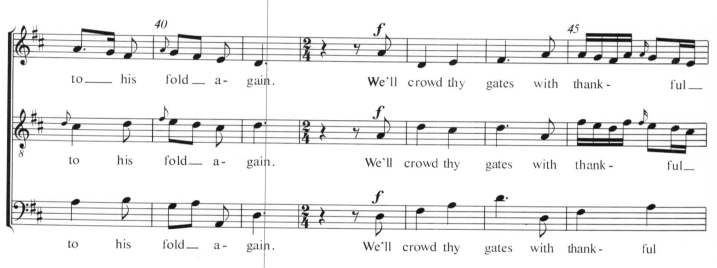

to＿ his fold＿ a- gain. We'll crowd thy gates with thank - ful＿

to his fold＿ a- gain. We'll crowd thy gates with thank - ful＿

to his fold＿ a- gain. We'll crowd thy gates with thank - ful

songs, High as the heav'ns our voic - es＿ raise, And earth, and earth, with her＿ ten

songs, High as the heav'ns our voic - es＿ raise, And earth, and earth, with her ten

songs, High as the heav'ns our voic - es raise, And earth, and earth, with her＿ ten

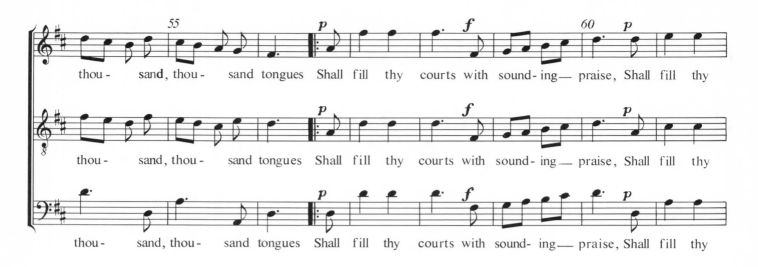

thou - sand, thou - sand tongues Shall fill thy courts with sound-ing— praise, Shall fill thy

thou - sand, thou - sand tongues Shall fill thy courts with sound-ing— praise, Shall fill thy

thou - sand, thou - sand tongues Shall fill thy courts with sound- ing— praise, Shall fill thy

courts with sound -ing— praise, Shall fill, Shall fill thy courts with sound - ing praise.

courts with sound- ing— praise, Shall— fill, Shall fill thy— courts with sound - ing praise.

courts with sound- ing— praise, Shall fill,— Shall fill thy courts with sound - ing praise.

praise. Wide, Wide as the world is thy com - mand, Vast as e -

praise. Wide, Wide as the world is thy com - mand, Vast as e -

praise. Wide, Wide as the world is thy com - mand, Vast as e -

[27.]Dunstan

Martin Madan, 1769

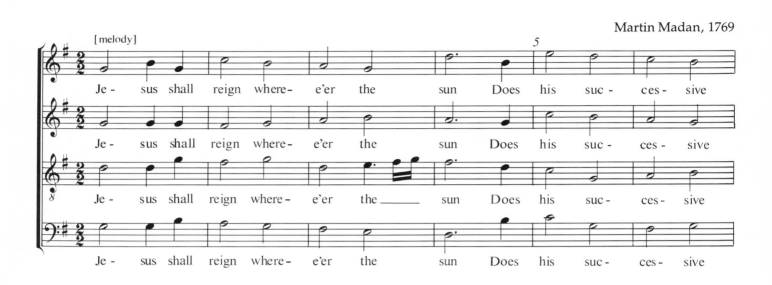

[melody]

Je - sus shall reign where- e'er the sun Does his suc - ces - sive

Je - sus shall reign where- e'er the sun Does his suc - ces - sive

Je - sus shall reign where- e'er the ____ sun Does his suc - ces - sive

Je - sus shall reign where- e'er the sun Does his suc - ces - sive

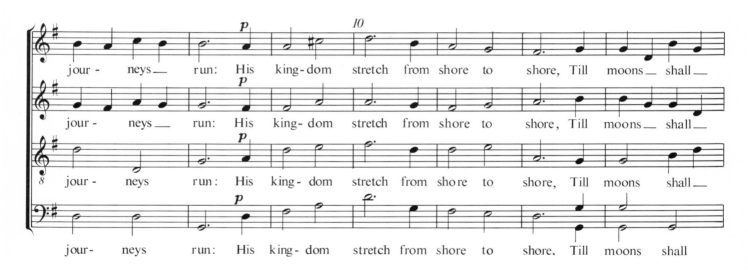

jour - neys ___ run: His king - dom stretch from shore to shore, Till moons ___ shall ___

jour - neys ___ run: His king - dom stretch from shore to shore, Till moons ___ shall ___

jour - neys run: His king - dom stretch from shore to shore, Till moons shall ___

jour - neys run: His king - dom stretch from shore to shore, Till moons shall

wax ___ and ___ wane no more, Till moons ___ shall ___ wax ___ and ___ wane no more.

wax ___ and ___ wane no more, Till moons ___ shall ___ wax ___ and ___ wane no more.

wax and wane no more, Till moons shall ___ wax ___ and ___ wane no more.

wax and wane no more, Till moons shall wax and wane no more.

2. Behold! the islands, with their kings,
   And Europe her best tribute brings:
   From north to south the princes meet,
   To pay their homage at his feet.

3. There Persia, glorious to behold,
   There India shines in Eastern gold;
   And barb'rous nations, at his word,
   Submit and bow, and own their Lord.

4. For this shall endless pray'r be made,
   And praises throng to crown his head;
   His name, like sweet perfume, shall rise
   With ev'ry morning sacrifice.

5. People and realms of ev'ry tongue
   Dwell on his love with sweetest song;
   And infant-voices shall proclaim,
   Their early blessings on his name.

6. Blessings abound where e'er he reigns;
   The pris'ner leaps to loose his chains;
   The weary find eternal rest,
   And all the sons of want are blest.

7. Where he displays his healing pow'r,
   Death and the curse are known no more;
   In him the tribes of Adam boast
   More blessings than their father lost.

8. Let every creature rise and bring
   Pecul'ar honors to our king;
   Angels descend with songs again,
   And earth repeat the long amen.

[28.] The Dying Christian

Edward Harwood, ca. 1770

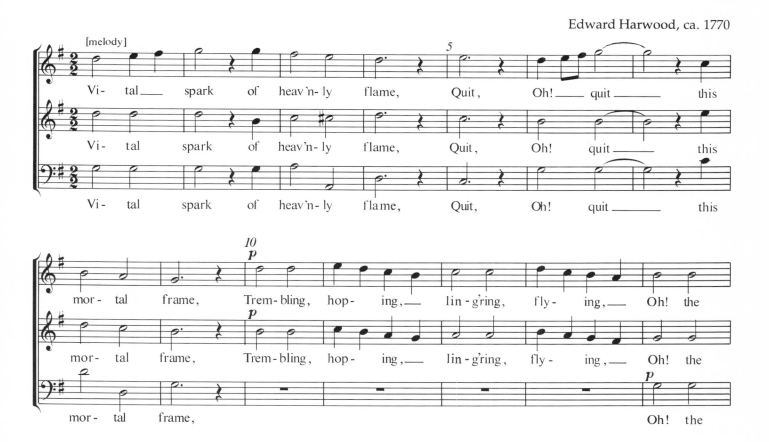

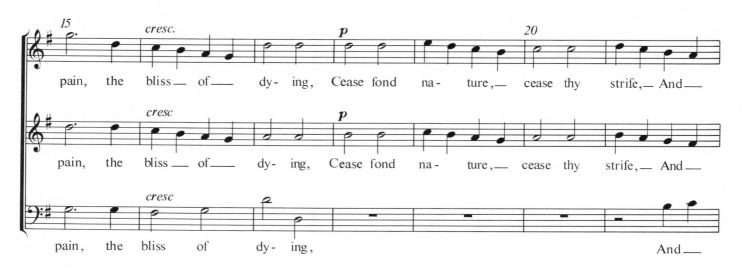

pain, the bliss — of — dy- ing, Cease fond na- ture,— cease thy strife,— And—

pain, the bliss — of — dy- ing, Cease fond na- ture,— cease thy strife,— And—

pain, the bliss of dy- ing, And—

let me lan- guish — in- to life. Hark, they whis- per— an- gels—

let me lan- guish — in- to life. Hark,

let me lan- guish — in- to life. Hark,

say, they whis- per— an- gels— say, Hark,

Hark, they whis- per— an- gels— Hark, they whis- per— an- gels— say,

Hark, Hark, they whis- per— an- gels— say,

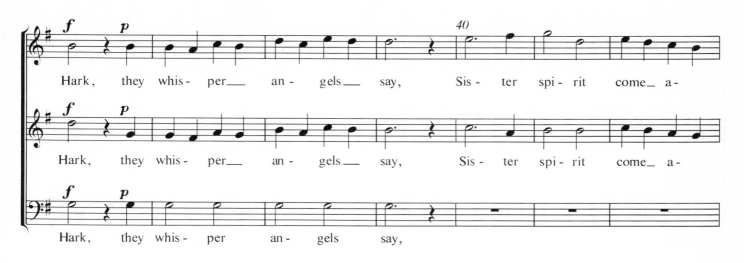

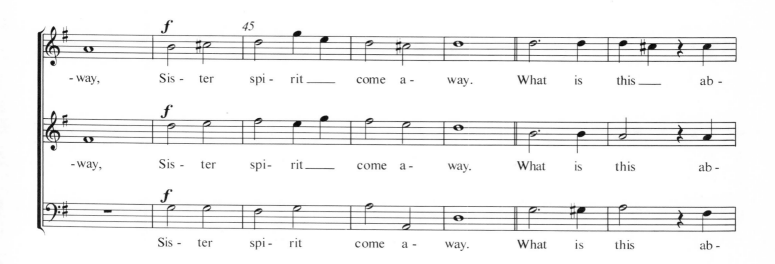

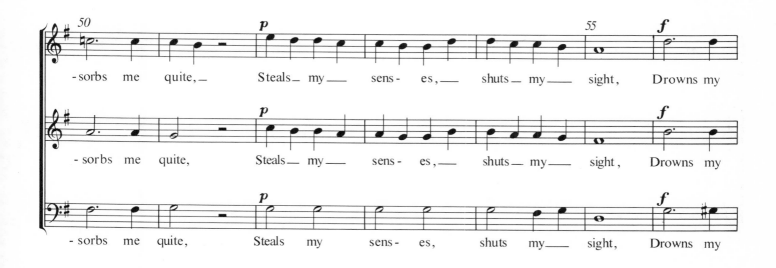

50

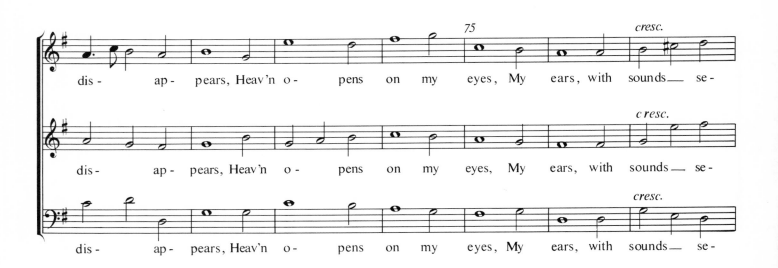

- raph - ic ring. Lend, lend your wings, I mount, I fly, O

- raph - ic ring. Lend, lend your wings, I mount, I fly, O

- raph - ic ring. Lend, lend your wings, I mount, I fly, O

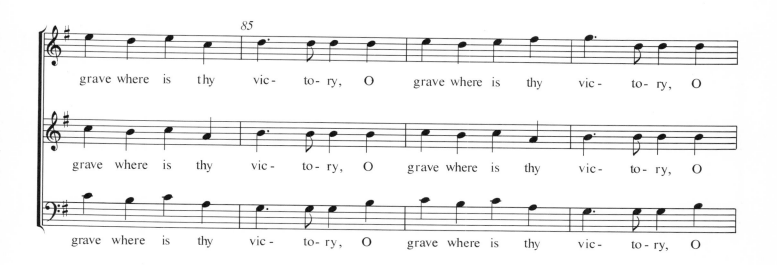

grave where is thy vic - to- ry, O grave where is thy vic - to- ry, O

grave where is thy vic - to- ry, O grave where is thy vic - to- ry, O

grave where is thy vic - to- ry, O grave where is thy vic - to- ry, O

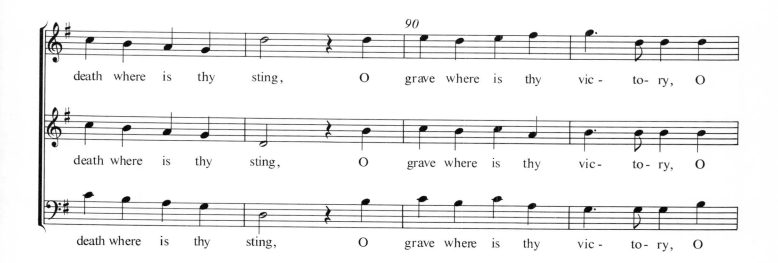

death where is thy sting, O grave where is thy vic - to- ry, O

death where is thy sting, O grave where is thy vic - to- ry, O

death where is thy sting, O grave where is thy vic - to- ry, O

52

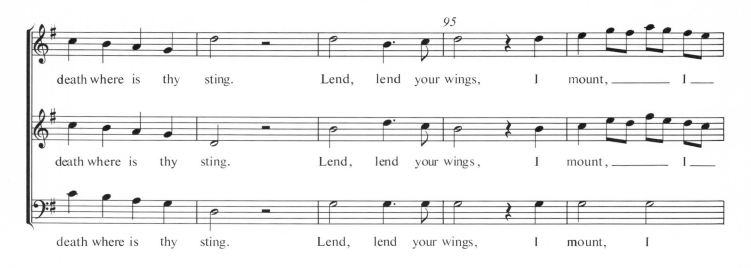

death where is thy sting. Lend, lend your wings, I mount, _____ I ___

death where is thy sting. Lend, lend your wings, I mount, _____ I ___

death where is thy sting. Lend, lend your wings, I mount, I

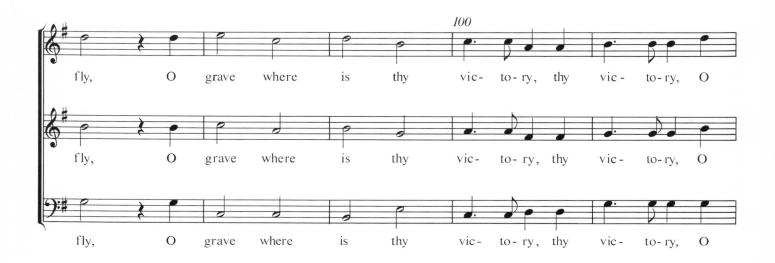

fly, O grave where is thy vic - to- ry, thy vic - to- ry, O

fly, O grave where is thy vic - to- ry, thy vic - to- ry, O

fly, O grave where is thy vic - to- ry, thy vic - to- ry, O

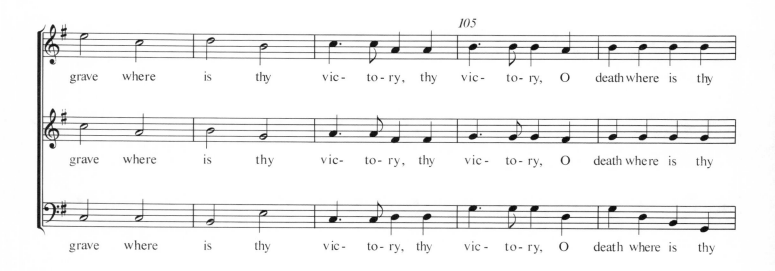

grave where is thy vic - to- ry, thy vic - to- ry, O death where is thy

grave where is thy vic - to- ry, thy vic - to- ry, O death where is thy

grave where is thy vic - to- ry, thy vic - to- ry, O death where is thy

sting.   O   death where is   thy   sting.   Lend,   lend   your   wings,   I   mount,   I

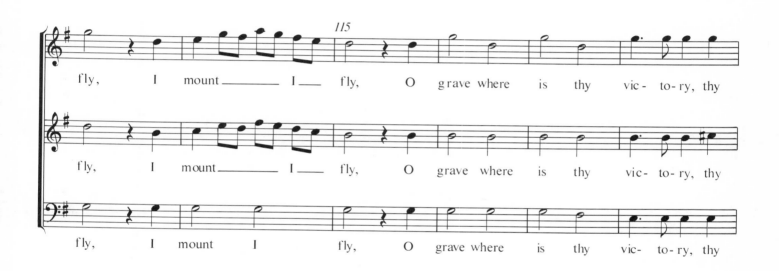

fly,   I   mount _____ I ___ fly,   O   grave where   is   thy   vic - to- ry,   thy

Slow

vic - to- ry, O   death,   O   death,   where   is   thy   sting.

[29.] Enfield

Solomon Chandler, 1785

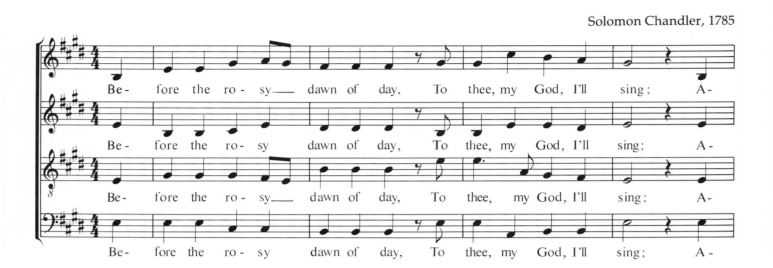

Be- fore the ro - sy___ dawn of day, To thee, my God, I'll sing; A-
Be- fore the ro- sy dawn of day, To thee, my God, I'll sing; A-
Be- fore the ro- sy___ dawn of day, To thee, my God, I'll sing; A-
Be- fore the ro- sy dawn of day, To thee, my God, I'll sing; A-

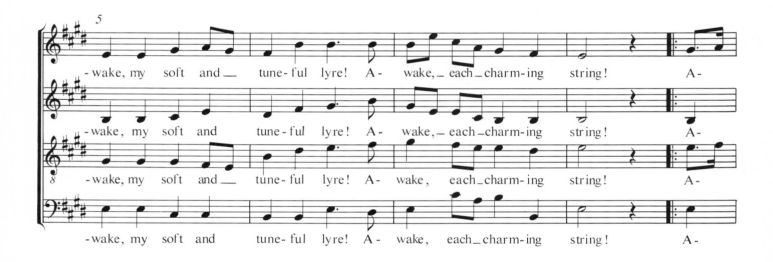

-wake, my soft and ___ tune-ful lyre! A- wake, ___ each ___ charm-ing string! A-
-wake, my soft and tune-ful lyre! A- wake, ___ each ___ charm-ing string! A-
-wake, my soft and ___ tune-ful lyre! A- wake, each ___ charm-ing string! A-
-wake, my soft and tune-ful lyre! A- wake, each ___ charm-ing string! A-

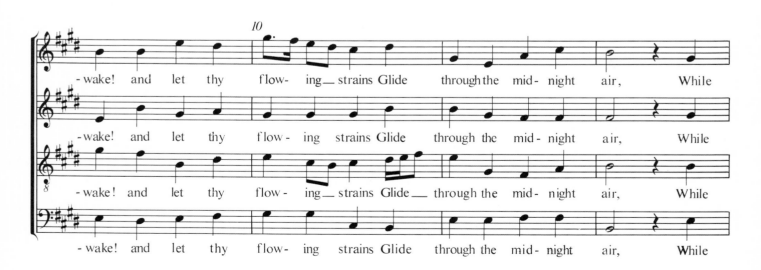

-wake! and let thy flow- ing ___ strains Glide through the mid- night air, While
-wake! and let thy flow- ing strains Glide through the mid- night air, While
-wake! and let thy flow- ing ___ strains Glide ___ through the mid- night air, While
-wake! and let thy flow- ing strains Glide through the mid- night air, While

high a- midst her si- lent orb The sil- ver moon rolls clear. clear.

high a- midst her si- lent orb The sil- ver moon rolls clear. clear.

high a- midst her si- lent orb The sil- ver moon rolls clear. clear.

high a- midst her si- lent orb The sil- ver moon rolls clear. clear.

2. While all the glitt'ring starry lamps
Are lighted in the sky,
And set their Maker's greatness forth
To thy admiring eye:
While watchful angels round the just
As nightly guardians wait,
In lofty strains of grateful praise
Thy spirit elevate.

3. Awake, my soft and tuneful lyre!
Awake each charming string!
Before the rosy dawn of day,
To thee, my God, I'll sing.
Thou round the heav'nly arch dost draw
A dark and sable veil,
And all the beauties of the world
From mortal eyes conceal.

4. Again, the sky with golden beams
Thy skilful hands adorn,
And paint, with chearful splendor gay,
The fair ascending morn.
And as the gloomy night returns,
Or smiling day renews,
Thy constant goodness still my soul
With benefits pursues.

[30.] Funeral Thought

English, 1763

Hark! from the tombs, a dole-full sound; My ears, at-tend the cry —
"Ye liv-ing men, come, view the ground Where you must short-ly lie."

2. "Princes, this clay must be your bed,
   In spite of all your tow'rs:
   The tall, the wise, the rev'rend head
   Must lie as low as our's."

3. Great God, is this our certain doom;
   And are we still secure:
   Still walking downwards to our tomb,
   And yet prepare no more!

4. Grant us the pow'rs of quick'ning grace,
   To fit our souls to fly;
   Then, when we drop this dying flesh,
   We'll rise above the sky.

57

[31.] Greenfield

Lewis Edson, 1782

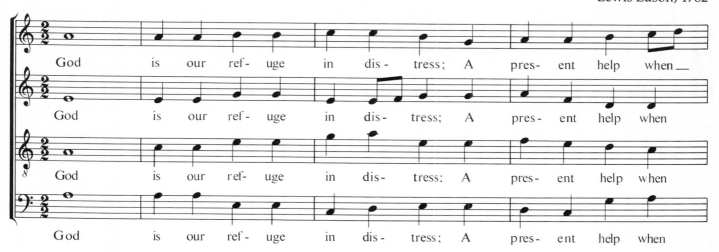

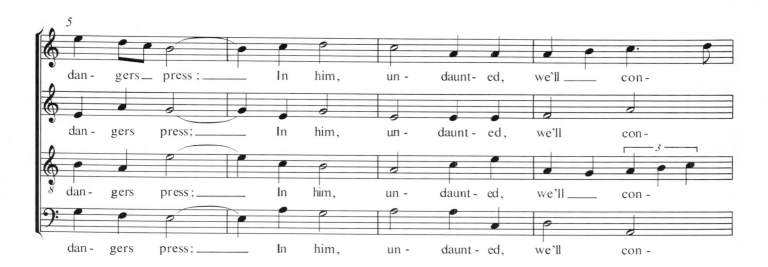

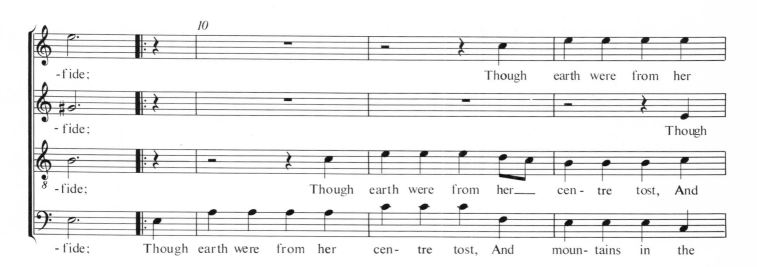

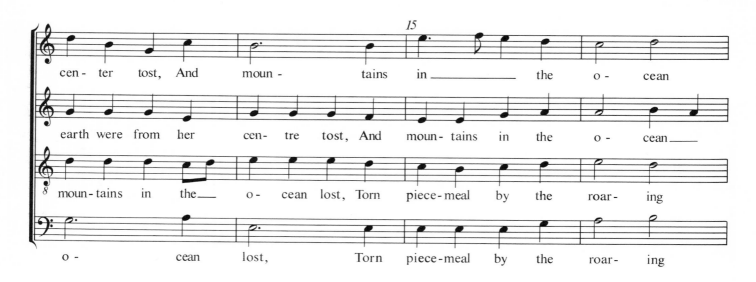

2. A gentler stream with gladness still
The city of our Lord shall fill,
The royal seat of God most high:
God dwells in Sion, whose fair tow'rs
Shall mock th'assaults of earthly pow'rs,
While his Almighty aid is nigh.

3. In tumults when the heathen rag'd,
And kingdoms war against us wag'd,
He thunder'd, and dispers'd their pow'rs:
The Lord of Hosts conducts our arms,
Our tow'r of refuge in alarms,
Our fathers' Guardian God, and ours.

4. Come, see the wonders he hath wrought,
On earth what desolation brought;
How he has calm'd the jarring world:
He broke the warlike spear and bow;
With them their thund'ring chariots too
Into devouring flames were hurl'd.

5. Submit to God's almighty sway;
For him the heathen shall obey,
And earth her sov'reign Lord confess:
The God of Hosts conducts our arms,
Our tow'r of refuge in alarms,
As to our fathers in distress.

[32.] Greenwich

Daniel Read, 1786

Lord, what a thought-less wretch was I, To mourn,___ and mur-mur, and re-

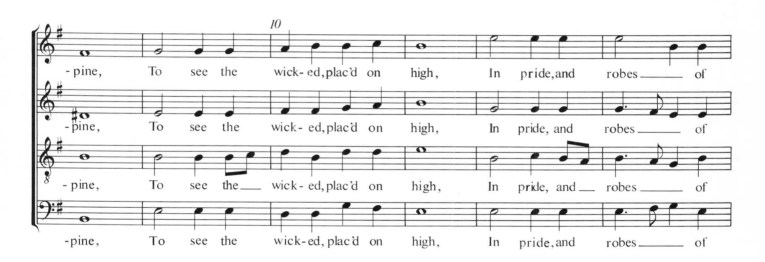

-pine, To see the wick-ed, plac'd on high, In pride, and robes___ of

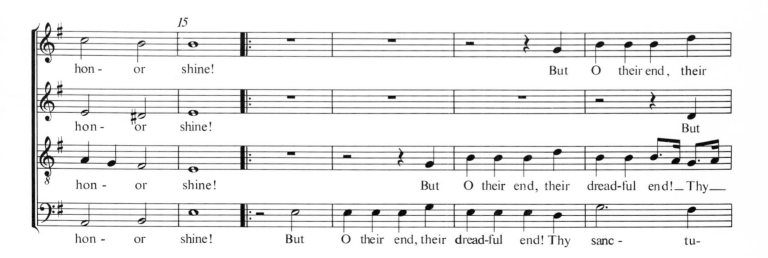

hon - or shine! But O their end, their dread-ful end! Thy sanc - tu-

60

2. Now let them boast how tall they rise,
   I'll never envy them again:
   There they may stand with haughty eyes,
   'Till they plunge deep in endless pain.
   Their fancy'd joys, how fast they flee!
   Just like a dream when man awakes;
   Their songs of softest harmony
   Are but a preface to their plagues.

[33.] Habakkuk

English, ca. 1760 or before

A- way, my ___ un- be- liev- ing ___ fears, Fear shall ___ in ___ me no ___

A- way, my un- be- liev- ing ___ fears, Fear shall ___ in me ___ no ___

A- way, my un- be- liev- ing ___ fears, Fear shall in me ___ no ___

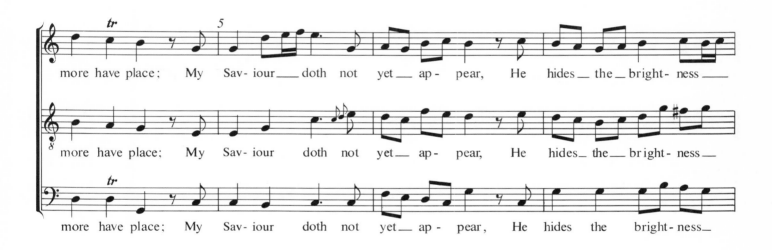

more have place; My Sav- iour ___ doth not yet ___ ap - pear, He hides ___ the ___ bright- ness ___

more have place; My Sav- iour doth not yet ___ ap- pear, He hides ___ the ___ bright- ness ___

more have place; My Sav- iour doth not yet ___ ap- pear, He hides the bright- ness ___

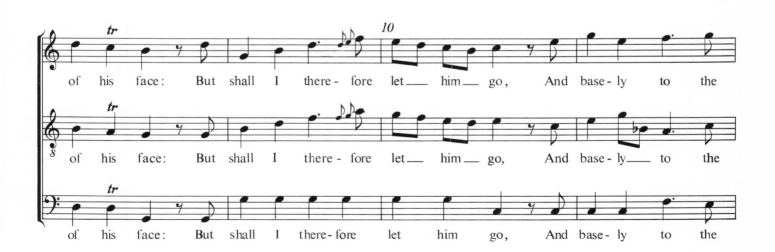

of his face: But shall I there - fore let ___ him ___ go, And base- ly to the

of his face: But shall I there - fore let ___ him go, And base- ly ___ to the

of his face: But shall I there - fore let him go, And base- ly to the

62

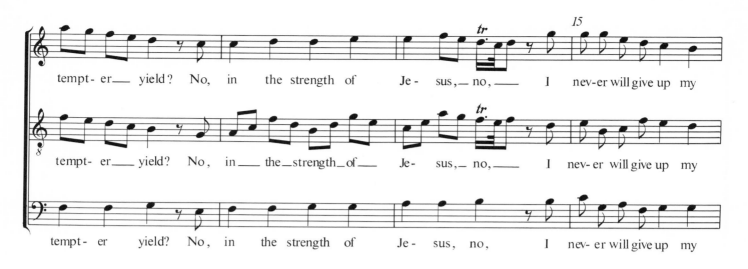

tempt- er___ yield? No, in the strength of Je - sus,— no,___ I nev-er will give up my

tempt- er___ yield? No, in___ the__strength_of___ Je - sus,— no,___ I nev-er will give up my

tempt- er yield? No, in the strength of Je - sus, no, I nev-er will give up my

shield. Al-tho' the vine its fruit__ de - ny, Al-tho' the ol- ive yield__ no___

shield. Al-tho' the vine its fruit__ de - ny, Al-tho' the ol- ive yield__ no___

shield. Al-tho' the vine its fruit de - ny, Al-tho' the ol- ive yield no

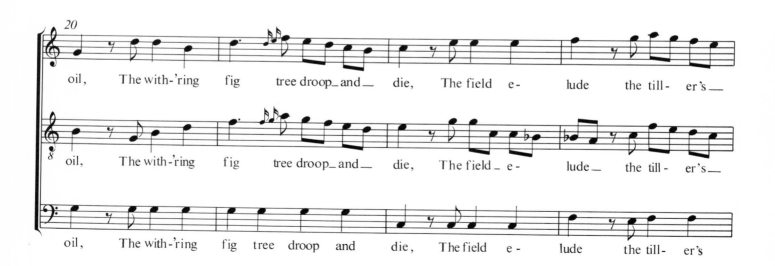

oil, The with-'ring fig tree droop_and__ die, The field e- lude the till- er's___

oil, The with-'ring fig tree droop_and__ die, The field_ e- lude_ the till- er's___

oil, The with-'ring fig tree droop and die, The field e- lude the till- er's

toil, The emp- ty stall no herd af - ford, And per- ish all the bleat- ing

toil, The emp- ty stall no herd af - ford, And per- ish all ___ the bleat- ing

toil, The emp- ty stall no herd af - ford, And per- ish all the bleat- ing ___

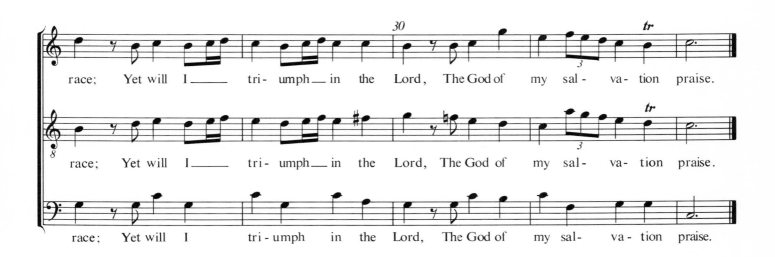

race; Yet will I ___ tri - umph ___ in the Lord, The God of my sal - va - tion praise.

race; Yet will I ___ tri - umph ___ in the Lord, The God of my sal - va - tion praise.

race; Yet will I tri - umph in the Lord, The God of my sal - va - tion praise.

64

[34.] Hartford

Elihu Carpenter, 1779

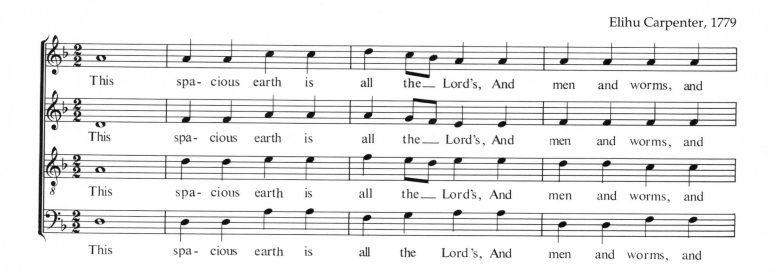

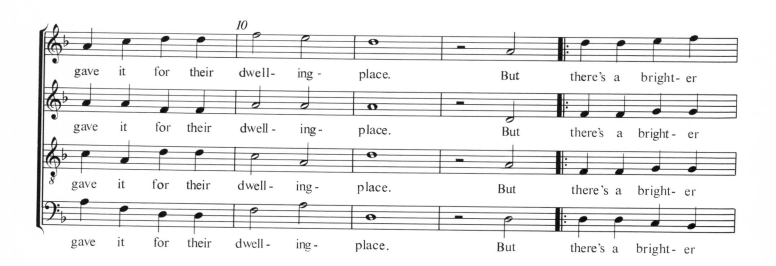

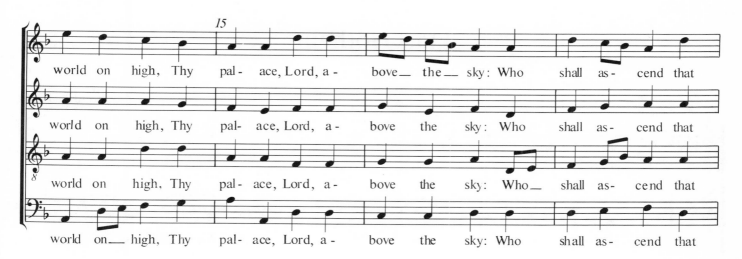

world on high, Thy pal - ace, Lord, a - bove__ the__ sky: Who shall as - cend that

world on high, Thy pal - ace, Lord, a - bove the sky: Who shall as - cend that

world on high, Thy pal - ace, Lord, a - bove the sky: Who__ shall as - ce nd that

world on__ high, Thy pal - ace, Lord, a - bove the sky: Who shall as - cend that

blest a - bode? And dwell__ so near his Ma - ker God. But God.

blest a - bode? And dwell so near his Ma - ker God. But God.

blest a - bode? And dwell so near his Ma - ker God. But God.

blest a - bode? And dwell__ so__ near his__ Ma - ker God. But God.

2. He who abhors and fears to sin,
   Whose heart is pure, whose hands are clean,
   Him shall the Lord the Saviour bless,
   And clothe his soul with right'ousness.
   These are the men, the pious race,
   Who seek the God of Jacob's face;
   These shall enjoy the blissful sight,
   And dwell in everlasting light.

3. Rejoice, ye shining worlds on high,
   Behold, the King of glory's nigh!
   Who can this King of glory be?
   The mighty Lord, the Saviour's he.
   Ye heavenly gates, your leaves display
   To make the Lord the Saviour way:
   Laden with spoils of earth and hell,
   The conqueror comes with God to dwell.

[35.] Hotham

English, 1769

Je - sus, lov - er of my soul, Let me to thy bo - som fly,

Je - sus, lov - er of my soul, Let me to thy bo - som fly,

Je - sus, lov - er of my soul, Le me to thy bo - som fly,

While the near - er wa - ters roll, While the __ tem - pest still is high: Hide __ me, O __ my

While the near - er wa - ters roll, While the tem - pest still is high: Hide me, O my

While the near - er wa - ters roll, While the tem - pest still is high: Hide me, O my

Sav - iour, __ hide, __ Till __ the __ storm __ of __ life is past: Safe in - to the

Sav - iour, __ hide, __ Till the __ storm of life is past: Safe in - to the

Sav - iour, hide, Till the storm of __ life is past: Safe in - to the

15
ha- ven— guide, O re- ceive,— O— re- ceive,— O— re- ceive_my— soul at last!
ha- ven guide, O re- ceive,— O re- ceive,— O re- ceive my— soul at last!
ha- ven guide, O re- ceive, O re- ceive, O re- ceive my soul at last!

2. Other refuge have I none,
Hangs my helpless soul on thee,
Leave, ah! leave me not alone,
Still support and comfort me;
All my trust on thee is stay'd,
All mine help from thee I bring,
Cover my defenceless head
With the shadow of thy wing.

3. Thou, O Christ, art all I want,
More than all in thee I find:
Raise the fallen, cheer the faint,
Heal the sick, and lead the blind.
Just and holy is thy name,
I am all unrighteousness!
Vile and full of sin I am,
Thou art full of truth and grace.

4. Plenteous grace with thee is found,
Grace to pardon all my sin;
Let the healing streams abound,
Make, and keep me pure within:
Thou of life the fountain art,
Freely let me take of thee,
Spring thou up within mine heart,
Rise to all eternity!

68

[36.] Irish

English or Irish, 1749

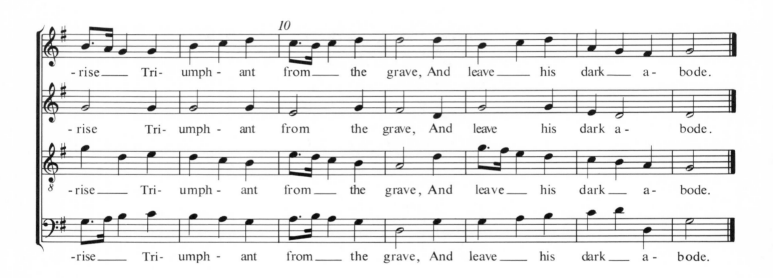

Blest morn- ing, whose young dawn- ing rays Be- held the son of God A- rise Tri- umph- ant from the grave, And leave his dark a- bode.

2. In the cold prison of a tomb
   The dead Redeemer lay;
   'Till the revolving skies had brought
   The third, th'appointed day.

3. Hell, and the grave, unite their force
   To hold our God, in vain;
   The sleeping conqueror arose,
   And burst their feeble chain.

4. To thy great name, almighty Lord,
   These sacred hours we pay;
   And loud Hosannas shall proclaim
   The triumph of the day.

5. Salvation and immortal praise
   To our victorious King;
   Let heaven, and earth, and rocks, and seas,
   With glad hosannas ring.

[37.] Isle of Wight

English, ca. 1720

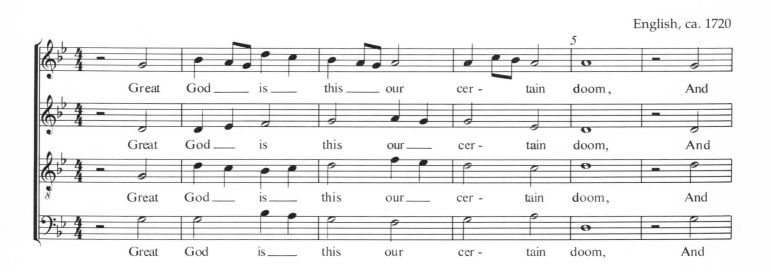

Great God ___ is ___ this ___ our ___ cer - tain doom, And

Great God ___ is this our ___ cer - tain doom, And

Great God ___ is ___ this our ___ cer - tain doom, And

Great God is ___ this our cer - tain doom, And

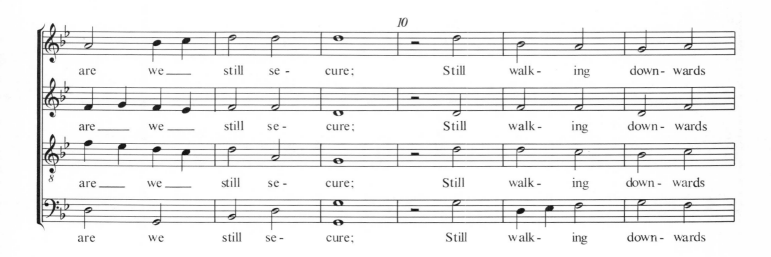

are we ___ still se - cure; Still walk - ing down- wards

are ___ we ___ still se - cure; Still walk - ing down- wards

are ___ we ___ still se - cure; Still walk - ing down - wards

are we still se - cure; Still walk - ing down - wards

to the tomb, And yet pre - pare ___ no more.

to the ___ tomb, And yet pre - pare no more.

to the ___ tomb, And yet pre - pare ___ no more.

to the tomb, And yet pre - pare no more.

2. Grant us the pow'rs of quick'ning grace,
   To fit our souls to fly;
   Then, when we drop this dying flesh,
   We'll rise above the sky.

[38.] Jordan

William Billings, 1786

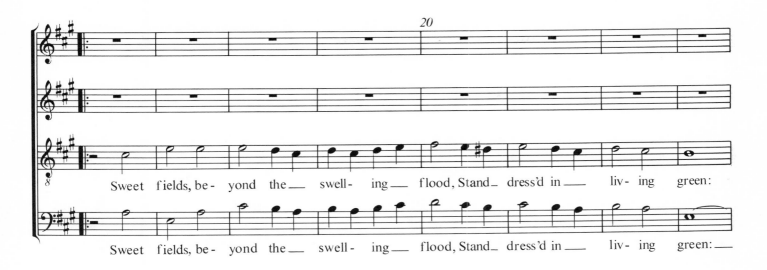

Sweet fields, be- yond the __ swell- ing __ flood, Stand__ dress'd in __ liv- ing green:

Sweet fields, be- yond the __ swell- ing __ flood, Stand__ dress'd in __ liv- ing green: __

So, to the __ Jews, old Ca- naan __ stood, While Jor - dan __ roll'd __ be- tween.

So, to the Jews, old Ca- naan stood, While Jor - dan __ roll'd be - tween.

So, to the Jews, old __ Ca- naan stood, While __ Jor - dan __ roll'd __ be- tween.

__ So, to the Jews old Ca- naan __ stood, While __ Jor - dan __ roll'd __ be- tween.

2. There everlasting spring abides,
   And never-with'ring flow'rs;
   Death, like a narrow sea, divides
   This heav'nly land from ours.
   But tim'rous mortals start and shrink,
   To cross this narrow sea,
   And linger, shiv'ring on the brink,
   Through fear to launch away.

3. Oh! could we make our doubts remove,
   Those gloomy doubts that rise—
   And see the Canaan, which we love,
   With unbeclouded eyes.
   Could we but climb where Moses stood,
   And view the landscape o'er;
   Not Jordan's streams, nor death's cold flood,
   Should fright us from the shore.

[39.] Judgment

Daniel Read, 1785

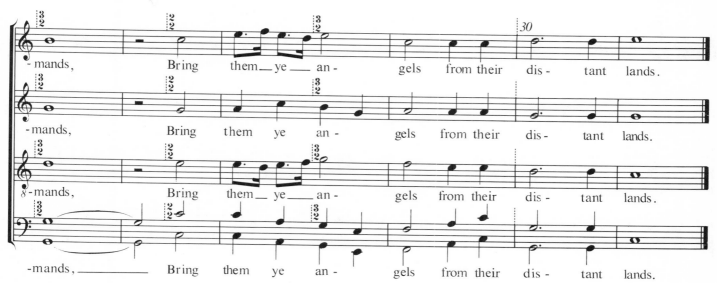

2. Behold! my cov'nant stands forever good,
Seal'd, by th'eternal Sacrifice, in blood,
And sign'd with all their names; the Greek, the Jew,
Who paid the ancient worship, or the new.
There's no distinction here; come, spread their thrones,
And near me seat my fav'rites and my sons.

3. I, their almighty Saviour and their God,
I am their Judge: ye heaven's proclaim abroad
My just eternal sentence, and declare
Those awful truths which sinners dread to hear,
Sinners in Sion, tremble and retire;
I doom the painted hypocrite to fire!

4. Not for the want of goats, or bullocks slain
Do I condemn thee: bulls and goats are vain
Without the flames of love: in vain the store
Of brutal off'rings which were mine before;
Mine are the tamer beasts and savage breed,
Flocks, herds and fields, and forests, where they feed.

5. If I were hungry, would I ask thee food?
When did I thirst, or drink thy bullock's blood?
Can I be flatter'd with thy cringing bows,
Thy solemn chatt'rings, and fantastic vows?
Are my eyes charm'd thy vestments to behold,
Glaring in gems, and gay in woven gold?

6. Unthinking wretch! how could'st thou hope to please
A God, a Spirit, with such toys as these?
While, with my grace and statutes on thy tongue,
Thou lov'st deceit, and dost thy brother wrong;
In vain to pious forms thy zeal pretends,
Thieves and adult'rers are thy chosen friends;

7. Silent I waited with long-suff'ring love,
But did'st thou hope that I should ne'er reprove?
And cherish such an imp'ous thought within,
That God, the right'ous, would indulge thy sin?
Behold my terrors now; my thunders roll,
And thy own crimes affright thy guilty soul!

8. Sinners, awake betimes; ye fools be wise;
Awake, before this dreadful morning rise:
Change your vain thoughts, your crooked ways amend;
Fly to the Saviour, make the Judge your friend,
Lest, like a lion, his last vengeance tear
Your trembling souls, and no deliv'rer near.

[40.] Kingsbridge

English, ca. 1760 or before

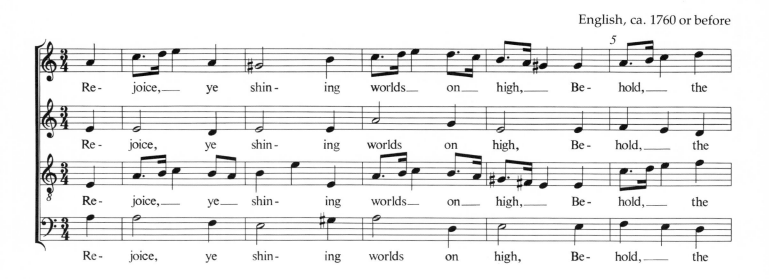

Re- joice,—— ye shin- ing worlds—— on—— high,—— Be- hold,—— the

Re- joice, ye shin- ing worlds on high, Be- hold,—— the

Re- joice,—— ye—— shin- ing worlds—— on—— high,—— Be- hold,—— the

Re- joice, ye shin- ing worlds on high, Be- hold,—— the

King—— of glo- ry nigh! Who can—— this King—— of

King—— of glo- ry nigh! Who can—— this King of

King—— of glo- ry—— nigh! Who can—— this King—— of

King of glo- ry nigh! Who can—— this King of

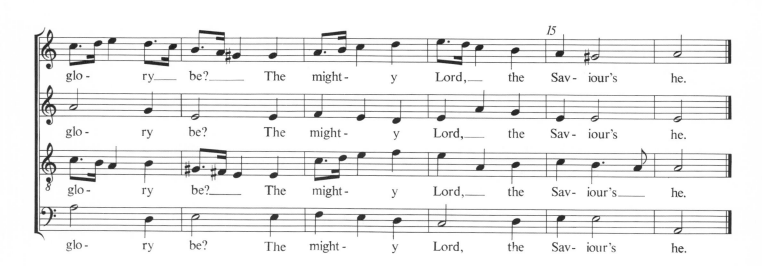

glo- ry—— be?—— The might- y Lord,—— the Sav- iour's he.

glo- ry be? The might- y Lord,—— the Sav- iour's he.

glo- ry be?—— The might- y Lord,—— the Sav- iour's—— he.

glo- ry be? The might- y Lord, the Sav- iour's he.

2. Would you behold the works of God,
   His wonders in the world abroad,
   Go with the mariners and trace
   The unknown regions of the seas.

3. They leave their native shores behind,
   And seize the favour of the wind;
   'Till God commands, and tempests rise,
   Which heave the ocean to the skies.

4. Now to the heav'ns they mount amain;
   Now sink to dreadful deeps again;
   What strange affrights young sailors feel,
   And like a stagg'ring drunkard reel!

5. When land is far, and death is nigh,
   Lost to all hope, to God they cry:
   His mercy hears their loud address,
   And sends salvation in distress.

6. He bids the winds their wrath assuage,
   The furious waves forget their rage;
   'Tis calm; and sailors smile to see
   The haven where they wish'd to be.

7. O may the sons of men record
   The wond'rous goodness of the Lord!
   Let them their private off'rings bring,
   And in the church his glory sing.

ALTERNATIVE TEXT

2. Ye heavenly gates, your leaves display
   To make the Lord the Saviour way:
   Laden with spoils of earth and hell,
   The conqu'ror comes with God to dwell.

3. Rais'd from the dead he goes before;
   He opens heav'ns eternal door,
   To give his saints a blest abode,
   Near their Redeemer and their God.

[41.] Landaff

European, 1558

The God of Glo- ry sends his sum-mons forth; Calls the South na- tions

The God of Glo- ry sends his sum-mons forth; Calls the South na- tions

The God of Glo- ry sends his sum-mons forth; Calls the South na- tions

The God of Glo- ry sends his sum-mons forth; Calls the South na- tions

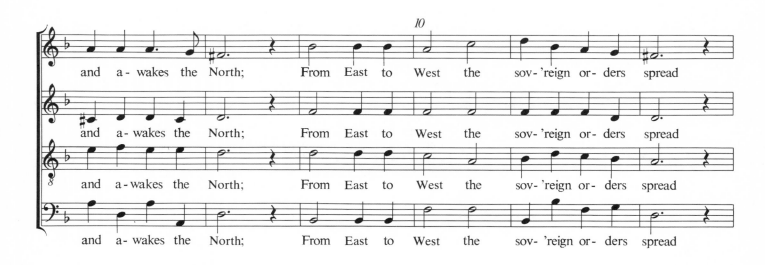

and a- wakes the North; From East to West the sov- 'reign or- ders spread

and a- wakes the North; From East to West the sov- 'reign or- ders spread

and a- wakes the North; From East to West the sov- 'reign or- ders spread

and a- wakes the North; From East to West the sov- 'reign or- ders spread

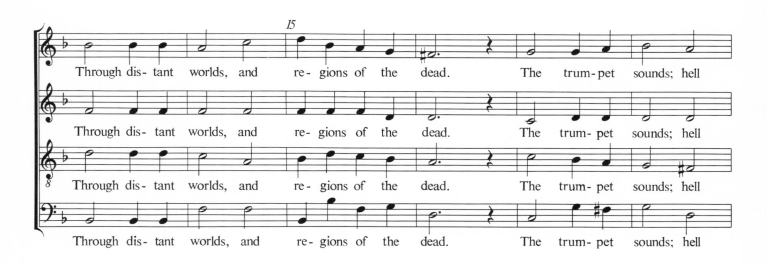

Through dis- tant worlds, and re- gions of the dead. The trum-pet sounds; hell

Through dis- tant worlds, and re- gions of the dead. The trum- pet sounds; hell

Through dis- tant worlds, and re- gions of the dead. The trum-pet sounds; hell

Through dis- tant worlds, and re- gions of the dead. The trum-pet sounds; hell

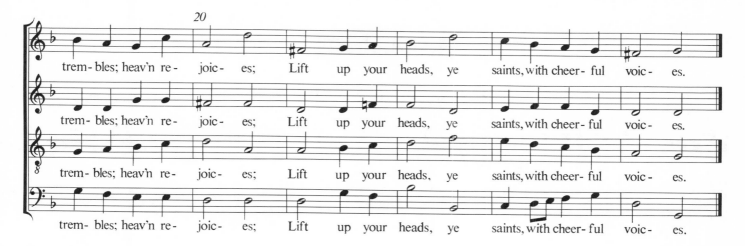

2. No more shall ath'ists mock his long delay,
His vengeance sleeps no more; behold the day!
Behold the Judge descends, his guards are nigh!
Tempest and fire attend him down the sky.
When God appears, all nature shall adore him:
While sinners tremble, saints rejoice before him.

3. "Heaven, earth, and hell, draw near; let all things come
To hear my justice and the sinner's doom;
But gather first my saints, the Judge commands;
Bring them, ye angels, from their distant lands."
When Christ returns, wake ev'ry cheerful passion,
And shout, ye saints, he comes for your salvation.

4. "Behold my cov'nant stands forever good,
Seal'd by the eternal sacrifice in blood!
And sign'd with all their names; the Greek, the Jew,
Who paid the ancient worship, or the new."
There's no distinction here, join all your voices,
And raise your heads, ye saints, for heav'n rejoices.

5. "Here, (saith the Lord) ye angels, spread their thrones,
And near me seat, my fav'rites and my sons:
Come, my redeem'd, possess the joy prepar'd,
E're time began; 'tis your divine reward."
When Christ returns, wake ev'ry cheerful passion,
And shout, ye saints, he comes for your salvation.

6. "I am the Saviour, I th'almighty God,
I am the Judge, ye heav'ns, proclaim abroad
My just eternal sentence, and declare
Those awful truths which sinners dread to hear."
When God appears, all nature shall adore him;
While sinners tremble, saints rejoice before him.

7. "Stand forth, thou bold blasphemer, and profane,
Now feel my wrath, nor call my threat'nings vain;
Thou hypocrite, once drest in saint's attire,
I doom the painted hypocrite to fire."
Judgment proceeds! hell trembles! heav'n rejoices!
Lift up your heads, ye saints, with cheerful voices.

8. "Not for the want of goats, or bullocks slain,
Do I condemn thee; bulls and goats are vain,
Without the flames of love; in vain the store
Of brutal off'rings, which were mine before."
Earth is the Lord's, all nature shall adore him:
While sinners tremble, saints rejoice before him.

9. "If I were hungry, would I ask thee food?
When did I thirst, or drink thy bullock's blood?
Mine are the tamer beasts and savage breed,
Flocks, herds, and fields, and forests where they feed."
All is the Lord's, he rules the wide creation;
Gives sinners vengeance, and the saints salvation.

10. "Can I be flatter'd with thy cringing bows,
Thy solemn chatt'rings, and fantastic vows?
Are my eyes charm'd thy vestments to behold
Glaring in gems, and gay in woven gold?"
God is the Judge of hearts: no fair disguises
Can screen the guilty when his vengeance rises.

11. "Unthinking wretch! how coulds't thou hope to please
A God, a spirit, with such toys as these?
While with my grace and statutes on thy tongue
Thou lov'st deceit, and dost thy brother wrong";
Judgment proceeds! hell trembles! heav'n rejoices!
Lift up your heads, ye saints, with cheerful voices.

12. "In vain to pious forms thy zeal pretends,
Thieves and adult'rers are thy chosen friends;
While the false flatt'rer at my altar waits,
His harden'd soul divine instruction hates."
God is the Judge of hearts; no fair disguises
Can screen the guilty, when his vengeance rises.

13. "Silent I waited, with long suff'ring love;
But did'st thou hope that I should ne'er reprove?
And cherish such an impious thought within
That the All Holy would indulge thy sin?"
See, God appears, all nature joins t'adore him,
Judgment proceeds, and sinners fall before him.

14. "Behold my terrors now; my thunders roll,
And thy own crimes affright thy guilty soul;
Now, like a lion, shall my vengeance tear
Thy bleeding heart, and no deliv'rer near."
Judgment concludes; hell trembles; heav'n rejoices;
Lift up your heads, ye saints, with cheerful voices.

15. "Sinners, awake betimes: ye fools, be wise;
Awake, before this dreadful morning rise;
Change your vain thoughts, your crooked works amend,
Fly to the Saviour, make the Judge your friend,"
Then join, ye saints, wake ev'ry cheerful passion;
When Christ returns, he comes for your salvation.

78

[42.] Lebanon

William Billings, 1770

Lord, what is man poor fee - ble man, Born of the earth at first?

His life a shad-ow, light and vain, Still hast-ing to the dust.

2. O what is feeble dying man,
   Or any of his race,
   That God should make it his concern
   To visit him with grace?

3. That God, who darts his lightnings down;
   Who shakes the world above,
   And mountains tremble at his frown,
   How wond'rous is his love!

[43.] Lenox

Lewis Edson, 1782

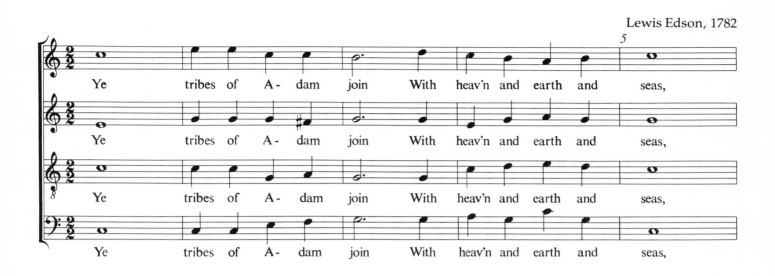

Ye tribes of A- dam join With heav'n and earth and seas,

Ye tribes of A- dam join With heav'n and earth and seas,

Ye tribes of A- dam join With heav'n and earth and seas,

Ye tribes of A- dam join With heav'n and earth and seas,

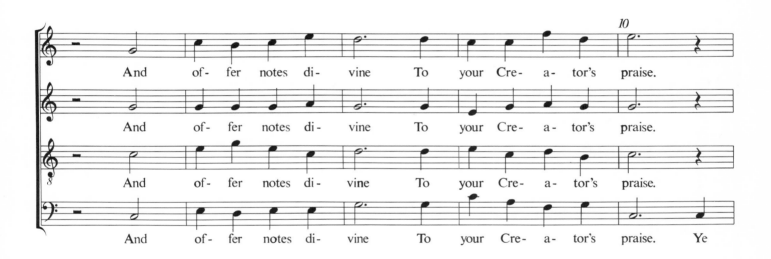

And of- fer notes di- vine To your Cre- a- tor's praise.

And of- fer notes di- vine To your Cre- a- tor's praise.

And of- fer notes di- vine To your Cre- a- tor's praise.

And of- fer notes di- vine To your Cre- a- tor's praise. Ye

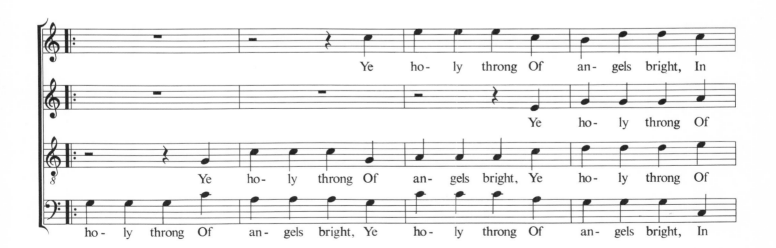

Ye ho- ly throng Of an- gels bright, In

Ye ho- ly throng Of

Ye ho- ly throng Of an- gels bright, Ye ho- ly throng Of

ho- ly throng Of an- gels bright, Ye ho- ly throng Of an- gels bright, In

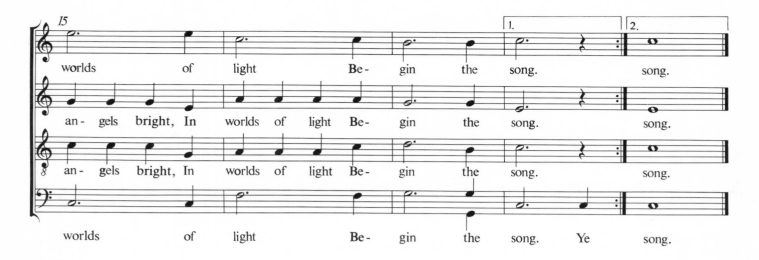

worlds of light Be - gin the song. song.

an - gels bright, In worlds of light Be - gin the song. song.

an - gels bright, In worlds of light Be - gin the song. song.

worlds of light Be - gin the song. Ye song.

2. Thou sun with dazzling rays,
   And moon which rul'st the night,
   Shine to your Maker's praise,
   With stars of twinkling light.
   His pow'r declare,
   Ye floods on high,
   And clouds which fly
   In empty air.

3. The shining worlds above
   In glor'ous order stand,
   Or in swift courses move
   By his supreme command:
   He spake the word,
   And all their frame
   From nothing came,
   To praise the Lord.

4. He mov'd their mighty wheels
   In unknown ages past,
   And each his word fulfils,
   While time and nature last.
   In diff'rent ways
   His works proclaim
   His wond'rous name,
   And speak his praise.

5. Let all the earth-born race,
   And monsters of the deep,
   The fish which cleave the seas,
   Or in their bosom sleep,
   From sea and shore
   Their tribute pay,
   And still display
   Their Maker's pow'r.

6. Ye vapours, hail and snow,
   Praise ye th'Almighty Lord,
   And stormy winds which blow
   To execute his word:
   When light'nings shine,
   Or thunders roar,
   Let earth adore
   His hand divine.

7. Ye mountains near the skies,
   With lofty cedars there,
   And trees of humbler size,
   Which fruit in plenty bear,
   Beasts, wild and tame,
   Birds, flies and worms,
   In var'ous forms
   Exalt his name.

8. Ye kings and judges fear
   The Lord, the sov'reign King
   And while you rule us here,
   His heav'nly honors sing:
   Nor let the dream
   Of pow'r and state
   Make you forget
   His pow'r supreme.

9. Virgins and youth engage
   To sound his praise divine,
   While infancy and age
   Their feebler voices join:
   Wide as he reigns
   His name be sung
   By ev'ry tongue
   In endless strains.

10. Let all the nations fear
    The God who rules above,
    He brings his people near
    And makes them taste his love:
    While earth and sky
    Attempt his praise,
    His saints shall raise
    His honors high.

[44.] Lisbon

Daniel Read, 1785

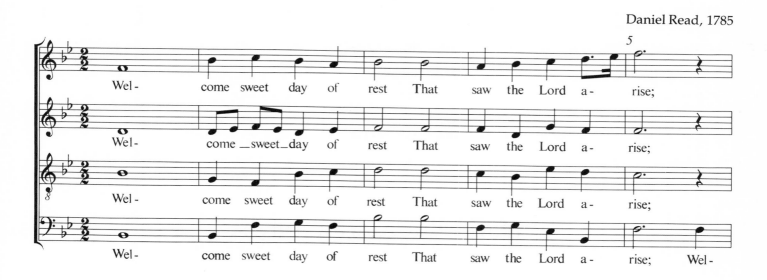

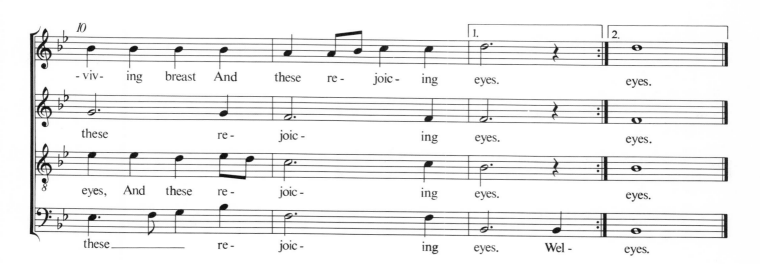

82

2. The King himself comes near
   And feasts his saints today;
   Here we may sit, and see him here,
   And love, and praise, and pray.

3. One day amidst the place
   Where my dear God has been,
   Is sweeter than ten thousand days
   Of pleasurable sin.

4. My willing soul would stay
   In such a frame as this;
   And sit, and sing herself away
   To everlasting bliss.

[45.] Little Marlborough

English, 1763

Wel-come, sweet day___ of rest, That saw the Lord a-rise; Wel-

Wel-come, sweet day of rest, That saw the Lord a-rise; Wel-

Wel-come, sweet day___ of rest, That saw the Lord a-rise; Wel-

Wel-come, sweet day of rest, That saw the Lord a-rise; Wel-

-come to this re-viv-ing breast, And these re-joic-ing eyes.

-come to this re-viv-ing breast, And these re-joic-ing eyes.

-come to this re-viv-ing breast, And these re-joic-ing eyes.

-come to this re-viv-ing breast, And these re-joic-ing eyes.

2. The King himself comes near
   And feasts his saints today;
   Here we may sit, and see him here,
   And love, and praise, and pray.

3. One day amidst the place
   Where my dear God has been,
   Is sweeter than ten thousand days
   Of pleasurable sin.

4. My willing soul would stay
   In such a frame as this;
   And sit, and sing herself away
   To everlasting bliss.

[46.] London New

Scottish, 1635

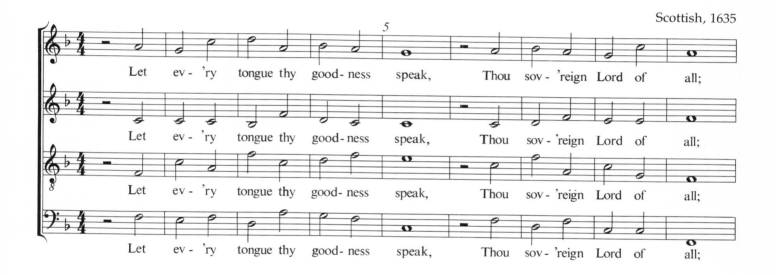

Let ev-'ry tongue thy good-ness speak, Thou sov-'reign Lord of all;

Thy strength-'ning hands up- hold the weak, And raise the poor who fall.

2. When sorrow bows the spirit down,
   Or virtue lies distrest
   Beneath some proud oppressor's frown,
   Thou giv'st the mourners rest.

3. The Lord supports our tott'ring days,
   And guides our giddy youth:
   Holy and just are all thy ways.
   And all thy words are truth.

4. He knows the pain his servants feel:
   He hears his children cry,
   And their best wishes to fulfil
   His grace is ever nigh.

5. His mercy never shall remove
   From men of heart sincere;
   He saves the souls whose humble love
   Is join'd with holy fear.

6. His stubborn foes his sword shall slay,
   And pierce their hearts with pain; -
   But none who serve the Lord shall say,
   "They sought his aid in vain."

7. My lips shall dwell upon his praise,
   And spread his fame abroad;
   Let all the sons of Adam raise
   The honors of their God.

[47.] Majesty

William Billings, 1778

85

2. And like a den most dark he made
His hid and secret place,
With waters black and airy clouds
Encompassed he was.
At his bright presence did thick clouds
In haste away retire,
And in the stead thereof did come
Hail stones and coals of fire.

3. The fiery darts and thunderbolts
Disperse them here and there,
And with his frequent lightnings he
Doth put them in great fear.
When thou, O Lord, with great rebuke
Thy anger dost declare,
The springs and the foundations of
The world discover'd are.

4. And from above the Lord sent down
To fetch me from below,
And pluck'd me out of waters great
That would me overflow:
And me deliver'd from my foes
That sought me to enthrall,
Yea, from such foes as were too strong
For me to deal withal.

[48.] Maryland

William Billings, 1778

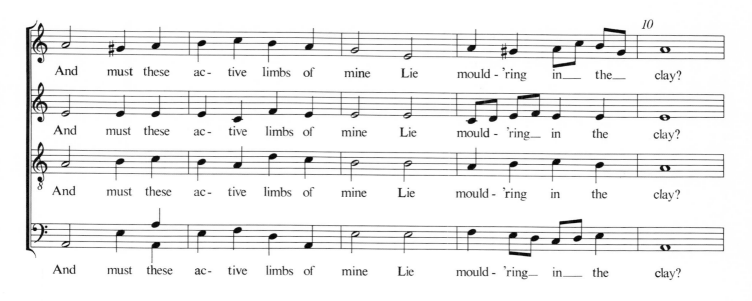

And must these ac - tive limbs of mine Lie mould - 'ring in___ the___ clay?

And must these ac - tive limbs of mine Lie mould - 'ring___ in the clay?

And must these ac - tive limbs of mine Lie mould - 'ring in the clay?

And must these ac - tive limbs of mine Lie mould - 'ring___ in___ the clay?

And must these ac - tive limbs of mine Lie mould - 'ring___ in the

And must___ these___ ac - tive

And must these ac - tive limbs of mine Lie___

And must these ac - tive limbs of mine Lie mould - 'ring in the clay?___

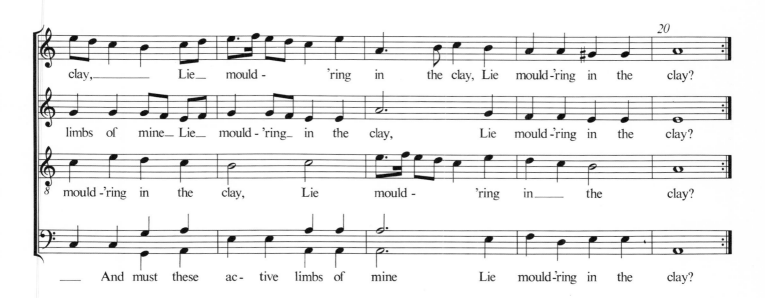

clay,___ Lie___ mould - 'ring in the clay, Lie mould-'ring in the clay?

limbs of mine___ Lie___ mould-'ring___ in the clay, Lie mould-'ring in the clay?

mould -'ring in the clay, Lie mould - 'ring in___ the clay?

___ And must these ac - tive limbs of mine Lie mould-'ring in the clay?

2. Corruption, earth, and worms
    Shall but refine this flesh;
    'Till my triumphant spirit comes,
    To put it on afresh.

3. God, my Redeemer, lives—
    And often, from the skies
    Looks down, and watches all my dust,
    'Till he shall bid it rise.

4. Array'd in glor'ous grace
    Shall these vile bodies shine;
    And ev'ry shape, and ev'ry face
    Look heav'nly and divine.

5. These lively hopes we owe
    To Jesus' dying love;
    We would adore his grace below,
    And sing his pow'r above.

6. Dear Lord, accept the praise
    Of these our humble songs—
    'Till tunes of nobler sound we raise
    With our immortal tongues.

[49.] Mear

English, ca. 1720

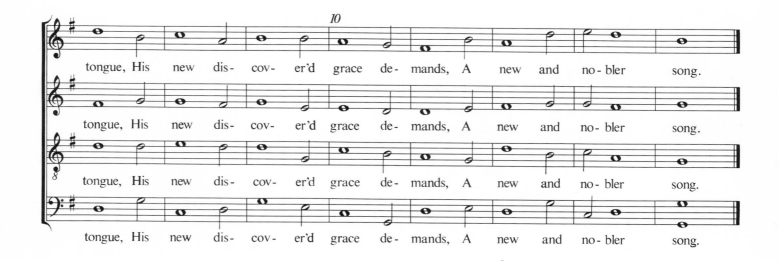

Sing to the Lord, ye dis- tant lands, Ye tribes of ev- 'ry tongue, His new dis- cov- er'd grace de- mands, A new and no- bler song.

2. Say to the nations, Jesus reigns,
   God's own almighty Son:
   His pow'r the sinking world sustains,
   And grace surrounds his throne.

3. Let heav'n proclaim the joyful day,
   Joy thro' the earth be seen;
   Let cities shine in bright array,
   And fields in cheerful green.

4. Let an unusual joy surprise
   The islands of the sea;
   Ye mountains sink, ye vallies rise,
   Prepare the Lord his way.

5. Behold! he comes, he comes to bless
   The nations as their God:
   To show the world his right'ousness,
   And send his truth abroad.

6. But, when his voice shall raise the dead,
   And bid the world draw near,
   How will the guilty nations dread
   To see their Judge appear?

[50.] Middletown

Amos Bull, 1779

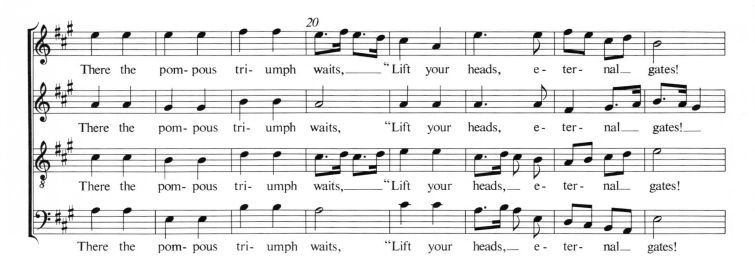

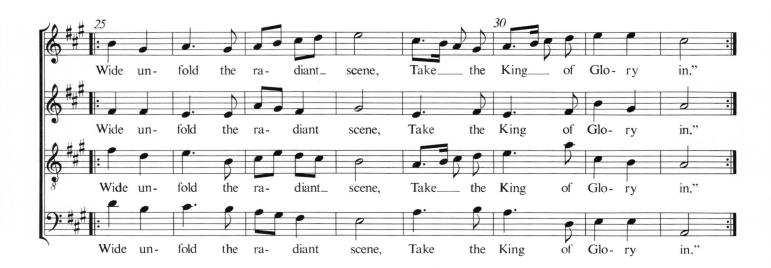

2. Circled around with angel-powers,
   Their triumphant Lord and ours,
   Conqu'ror o'er death, hell and sin,
   Take the King of Glory in.
   Him, though highest heaven receives,
   Still he loves the earth he leaves;
   Though returning to his throne,
   Still he calls mankind his own.

3. See, he lifts his hand above;
   See, he shows the prints of love;
   Hark! his gracious lips bestow
   Blessings on his church below:
   Still for us he intercedes,
   Prevalent his death he pleads;
   Next himself prepares our place,
   Harbinger of human race.

4. Master (may we ever say)
   Taken from our head to-day,
   See, thy faithful servants see,
   Ever gazing up to thee!
   Grant, though parted from our sight,
   High above yon azure height,
   Grant our hearts may thither rise,
   Seeking thee beyond the skies.

5. Ever upward may we move,
   Wafted on the wings of love;
   Looking when our Lord shall come,
   Longing, gasping after home!
   There may we with thee remain,
   Partners of thine endless reign;
   There thy face unclouded see,
   Find our heaven of heavens in thee.

[51.] Milford

Joseph Stephenson, 1760

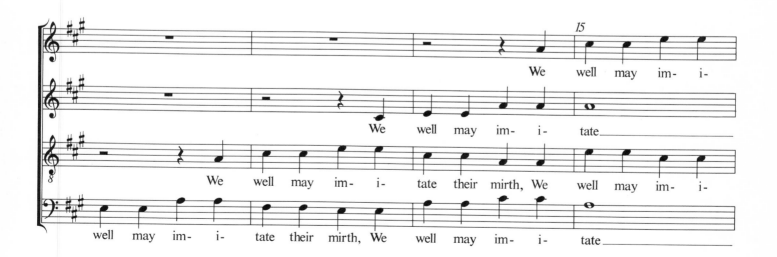

92

2. Grieve not vain man, who mortal art,
   That thou to earth must fall,
   It was his portion, 'twas the part,
   Of him, who made us all.

3. Himself he humbled to the grave
   Made flesh, like us, to show;
   That we as certainly shall have,
   A resurrection too.

4. To Father, Son, and Holy Ghost,
   The God whom we adore:
   As in beginning was is now,
   And shall be evermore.

[52.] Montague

Timothy Swan, 1783

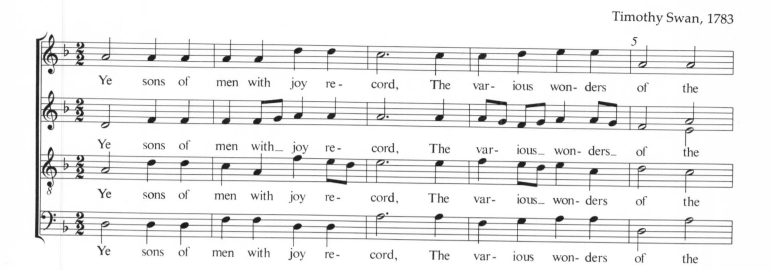

Ye sons of men with joy re-cord, The var-ious won-ders of the

Lord, And let his pow'r and good-ness sound, Thro'

all your tribes the world a-round: Let the high heav'ns your

94

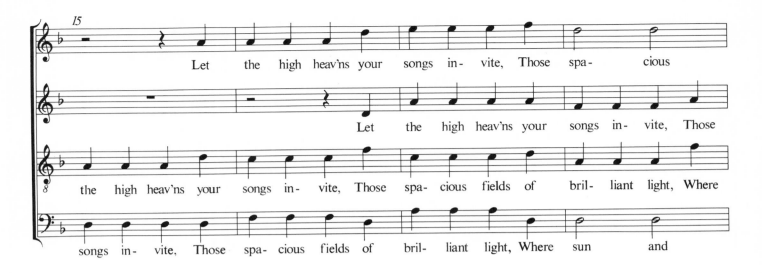

2. Sing earth, in verdant robes array'd,
   Its herbs and flow'rs, its fruit and shade;
   Peopl'd with life of various forms,
   Fishes, and fowls, and beasts, and worms.
   View the broad sea's majestic plains,
   And think how wide its Maker reigns;
   That band remotest nations join,
   And on each wave his goodness shines.

3. But, O that brighter world above,
   Where lives and reigns incarnate love;
   God's only Son in flesh array'd,
   For man a bleeding victim made.
   Thither, my soul, with rapture soar;
   There in the land of praise adore:
   This theme demands an angel's tongue,
   Demands a never-ending song.

[53.] Montgomery

Justin Morgan, 1790

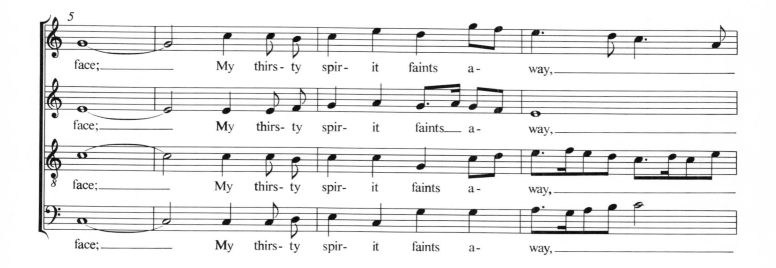

With- out thy chear- ing grace:

With- out thy chear- ing grace:

With- out thy chear- ing grace: So

With- out thy chear- ing grace: So pil- grims on the

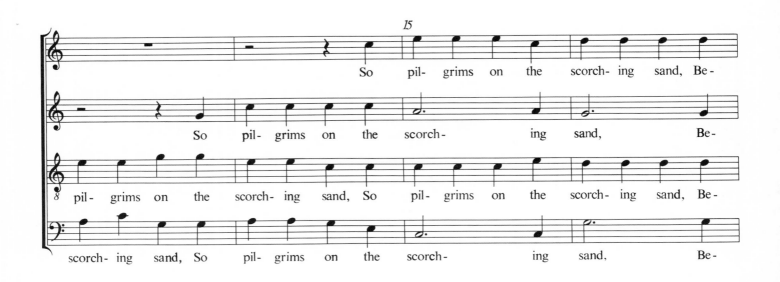

So pil- grims on the scorch- ing sand, Be-

So pil- grims on the scorch- ing sand, Be-

pil- grims on the scorch- ing sand, So pil- grims on the scorch- ing sand, Be-

scorch- ing sand, So pil- grims on the scorch- ing sand, Be-

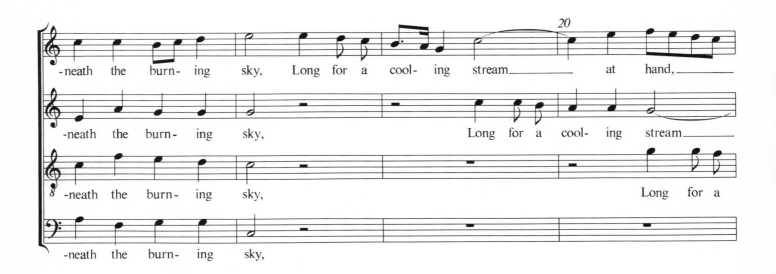

-neath the burn- ing sky, Long for a cool- ing stream____ at hand,____

-neath the burn- ing sky, Long for a cool- ing stream____

-neath the burn- ing sky, Long for a

-neath the burn- ing sky,

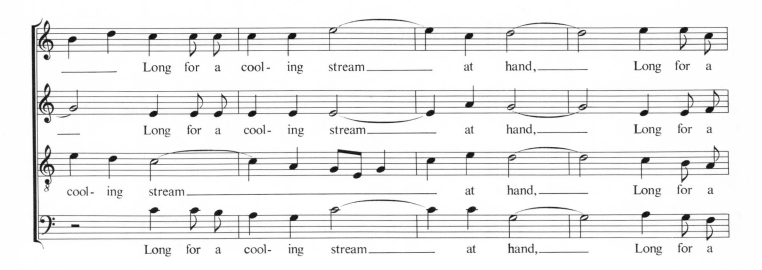

2. I've seen thy glory and thy pow'r
   Through all thy temple shine;
   My God, repeat that heav'nly hour,
   That vision so divine.
   Not all the blessings of a feast
   Can please my soul so well,
   As when thy richer grace I taste,
   And in thy presence dwell.

3. Not life itself, with all her joys,
   Can my best passions move,
   Or raise so high my chearful voice
   As thy forgiving love.
   Thus, 'till my last expiring day,
   I'll bless my God and King,
   Thus will I lift my hands to pray,
   And tune my lips to sing.

[54.] Morning Hymn

Probably American, probably 1761

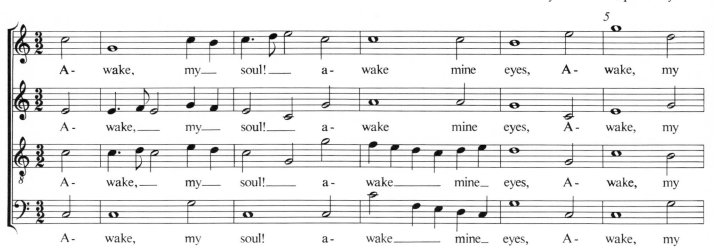

A- wake, my soul! a- wake mine eyes, A- wake, my

A- wake, my soul! a- wake mine eyes, A- wake, my

A- wake, my soul! a- wake mine eyes, A- wake, my

A- wake, my soul! a- wake mine eyes, A- wake, my

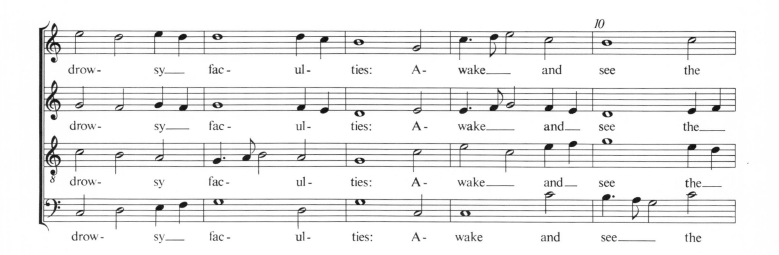

drow- sy fac- ul- ties: A- wake and see the

drow- sy fac- ul- ties: A- wake and see the

drow- sy fac- ul- ties: A- wake and see the

drow- sy fac- ul- ties: A- wake and see the

new- born light, Sprung from the dark- some womb of night.

new- born light, Sprung from the dark- some womb of night.

new- born light, Sprung from the dark- some womb of night.

new- born light, Sprung from the dark- some womb of night.

2. Look up, and see the unwearied sun
   Already has his race begun.
   The pretty lark is mounted high,
   And sings his matins in the sky.

3. Arise, my soul, and thou, my voice,
   In songs of praise early rejoice.
   O great Creator, heav'nly King,
   Thy praises let me ever sing,

4. Thy pow'r has made, Thy goodness kept,
   This senceless body while I slept:
   Yet one night more hast kept me
   From all the pow'rs of darkness free.

5. O keep my heart from sin secure,
   My life unblameable and pure;
   That when the last of days shall come,
   I chearfully may meet my doom.

[55.] New Jerusalem

Jeremiah Ingalls, 1796

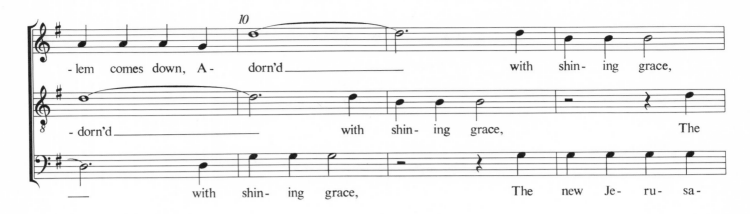

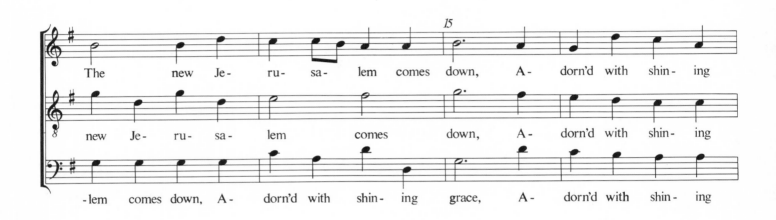

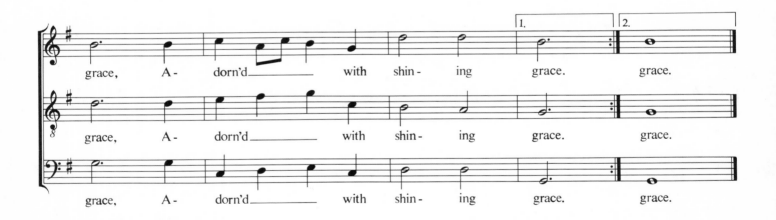

2. Attending angels shout for joy,
   And the bright armies sing,
   "Mortals, behold the sacred seat
   Of your descending king!

3. The God of glory down to men
   Removes his bless'd abode!
   Men, the dear objects of his grace,
   And he the loving God.

4. His own soft hand shall wipe the tears
   From ev'ry weeping eye,
   And pains, and groans, and griefs, and fears,
   And death itself shall die."

5. How long, dear Saviour! O how long
   Shall this bright hour delay?
   Fly swifter round, ye wheels of time,
   And bring the welcome day.

[56.] Newbury

English, 1749

How aw-ful is ___ thy chas-t'ning rod May thy ___ own

chil-dren say, The great, the wise ___ the dread-ful God! How ho-

2. I'll meditate his works of old;
   The King who reigns above,
   I'll hear his ancient wonders told,
   And learn to trust his love.

3. Long did the house of Joseph lie
   With Egypt's yoke opprest;
   Long he delay'd to hear their cry,
   Nor gave his people rest.

4. The sons of good old Jacob seem'd
   Abandon'd to their foes:
   But his almighty arm redeem'd
   The nation which he chose.

5. Isr'el, his people and his sheep,
   Must follow where he calls;
   He bade them venture through the deep,
   And made the waves their walls.

6. The waters saw thee, mighty God!
   The waters saw thee come!
   Backward they fled, and frighted stood,
   To make thine armies room.

7. Strange was thy journey through the sea,
   Thy footsteps, Lord, unknown!
   Terrors attend the wond'rous way
   Which brings thy mercy down.

8. Thy voice, with terror in the sound,
   Through clouds and darkness broke;
   All heav'n in light'ning shown around,
   And earth with thunder shook.

9. Thine arrows through the sky were hurl'd;
   How glor'ous is the Lord!
   Surprise and trembling seiz'd the world,
   And humbled saints ador'd.

10. He gave them water from the rock;
    And safe, by Moses' hand
    Through a dry desert led his flock
    Home to the promis'd land.

[57.] Newton

English, ca. 1780

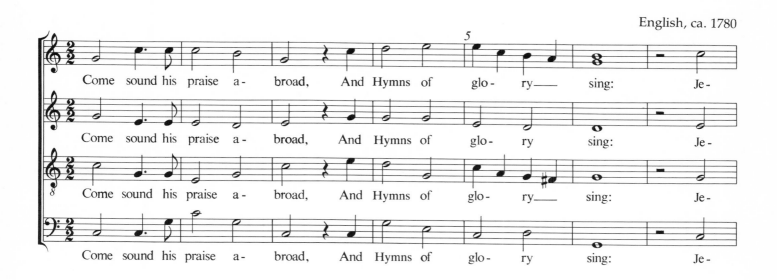

Come sound his praise a- broad, And Hymns of glo- ry —— sing: Je-

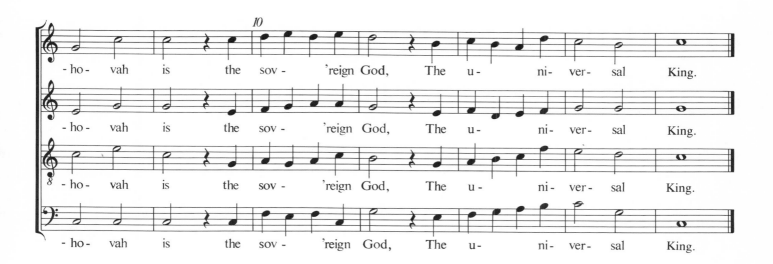

-ho- vah is the sov- 'reign God, The u- ni- ver- sal King.

2. He form'd the deeps unknown;
   He gave the seas their bound;
   The watry worlds are all his own:
   And all the solid ground.

3. Come, worship at his throne;
   Come, bow before the Lord;
   We are his works, and not our own:
   He form'd us by his word.

4. To day attend his voice;
   Nor dare provoke his rod;
   Come, like the people of his choice,
   And own your gracious God.

5. But, if your ears refuse
   The language of his grace,
   And hearts grow hard, like stubborn Jews,
   That unbelieving race.

6. The Lord, in vengeance drest,
   Will lift his hand and swear,
   "You who despise my promis'd rest,
   Shall have no portion there."

104

[58.] Norwich

Hibbard?, 1779

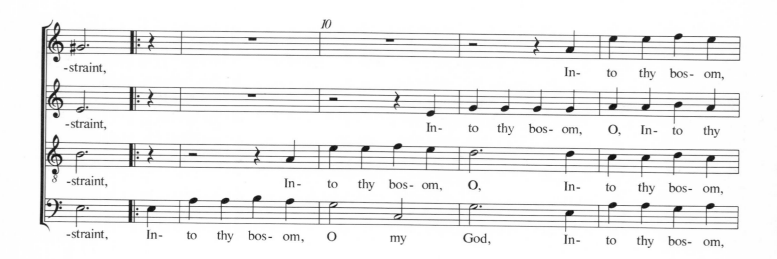

2. How often have I stood,
   A rebel to the skies!
   Yet, O the patience of my God,
   Thy thunder silent lies.

3. Now by a powerful glance,
   My Saviour, from thy face,
   This rebel heart no more withstands
   But yields to sovereign grace.

4. I see the prince of life
   Display his wounded veins;
   I see the fountain opened wide,
   To wash away my stains.

5. My God is reconcil'd,
   My tears his pity move;
   He calls me his adopted child,
   The object of his love.

6. Now let me not receive
   In vain this heavenly grace;
   But let it be a fruitful seed
   Producing holiness.

[59.] Ocean

American, 1787–90

Thy works of glo-ry, might-y Lord, That rule the bois-t'rous

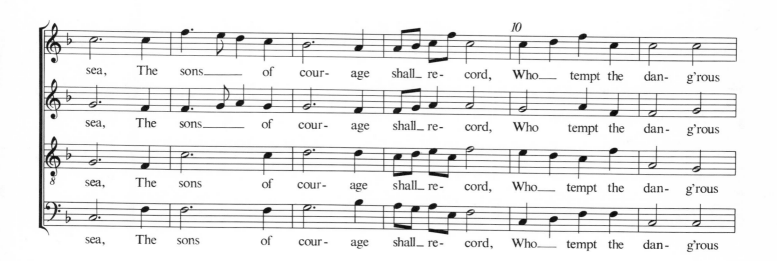

sea, The sons of cour-age shall re-cord, Who tempt the dan-g'rous

106

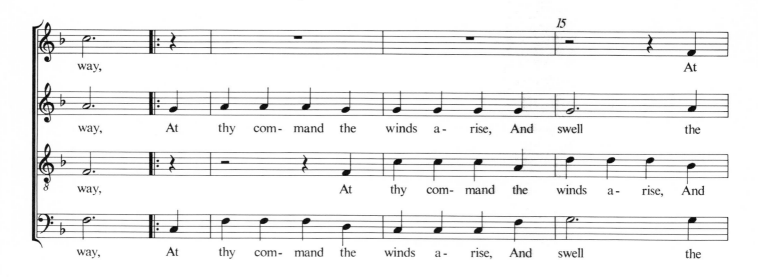

2. Again they climb the wat'ry hills,
   And plunge in deeps again:
   Each, like a tott'ring drunkard, reels,
   And finds his courage vain.
   Frighted to hear the tempest roar,
   They pant, with flutt'ring breath;
   And, hopeless of the distant shore,
   Expect immed'ate death.

3. Then to the Lord they raise their cries;
   He hears the loud request;
   And orders silence through the skies,
   And lays the floods to rest.
   Sailors rejoice to loose their fears,
   And see the storm allay'd;
   Now to their eyes the port appears,
   There let their vows be paid.

4. 'Tis God who brings them safe to land;
   Let stupid mortals know
   That waves are under his command,
   And all the winds which blow.
   O that the sons of men would praise
   The goodness of the Lord!
   And those who see thy wond'rous ways
   Thy wond'rous love record!

[60.] Plymouth

William Tans'ur, 1735

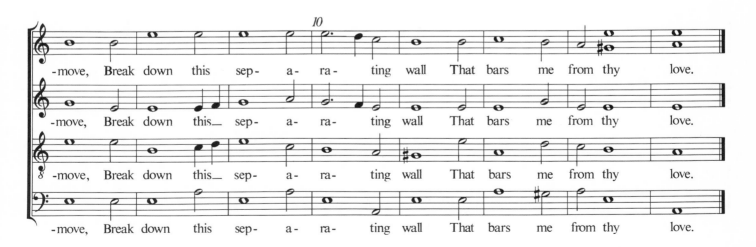

2. Give me the presence of thy grace,
   Then my rejoicing tongue
   Shall speak aloud thy right'ousness,
   And make thy praise my song.

3. No blood of goats nor heifers slain
   For sin could e'er atone;
   The death of Christ shall still remain
   Sufficient and alone.

4. A soul oppress'd with sin's desert
   My God will ne'er despise;
   A humble groan, a broken heart
   Is our best sacrifice.

[61.] Portsmouth

English, 1711

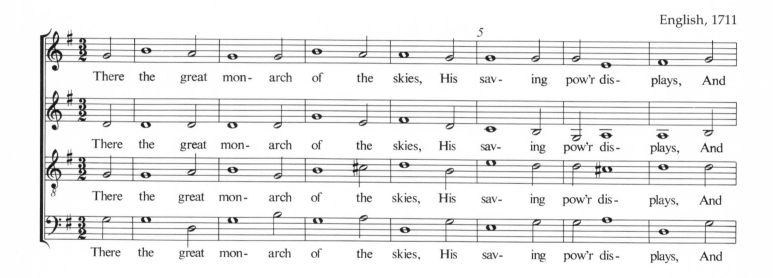

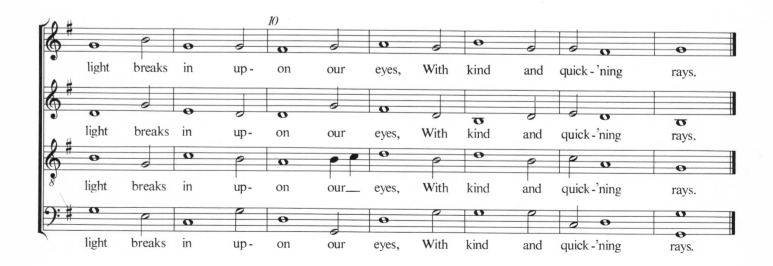

2. With his rich gifts the heav'nly dove
Descends and fills the place,
While Christ reveals his wond'rous love,
And sheds abroad his grace.

3. There, mighty God, thy words declare
The secrets of thy will;
Still we will seek thy mercy there,
And sing thy praises still.

4. My heart and flesh cry out for thee,
While far from thine abode;
When shall I tread thy courts and see
My Saviour and my God?

5. The sparrow builds herself a nest,
And suffers no remove;
O make me like the sparrow blest,
To dwell but where I love!

6. To sit one day beneath thine eye,
And hear thy gracious voice,
Exceeds a whole eternity
Employ'd in carnal joys.

7. Lord, at thy threshold I would wait,
While Jesus is within,
Rather than fill a throne of state,
Or live in tents of sin!

8. Could I command the spacious land,
And the more boundless sea,
For one blest hour at thy right hand,
I'd give them both away.

[62.] Portsmouth

English, ca. 1760 or before

110

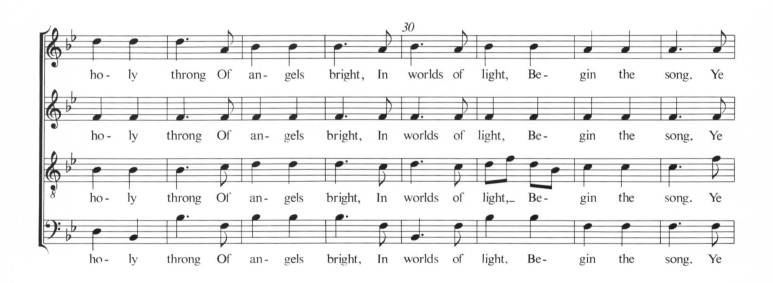

2. Thou moon, that rul'st the night,
   And sun, that guid'st the day,
   Ye glitt'ring stars of light,
   To him your homage pay:
   His praise declare,
   Ye heav'ns above,
   And clouds that move
   In liquid air.

3. Let them adore the Lord,
   And praise his holy Name,
   By whose Almighty word
   They all from nothing came:
   And all shall last,
   From changes free;
   His firm decree
   Stands ever fast.

4. Let earth her tribute pay;
   Praise him, ye dreadful whales,
   And fish that through the sea
   Glide swift with glitt'ring scales;
   Fire, hail, and snow,
   And misty air,
   And winds that, where
   He bids them, blow.

5. By hills and mountains, all
   In grateful concert join'd;
   By cedars stately tall,
   And trees for fruit design'd;
   By ev'ry beast,
   And creeping thing,
   And fowl of wing,
   His Name be blest.

6. Let all of royal birth,
   With those of humbler frame,
   And judges of the earth,
   His matchless praise proclaim:
   In this design,
   Let youths with maids,
   And hoary heads
   With children join.

7. United zeal be shown,
   His wond'rous fame to raise,
   Whose glorious name alone
   Deserves our endless praise:
   Earth's utmost ends
   His pow'r obey;
   His glorious sway
   The sky transcends.

8. His chosen saints to grace,
   He sets them up on high,
   And favours Israel's race,
   Who still to him are nigh:
   O therefore raise
   Your grateful voice,
   And still rejoice
   The Lord to praise.

[63.] Portugal

Thomas Thorley, 1789 or before

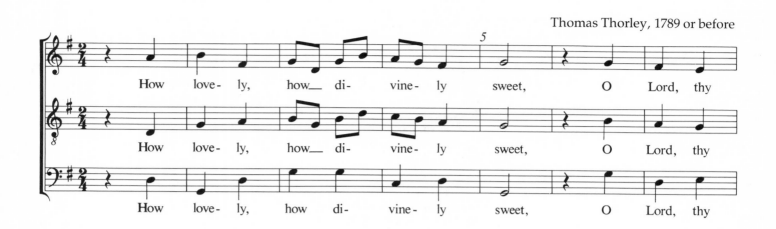

How love- ly, how di- vine- ly sweet, O Lord, thy

How love- ly, how di- vine- ly sweet, O Lord, thy

How love- ly, how di- vine- ly sweet, O Lord, thy

sa - cred courts ap- pear! Fain would my long- ing

sa - cred courts ap- pear! Fain would my long- ing

sa - cred courts ap- pear! Fain would my long- ing

pas- sions meet The glo- ry of thy pres- ence there.

pas- sions meet The glo- ry of thy pres- ence there.

pas- sions meet The glo- ry of thy pres- ence there.

2. O, blest the men, blest their employ,
Whom thy indulgent favors raise
To dwell in these abodes of joy,
And sing thy never ceasing praise.

3. Happy the men whom strength divine,
With ardent love and zeal inspires;
Whose steps to thy blest way incline,
With willing hearts and warm desires.

4. One day within thy sacred gate,
Affords more real joy to me,
Than thousands in the tents of state;
The meanest place is bliss with thee.

5. God is a sun; our brightest day
From his reviving presence flows;
God is a shield, thro' all the way,
To guard us from surrounding foes.

6. He pours his kindest blessings down,
Profusely down on souls sincere;
And grace shall guide, and glory crown
The happy favorites of his care.

7. O Lord of hosts, thou God of grace,
How blest, divinely blest, is he,
Who trusts thy love and seeks thy face,
And fixes all his hopes on thee!

[64.] Psalm 25

Alexander Gillet, 1779

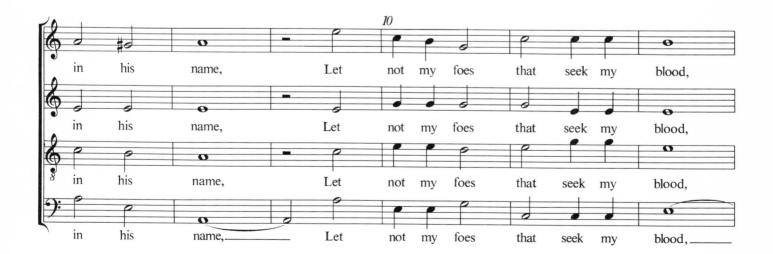

Still tri-umph in my shame, Still tri-umph in my shame.

2. Sin and the pow'rs of hell
   Persuade me to despair;
   Lord, make me know thy cov'nant well,
   That I may 'scape the snare.

3. From the first dawning light,
   'Till the dark ev'ning rise,
   For thy salvation, Lord, I wait
   With ever longing eyes.

4. Remember all thy grace,
   And lead me in thy truth;
   Forgive the sins of riper day
   And follies of my youth.

5. The Lord is just and kind,
   The meek shall learn his ways,
   And ev'ry humble sinner find
   The methods of his grace.

6. For his own goodness sake,
   He saves my soul from shame,
   He pardons (though my guilt be great)
   Thro' my redeemer's name.

[65.] Psalm 33

William Tuckey, 1761

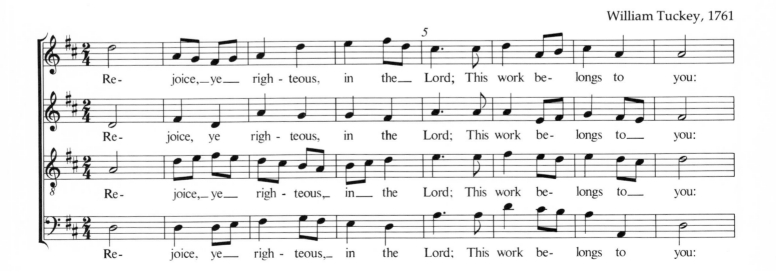

Re-joice, ye righteous, in the Lord; This work belongs to you:

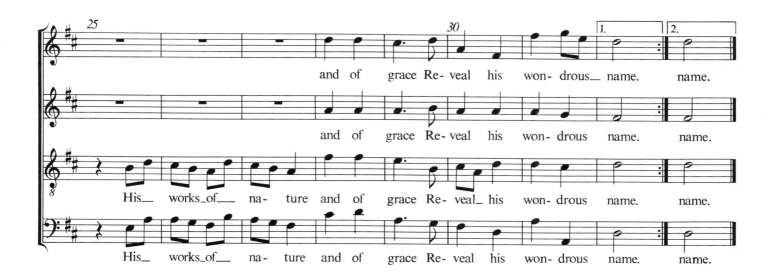

2. His wisdom and almighty word
   The heav'nly arches spread;
   And by the spirit of the Lord
   Their shining hosts were made.
   He bade the liquid waters flow
   To their appointed deep;
   The flowing seas their limits know,
   And their own station keep.

3. Ye tenants of the spacious earth,
   With fear before him stand:
   He spake, and nature took its birth,
   And rests on his command.
   He scorns the angry nation's rage,
   And breaks their vain designs;
   His counsel stands thro' ev'ry age,
   And in full glory shines.

[66.] Psalm 34

Joseph Stephenson, 1760

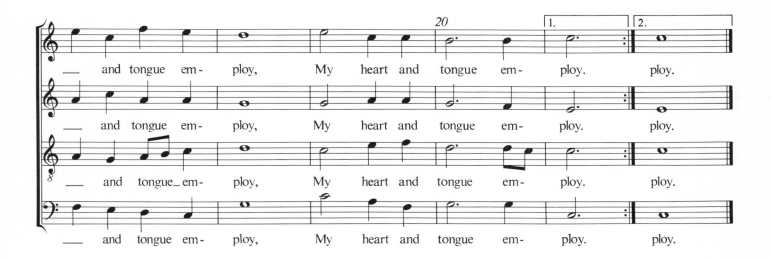

2. Of his deliv'rance I will boast,
   Till all that are distrest,
   From my example comfort take,
   And charm their griefs to rest.

3. O! magnify the Lord with me,
   With me exalt his name:
   When in distress to him I call'd,
   He to my rescue came.

4. Their drooping hearts were soon refresh'd,
   Who look'd to him for aid;
   Desir'd success in ev'ry face
   A cheerful air display'd.

5. "Behold, (say they) behold the man,
   Whom Providence reliev'd;
   The man so dang'rously beset,
   So wond'rously retriev'd!"

6. The hosts of God encamp around
   The dwellings of the just;
   Deliv'rance he affords to all,
   Who on his succour trust.

7. O! make but trial of his love,
   Experience will decide
   How blest they are, and only they,
   Who in his truth confide.

8. Fear him, ye saints; and you will then
   Have nothing else to fear:
   Make you his service your delight,
   Your wants shall be his care.

9. While hungry lions lack their prey,
   The Lord will food provide
   For such as put their trust in him,
   And see their needs supply'd.

[67.] Psalm 46

Amos Bull, 1784

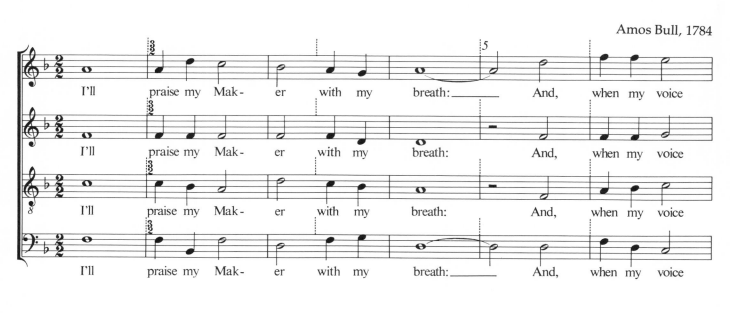

I'll praise my Mak- er with my breath:_____ And, when my voice

is lost in death,_____ Praise shall em- ploy my no- bler pow'rs:_____

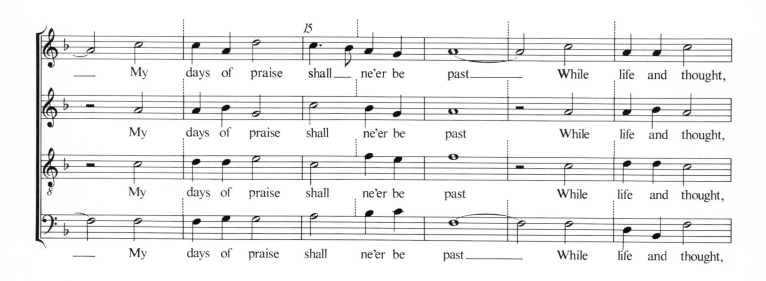

—— My days of praise shall___ ne'er be past_____ While life and thought,

2. Why should I make a man my trust?
   Princes must die, and turn to dust;
   Vain is the help of flesh and blood;
   Their breath departs, their pomp and pow'r,
   And thoughts all vanish in an hour,
   Nor can they make their promise good.

3. Happy the man whose hopes rely
   On Isr'el's God; he made the sky,
   And earth and seas, with all their train;
   His truth forever stands secure;
   He saves th'opprest, he feeds the poor,
   And none shall find his promise vain.

4. The Lord hath eyes to give the blind;
   The Lord supports the sinking mind;
   He sends the lab'ring conscience peace;
   He helps the stranger in distress,
   The widow and the fatherless,
   And grants the pris'ner sweet release.

5. He loves his saints; he knows them well,
   But turns the wicked down to hell:
   Thy God, O Zion! ever reigns:
   Let ev'ry tongue, let ev'ry age,
   In this exalted work engage:
   Praise him in everlasting strains.

6. I'll praise him while he lends me breath,
   And when my voice is lost in death,
   Praise shall employ my nobler pow'rs:
   My days of praise shall ne'er be past
   While life and thought and being last,
   And immortality endures.

[68.] Psalm 100 [Old]

European, 1551

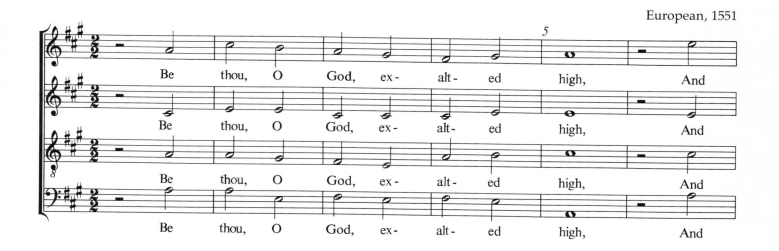

120

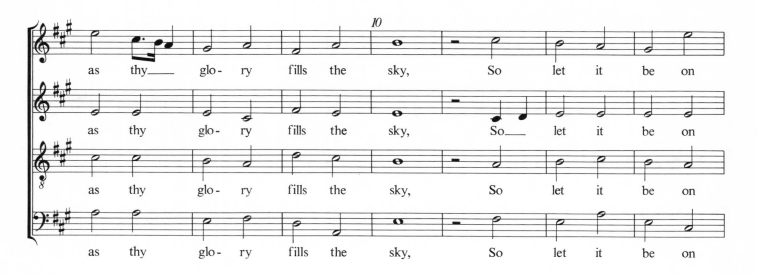

as thy___ glo - ry fills the sky, So let it be on
as thy glo - ry fills the sky, So__ let it be on
as thy glo - ry fills the sky, So let it be on
as thy glo - ry fills the sky, So let it be on

earth dis - play'd, 'Till thou art here as there o - bey'd.
earth dis - play'd, 'Till thou art__ here as there o - bey'd.
earth dis - play'd, 'Till thou art here as there o - bey'd.
earth dis - play'd, 'Till thou art here as there o - bey'd.

2. To take me they their net prepar'd,
And had almost my soul ensnar'd;
But fell themselves, by just decree,
Into the pit they made for me.

3. O God, my heart is fix'd, 'tis bent,
Its thankful tribute to present;
And, with my heart, my voice I'll raise,
To thee, my God, in songs of praise:

4. Awake, my glory; harp and lute,
No longer let your strings be mute;
And I, my tuneful part to take,
Will with the early dawn awake.

5. Thy praises, Lord, I will resound
To all the list'ning nations round;
Thy mercy highest Heav'n transcends;
Thy truth beyond the clouds extends.

6. Be thou, O God, exalted high;
And, as thy glory fills the sky,
So let it be on earth display'd,
Till thou art here, as there, obey'd.

[69.] Psalm 100 [New]

American, 1723

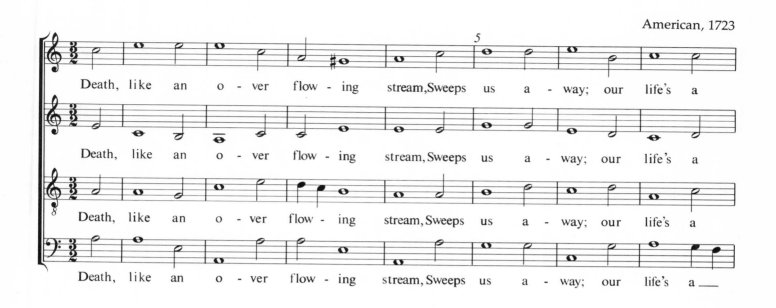

Death, like an o-ver flow-ing stream, Sweeps us a-way; our life's a

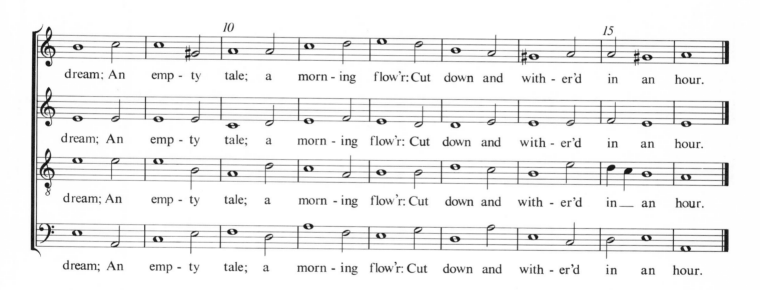

dream; An emp-ty tale; a morn-ing flow'r: Cut down and with-er'd in an hour.

2. Our age to sev'nty years is set;
   How short the term! how frail the state!
   And if to eighty we arrive,
   We rather sigh and groan than live.

3. But O! how oft thy wrath appears,
   And cuts off our expected years!
   Thy wrath awakes our humble dread:
   We fear that pow'r which strikes us dead.

4. Teach us, O Lord, how frail is man!
   And kindly lengthen out our span,
   'Till a wise care of piety
   Fit us to die, and dwell with thee.

[70.] Psalm 136

Deaolph, 1778

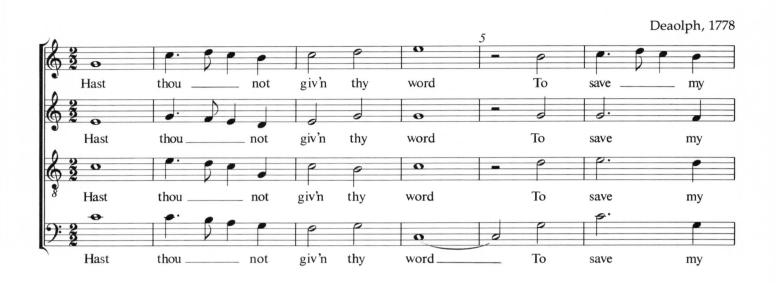

Hast thou _____ not giv'n thy word To save _____ my

Hast thou _____ not giv'n thy word To save my

Hast thou _____ not giv'n thy word To save my

Hast thou _____ not giv'n thy word _____ To save my

soul from _____ death? And

soul from death? And I can trust, And

soul from _____ death? And I can trust my Lord, _____ And

soul from death? And I can trust, And I can trust, And

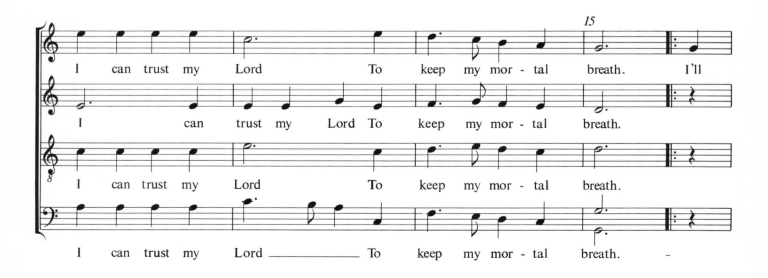

I can trust my Lord To keep my mor - tal breath. I'll

I can trust my Lord To keep my mor - tal breath.

I can trust my Lord To keep my mor - tal breath.

I can trust my Lord _____ To keep my mor - tal breath. -

go and come, Nor fear _____ to die, I'll go and

I'll go and come, Nor fear to die, I'll go and

I'll go and come, Nor fear to

I'll go and come, Nor

20

come, Nor fear to die, 'Till from on high Thou call me home. home.

come, Nor fear to die, 'Till from on high Thou call me home. home.

die, 'Till from on high _____ Thou call me home. home.

fear to die, 'Till from on high Thou call me home. home.

[71.] Psalm 148

European, 1558

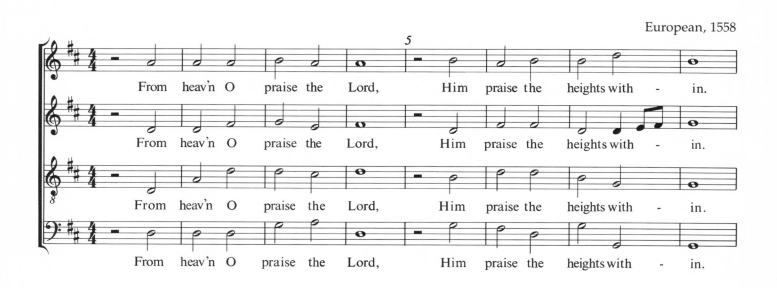

From heav'n O praise the Lord, Him praise the heights with - in.

From heav'n O praise the Lord, Him praise the heights with - in.

From heav'n O praise the Lord, Him praise the heights with - in.

From heav'n O praise the Lord, Him praise the heights with - in.

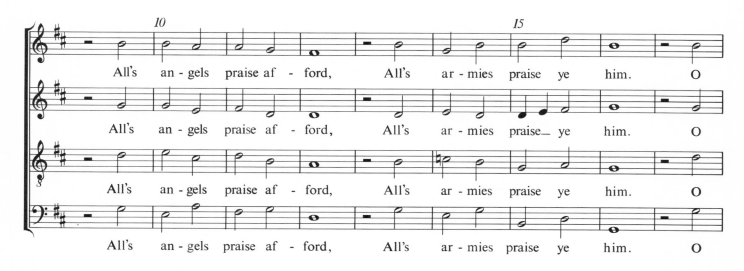

All's an - gels praise af - ford, All's ar - mies praise ye him. O

All's an - gels praise af - ford, All's ar - mies praise ye him. O

All's an - gels praise af - ford, All's ar - mies praise ye him. O

All's an - gels praise af - ford, All's ar - mies praise ye him. O

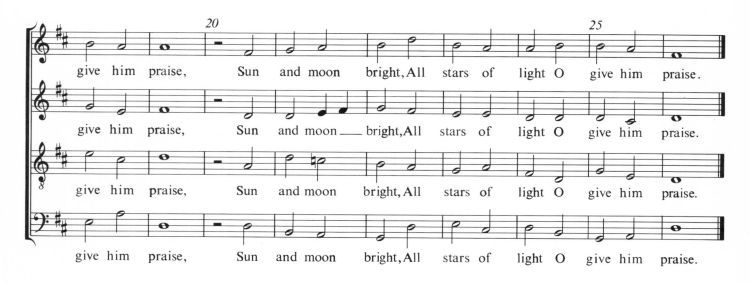

give him praise, Sun and moon bright, All stars of light O give him praise.

give him praise, Sun and moon bright, All stars of light O give him praise.

give him praise, Sun and moon bright, All stars of light O give him praise.

give him praise, Sun and moon bright, All stars of light O give him praise.

2. Ye heav'ns of heav'ns him praise,
   'Bove heav'ns ye waters clear.
   The Lords name let them praise:
   For he spake made they were.
   Them stablish'd he
   For ever and aye;
   Nor pass away
   Shall his decree.

3. Praise God from th'earth below,
   Ye dragons and each deep.
   Fire hail and mist, and snow,
   Whirlwinds his word which keep.
   Mountains also
   And hills all ye:
   Each fruitful tree,
   All cedars too.

4. Beasts also cattle all,
   Things creeping, fowls that fly,
   Earths kings, and peoples all
   Peers all, th'earths judges high.
   Do ye always.
   Young men and maids,
   Old men and babes.
   The Lords name praise.

5. For his name's only high,
   His glory 'bove earth and heav'n.
   His folks horn he lifts high:
   Of all his Saints the praise.
   The sons who be
   Of Isra'l dear,
   His people near,
   The Lord praise ye.

[72.] Psalm 149

English, 1708

Is - r'el re - joice, And chil - dren of Si - on Be glad in their King.

Is - r'el re - joice, And chil - dren of Si - on Be__ glad in__ their King.

Is - r'el re - joice, And chil - dren of Si - on Be glad in their King.

Is - r'el re - joice, And chil - dren of Si - on Be glad__ in their King.

2. Let them his great Name
   Extol in the dance;
   With timbrel and harp
   His praises express;
   Who always takes pleasure
   His saints to advance,
   And with his salvation
   The humble to bless.

3. With glory adorn'd,
   His people shall sing
   To God, who their beds
   With safety does shield;
   Their mouths fill'd with praises
   Of him, their great King;
   Whilst a two-edged sword
   Their right-hand shall wield;

4. Just vengeance to take
   For injuries past;
   To punish those lands
   For ruin design'd;
   With chains, as their captives,
   To tie their kings fast,
   With fetters of iron
   Their nobles to bind.

5. Thus shall they make good,
   When them they destroy,
   The dreadful decree
   Which God does proclaim;
   Such honour and triumph
   His saints shall enjoy:
   O therefore for ever
   Exalt his great Name.

[73.] Putney

Aaron Williams, 1763

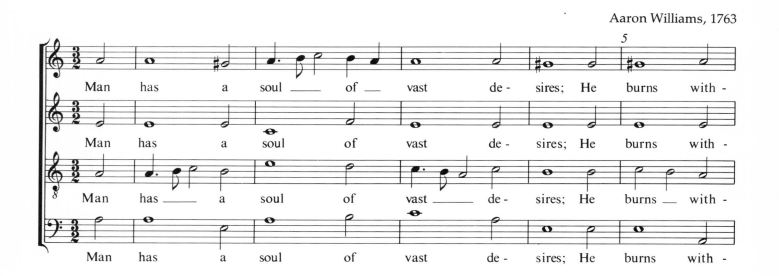

Man has a soul __ of __ vast de - sires; He burns with -

Man has a soul of vast de - sires; He burns with -

Man has __ a soul of vast __ de - sires; He burns __ with -

Man has a soul of vast de - sires; He burns with -

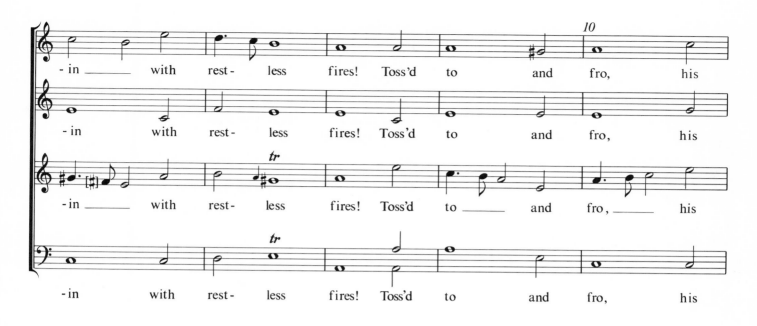

-in _____ with rest- less fires! Toss'd to and fro, his

-in with rest- less fires! Toss'd to and fro, his

-in _____ with rest- less fires! Toss'd to _____ and fro, _____ his

-in with rest- less fires! Toss'd to and fro, his

pas- sions fly From van- i- ty to van- i- ty.

pas- sions fly From van- i- ty to van- i- ty.

pas- sions fly From van- i- ty _____ to van- i- ty.

pas- sions fly From van- i- ty to van- i- ty.

2. In vain, on earth, we hope to find
   Some solid good to fill the mind:
   We try new pleasures—but we feel
   The inward thirst, and torment still.

3. So when a raging fever burns,
   We shift from side to side, by turns;
   And 'tis a poor relief we gain,
   To change the place, but keep the pain.

4. Great God! subdue this vicious thirst,
   This love to vanity and dust;
   Cure this vile fever of the mind,
   And feed our souls with joys refin'd.

[74.] Rainbow

Timothy Swan, 1785

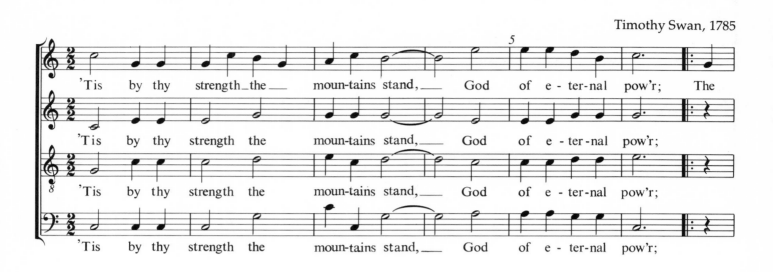

'Tis by thy strength the moun-tains stand, God of e - ter - nal pow'r; The

'Tis by thy strength the moun-tains stand, God of e - ter - nal pow'r;

'Tis by thy strength the moun-tains stand, God of e - ter - nal pow'r;

'Tis by thy strength the moun-tains stand, God of e - ter - nal pow'r;

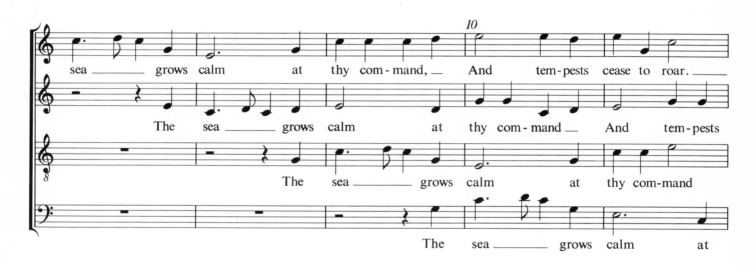

sea grows calm at thy com - mand, And tem-pests cease to roar.

The sea grows calm at thy com - mand And tem-pests

The sea grows calm at thy com-mand

The sea grows calm at

cease to roar. And

And tem-pests cease to roar. And

And tem-pests cease to roar. And

thy com-mand And tem-pests cease to roar. And

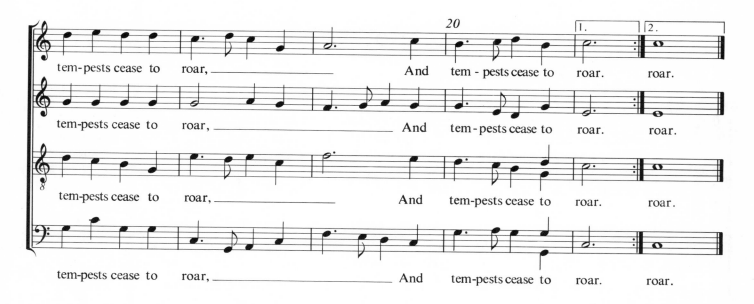

tem-pests cease to roar, _____ And tem - pests cease to roar. roar.

tem-pests cease to roar, _____ And tem - pests cease to roar. roar.

tem-pests cease to roar, _____ And tem-pests cease to roar. roar.

tem-pests cease to roar, _____ And tem-pests cease to roar. roar.

2. The morning light and ev'ning shade
Successive comforts bring:
Thy plent'ous fruits make harvest glad,
Thy flow'rs adorn the spring.

3. Seasons and times, and moons and hours,
Heav'n, earth and air are thine;
When clouds distil their fruitful show'rs,
The author is divine.

4. Those wand'ring cisterns in the sky,
Borne by the winds around,
With wat'ry treasures well supply
The furrows of the ground.

5. The thirsty ridges drink their fill,
And ranks of corn appear:
Thy ways abound with blessings still,
Thy goodness crowns the year.

[75.] Rochester

Israel Holdroyd, ca. 1724

God, my sup - port - er and my hope, My help for - ev - er near,
God, my sup - port - er and my hope, My help for - ev - er near,
God, my sup - port - er and my hope, My help for - ev - er near,
God, my sup - port - er and my hope, My help for - ev - er near,

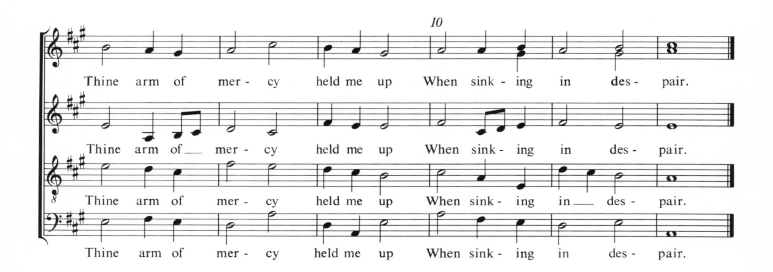

Thine arm of mer - cy held me up When sink - ing in des - pair.
Thine arm of mer - cy held me up When sink - ing in des - pair.
Thine arm of mer - cy held me up When sink - ing in des - pair.
Thine arm of mer - cy held me up When sink - ing in des - pair.

2. Thy counsels, Lord, shall guide my feet
Through this dark wilderness!
Thine hand conduct me near thy seat,
To dwell before thy face.

3. Were I in heav'n, without my God,
'Twould be no joy to me;
And whilst this earth is my abode,
I long for none but thee.

4. What if the springs of life were broke,
And flesh and heart should faint?
God is my soul's eternal Rock,
The strength of ev'ry saint.

5. Behold the sinners who remove
Far from thy presence, die;
Not all the idol gods they love,
Can save them, when they cry.

6. But, to draw near to thee, my God,
Shall be my sweet employ;
My tongue shall sound thy works abroad,
And tell the world my joy.

[76.] Russia

Daniel Read, 1786

False are the men of high de- gree, The bas- er sort are van - i - ty;

False are the men of high de- gree, The bas- er sort are van - i - ty;

False are the men of high de- gree, The bas- er sort are van - i - ty;

False are the men of high de- gree, The bas- er_ sort are van- i - ty; Laid

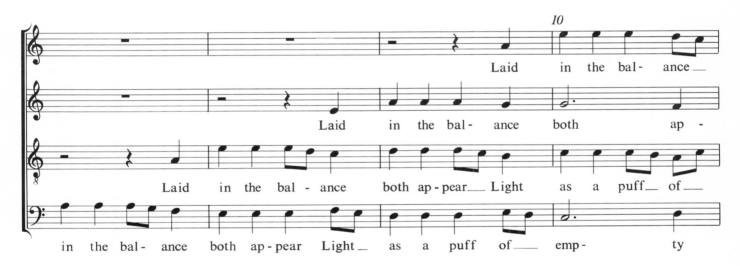

Laid in the bal- ance_

Laid in the bal- ance both ap -

Laid in the bal - ance both ap- pear_ Light as a puff_ of_

in the bal - ance both ap - pear Light_ as a puff of_ emp - ty

both ap - pear Light as a puff of emp - ty air. air.

-pear Light as a puff of emp - ty air. air.

emp - ty air_ Light as_ a _ puff of _ emp - ty air. air.

air, Light as a puff of emp - ty air. air.

2. Make not increasing gold your trust,
   Nor set your heart on glitt'ring dust;
   Why will you grasp the fleeting smoke,
   And not believe what God has spoke?

3. Once has his awful voice declar'd,
   Once and again my ears have heard,
   "All pow'r is his eternal due;
   He must be fear'd and trusted too."

4. For sov'reign power reigns not alone,
   Grace is a partner of the throne:
   Thy grace and justice, mighty Lord,
   Shall well divide our last reward.

[77.] St. Anne

William Croft, 1708

My God, my por-tion and my love, My ev-er-last-ing all;

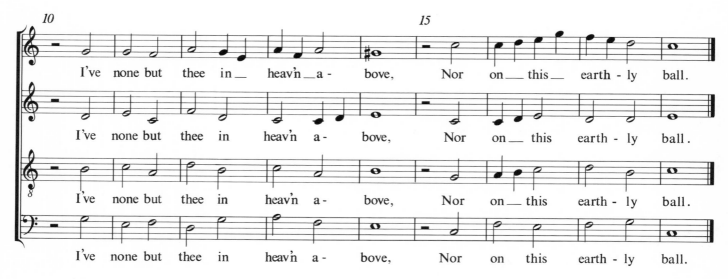

I've none but thee in heav'n a-bove, Nor on this earth-ly ball.

2. What empty things are all the skies,
   And this infer'or clod!
   There's nothing here deserves my joys;
   There's nothing like my God.

3. In vain the bright, the burning sun
   Scatters his feeble light:
   'Tis thy sweet beams create my noon;
   If thou withdraw, 'tis night.

4. And whilst upon my restless bed
   Among the shades I roll;
   If my Redeemer shows his head,
   'Tis morning with my soul.

5. To Thee I owe my wealth and friends,
   And health, and safe abode;
   Thanks to thy name for meaner things,
   But they are not my God.

6. How vain a toy is glitt'ring wealth,
   If once compar'd to Thee!
   Or what's my safety, or my health,
   Or all my friends, to me?

7. Were I possessor of the earth,
   And call'd the stars my own:
   Without thy graces, and thy Self,
   I were a wretch undone.

8. Let others stretch their arms, like seas,
   And grasp in all the shore;
   Grant me the visits of thy face,
   And I desire no more.

[78.] St. David's

English, 1621

2. With fierce intent my flesh to tear,
   When foes beset me round,
   They stumbled, and their haughty crests
   Were made to strike the ground.

3. Through him my heart, undaunted, dares
   With mighty hosts to cope;
   Through him, in doubtful straits of war,
   For good success I hope.

4. Henceforth, within his house to dwell
   I earnestly desire;
   His wond'rous beauty there to view,
   And of his will inquire.

5. For there I may with comfort rest,
   In times of deep distress;
   And safe, as on a rock, abide
   In that secure recess:

6. Whilst God o'er all my haughty foes
   My lofty head shall raise;
   And I my joyful tribute bring,
   With grateful songs of praise.

[79.] St. George's

English, ca. 1760 or before

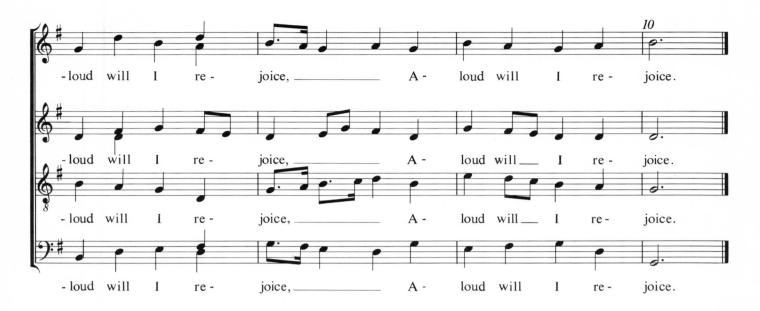

2. 'Tis he adorn'd my naked soul,
   And made salvation mine;
   Upon a poor polluted worm
   He made his grace to shine.

3. And lest the shadow of a spot
   Should on my soul be found,
   He took the robe the Saviour wrought,
   And cast it all around.

4. How far the heav'nly robe exceeds
   What earthly princes wear!
   These ornaments, how bright they shine!
   How white the garments are!

5. The Spirit wrought my faith and love,
   And hope, and ev'ry grace;
   But Jesus spent his life to work
   The robe of right'ousness.

6. Strangely, my soul, art thou array'd
   By the great sacred Three!
   In sweetest harmony of praise
   Let all thy pow'rs agree.

136

[80.] St. Helen's

English, 1763 or before

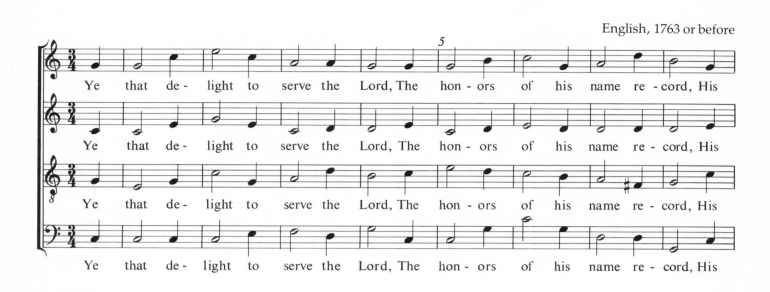

Ye that de - light to serve the Lord, The hon - ors of his name re - cord, His

sa - cred name _ for - ev - er bless; Where - e'er the cir - cling sun dis - plays His

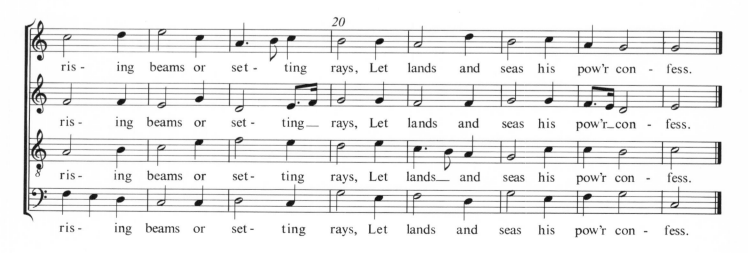

ris - ing beams or set - ting rays, Let lands and seas his pow'r con - fess.

2. Not time nor nature's narrow rounds,
   Can give his vast dominion bounds;
   The heav'ns are far below his height;
   Let no created greatness dare
   With our eternal God compare,
   Arm'd with his uncreated might.

3. He bows his glor'ous head to view
   What the bright hosts of angels do,
   And bends his care to mortal things;
   His sov'reign hand exalts the poor;
   He takes the needy from the door,
   And makes them company for kings.

4. When childless families despair,
   He sends the blessing of an heir,
   To rescue their expiring name:
   The mother, with a thankful voice
   Proclaims his praises and her joys:
   Let ev'ry age advance his fame.

[81.] St. James

Rafael Courtville, 1697

O thou, to whom all crea-tures bow, With-in this earth-ly frame!

Through all the world, how great art thou! How glo-rious is thy name.

138

2. In heav'n thy wond'rous acts are sung,
   Nor fully reckon'd there;
   And yet thou mak'st the infant tongue
   Thy boundless praise declare.

3. Through thee the weak confound the strong,
   And crush their haughty foes;
   And so thou quell'st the wicked throng,
   That thee and thine oppose.

4. When heav'n, thy beauteous work on high,
   Employs my wond'rous sight;
   The moon, that nightly rules the sky,
   With stars of feebler light;

5. What's man, say I, that, Lord, thou lov'st
   To keep him in thy mind?
   Or what his offspring, that thou prov'st
   To them so wond'rous kind?

6. Him next in pow'r thou didst create
   To thy celestial train;
   Ordain'd, with dignity and state,
   O'er all thy works to reign.

7. They jointly own his pow'rful sway;
   The beasts that prey or graze;
   The bird that wings its airy way;
   The fish that cuts the seas.

8. O thou, to whom all creatures bow
   Within this earthly frame,
   Through all the world how great art thou!
   How glorious is thy name!

[82.] St. Martin's

William Tans'ur, 1735

for his name, And songs be - fore un - known.

for his name, And songs be - fore un - known.

for his name, And songs be - fore un - known.

for his name, And songs be - fore un - known.

2. Let elders worship at his feet,
   The church adore around,
   With vials full of odours sweet,
   And harps of sweetest sound.

3. Those are the prayers of the saints,
   And these the hymns they raise:
   Jesus is kind to our complaints,
   He loves to hear our praise.

4. Eternal Father, who shall look
   Into thy secret will?
   Who but the Son shall take that book,
   And open ev'ry seal?

5. He shall fulfill thy great decrees;
   The Son deserves it well:
   Lo, in his hand the sov'reign keys
   Of heav'n, and death, and hell!

6. Now to the Lamb that once was slain,
   Be endless blessings paid;
   Salvation, glory, joy, remain
   Forever on thy head.

7. Thou hast redeem'd our souls with blood;
   Hast set the pris'ners free;
   Hast made us kings and priests to God,
   And we shall reign with thee.

8. The worlds of nature and of grace
   Are put beneath thy pow'r;
   Then shorten these delaying days,
   And bring the promis'd hour.

140

[83.] St. Thomas

Aaron Williams, 1770

Let ev - ery crea - ture ___ join To praise th'e - ter - nal God

Let ev - ery crea - ture ___ join To praise th'e - ter - nal God

Let ev - ery crea - ture ___ join To ___ praise th'e - ter - nal God

Let ev - ery crea - ture ___ join ___ To praise th'e - ter - nal God ___

Ye heav'n - ly hosts the ___ song be - gin And sound his ___ name a - broad.

Ye heav'n - ly hosts the ___ song be - gin And sound his ___ name a - broad.

Ye heav'n - ly hosts the ___ song be - gin And sound his ___ name a - broad.

___ Ye heav'n - ly hosts the ___ song be - gin And sound his ___ name a - broad.

2. Thou sun with golden beams,
   And moon with paler rays,
   Ye starry lights, ye twinking flames,
   Shine to your Maker's praise.

3. He built those worlds above,
   And fix'd their wond'rous frame;
   By his command they stand or move,
   And ever speak his name.

4. Ye vapours, when ye rise,
   Or fall in show'rs of snow,
   Ye thunders, murm'ring round the skies,
   His pow'r and glory show.

5. Wind, hail, and flashing fire,
   Agree to praise the Lord,
   When ye in dreadful storms conspire
   To execute his word.

6. By all his works above
   His honors be exprest;
   But saints who taste his saving love
   Should sing his praises best.

7. Let earth and ocean know
   They owe their Maker praise;
   Praise him, ye wat'ry worlds below,
   And monsters of the seas.

8. From mountains near the sky
   Let his high praise resound,
   From humble shrubs and cedars high,
   And vales and fields around.

9. Ye lions of the wood,
   And tamer beasts which graze,
   Ye live upon his daily food,
   And he expects your praise.

10. Ye birds of lofty wing,
    On high his praises bear,
    Or sit on flow'ry boughs; and sing
    Your Maker's glory there.

11. Ye creeping ants and worms,
    His var'ous wisdom show;
    And flies, in all your shining swarms,
    Praise him who drest you so.

12. By all the earth-born race,
    His honors be exprest;
    But saints who know his heav'nly grace,
    Should learn to praise him best.

13. Monarchs of wide command,
    Praise ye th'eternal King;
    Judges, adore that sov'reign hand
    Whence all your honors spring.

14. Let vig'rous youth engage
    To sound his praises high;
    While growing babes and with'ring age
    Their feebler voices try.

15. United zeal be shown
    His wond'rous fame to raise;
    God is the Lord; his name alone
    Deserves our endless praise.

16. Let nature join with art,
    And all pronounce him blest,
    But saints who dwell so near his heart
    Should sing his praises best.

[84.] Sherburne

Daniel Read, 1785

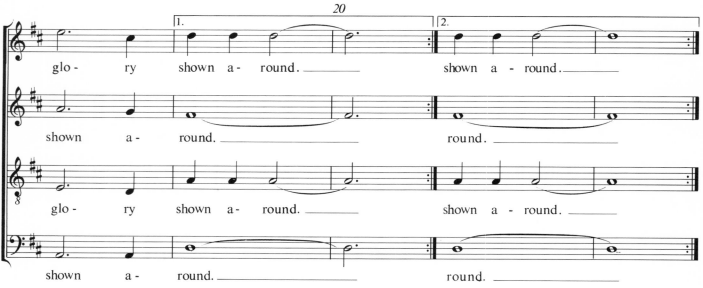

2. "Fear not," said he, for mighty dread
   Had seiz'd their troubled mind;
   "Glad tidings of great joy I bring
   To you, and all mankind.

3. To you, in David's town, this day
   Is born of David's line,
   The Saviour, who is Christ the Lord;
   And this shall be the sign:

4. The Heav'nly Babe you there shall find,
   To human view display'd,
   All meanly wrapp'd in swathing bands,
   And in a manger laid."

5. Thus spake the seraph, and forthwith
   Appear'd a shining throng
   Of angels, praising God, who thus
   Address'd their joyful song:

6. "All glory be to God on high,
   And to the earth be peace;
   Good will, henceforth, from heav'n to men
   Begin, and never cease."

[85.] Southwell

English, 1579

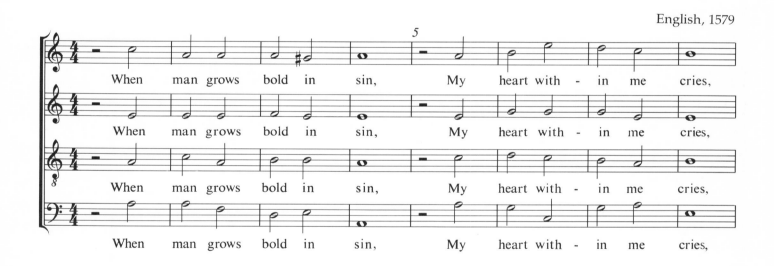

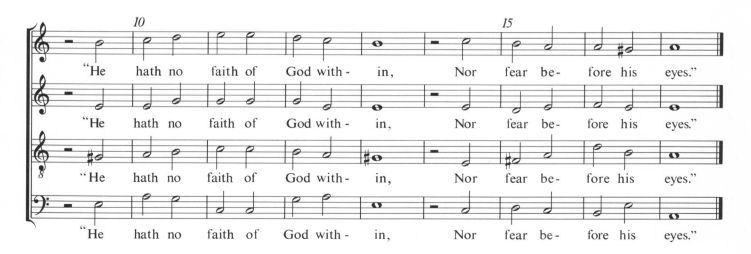

144

2. He walks a while, conceal'd
   In a self flatt'ring dream,
   'Till his dark crimes, at once reveal'd,
   Expose his hateful name.

3. His heart is false and foul,
   His words are smooth and fair;
   Wisdom is banish'd from his soul,
   And leaves no goodness there.

4. He plots upon his bed,
   New mischiefs to fulfil,
   He sets his heart, and hand, and head,
   To practice all that's ill.

5. But there's a dreadful God,
   Though men renounce his fear:
   His justice, hid behind the cloud,
   Shall one great day appear.

6. His truth transcends the sky,
   In heav'n his mercies dwell;
   Deep as the sea his judgments lie,
   His anger burns to hell.

7. How excellent his love,
   Whence all our safety springs!
   O never let my soul remove
   From underneath his wings!

[86.] Stafford

Daniel Read, 1782

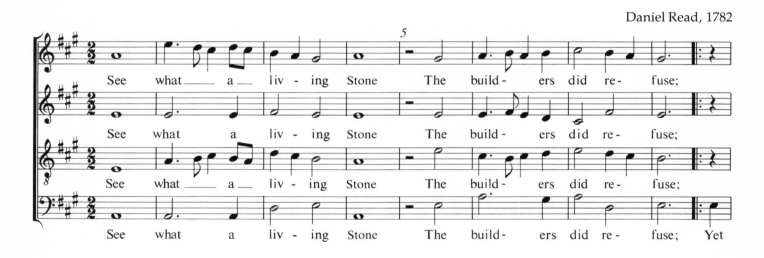

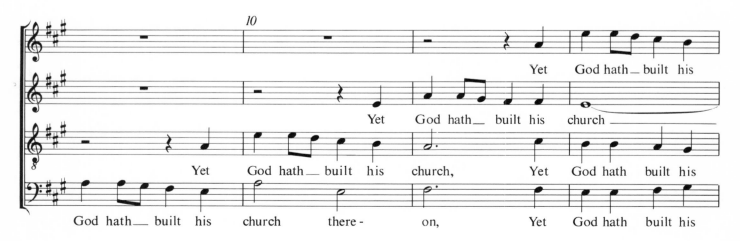

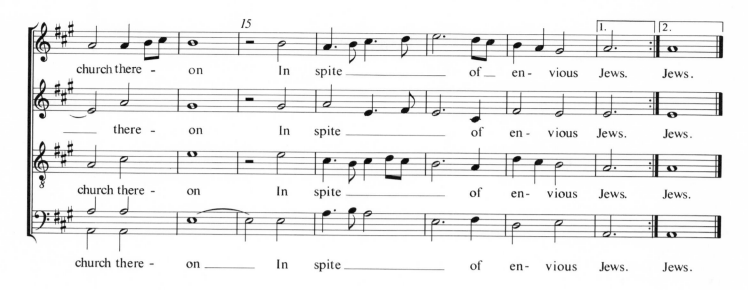

2. The scribe and angry priest
   Reject thine only Son:
   Yet on this rock shall Zion rest
   As the chief corner-stone.

3. The work, O Lord, is thine,
   And wond'rous in our eyes:
   This day declares it all divine,
   This day did Jesus rise!

4. This is the glor'ous day
   Which our Redeemer made;
   Let us rejoice, and sing, and pray;
   Let all the church be glad.

5. Hosanna to the King
   Of David's royal blood;
   Bless him, ye saints, he comes to bring
   Salvation from your God.

6. We bless thine holy word
   Which all this grace displays;
   And offer on thy altar, Lord,
   Our sacrifice of praise.

[87.] Standish

English, 1700

How shall the young se- cure their hearts, And guard their lives from sin?

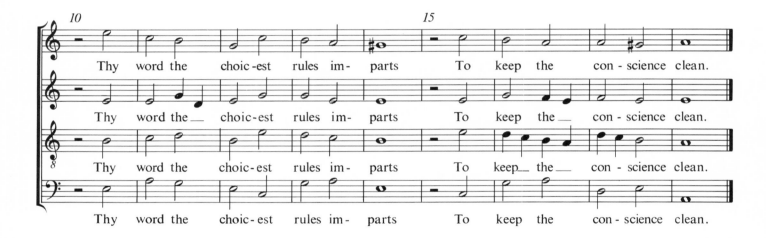

Thy word the choic-est rules im- parts To keep the con - science clean.

2. When once it enters to the mind,
   It spreads such light abroad,
   The meanest souls instruction find,
   And raise their thoughts to God.

3. 'Tis like the sun, a heav'nly light,
   Which guides us all the day;
   And through the dangers of the night,
   A lamp to lead our way. ·

4. The men who keep thy law with care,
   And meditate thy word,
   Grow wiser than their teachers are,
   And better know the Lord.

5. Thy precepts make me truly wise:
   I hate the sinners' road:
   I hate my own vain thoughts which rise,
   But love thy law, my God.

6. The starry heav'ns thy rule obey;
   The earth maintains her place;
   And these thy servants, night and day
   Thy skill and pow'r express.

7. But still thy law and gospel, Lord,
   Have lessons more divine:
   Not earth stands firmer than thy word,
   Nor stars so nobly shine.

8. Thy word is everlasting truth;
   How pure is ev'ry page!
   That holy book shall guide our youth,
   And well support our age.

147

[88.] Suffield

Oliver King, 1779

2. A span is all which we can boast,
   An inch or two of time:
   Man is but vanity and dust,
   In all his flow'r and prime.

3. See the vain race of mortals move,
   Like shadows, o'er the plain,
   They rage and strive, desire and love,
   But all their noise is vain.

4. Some walk in honor's gaudy show;
   Some dig for golden ore;
   They toil for heirs, they know not who,
   And straight are seen no more.

5. What could I wish or wait for then
   From creatures, earth and dust?
   They make our expectations vain,
   And disappoint our trust.

6. Now I forbid my carnal hope,
   My fond desires recall;
   I give my mortal int'rest up,
   And make my God my All.

[89.] Sutton

English, ca. 1760 or before

2. The darkness and the light
   Still keep their course the same;
   While night to day, and day to night,
   Divinely teach his name.

3. In ev'ry diff'rent land
   Their gen'ral voice is known,
   They show the wonders of his hand,
   And orders of his throne.

4. America, rejoice!
   He here reveals his word;
   We are not left to nature's voice
   To bid us know the Lord.

5. His statutes and commands
   Are set before our eyes;
   He puts his gospel in our hands,
   Where our salvation lies.

6. His laws are just and pure;
   His truth without deceit;
   His promises forever sure,
   And his rewards are great.

7. Not honey to the taste
   Affords so much delight;
   Nor gold which has the furnace past
   So much allures the sight.

8. While of thy works I sing,
   Thy glory to proclaim,
   Accept the praise, my God, my King,
   In my Redeemer's name.

[90.] Sutton

Ezra Goff, 1793

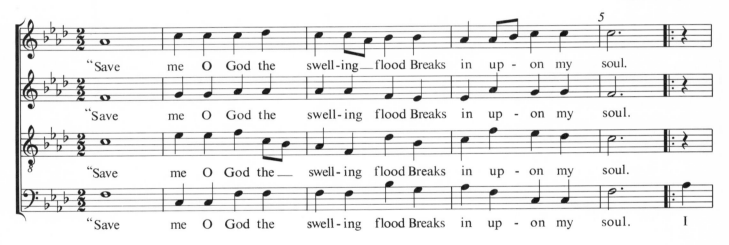

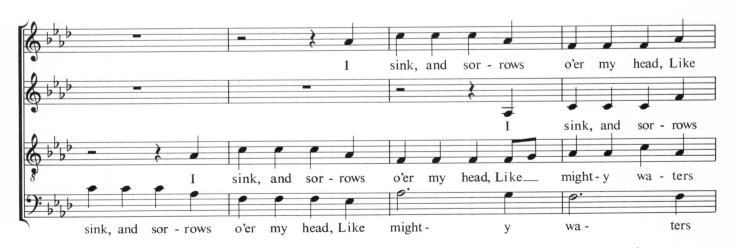

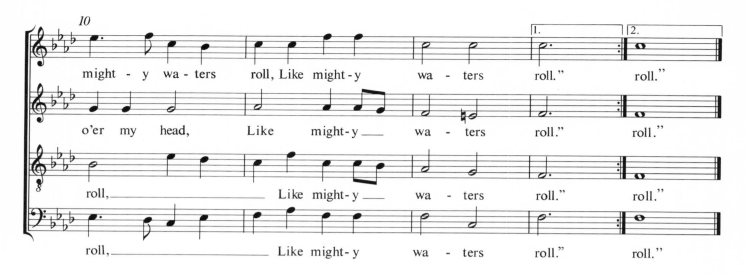

2. "I cry, till all my voice be gone,
   In tears I waste the day;
   My God, behold my longing eyes!
   And shorten thy delay.

3. They hate my soul without a cause,
   And still their number grows
   More than the hairs around my head,
   And mighty are my foes.

4. 'Twas then I paid that dreadful debt,
   Which men could never pay,
   And gave those honors to thy law,
   Which sinners took away."

5. Thus, in the great Messiah's name,
   The royal prophet mourns;
   Thus he awakes our hearts to grief,
   And gives us joy by turns.

6. "Now shall the saints rejoice and find
   Salvation in my name,
   For I have borne their heavy load
   Of sorrow, pain and shame.

7. Grief, like a garment, cloth'd me round,
   And sackcloth was my dress,
   While I procur'd for naked souls
   A robe of right'ousness.

8. Among my brethren and the Jews,
   I, like a stranger stood,
   And bore their vile reproach, to bring
   The Gentiles near to God.

9. I came in sinful mortals' stead
   To do my Father's will;
   Yet, when I cleans'd my Father's house,
   They scandaliz'd my zeal.

10. My fasting and my holy groans
    Were made the drunkard's song,
    But God, from his celest'al throne
    Heard my complaining tongue.

11. He sav'd me from the dreadful deep,
    Nor let my soul be drown'd;
    He rais'd and fix'd my sinking feet
    On well-established ground.

12. 'Twas in a most accepted hour
    My pray'r arose on high,
    And, for my sake, my God shall hear
    The dying sinners' cry."

[91.] Virginia

Oliver Brownson, 1782

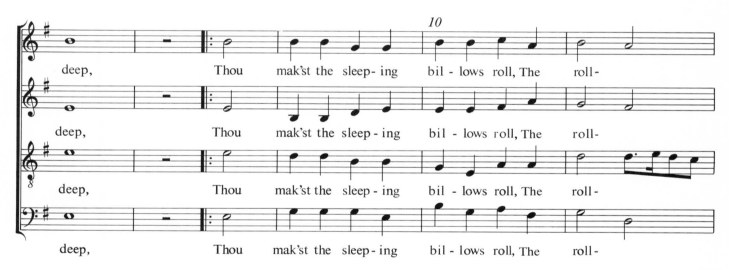

2. Heav'n, earth and air, and sea are thine,
   And the dark world of hell;
   How did thine arm in vengeance shine
   When Egypt durst rebel!

3. Justice and judgment are thy throne;
   Yet wond'rous is thy grace;
   While truth and mercy join'd in one
   Invite us near thy face.

[92.] Walsall

English, ca. 1726?

Lord, in the morn-ing thou shalt hear My voice as-cend-ing high:

To thee will I di-rect my pray'r, To thee lift up my eye.

2. Up to the hills, where Christ is gone
To plead for all his saints,
Presenting at his father's throne
Our songs and our complaints.

3. Thou art a God before whose sight
The wicked shall not stand;
Sinners shall ne'er be thy delight,
Nor dwell at thy right hand.

4. But to thy house will I resort,
To taste thy mercies there;
I will frequent thine holy court,
And worship in thy fear.

5. O may thy spirit guide my feet
In ways of right'ousness!
Make every path of duty straight,
And plain before my face.

6. My watchful enemies combine
To tempt my feet astray;
They flatter with a base design,
To make my soul their prey.

7. Lord, crush the serpent into dust,
And all his plots destroy;
While those who in thy mercy trust,
For ever shout for joy.

8. The men who love and fear thy name,
Shall see their hopes fulfill'd;
The mighty God will compass them
With favor, as a shield.

[93.] Wantage

English, 1763 or before

154

2. How terrible thy glories be!
   How bright thine armies shine!
   Where is the pow'r which vies with thee?
   Or truth compar'd to thine?

3. The Northern pole and Southern rest
   On thy supporting hand;
   Darkness and day from East to West
   Move round at thy command.

4. Thy words the raging winds controul,
   And rule the boist'rous deep!
   Thou mak'st the sleeping billows roll,
   The rolling billows sleep.

5. Heav'n, earth and air, and sea are thine,
   And the dark world of hell;
   How did thine arm in vengeance shine
   When Egypt durst rebel!

6. Justice and judgment are thy throne;
   Yet wond'rous is thy grace:
   While truth and mercy join'd in one
   Invite us near thy face.

[94.] Wells

Israel Holdroyd, ca. 1724

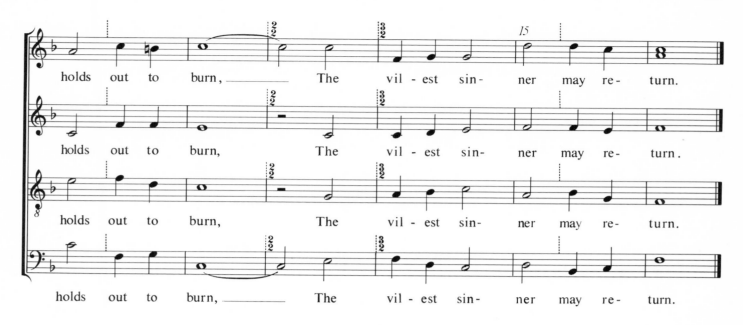

holds out to burn, _____ The vil - est sin - ner may re - turn.

holds out to burn, The vil - est sin - ner may re - turn.

holds out to burn, The vil - est sin - ner may re - turn.

holds out to burn, _____ The vil - est sin - ner may re - turn.

2. Life is the hour which God has giv'n
   To 'scape from hell, and fly to heav'n;
   The day of grace, when mortals may
   Secure the blessings of the day.

3. The living know that they must die,
   But all the dead forgotten lie;
   Their mem'ry and their sense are gone,
   Alike unknowing and unknown.

4. Their hatred and their love are lost,
   Their envy bury'd in the dust;
   They have no share in all that's done
   Beneath the circuit of the sun.

5. Then what my thoughts design to do,
   My hands, with all your might pursue;
   Since no device, nor work is found,
   Nor faith, nor hope, beneath the ground.

6. There are no acts of pardon past
   In the cold grave, to which we haste;
   But darkness, death, and long despair
   Reign in eternal silence there.

[95.] Weston Favel

William Knapp, 1738

2. "Worthy the Lamb, that di'd," they cry,
   "To be exalted thus";
   "Worthy the lamb," our lips reply,
   For he was slain for us.

3. Jesus is worthy to receive
   Honor and pow'r divine;
   And blessings, more than we can give,
   Be, Lord, forever thine.

4. Let all who dwell above the sky,
   And air, and earth, and seas,
   Conspire to raise thy glories high,
   And speak thine endless praise.

5. Let all creation join in one,
   To bless the sacred name
   Of him, who sits upon the throne,
   And to adore the Lamb.

[96.] Winchester

German, 1690

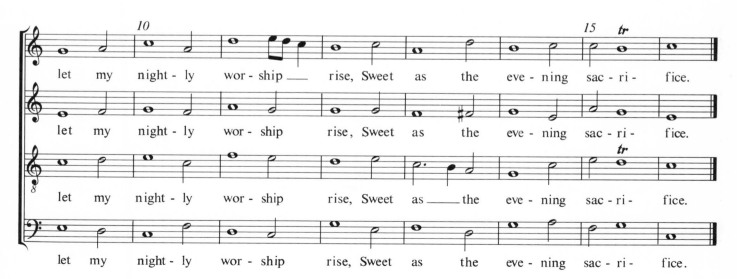

2. Watch o'er my lips, and guard them, Lord,
From ev'ry rash and heedless word;
Nor let my feet incline to tread
The guilty path where sinners lead.

3. O may the right'ous, when I stray,
Smite and reprove my wand'ring way!
Their gentle words, like ointment shed,
Shall never bruise, but cheer my head.

4. When I behold them prest with grief
I'll cry to heav'n for their relief;
And by my warm petitions prove
How much I prize their faithful love.

[97.] Windham

Daniel Read, 1785

Broad is the road that leads to death, And

Broad is the road that leads to death, And

Broad is the road that leads to death, And

Broad is the road that leads to death, And

thou - sands walk to - geth - er there, But wis - dom shows

thou - sands walk to - geth - er there, But wis - dom shows

thou - sands walk to - geth - er there, But wis - dom shows

thou - sands walk to - geth - er there, But wis - dom shows

159

a   nar - row   path, _____   With   here and there __ a __ trav - el -   ler.

a   nar - row   path,   With   here and there   a   trav - el -   ler.

a   nar - row   path,   With   here and there   a   trav - el -   ler.

a   nar - row   path, _____   With   here and there   a   trav - el -   ler.

2. "Deny thyself, and take thy cross,"
Is the Redeemer's great command!
Nature must count her gold but dross,
If she would gain this heav'nly land.

3. The fearful soul, who tires and faints,
And walks the ways of God no more,
Is but esteem'd almost a saint,
And makes his own destruction sure.

4. Lord, let not all my hopes be vain;
Create my heart entirely new;
This Hypocrites did ne'er attain,
And false Apostates never knew.

[98.] Windsor

English, 1591

That aw-ful day will sure-ly come, Th'ap-point-ed hour makes haste,

That aw-ful day will sure-ly come, Th'ap-point-ed hour makes haste,

That aw-ful day will sure-ly come, Th'ap-point-ed hour makes haste,

That aw-ful day will sure-ly come, Th'ap-point-ed hour makes haste,

When I must stand be-fore my Judge, And pass the sol-emn test.

When I must stand be-fore my Judge, And pass the sol-emn test.

When I must stand be-fore my Judge, And pass the sol-emn test.

When I must stand be-fore my Judge, And pass the sol-emn test.

2. Thou lovely Chief of all my joys,
Thou Sov'reign of my heart,
How could I bear to hear thy voice
Pronouce the sound—*depart*?

3. The thunder of that dismal word
Would so torment my ear,
'Twould tear my soul asunder, Lord,
With most tormenting fear.

4. What to be banish'd from my life,
And yet forbid to die!
To linger in eternal pain,
Yet death forever fly!

5. Oh! wretched state of deep despair.
To see my God remove,
And fix my doleful station where
I must not taste his love!

6. Jesus, I throw my arms around,
And hang upon thy breast:
Without a gracious smile from Thee,
My spirit cannot rest.

7. Oh! tell me that my worthless name
Is graven on thy hands;
Show me some promise, in thy book,
Where my salvation stands.

8. Give me one kind, assuring word
To sink my fears again;
And cheerfully my soul shall wait
Her three-score years and ten.

[99.] Winter

Daniel Read, 1785

2. When, from his dreadful stores on high,
He pours the rattl'ing hail,
The wretch who dares this God defy,
Shall find his courage fail.

3. He sends his word, and melts the snow,
The fields no longer mourn;
He calls the warmer gales to blow,
And bids the spring return.

4. The changing wind, the flying cloud,
Obey his mighty word:
With songs and honors sounding loud,
Praise ye the sovereign Lord.

[100.] Worcester

Abraham Wood, 1778

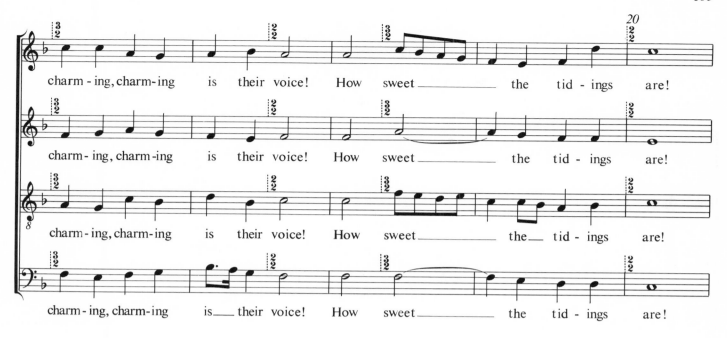

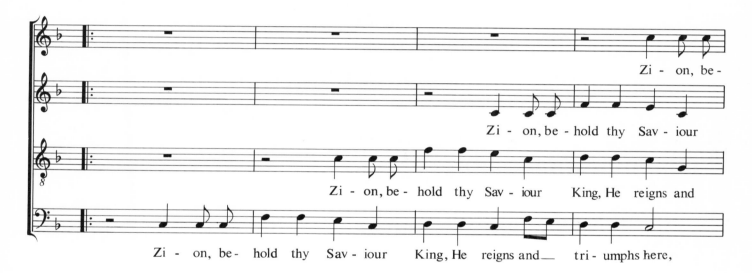

Zi - on be - hold thy Sav - iour King, _____ He reigns and tri - umphs here.

here. Zi - on be - hold thy Sav - iour King, _____ He reigns and tri - umphs here.

here. Zi - on be - hold thy Sav - iour King, _____ He __ reigns and __ tri - umphs here.

here. Zi - on be - hold thy Sav - iour King, _____ He __ reigns and tri - umphs here.

2. How happy are our ears,
That hear this joyful sound,
Which kings and prophets waited for,
And sought, but never found!
How blessed are our eyes,
That see this heav'nly light;
Prophets and kings desir'd it long,
But dy'd without the sight!

3. The watchmen join their voice,
And tuneful notes employ:
Jerusalem breaks forth in songs,
And deserts learn the joy.
The Lord makes bare his arm
Through all the earth abroad;
Let ev'ry nation now behold
Their Saviour and their God.

[101.] York

Scottish, 1615

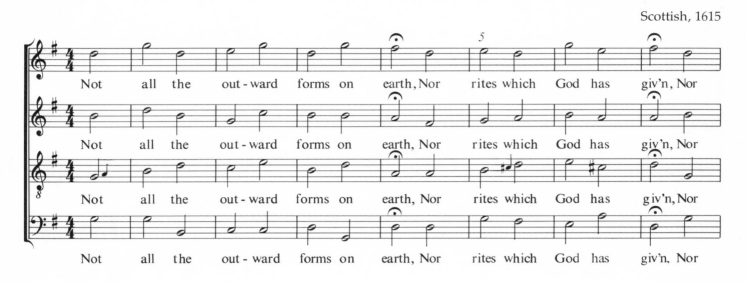

Not all the out-ward forms on earth, Nor rites which God has giv'n, Nor

Not all the out-ward forms on earth, Nor rites which God has giv'n, Nor

Not all the out-ward forms on earth, Nor rites which God has giv'n, Nor

Not all the out-ward forms on earth, Nor rites which God has giv'n, Nor

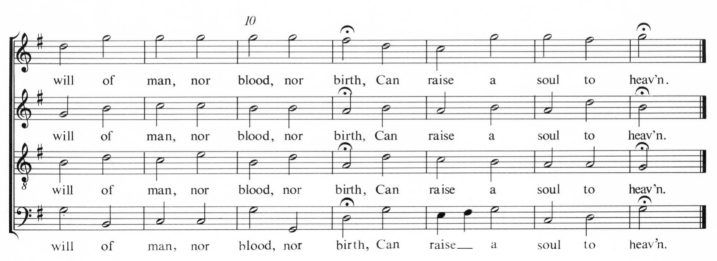

will of man, nor blood, nor birth, Can raise a soul to heav'n.

will of man, nor blood, nor birth, Can raise a soul to heav'n.

will of man, nor blood, nor birth, Can raise a soul to heav'n.

will of man, nor blood, nor birth, Can raise__ a soul to heav'n.

2. The sov'reign will of God, alone
   Creates us heirs of grace;
   Born in the image of his son,
   A new pecul'ar race.

3. The Spirit, like some heav'nly wind,
   Blows on the sons of flesh;
   New-models all the carnal mind,
   And forms the man afresh.

4. Our quick'ned souls awake—and rise
   From the long sleep of death;
   On heav'nly things we fix our eyes,
   And praise employs our breath.